ISRAEL
The Land and the People

ISRAEL
The Land and the People

An Evangelical Affirmation of God's Promises

H. Wayne House
General Editor

kregel
PUBLICATIONS

Grand Rapids, MI 49501

For more information about Kregel Publications, visit our web site at http:\\www.kregel.com.

Cover design: Alan G. Hartman
Book design: Nicholas G. Richardson

Library of Congress Cataloging-in-Publication Data
    Israel, the land and the people: an evangelical affirmation of God's promises / H. Wayne House, editor.
        p.   cm.
    Includes bibliographical references and indexes.
    1. Israel (Christian Theology). 2. Christianity and other relations—Judaism. 3. Judaism—Relations—Christianity. 4. Covenants—Religious aspects—Christianity
I. House, H. Wayne.
BT590.J8I77   1998   231.7'6—dc21   97-50516
                                                    CIP

ISBN 0-8254-2878-5 (paperback)
ISBN 0-8254-2879-3 (hardcover)

Printed in the United States of America

2 3 4 / 04 03 02 01 00 99 98

CONTENTS

FOREWORD

This book is long overdue. Finally a group of scholars have united to help us sort through issues regarding Israel. For almost two thousand years the church has attempted the impossible task of transforming itself into Israel. This has never been God's intention. Each of the scholars involved in this project was asked to respond to the question, "Who is Israel today, and how is Israel different from the church?"

Regarding this important question, let me state clearly three truths: (1) the church is not Israel; (2) God is not finished with His people, the Jews; (3) the church (made up primarily of Gentiles and a remnant of Jews) is comprised of God's people but has a different goal and different future than Israel has. The authors of this book affirm these truths and, in the finest tradition of scholarship, set forth a historical and biblical defense of these truths.

When the church confuses itself with Israel, it falls into at least one or more of three extremes, that of legalism, spiritualizing Scriptures that should be taken literally, or embracing a mission of dominion to which God never called it.

The latter concern may be discerned in what Paul declared in Romans 11:25 regarding the relationship of Israel to the church: "For I do not desire, brethren, that you should be ignorant of this mystery, lest you be wise in your own opinion, that blindness in part has happened to Israel until the fulness of the Gentiles has come in." The King James Version puts it more succinctly, "lest ye should be wise in your own conceits; . . ." The Gentile Christian community needs to heed these admonitions today as much as in Paul's day so as not to miss the important truth of God that only for a season Israel would fail to see Messiah, be converted, and be healed. The church must not think that it has somehow replaced Israel forever in God's plan.

7

8FOREWORD

This book deals with many of the difficult questions regarding the relationship between Israel and the church. It is important reading for those who desire that the body of Christ fulfill its glorious destiny but also yearn for the fulfillment of Paul's vision "that all Israel shall be saved."

Israel: The Land and the People could not have been the work of one person or one faculty of a theological school. It had to be a compendium and consensus of thought, with various theological scholars uniting over the fundamentals and distinguishing the essential from the nonessential.

Special commendation is due to the Board of Directors of Jews for Jesus, who had the vision and saw the need for such a consultation and compendium.

—MOISHES ROSEN
founder of Jews for Jesus

INTRODUCTION

Israel! Israel, the land given to Abraham, Isaac, and Jacob; Israel, the people who are physical descendants of the man Israel (Jacob); Israel, the remnant of God among the Jewish people who continue to show God's faithfulness to His covenants with the patriarchs until the present day.

As I look out my window at the kibbutz at Mitzpeh Ramat Rachel, I can see Bethlehem, the birthplace of Jesus, King of the Jews. Just a short distance to the north is Jerusalem, city of peace. Most of my life I envisioned traveling to the land of the Bible, the Holy Land, to see for myself the place where Abraham put his tents and trusted in God; where David fought for the mighty God of Jacob; where the prophet Elijah (which means "Yahweh is my God") demonstrated the truth of his name against the false religions of the Canaanites; where Jesus, God incarnate, came as Messiah to the Jewish people and ultimately to the whole world; where the early church had its birth among Israel, God's people. Each trip to the land of Israel brings me closer to the people and events of biblical history, the foundations of my Christian faith.

Along with my enchantment with the land of the Bible, I share an attachment to Israel, the people of promise. Among all the nations, God chose a special people through whom to work his covenants and reveal Himself. They were not special because of certain qualities they possessed, but in His electing grace He made them special. Of all the peoples of the earth it was through the Jewish people that He chose to enter into the world, offering Himself as Messiah, Savior, and King.

Israel! Just the mention of this one word brings a flood of images and emotions to me. Although a Gentile, an outsider to the Jewish experience, I am a

9

person who is very aware of the biblical perspective on the land and the people. Other than the missionary journeys of Paul and the exilic books of the Hebrew Scriptures, the overwhelming context of the Bible is this land. The covenants God made here with Israel, the people, are everlasting and are not vitiated by the advent of the church. Paul makes it clear that God has not set aside Israel but rather has kept for Himself a remnant of faith among this people. He intends to bring His covenant people back to Himself at the end of the age, to fulfill all the blessings He desired for them.

Not all Christians share the same enthusiasm that I have for Israel. Many believers today think that the church has replaced the people Israel in the plan of God, with the church being the "New Israel." This is replacement theology, which conditions Old Testament covenants on Israel's obedience. Disobedience, those adhering to this view believe, caused the transfer of the covenants and attendant blessings to the church. Belief in replacement theology has given rise to considerable anti-Semitism at times.

The other extreme, the opposite of replacement theology, is Christian Zionism. The views of those who are a part of this movement could be summed up as "Israel, right or wrong!" These Christians have made idols of the Jewish people and the state of Israel. Since God gave the land to the Jews and now the state of Israel is in existence, whatever the Jewish state does to those within its borders should go unquestioned, regardless of human rights concerns. Some within this camp have advocated a view called "two-covenant theology," believing that Jewish people are saved simply by being Jewish and being connected to the Abrahamic covenant, while Gentiles must be saved through faith in Christ.

The majority of Christians today do not hold either of these incorrect perspectives but simply do not give thought to Israel at all. They don't think of the church as being made up of Jews and Gentiles, but Gentiles alone. The Jewish people are marginalized; there is no heart for evangelism.

This lack of concern has been encouraged by many Jewish leaders, inside and outside the nation of Israel, who view evangelical action as tantamount to anti-Semitism, believing that turning to Christ is turning their backs on their Jewishness. In so doing they deny their people the promises given to Israel and ostracize those who embrace Yeshua, Israel's Messiah. Unfortunately, many Gentile Christians participate, ignorantly or not, in denying the current remnant within Israel and expect or demand that those Jews who become believers in Jesus cease to be Jewish.

In order to address these concerns, a group of evangelical biblical scholars met together in Jerusalem in early June of 1997. This group set forth correctives to what they view as the mistaken understanding of the Bible on the nature and purpose of Israel and made an affirmation of God's promises to His people Israel. To do so now is significant because Israel in 1998 celebrates its fiftieth year as a nation. This will truly be a year of Jubilee (Lev. 25:8; Luke 4:18–19).

Our prayer is that this book encourages the reader and the broader Christian family, both Jew and Gentile, to rejoice in the special place that God has for His chosen people, the Jews, and that more of this remnant will be led to completeness in the recognition that Yeshua came as Savior, first to the Jew and then to the Gentile.

—H. WAYNE HOUSE

CONTRIBUTORS

Ralph H. Alexander — Director of Educational Development in the former Soviet Union; Church Leadership International

Ronald B. Allen — Professor of Bible Exposition, Dallas Theological Seminary, Dallas, Texas

Louis Goldberg — Scholar in Residence, Jews for Jesus, New York, New York; formerly Professor of Theology and Jewish Studies, Moody Bible Institute, Chicago, Illinois

Harold W. Hoehner — Chairman and Senior Professor of New Testament, Director of Ph.D. Studies, Dallas Theological Seminary, Dallas, Texas

H. Wayne House — Professor of Theology and Culture, Trinity Graduate School, and Professor of Law, Trinity Law School, Trinity International University, Anaheim, California

John A. Jelinek — Associate Professor, Baptist Bible Seminary, Clarks Summit, Pennsylvania

Walter C. Kaiser Jr. — Colman M. Mockler Distinguished Professor of Old Testament and President, Gordon-Conwell Theological Seminary, South Hamilton, Massachucetts

David L. Larsen — Professor Emeritus of Preaching, Trinity Evangelical Divinity School, Deerfield, Illinois

A. Boyd Luter   Associate Professor of Bible, Cedarville College, Cedarville, Ohio

Ray A. Pritz   Study Notes Editor, United Bible Societies and Hebrew Studies Program, Caspari Center, Jerusalem, Israel

Robert L. Thomas   Professor of New Testament, The Master's Seminary, Sun Valley, California

Tuvya Zaretsky   Director, Jews for Jesus, Southern California District, Los Angeles, California

PART ONE

IDENTITY ISSUES

Sunrise in Jerusalem, looking toward the northwest.

CHAPTER ONE

THE LAND OF ISRAEL

Ronald B. Allen

THE NAME OF THE LAND

Israel has not always been called Israel, of course. Only God knows how many names this little territory has had. Principal names include the Land of Canaan, the Land of Israel, and Palestine. The area has also been called the Land of the Ammorites (see Josh. 10:5; compare Gen. 15:16). Indeed, at the beginning of the main story line of the Bible (Gen. 12:1),[1] the land was inhabited by numerous people groups identified, perhaps only in part, as "the Kenites, the Kenezzites, the Kadmonites, the Hittites, the Perizzites, the Rephaim, the Amorites, the Canaanites, the Girgashites, and the Jebusites" (Gen. 15:19–21).[2] Any one of these people groups would have regarded the land as theirs; thus, "the land of the Kenites" would have been a proper designation at a given point in history. Indeed, in Joshua 17:15 the land is called, at least in part, "the land of the Perizzites."

Nonetheless, for those whose ideas are shaped by biblical theology, no name for the land is as important as the designation "the land of Israel" (or, *Eretz Israel*, as the Hebrew words are commonly styled in English). And no place is as important for our understanding of the Bible. "The land where the Word-made-flesh dwelt with men is, and must ever be, an integral part of the Divine Revelation."[3] Norman C. Habel, in an informative study of the theology of the land avers, "Land, after all, is such a comprehensive symbol in the Old Testament that it could be ranked next to God in importance."[4]

With all of its importance, there is a surprise in store for many. Even some of the most knowledgeable Bible readers are suprised to find on initial journey to the modern State of Israel that the land of Israel is astonishingly small. The

traditional boundaries include a territory that extends only about 150 miles north
to south (going from Dan to Beersheba), and an average of thirty miles east to
west (from the Mediterranean to the Jordan River Valley).[5] The maps of the
modern state become quite confusing to the first-time visitor; few of the modern
borders match the ancient boundaries.

Throughout time this tiny region of the globe has been known by a wide variety
of names as it has come under the sway of numerous people groups. Wave after
wave of peoples has washed across this meager little land-bridge that connects
the three continents of Asia, Africa, and—by extension—Europe.[6] The trunk
highways that traverse the land from north to south have borne the weight of
innumerable marching boots and war machines through the ages. It is difficult
to imagine a region of similar dimension that has been more significant in world
history than the little land of Israel.

O LAND, LAND, LAND!

But the land of Israel is not just the marching ground of armies, ancient and
modern. It is the particular place on the planet that the sovereign, living God has
enacted events that are of greater significance than any other in world history. It
was to this little territory that Yahweh first brought Abram and Sarai, the father
and mother of the Hebrew peoples, at the beginning of the biblical story (Genesis 12). It was to this region that the Lord brought again the Hebrew nation whom
He had redeemed from Egypt at the beginning of their national story (Joshua
1–12; see also Deut. 8:6–10). It was from this region that He subsequently drove
His people when they proved faithless to Him and undeserving of His gift of the
land (e.g., see 2 Kings 25). But to this land He subsequently caused them to return (see the books of Ezra and Nehemiah). For this land, *Eretz Israel*, the land
of Israel, is the geographical platform on which the story of the Bible is staged.
No other land on the planet is as important in terms of God's work of salvation
as the little land of Israel.

It was in this small place that the King of Glory came in the central miracle of
all time, the Incarnation. It was here that the Savior lived, taught, suffered, and
died. It was here that He rose again, it was from here that He ascended to the
Father, and it is here that one day He will return in great glory. What a land—in
the providence of God! Surely one does not misconstrue the matter when he or
she speaks of the land of Israel as the most important single location on the planet,
being the geographical setting for the enactment of the work of God among His
people. No place is more significant to God—or man—than the land of Israel!

The prophet Jeremiah, anticipating the action of the Savior Jesus (see Luke
19:41), wept often over this land because of the judgment that was about to come
upon its people due to their sinfulness. Jeremiah lived in the last days of the
monarchy, a period marked by unremitting apostasy, unbridled idolatry, unimag-
inable debauchery—all within the sacred precincts of the once-holy land.[7]

In a moment of deep emotion concerning God's impending judgment on Jehoiakim's brief reign as a puppet king of Judah in 598 B.C., Jeremiah gasped, "O earth, earth, earth, Hear the word of Yahweh!" The Hebrew word here is 'ereṣ, a word that can also be rendered "land." In anticipation of the coming destruction of the household of the king, the land, the city, the Temple, the prophet repeated the term "land" three times. This is a very unusual phenomenon, perhaps not unlike the threefold use of the word "holy" in Isaiah when that prophet heard the seraphs singing of the supernal holiness of Yahweh (see Isa. 6:3). When Jeremiah weepingly said, "O earth, earth, earth," he evinced the depths of his emotion concerning his attachment to this little land.

A recurring theme in the Bible is that the land of Israel is God's land. We affirm that not just the land of Israel belongs to the Lord; everything belongs to Yahweh, as David writes:

> The earth is Yahweh's, and all its fullness,
> The world and those who dwell therein.
> For He has founded it upon the seas,
> And established it upon the waters. (Ps. 24:1)

Nonetheless, Yahweh shows a special and particular pleasure in speaking of the land of Israel as *His own land.* Yahweh declares in Torah, "the land is Mine" (Lev. 25:23). This emphasis carries through to the prophets. Joel, for example, reports the words of God responding in mock incredulity to the horrendous locust plague that had swept across the land of Judah, likely in the last decades of the monarchy.[8] The Lord says of the locusts, "For a nation has come up against My land, Strong and without number" (Joel 1:6). Similarly, Jeremiah reports the words of God in judgment on His people who betrayed His love when they entered the land that He had given to them:

> I brought you to a bountiful country,
> To eat its fruit and its goodness.
> But when you entered, you defiled My land
> And made My heritage an abomination. (Jer. 2:7)

The point is clear throughout the pages of the Hebrew Bible. "Canaan is YHWH's land grant to Israel."[9] Urbach writes, "Scripture states that the ultimate owner of the land of Israel is the Lord (Lev. 25:23) and that he alone can give the land to whomever he wishes."[10] The sadness, of course, is that the sinfulness of the people caused them to lose the land for a time in the two catastrophes in the period of the Hebrew Scriptures (the fall of Samaria in 722 B.C. and in the fall of Jerusalem in 586 B.C.) and then to lose it again in the catastrophe of the fall of Jerusalem to the Romans in A.D. 70.

But now, in the late twentieth century, we know that Jewish people are back in the land of Israel, and the old claims are heard anew. After centuries of history, it is again *Eretz Israel!*

WHOSE LAND?

The changing of the year from A.D. 1996 to 1997 brought little change in attitudes among the peoples living in and near the ancient biblical site of Hebron in what is now called "a disputed territory"; this region is believed by many Jewish people to be a part of the land of Israel. Nearly four millennia have passed since the Hebrew patriarch once named Abram of Ur purchased a bit of land in Canaan, after having lived there for many decades. The land he bought was intended as a burial cave for his beloved wife, Sarai, later named Sarah (Genesis 23). And it was in that cave that he and several others of his immediate family would subsequently be buried.

The land bought by Abraham so long ago is a small part of one of the most significant issues of international dispute in our own day. Even though Abraham bought a piece of it, and despite the fact that the Bible records the divine promise of the land, the question remains—Who owns the land?

As reported in *The Sunday (Portland) Oregonian*, more than a thousand Jewish people came to Hebron in a show of force on Saturday, December 28, 1996, to show their resistance to the negotiations then in process to turn the city and area over to Palestinian control.

Tamar Halfron, a settler from Nefim in the West Bank, is reported to have said, "This is our land. I don't think anyone has the right to give away what God gave us."[11]

And that is the crux of the issue: *Was the land a promise of God to Israel, to the Jewish people? If so, is that promise still in force? And if so, how and by what means may that land be secured by the Hebrew people?* These are the issues of this chapter.

THE PROMISE

It would seem that the fact of a biblical divine promise of the ancient land of Canaan to Abraham is unquestionable. This must be the case in any fair reading. The language of Hebrew Scriptures is clear that God certainly did vow to give the land of Canaan to His servant Abraham and to His descendants. The first instance of the promise is given biblical pride of place; it is found in Genesis 12, the very setting in which the story really begins.[12]

Genesis 12 begins in words that are so impressive as to be unforgettable. The promise of Yahweh to Abram of Ur was as monumental as His demands were unprecedented. Abram was commanded to leave all that made him who and what he was (Gen. 12:1) so that he would be able to become someone entirely new, the blessed and protected of Yahweh. With his wife, Sarai, Abram would be the founding person of an entirely new people, from whom God would bring the means and message of His gracious salvation to all peoples everywhere (Gen. 12:2–3).[13]

When Abram did just as God had commanded (Gen. 12:4–6) and became a "nonperson" in a period and place in history in which one's very meaning was directly connected to place and people, God extended the words of promise to include the explicit provision of a new land.

Because of his faithfulness to the commands of God, the promise was now made to Abraham in clear words and in the context of a dramatic theophany—an appearance of the divine:

> Then Yahweh appeared to Abram and said,
> "To your descendants I will give this land." (Gen. 12:7)

One of the emphases made repeatedly in the narrative of Torah is that the land Yahweh promised to Abraham and his descendants was not an empty land. Indeed, from the beginning we observe that the Bible writers insist that the land was already heavily populated by numerous groups. Immediately after describing Abram's remarkable obedience to the command of Yahweh to leave all that he had and all that identified him as who he was and go to a land that he would know nothing about and in which he would have no prior identity (Gen. 12:1), we read the circumstantial clause, "Now the Canaanites were then in the land" (Gen. 12:6).[14] This reminds us at the very start of the account that Abram and Sarai had not entered a land that was theirs for the taking; it was already populated. Similarly, when Abram and Sarai returned to Canaan from Egypt, the reader is again reminded of the populations already present there: "The Canaanites and the Perizzites then dwelt in the land" (Gen. 13:7; Gen. 34:30).

THE GOOD LAND

That the land was populated is one of the evidences that it was regarded as a "good land." An empty land might have been unpopulated because it was not regarded as a good place to live. Not so the land of Canaan; it had people aplenty! Yahweh's promise to Moses, given at the time of the revelation of the divine name,[15] included these words: "[I am leading you] to the place of the Canaanites and the Hittites and the Amorites and the Perizzites, and the Hivites and the Jebusites" (Exod. 3:8; see also 3:17).[16]

Thus, from the start, there was something of a jarring element in the land as God's gift to His people. The people who then were present would have to be displaced.[17] In His mercy, Yahweh was to allow the Amorites and their compatriots to continue in the land for four centuries from the time that He first made his promise to Abram (see Gen. 15:13). But His patience would not last forever.[18] At last, "the iniquity of the Amorites" would be complete (Gen. 15:16), as the filling of a cup with wine. But finally, judgment would come.

There is another aspect of the gift of the land to the people of Israel that we have anticipated. The land is "good." The promise to Moses included these words: "So I have come down to deliver them out of the hand of the Egyptians, and to bring them up from that land to a good and large land, to a land flowing with milk and honey" (Exod. 3:8). Another elaboration is found in Deuteronomy 8:7–10.

> For Yahweh your God is bringing you into a good land, a land of brooks of water, of fountains and springs, that flow out of valleys and hills; a land of wheat and barley, of vines and fig trees and pomegranates, a land of olive oil and honey; a land in which you will eat bread without scarcity, in which you will lack nothing; a land whose stones are iron and out of whose hills you can dig copper. When you have eaten and are full, then you shall bless Yahweh your God for the good land which He has given you.

Habel writes that "the hyperbole of this lyrical propaganda emphasizes that Israel 'will lack nothing.' The land provided by the celestial ruler is expected to make the Israelite vassals totally self-sufficient."[19] The expression "flowing with milk and honey" does not denote a paradise, but a land that will be sufficient for their needs.[20] The term *milk* speaks of the herds and flocks of the Hebrew peoples. The modern dairy cow is not indicated; rather, the milk would come from goats. This means that the land will provide the forage necessary for the care and raising of goats and attendant sheep and cattle. There would be milk—dairy goat milk. The modern, Western reader may not appreciate this fact, having perhaps a negative attitude toward goat milk. But in many places even in our modern world, the care and breeding of goats is highly valued, for it produces delicious milk that has many uses, both fresh for drinking and processed for cheese and yogurt; not to mention the meat that the herds provide.

The term *honey* refers to the bee, of course, and that which the bee represents, agriculture. In addition to the seminomadic herdsmen of Israel who would follow their flocks and herds in search of green grass,[21] the possibility of a truly settled agriculture was very important. This would allow many of the people of Israel to live in the cities and to benefit from the productivity of the land. It is not necessary to argue for a development of apiculture (the management of bee colonies in agriculture) in this period.[22] Wild bees (producing honey) would still be a part of the agricultural life of the farmers of the land of promise. Thus, God's gift of the land of Canaan to His people Israel was to be regarded by them as an altogether good gift, just what we would expect from His kind hand.

THE GOOD LIFE

The prospect of Israel's enjoyment of the goodness of the land is a central part of what Elmer Martens calls "God's design." Taking His lead from the seminal text of Exodus 5:22–6:8, Martens observes that there are four aspects to God's design for Israel. These are summarized here:

(1) Yahweh's initial design for His people is deliverance.
I am Yahweh. I will bring you out from under the burdens of the Egyptians, I will rescue you from their bondage, and I will redeem you with an outstretched arm and with great judgments (Exod. 6:6).
(2) Yahweh's design is to form a godly community.
I will take you as My people, and I will be your God (Exod. 6:7a).
(3) Yahweh's intention is that there be an ongoing relationship with His people.
Then you shall know that I am Yahweh your God who brings you out from under the burdens of the Egyptians (Exod. 6:7b).
(4) Yahweh's intention for His people is that they are to enjoy the good life.
And I will bring you into the land which I swore to give to Abraham, Isaac, and Jacob; and I will give it to you as a heritage: I am Yahweh (Exod. 6:8).[23]

It is particularly the last point that is germane to this chapter. Martens writes,

The land was already the object of promise where it was the concrete part of God's blessing for His people. Elsewhere the land is described as the land flowing with milk and honey (Exod. 3:17), which is to say that it is a land in which life is pleasant and in which living is marked by abundance. The land comes before long to symbolize the life with Yahweh in ideal conditions, a quality of life which might be characterized as the abundant life.[24]

Thus, when we think of the land in the context of God's intention in His ongoing promises, it was far more than real estate. It was the symbol of all that was good in living as His people under His blessing. So the expression, "the land of Israel," is a phrase that is filled with meaning. It is so important in the flow of biblical theology that were it lacking in the biblical record, the entire story would be affected.

THE MAKING OF THE COVENANT

The making of the covenant with Abram is stunningly recorded in the Bible. Abram was commanded to bring three animals and two birds, to slay them, to cut the animal carcasses in two, and then to make a grisly pathway by aligning the parts of these dead animals. Vultures circled over this carrion feast, but Abram was not preparing a meal for the birds; he spent the day driving the birds away from the meat (see Gen. 15:9–11). Then, at dusk, God put him into the same type of supernatural, trancelike sleep that He had brought upon Adam in the Garden (Gen. 15:12; see also Gen. 2:21 where the same Heb. word is used, *tardemâ*).

Abram's response was an overwhelming sense of horror. The moment was ripe for the appearance of the living God!

In the signs of smoke and burning emblems (see Exod. 19:16–20; Ps. 97:2–6; Isa. 6:1–5; Joel 2:2–3; Zeph. 1:14–16 for the use of smoke and fire in association with the revelation of Yahweh), Yahweh passed between the parts of the dead beasts and the birds. Presumably, in ordinary events, two persons might make such a grisly pathway and both would walk between the slain animals as a sign, each to the other, that if one of them was not faithful to a mutual promise, then let it happen to him what had happened to the animals. In this case, Abram was a silent witness; he does not move. Only God passed between the parts. The onus of the covenant is entirely on Him. How stunning this is! The keeping of this covenant is as sure as the fact of the living God!

With this solemn, unforgettable event, the words of God become truly memorable: "To your descendants I have given this land" (Gen. 15:18). The words of the earlier promise (Gen. 12:7, "To your descendants I will give this land") have now become the words of the divine, irrevocable covenant. The words *this land* serve as the key for the text. The land of Canaan was to become the land of Israel, and the eternal God of heaven would now guarantee that fact by His own life. The promise would be repeated and reaffirmed in later events (see Gen. 17:6–8). God would remove His people from their land because of their sin, but He would also bring them back because of His faithfulness. He has never revoked the promise that is based on His character. This is an irrevocable, everlasting promise.

The dimensions of the land grant to Abram were never fully realized in the experience of Israel in the pages of the Hebrew Scriptures. The words of the promise include regions of ancient Aram as well as Israel proper. Although the period of conquest and the later expansions under Saul, David, and Solomon began a fulfillment of the extent of the promises, the pattern was still only a partial fulfillment.[25] The ultimate extension of the land that would one day be called *Eretz Israel* in the original promise of Genesis 15, is estimated by Charles L. Feinberg to call "for a stretch of land of 300,000 square miles or twelve and one-half times the size of Great Britain and Ireland."[26] This contrasts strongly with the borders of the modern State of Israel, with an area of about 10,000 square miles.[27]

Perhaps the most troubling thing about God's promise and covenant to Abraham is that Abraham himself never realized more than a smidgen of the fulfillment of the promises. His life was that of a sojourner, a traveler, a passerthrough. The words of Genesis 12:9 mark much of the course of Abraham's life: "So Abram journeyed, going on still toward the South." When he settled in places such as Hebron or Beersheba, he knew that he and Sarah and their family were temporary dwellers in a land that God had promised to their seed.

The death of Sarah provided for the one exception; Abraham, who had been promised the land, wound up possessing only the burial ground for his wife.

Abraham's words to the sons of Heth are typical: "I am a foreigner and a visitor among you" (Gen. 23:3). He was but a resident alien, and at the end of the marvelous exchange described in chapter 23 of Genesis, he had become the owner of a burial cave along with attendant fields and trees. Owning only this place of sadness, Abraham was later described by the writer of Hebrews in the New Testament in these marvelous words:

> By faith he dwelt in the land of promise as in a foreign country, dwelling in tents with Isaac and Jacob, the heirs with him of the same promise; for he waited for the city which has foundations, whose building and maker is God. (Heb. 11:9–10)

Abraham's ultimate promise was not to be realized in his lifetime, but his descendants will one day possess all of the land that God promised. This realization of God's promise, we believe, will be fulfilled when the Lord Jesus returns to the earth to establish His glorious kingdom. Then the land promise of the covenant will be realized, for the promises of God, guaranteed by His character, may not be revoked.

THE LAND TODAY

The inevitable questions come. Is the modern State of Israel the fulfillment, or a fulfillment, of God's promises of the land to Israel? Did 1948 bring about the fulfillment of Yahweh's purpose in *Eretz Israel?* To these questions there are some who respond with a resounding (and angry) no. One is Theodore Winston Pike. His book, written to Christians, appears to be an unrelieved tract of hatred of all things Jewish. He claims to have "unearthed irrefutable evidence that Israel is a dominant and moving force behind the present and coming evils of our day. . . . She is a misshapen facsimile of everything we had so fondly bid godspeed to . . . a monstrous system of evil"—well, one gets the idea.[28] For Pike, the situation is obvious: Israel has long ago lost her right to the land. It was only leased to her by God in times past as the physical means for the spiritual objective of the birth of Jesus Christ to be accomplished. Once that was done, they were to be banished and scattered among the nations.[29]

A far more balanced and biblical presentation is given by Stanley A. Ellisen, long-time professor at Western Seminary in Portland, Oregon. His book *Who Owns the Land?* presents a sympathetic, but not uncritical, survey of the issues leading up to the founding of the State of Israel and the aftermath, with a strong Christian perspective.[30] One of his closing paragraphs is based on a recital of the story of Jacob's wrestling with the mysterious Man (perhaps the Angel of Yahweh, or more precisely, the Preincarnate One; see the description in Gen. 32:22–32). It was in the aftermath of that encounter that Jacob received his new name, Israel. Ellisen writes,

The analogy speaks for itself. Israel's basic need today is not peace with the Arabs; it is peace with God. The national turmoil and heart-ache of both clans is spiritual in nature rather than merely racial. Israel's deepest need is not economic, political, or military, but one she yet firmly resists—a history tryst with her covenant Lord, similar to that of Jacob returning from exile. That meeting will do what no military victory could accomplish—inaugurate permanent peace with good will toward all.[31]

And Israel's claim to the land as the fulfillment of biblical prophecy? Ellisen rightly concludes:

> Judged on biblical grounds, the nation today does not pass divine mus-ter. The promise of the land is directly tied to the nation's response to Messiah. Though her international right to the land can be well defended, her divine right by covenant has only sentiment in its favor.[32]

This assessment appears to be correct. Israel certainly has a right to exist as a nation. Israel has a right to remain in the land that became hers through the international actions of the United Nations following World War II. But a critical factor seems to be lacking for one to declare the present State of Israel to be the ultimate fulfillment of biblical prophecy for the return of the Jewish people to their ancient land—that factor is faith in the Savior of the Scriptures, the Lord Jesus, the Messiah.[33] Nonetheless, neither may one minimize the significance of two facts that seem to be almost unbelievable: (1) the perseverance of the Jewish people through the centuries and (2) the formation of the Jewish State of Israel in the land long ago promised to them by God. Israel is a modern miracle. The very fact of the existence of the state is simply astonishing.

There is likely nothing in history that can compare to the restoration of the Hebrew people to their ancient land. What other people of any time, any conti-nent, any lineage can claim what the people of modern Israel can claim? No people group has ever been removed from its land, dispersed among the nations, sur-vived with a sense of self-awareness and identity, and—many hundreds of years later—been regathered to one place, their old place, and has become a nation and state once again. This is simply without parallel.[34]

Now, the Christian believer, observing this isolated phenomenon, finds it ex-ceedingly difficult to say that this is not of God. Indeed, as we read the words of Deuteronomy 4:32–40, we are reminded that the past acts of God for His people also were unparalleled. Never had a people been taken by their god, as Israel was taken by her God, from a land of slavery to a land of freedom in the midst of incontrovertible signs and wonders. That passage concludes, however, with a strong emphasis on the responsibility of the people so delivered by God to live in a conscious sense of awareness of their Redeemer and in a conscientious obedience to His commands.

We observe with sadness that these characteristics simply do not describe the people of the modern State of Israel. To put it bluntly, Israel is a secular state with a veneer of religious interests. Aside from a small minority of Jewish believers in Yeshua, the State of Israel is as dissimilar to the visions of the prophets of the future, glorious promises of the New Covenant, as is the most jaded Western democracy distant from a once-claimed participation in "Christendom."

So what is the land of Israel? First, it is a geographical region. It is the old land of Canaan, once populated by numerous clans and people groups. It is the locale where God brought about the Hebrew kingdom in biblical times. It was the stage for Israel's enjoyment of the good life under God's mercy. But it is also other things such as the land of Palestine, the place where the Philistines lived who were among the adversaries of Israel, and is a title used by other enemies of Israel in subsequent centuries. It is also the enormously significant land bridge joining three continents: its boundaries include the westernmost edge of Asia, where it borders on the Mediterranean Sea, joining that region to Egypt and Africa to the southwest; and it reaches out to Europe in the northwest.

But the land of Israel is not just dirt and rock. It is more than mountain and plain. The land of Israel is a promise of God. It is a promise so strongly held by Him that He stakes His promise concerning the land to His eternal character.

Was there a conditionality to the divine promise?[35] We would like to answer yes and no. All of God's promises have conditions, sometimes stated and sometimes implicit. The subsequent history of Israel following the promises in Torah demonstrate that faith and obedience were requisites for the people to enjoy the good life in the good land. Therefore, at each point, in each generation, and for each individual, there was the obligation to be in a personal relationship with God through faith and in an ongoing response to God in gratitude, worship, and obedience. So even the "unconditional covenants" had conditions to them. But we rush to add that these conditions pertain to the enjoyment of or participation in the promises and covenants by particular persons or generations; the unconditional covenants are unconditional in terms of their final fulfillment.

When individuals, generations, and populaces turned from God, He turned from them, and eventually turned them out of their land. But at one moment in their history, the very point where all seemed hopeless, with the siege machines of the Babylonians at the walls of the city of Jerusalem, the prophet Jeremiah was given the promise of Yahweh for a New Covenant. God will again work within the lives of His people to bring them back to His land (their land) and to help ensure that His will will be done by them joyfully and obediently (see Jer. 31:31–34 and the larger context of 31:23–40).[36]

Yahweh's plan would make it possible for the people of His promise to live as His people once again in order to complete His promise which is ultimately

irrevocable! The land of Israel is the place where the people of God will enjoy
the presence of God under the reign of God in the kingdom of God. Ultimately,
the land of Israel is the center of the planet, the focal point of the universe—for
the outworking of the purposes of God. *Eretz Israel!* The land of Israel is the
enduring physical place for the outworking of God's plan.

UNTIL THEN

In A.D. 1141 a Spanish Jew set out on a pilgrimage to Palestine, the trip of a
lifetime—and the journey that, sadly, brought his life to an end. Jehudah Halevi
expressed his love for the land of Israel from afar. This love was centered particularly on the site of the holy Temple. Although the Temple was no longer
present, just the place—the dust alone—would suffice for the pilgrim, as expressed in his poetry:

> My heart is in the east, and I in the uttermost west—
> How can I find savour in food? How shall it be sweet to me?
> How shall I render my vows and my bonds, while yet
> Zion lieth beneath the fetter of Edom, and in Arab chains?
> A light thing would it seem to me to leave all the good things of
>   Spain—
> Seeing how precious in mine eyes to behold the dust of the desolate
>   sanctuary.[37]

So, in the tradition of Judah Halevi, the modern Christian has a longing for
the land of Israel and the fulfillment of the promises of God. We too can journey
to the present land. We can walk in places made holy and places made
horrendous by events long ago. We can marvel at the present nation, rejoicing
at the victories and accomplishments of the Jewish people even as we may also
weep at the distress of those in its midst and beside its tortured borders who
are marginalized by its presence. The sadness is not unparalleled, of course,
when people and people groups become victims of history, enmeshed in
movements that are beyond their control and concerning which they may have
no full knowledge.

But we live as well in hope. "The dust of the desolate sanctuary" will one
day be replaced by the palace of the King, the Temple of the Savior, and the
fulfillment of all of the promises of the living God. Then—at last—the land
of Israel will truly be the holy land! We agree with Ray Pritz that "no physical
place is intrinsically holy."[38] But when the Savior is present in His land,
surrounded by His people in glorious array—ah, then, dust particles of old
will dissipate, and the land made holy will be the true land, Yahweh's land of
Israel!

APPENDIX

A Sample Listing of the Nations of Canaan Before It Became the Land of Israel

Note: This arrangement is from the longer lists to the smaller; one may observe the variety in these listings of names and the varied order to them.

The longest list is that of Genesis 15:19–21 that has ten names for people groups: the Kenites, the Kenezzites, the Kadmonites, the Hittites, the Perizzites, the Rephaim, the Amorites, the Canaanites, the Girgashites, and the Jebusites.

Deuteronomy 7:1 lists seven nations: Hittites, Girgashites, Amorites, Canaanites, Perizzites, Hivites, and Jebusites. So also in Joshua 3:10, but in this order: Canaanites, Hittites, Hivites, Perizzites, Girgashites, Amorites, Jebusites; so also in Joshua 24:11, but in this order: Amorites, Perizzites, Canaanites, Hittites, Girgashites, Hivites, and the Jebusites.

Exodus 3:8, 17 lists six entities in this order: Canaanites, Hittites, Amorites, Perizzites, Hivites, and Jebusites. Exodus 23:23 lists the same in this order: Amorites, Hittites, Perizzites, Canaanites, Hivites, and Jebusites; Joshua 12:8 has the same six nations in this order: Hittites, Amorites, Canaanites, Perizzites, Hivites, and Jebusites. Judges 3:5 has the same six nations in this order: Canaanites, Hittites, Amorites, Perizzites, Hivites, and Jebusites.

Nehemiah 9:8 has six nations, but a different list than Exodus 3:8: Canaanites, Hittites, Amorites, Perizzites, Jebusites, and Girgashites.

Exodus 13:5 has five nations in this order: Canaanites, Hittites, Amorites, Hivites, and Jebusites.

First Kings 9:20 has a different list of five nations in this order: Amorites, Hittites, Perizzites, Hivites, and Jebusites. So also 2 Chronicles 8:7, but in this order: Hittites, Amorites, Perizzites, Hivites, and Jebusites.

Ezra 9:1 is a little different as it includes "peoples of the lands" extending from Canaan to Egypt, Ammon, and Moab. But among the familiar words from Canaan we read these five: Canaanites, Hittites, Perizzites, Jebusites, Amorites.

From these and other lists we may observe that there is a certain lack of pattern to the litany of the nations. The number of the nations and their order in listing seems not so important as the general idea that the land was filled with people at the time of God's promise to Israel that the land would become theirs. Thus, it matters little if there were five people groups or ten; the important issue is that the land was going to be given to Israel, no matter who lived there at the time.

DISCUSSION QUESTIONS

1. What is the meaning of the expression "the land of Israel"? What elements contribute to your understanding?

2. What makes the land of Israel so special in the views of some Christians? What elements have led others to view the land of Israel in a more negative manner?

3. Why or why not are the land promises of God to the people of Israel still in effect?

4. In your view, is the present State of Israel (founded in 1948) the fulfillment of biblical prophecy? Why or why not?

ENDNOTES

1. The concept of Genesis 1–11 as a prologue and Genesis 12–50 as the main story line is developed in the Introduction to Genesis in *The Nelson Study Bible* [henceforth, *NSB*], ed. Earl D. Radmacher, Ronald B. Allen, and H. Wayne House (Nashville: Nelson, 1997), 1–2.
2. Genesis 15:19–21 has the longer list; other passages list some, but not all of these people groups. See, for example, Exodus 33:2: "the Canaanite and the Amorite and the Hittite and the Perizzite and the Hivite and the Jebusite," and compare the relatively sparse list in Gen. 34:30, "the Canaanites and the Perizzites." We will return to these lists at the end of this chapter.
3. W. M. Thomson, *The Land and the Book*, reprint ed. (Grand Rapids: Baker Book House, 1954), xvi.
4. Norman C. Habel, *The Land Is Mine: Six Biblical Land Ideologies, Overtures to Biblical Theology* (Minneapolis: Fortress Press, 1995), 6. See also the article in this volume by Walter C. Kaiser, Jr., "The Land of Israel and the Future Return (Zechariah 10)," particularly the beginning paragraphs where he develops the importance of the notion of "land" in Hebrew Scripture.
5. Some would suggest an east to west average of from thirty to fifty miles. A convenient, brief description of the geography of Canaan and the broader biblical world is given by Keith N. Schoville, "Geography of the Bible Lands," in David S. Dockery, Kenneth A. Mathews, and Robert B. Sloan, eds., *Foundations for Biblical Interpretation: A Complete Library of Tools and Resources* (Nashville: Broadman & Holman Publishers, 1994), 73–96. A standard full treatment is by Yohanan Aharoni, *The Land of the Bible: A Historical Geography*, rev. and enlarged ed., trans. by A. F. Rainey (Philadelphia: Westminster, 1979).
6. Aharoni begins his magisterial treatment on the geography of the land with these words: "The history of any land and people is influenced to a considerable degree by their geographical environment. This includes not only natural features such as climate, soil, topography, etc., but also the geopolitical relationships with neighboring areas. This is especially true for Palestine, a small and relatively poor country, which derives its main importance from its unique centralized location at a juncture of continents and a crossroads for the nations." Aharoni, *The Land of the Bible*, 3.
7. See, for example, the words of the Lord through His prophet in Jeremiah 7:30–31, "For the children of Judah have done evil in My sight," says Yahweh. "They have set their abominations in the house which is called by My name, to pollute it. And they have built the high places of Tophet, which is in the Valley of the Son of Hinnom, to burn their sons and their daughters in the fire, which I did not command, nor did

it come into My heart." All Scripture quotations in this chapter, unless otherwise identified, are from the *New King James Version*; except the phrase "the LORD" is rendered as "Yahweh."

8. The Book of Joel is variously dated from 835 to 350 B.C., but some recent evangelical scholars date the book about 600 B.C. because of its strong connections with the prophecy of Zephaniah, particularly in the presentations concerning the Day of Yahweh (compare Joel 2:1, 2 with Zeph. 1:14–16). See William Sanford LaSor, David Allen Hubbard, and Frederic Wm. Bush, *Old Testament Survey: The Message, Form and Background of the Old Testament* (Grand Rapids: Wm. B. Eerdmans, 1982), 438–41. See also Ronald B. Allen, *Bible Study Commentary: Joel* (Grand Rapids: Zondervan/Lamplighter Books, 1988), 19–23. Richard D. Patterson makes a strong case for an early eighth-century date, "Joel," in *The Expositor's Bible Commentary*, ed. Frank E. Gaebelein and Richard P. Polcyn, vol. 7 (Grand Rapids: Regency/Zondervan, 1985), 229–35.

9. Habel, *The Land Is Mine*, 39.

10. Chaim Urbach, "The Land of Israel in Scripture," *Mishkan* 26 (1/1997), 22. This entire issue of this publication is devoted to a study of the notion of the land of Israel. *Mishkan*, subtitled "A Forum on the Gospel and the Jewish People," is published in Jerusalem, Israel.

11. "Israelis Visit Hebron to Support Settlers before Withdrawal," *The Sunday (Portland) Oregonian* (29 December 1996), A3.

12. A focus on the grace of Yahweh in this formative act in the Bible is found in Ronald B. Allen, "When God Reached Out to Abraham," *Moody* (November 1989), 36–40.

13. See Ronald B. Allen, "Abraham—Friend of God and Father of the Faithful," *Decision* (May, 1987), 31–33.

14. Author's translation. This clause is a fine example of a circumstantial clause. Made of just three words in Hebrew, the clause begins with a *Waw* disjunctive and is followed by a noun phrase. The disjunctive element is better rendered "now," than "and," to show the circumstantial nature of the words.

15. See Ronald B. Allen, "What Is in a Name?" in *God: What Is He Like?* ed. William F. Kerr (Wheaton, Ill.: Tyndale Press, 1977), 107–27.

16. The lists vary a bit, ranging from ten nations (Gen. 15:19–21) to five (as in Exod. 13:5). See Appendix to this chapter.

17. At one point Habel says, "What a gift! Entrenched enemy nations in your own land!" *This Land Is Mine*, 64.

18. The pictorial term for the patience of God may be translated rather literally as "long of nose," see Ex. 34:6; in our idiom we might say that God has a very long fuse. His anger is not to be minimized for He does visit iniquity upon peoples; but neither is it to be thought as the basic characteristic of God—as is the error of so many who wrongly speak darkly of "the Old Testament God." Indeed, His wrath is best thought of as His strange work, His alien task (see Isa. 28:21). In the note at this verse in the *NSB* we find this comment: "God's judgment on Israel was unusual, or 'alien,' in that He rarely struck out in wrath against His own sinful people. The Hebrew Scripture is not a record of the wrath of God, but of His long patience toward His erring people, whom He still desires to call 'My people' (Ex. 6:2–8)" (p. 1154).

19. Habel, *This Land Is Mine*, 42.

20. One should observe that not all interpreters believe that the phrase "a land flowing with milk and honey" is a positive one. Hareuveni, for example, believes that the phrase is descriptive not of a land fitted for both flocks and herds as well as settled agriculture, but of a land that was suitable only for herdsmen but *not* for agriculture.

When the "milk and honey" areas were cleared for agricultural use, the phrase would be a "frightening description associated with the destruction of productive farmland." See N. Hareuveni, *Nature in Our Biblical Heritage* (Kiryat Ono, Israel: Neot Kedumim, 1980), 22. He comes to this conclusion by his reading of passages such as Isaiah 7:21–24 where milk and honey phrasing is used to describe conditions following the Assyrian incursions into Judah. Hareuveni agrees that the "milk" refers to a land suited for flocks and herds, but he believes that the "honey" is from areas not cultivated but filled with wild flowers (and, hence, also with bees), as biblical passages concerning the bee seem to be "wild bees" rather than not (see, e.g., Prov. 25:16; Judg. 14:8, 9; 1 Sam. 14:25–26). We may observe that Hareuveni makes some persuasive points (ibid., 11–22), but that the phrasing as found in the context of Deuteronomy 8:7–10, as quoted above, is one that is *entirely positive in nature, and that it includes celebrated instances of settled agriculture in the list!* I am indebted to Ray Pritz for alerting me to the material by Hareuveni. Further, the Egyptian traveler Si-nuhe (mid-20th century, B.C.) describes Canaan in terms that fit very nicely with the biblical promise in Deuteronomy 8:7–10. The land of Yaa (presumed to be in northern Canaan) is described as having abundant agriculture, sustaining many herds and flocks, and was proximate to hunting. See the story in *ANET*, pp. 18–22; note especially lines 78–92, pp. 19–20.

21. See, for example, the later stories of Saul looking for his donkeys (1 Sam. 9) and David tending sheep (1 Sam. 17:12–20).
22. See the argument made by Hareuveni, referred to in note 20.
23. Adapted from Elmer A. Martens, *God's Design: A Focus on Old Testament Theology* (Grand Rapids: Baker Book House, 1981), 18–19.
24. Ibid., 19.
25. John Bright writes that the promise "began to find fulfillment—though never a complete fulfillment—in the giving of the Promised Land." John Bright, *A History of Israel*, 3d. ed. (Philadelphia: Westminster, 1981), 96–97.
26. Charles L. Feinberg, *Israel: At the Center of History & Revelation*, 3d. ed. (Portland: Multnomah, 1980), 168. For a discussion of the extent of the borders of the original promise, see Kaiser, "The Land of Israel and the Future Return (Zechariah 10)," in this volume. For a discussion of the extent of the future borders of the land in the promise found in the Book of Ezekiel, see Louis Goldberg, "The Borders of the Land of Israel according to Ezekiel," *Mishkan* 26 (1/1997), 44–48.
27. Hanan Sher, et al., *Facts About Israel* (Jerusalem: The Ministry of Foreign Affairs, 1979), 2. A comparison of the maps of the modern state with selected maps of the biblical pre-exilic periods reveals a most curious fact—today's borders are, in a sense, a mirror image of those in the past. Today's borders include the triangular section of the Negev (the south), the narrow strip of coastal land, the area near to and including the Sea of Galilee, and the wedge from the central coastland that reaches to and includes much of Jerusalem. In much of biblical history the Hebrew people were settled in the mountains of the central part of Canaan (Israel), the Negev was a place for nomads, and the coastal plains were under control of Philistines and Phoenicians.
28. Theodore Winston Pike, *Israel: Our Duty . . . Our Dilemma* ([n.p.]: Big Sky Press, 1984), 280.
29. Ibid., 272–73.
30. Stanley A. Ellisen, *The Arab-Israeli Conflict: Who Owns the Land?* (Portland: Multnomah, 1991).
31. Ibid., 186.
32. Ibid., 174.

33. Goldberg writes, "Some Israelis lay claim to [the whole of] the land now, but it will only be a reality when everyone in Israel undergoes the experience of having their heart of stone removed and a heart of flesh implanted in them (Ezek 36:26)" ("The Borders," p. 48).

34. The writer recalls a marvelous experience when he was in college more than thirty years ago. An invitation was afforded to hear a public lecture by the esteemed historian Arnold Toynbee in Los Angeles. During the course of his presentation, Toynbee spoke of the historically unparalleled phenomenon of the formation of the State of Israel.

35. This is a nagging question, of course. It is addressed by Bruce K. Waltke, "The Phenomenon of Conditionality within Unconditional Covenants," in *Israel's Apostasy and Restoration: Essays in Honor of Roland K. Harrison,* ed. Avraham Gileadi (Grand Rapids: Baker Book House, 1988), 123–39. Waltke concludes that the unconditional nature of the Abrahamic covenant "will finally come to fruition" (p. 137) on the basis of the outworking of the New Covenant.

36. The reader is directed to the chapter in this volume by Ralph H. Alexander, "A New Covenant—An Eternal People."

37. Heinrich Brody, ed., *Selected Poems of Jehudah Halevi* (Philadelphia: The Jewish Publication Society of America, 1952), 2. I am deeply indebted to my friend Stuart Dauerman for introducing me to this poet, and in giving me this book (June 1985, Jerusalem). A modern Jewish writer captures some of the same pathos (and glory) concerning the memory of the Holy Temple that we find in the writings of Halevi. This is the way Richman puts it, "One of the most important principles of Jewish belief is that man has the capacity to engage in a direct, constant, and fulfilling relationship with his Creator. The memory of that relationship and the dream of its renewal keep the fires of the Temple altar burning within the collective heart of the nation of Israel, and the hearts of all those who cherish God. (Chaim Richman, *A House of Prayer for All Nations: The Holy Temple of Jerusalem* [Jerusalem: The Temple Institute/Carta, 1997], 5.)

38. Ray Pritz, "Jerusalem, the Holy City?" *Mishkan* 26 (1/1997), 43.

Young orthodox Jews in Israel.

CHAPTER TWO

ISRAEL THE PEOPLE

Tuvya Zaretsky

Followers of Jesus Christ have been excited about the regathering of the descendants of Abraham, Isaac, and Jacob into their historic homeland. With the founding of the modern political State of Israel, a new act began in the unfolding drama of the sons of Jacob. Another voice was being added to the crowd of opinions in the dispute over who is a Jew.

Meanwhile, in the United States, the Jewish community is experiencing deconstruction. That trend is powered by an intermarriage rate that has exceeded sixty-two percent, a divorce rate that reflects the meltdown in American family values, a declining birth rate, and a departure from synagogue memberships (nationally, fewer than thirty-seven percent are still affiliated). The definition of Jewishness in America is dynamic indeed.

> In an individualistic, free society, where ethnicity and religion are voluntary, the authority of tradition, family, kinship and community has decreasing force and validity. Anybody is Jewish if he or she wants to be and usually on individualistic terms. In practice, everyone is a Jew by Choice.[1]

In this relativistic environment, Christians must take a biblical look at Israel the people. God has the final word about this nation because He has chosen it for His purposes. So, we will look at the identity of Israel the people, then consider the significance of that chosen nation, and finally look into the purposes for which God singled out the nation among all others.

WHO IS ISRAEL?

In the Hebrew Scriptures

The Sons of Jacob

In the attempt to identify who Israel is, we need to consider the possible candidates. The first Bible reference to Israel is made of the individual formerly known as Jacob. At Peniel, Jacob experienced a theophany, an encounter with a physical presence of God, on the bank of the river Jabbok.

> So He said to him, "What *is* your name?" He said, "Jacob." And He said, "Your name shall no longer be called Jacob, but Israel; for you have struggled with God and with men, and have prevailed." (Gen. 32:27–28, NKJV)[2]

God blessed Jacob with a new name, יִשְׂרָאֵל (*Yisrael*), meaning that he had persisted with God. It was Jacob's nature to struggle, relying on his own strength to gain the upper hand with others (e.g., his sometimes contentious relationship with Laban). As he exerted himself with others, so he would persist no less with the God of his father, Isaac, and his grandfather, Abraham.[3]

Second, we find mention of the descendants of the person Israel. Beginning with the book of Genesis, there are fifteen references in the Hebrew Scriptures[4] in which Jacob's children are called the sons of Israel, בְּנֵי יִשְׂרָאֵל (*b'nai yisrael*) (Gen. 45:21; 46:8; 50:25; Exod. 1:1; 13:19; 28:9, 11–12, 21, 29; 39:6–7, 14; Deut. 32:8; 1 Chron. 2:1). This became the biblical designation for all of the physical offspring of the patriarch Israel, including the original tribal heads and their offspring "who went to Egypt" (Gen. 46:8). *Israel* was their national name when they were delivered by God from Egyptian bondage (Exod. 1:9, 12; 2:23, 25) and for those who came from them afterward (Exod. 19:5–6).

Some of the other possibilities for what Israel might mean include

- The land in which the physical descendants of Israel came to live. The geographic distinction is called "the land of Israel." There are twenty such references in Hebrew Scriptures and one in the New Testament (Matt. 2:19–21).
- The royal monarchy under the unified rule of Saul, David, and then his descendants. The first time Israel was designated a political entity or nation state was as the kingdom of Israel (1 Sam. 15:28; 24:20; 1 Chron. 11:10).
- The northern confederation of tribes that resulted from the rupture of the Davidic monarchy was called Israel. That was a geopolitical distinction between the kingdoms of Judah and Israel. An example of the distinction was at the end of the northern kingdom's rule when God said, "I will put an end to the kingdom of Israel" (Hos. 1:4).

- Israel, the modern state, declared its independence in May of 1948. It is a sovereign country in the Middle East and has designated Jerusalem as its undivided and eternal capital.
- The Israel of God: a unique reference to Jewish followers of Jesus, who, according to the argument of Paul in the book of Galatians, had trusted in the saving righteousness of the Messiah alone. By definition, this group bears a dual identity as both a remnant within Israel the people and as a particular community within the body of Christ.

For in Christ Jesus neither circumcision nor uncircumcision avails anything, but a new creation. And as many as walk according to this rule, peace and mercy *be* upon them, and upon the Israel of God. (Gal. 6:15–16)

Israel was first a nation of people, an anthropological entity. As early as the thirteenth century B.C., during the time of the judges, Pharaoh Merneptah provided the first archaeological evidence for the people of Israel. By the grammar used in his Israel Stela, the king indicated that Israel was a nation or a tribe, a people that was greater than a local city-state.[5]

At the holy tent of meeting, the whole nation was symbolically carried into the presence of God upon the shoulders of Aaron, the high priest. Mounted upon the shoulder pieces of his garments were the ephod, the gold filigree with twelve memorial stones naming each one of the "sons of Israel" (Exod. 28:9, 11–12).

Unique Relationship

Yahweh gave Israel its unique identity, significance, and purpose. For example, in the time of Moses, God spoke of the nation as "Israel is my son, even my firstborn" (Exod. 4:22). Of all the nations of the earth, Israel was singled out as the one that would experience an exceptional and intimate relationship with God.

Also, the same Yahweh who is sovereign over the whole earth (Ps. 47:7; 95:3) would uniquely be the King of the people Israel. After the exodus from Egypt, Moses led the people in an anthem of praise: "Yahweh shall reign forever and ever" (Exod. 15:18). Gideon, the judge, did not want to be Israel's ruler. He recognized that Yahweh alone was the rightful monarch over the nation (Judg. 8:23). Later, when the people desired a human king, God admonished Israel through the prophet Samuel, saying, ". . . they have rejected Me from being king over them" (1 Sam. 8:7). King David knew that Yahweh was rightful master of the nation, so he led Israel to worship and enthrone her true Lord.[6] "Let Israel be glad in his Maker; Let the sons of Zion rejoice in their King" (Ps. 149:2).

Israel's identity is unique among the nations in that her significance was based upon being chosen by Yahweh to serve Him. It is important to understand that Israel was God's chosen people, whether or not they ever, as individuals, believed in Him unto salvation. "O descendants of Israel his servant, O sons of Jacob, his chosen ones" (1 Chron. 16:13). Israel was called the "servant of the LORD" forever to express God's gracious choosing (Ps. 136:22). God spoke of both Israel the people and of His Messiah the person as His servant.[7] He had a unique purpose for the nation. It could be said that, as God's chosen servant, the nation Israel would be the delivery system for the Savior of all the nations.

The Nation

In exploring what the Bible means by "the people of God," it would appear that the Hebrew Scriptures recognize the community of Israel as a nation. It was God's stated intent at the establishment of His covenant with Abraham that the people from the patriarch's loins would be a nation that was set apart to be a people of His own: "I will make you a great nation" (Gen. 12:3).[8] It was to be an eternal relationship, even after a time of dispersion: "Then they shall be My people and I will be their God" (Ezek. 37:23c). Thus, the nation of people has had a special relationship to God, a people who derive their significance from a unique service to the Sovereign of all the earth. It is distinguished by an ancestral line of people called into being by God. Israel is the people who are the physical descendants of Abraham, Isaac, and Jacob.

In the New Testament

The term *Israel* occurs over fifty times in the New Testament. It is used most often in the Acts of the Apostles (eighteen) and then in the writings of Paul, where eleven of the sixteen occurrences are in Romans 9–11. In the Gospels, *Israel* appears twelve times each in Matthew and Luke, three times in John, and twice in Mark.[9]

The New Testament widely uses *Israel* to refer to the historic nation of people who descended from Jacob, otherwise known as the house of Israel.[10] Other occurrences are to the God of Israel,[11] the King of Israel (Jesus),[12] the "lost sheep" of Israel, the tribes of Israel, the elders of Israel, and the land.[13] In the New Testament, *Israel* is used for neither the church nor the Gentiles.[14]

Indeed, Paul consistently affirms in his epistles that salvation has come to the Gentiles and to Israel. There is a fullness of the Gentiles and a fullness whereby "all Israel will be saved" (Rom. 11:26). From the disputed passages about the meaning of *Israel* in the New Testament, some Christian scholars have arrived at the understanding that the church is *the new Israel*.[15] Apart from those disputed texts, the general use of *Israel* in the New Testament does not compel us to change the meaning of the term to include Gentiles or to infer the church.[16] This subject will be better taken up and developed by other authors in this book.[17]

Israel in Modern Understanding

We are defining Israel as a unique nation of people who were linked by bloodline back to Abraham through Jacob. Israel in this sense would not be delineated by territory, government, or a particular faith. This identity as a distinct nation was seen throughout the Hebrew Scriptures and the New Testament. Whether identified as a people (עַם 'am) or a nation (גּוֹי goy), Israel was distinguished as the people of God.[18] Did that mean that the nation was godly at all times or in any way defined by a particular faith?

Religion

Christian people who think about Israel are often confused about the relationship between the faith and the nationality of the people. Maybe that is partly because, among Jewish people today, reference to nationality and religion is often indiscriminate. Terms like *Jewishness* and *Judaism* might regularly be used interchangeably in conversation without giving thought to the distinction.

The link between religion and national identity is tightly fixed in traditional Jewish culture. That amalgamation has created a false perception of seamlessness between the two.[19] A Jewish Christian scholar, Jacob Jocz,[20] rightly observed an attitude of Jewish particularism when he wrote, "It is a peculiar fact about Judaism that religion and nationhood are inseparably welded together."[21]

This perception has led many Jewish and Gentile people to wrongly assume that the religion of Judaism defines the Jewish people. For example, in his recent book, Elliott Abrams, the former Assistant Secretary of State, suggested that the national integrity of the people depended on the continuation of a traditional belief that "Jewishness without Judaism cannot be transmitted from generation to generation."[22] Is the birthright of Israelite nationality really pinned upon what every child believes? The source of birthright is found in the genes. Jews are born to other Jews. Descendants of Israel produce more Israelites.

Abrams is correct in one observation. Children are not born with a religious faith, though they might be born into the tradition of a particular religious community. Each individual child must come to his or her own personal faith conviction. So, we are suggesting that the traditional faith of Judaism might be the conventional religion of many Jewish people, but it cannot be the element that ultimately defines who is a Jew. To better understand the people of Israel one must see that religion and nationhood are not seamlessly woven together.

National identity, cultural self-expression, and traditional religious forms of the Jewish community are closely linked, but only the first of those three is determinative. For example, Jewish communities internationally and within the same countries display varieties of unique cultural expressions, yet all are descendants of Israel (e.g., the different Passover traditions of the Ashkenazi, Sephardi, or Mizrachi, "Oriental" Jewish communities). Likewise, there are countless beliefs and religious practices among contemporary Jewish people, including the right to have no faith at all, yet not one single religious position defines Israel. Judaism, though it is the religion of many descendants of Israel, cannot be the defining element for national identity. Nationality stands alone as a birthright. Religious

belief does matter, and later we will examine why every Israelite must still find a
relationship with God.

There is a continuing debate in the international Jewish community today about
the status of Gentiles who choose to follow the God of Israel or who participate
in the varieties of Judaism. That discussion is reserved for the brief excursus at
the end of this chapter.

Terminology

A definition of terms would be helpful in this study. The term *Jew* is a noun that
can also be used of an individual descendant of Israel. It was derived from the Hebrew term *Yehuda* (Judah), which was used of people and territory. The term *Jew*
first appears in the biblical canon in the book of Esther. In all eight occurrences it
refers to Mordecai ben Yair; and in six of those he is simply called "Mordecai the
Jew."[23] In total, the term is used fourteen times in the masculine singular, six times in
the feminine, and seventy-one times in the plural form *Yehudim.*[24] It might sound
strange, but in the hearing of North American Jewish people, use of the words *Jew*
and *Jews,* especially when applied to them by Gentiles, has an edge. This may help
to explain the widely held Jewish fear that the New Testament is anti-Semitic because of the many references to "the Jews" found in it.[25]

While the adjective *Jewish* is used to describe one who is a descendant of Israel, the noun *Jewishness* speaks of the state or the manner in which one expresses
being a Jew. Those expressions are relative to the various cultures and countries
where Jewish people are found. Jews have tended to reflect a cultural adaptation
in their self-expression. Since they are a people who have been dispersed for over
two millennia, that cultural manifestation has often included something of the
national identity where they have settled. Emma Lazerus was quoted in a piece
that was featured in the exhibition "Too Jewish?" at the Armand Hammer Museum in Los Angeles during the spring of 1997: "Jews are the intensive form of
any nationality whose language and customs they adopt." Although Jewish people
have been scattered among the nations, they still have maintained a national self-
distinction, even when that has picked up elements from the host cultures.

English-speaking Jewish people today would not refer to themselves as *Hebrews* or *Israelites.* The archaic term *Hebrews* (*ivrim*), from *ever*, meaning
"across" or "from the other side," originated with Abraham, who is identified as
the first Jew, and who came across the river Euphrates. The term *Israelite* (*Israeli*) is a familiar term primarily in the State of Israel. The birth of the modern
political State of Israel brought with it altogether new dimensions for defining
terminology. The State entered the discussion about "Who is a Jew?" as it sought
guidelines for citizenship. This has also produced some confusion for Christians
who preferred to look in the Bible for definitions about Israel.

In 1950 the Israeli *Knesset* enacted the Law of Return guaranteeing the right
of "every Jew" from anywhere in the world to be granted citizenship on arrival

in the new State. Initially, the status was granted to people with only one Jewish grandparent. Rejected in the discussion was the ultra-Orthodox proposal that a person's Jewishness be established "according to Jewish law" or *halakha*. Now three sources for opinion to define Jewishness are available: the Bible, the Israeli courts, and the historic rabbinic tradition.

In 1970 the Supreme Court of the State of Israel ruled that "membership" in the Jewish faith is separate from citizenship in the Jewish nation (meaning the State of Israel). The Chief Justice, Shimon Agranat, wrote that the goal of integrating Jewish people who are dispersed or exiled "obligates us to see the term 'Jew' as a secular, liberal, dynamic concept." Later that same year, Orthodox members of the *Knesset* gained some ground with an amendment to the Law of Return which defined a Jew as "a person who was born of a Jewish mother or who was converted to Judaism."[26] Once again religion and Jewishness were intertwined! Eventually, this compromise to include a religious definition of Jewishness has been employed to bar Gentiles from receiving Israeli citizenship if they were converted to Judaism by Reform and Conservative rabbis. Jews who have believed in Jesus the Messiah were at one time simply rejected for their faith and are now excluded by law from receiving Israeli citizenship.

We must remember that it was God who called the Jewish people into existence and who created the nation. He alone has the right to define the identity of the nation. The significance of Israel among all the nations of the earth would come from their relationship with Yahweh. He gave the nation its purpose according to His divine plan to make Himself known and to bring about the salvation of humanity.

Let us next consider why God called Israel into existence. What was the significance that God made them a peculiar people among the nations? If they were given the covenant promise by God as a nation, why were they challenged to personally believe in Him and be obedient to His instruction? What difference did it make if they personally participated in the blessings promised?

WHAT IS THE SIGNIFICANCE OF ISRAEL?

A Holy People

> "For you *are* a holy people to the LORD your God; The LORD your God has chosen you to be a people for Himself, a special treasure above all the peoples on the face of the earth." (Deut. 7:6)

Israel derived her true identity from God. He also provided the nation with significance. Israel was chosen to be a "holy people" (*'am kadosh*), set apart out of all the peoples (*'amim*) on the face of the earth. In this section we consider what it meant that the nation of Israel was set apart. We will later explore in depth the purpose for which Israel was sanctified. In this section we are examining what it meant to be an elect people.

A Holy People

Through the covenant that God made with Abram, He made known His intent to use the nation as a channel through which He would pour a blessing out to the nations: "And in you all the families of the earth shall be blessed" (Gen. 12:3). Here was Israel's significance. It was the only nation so chosen to carry out the unique plan of God.

The Hebrew word עַם ('am.) describes the unity and interrelatedness of a people. The nation Israel is 'am echad, one people, bound to one another. However, the significance of that nation is not in its unity, but in the fact that it is the only people of its kind so set apart by God's choosing. In the Hebrew Scriptures, Israel is uniquely called עַם קָדוֹשׁ ('am kadosh), "a holy people" (Deut. 7:6 [3x]); עַם קְדוֹשִׁים ('am ke'doshim), "holy people" (Dan. 8:24); עַם הַקֹּדֶשׁ ('am hakodesh), "the holy people" (Isa. 62:12; 63:18; Dan. 12:7); עַם סְגֻלָּה ('am se'gulah), "a treasured possession" (Deut. 7:6; 14:2; 26:18). God set this nation apart from the other nations. That was the significance of Israel.

What made Israel holy? The nation was given a covenant that stipulated the Lord's promises to Abraham. There would be offspring, an honored name among the nations, a land, and a blessing. These were the benefits of the relationship with Yahweh. He expressed His personal commitment to the nation: ". . . I will be their God" (Gen. 17:8). Yahweh would take Israel as His special people, elect, set apart, sanctified for His purpose. The holy God would always be there with His holy (set-apart or sanctified) people.

In the Sinai wilderness, God pledged Himself to the nation: "I will walk among you and be your God, and you shall be My people" (Lev. 26:12). He committed Himself to a loyal love (hesed), as though married to the nation. The intimacy of God demanded that the nation regard itself, and be regarded by others, as set apart to Yahweh. Israel's significance was that she was set apart to Yahweh.

A Chosen People

"The LORD your God has chosen you to be a people for Himself, a special treasure above all the peoples on the face of the earth." (Deut. 7:6)

Thou hast chosen us from all peoples; thou hast loved us and taken pleasure in us, and has exulted us above all nations; Thou hast sanctified us by thy commandments and brought us near unto thy service, O our King, and hast called us by thy great and holy Name.[27]

When, how, and why did God appoint Israel for a particular destiny
out of all the other potential peoples? The consensus of traditional rabbinic thought is that "Israel's election was . . . predestined before the
creation of the world (just as was the name of the Messiah), and sanctified under the name of God even before the universe was called into
existence."[28]

In rabbinic tradition there is voiced a discomfort about God's seeming partiality
for Israel. Since the two tablets of the commandments were brought down from
Sinai to the children of Israel alone, Moses is seen as being caused to wonder.
One tradition has depicted Moses as asking God, "Of all the seventy great nations
thou hast created in the world thou givest me commands only about Israel?"[29]

Israel was not elect because she was first in chronology among the table of
nations (see Genesis 10). The nation was not chosen because it was the largest or
most prestigious among the powerhouses of the ancient Near East (Deut. 7:6–8).
God's elective grace was not based on size or merit. God owed nothing to Israel,
since He "shows no partiality and accepts no bribes" (Deut. 10:17).

God did not set His affection upon Israel for any other reason but that He decided a human instrument would be central to His salvation plan. All was done
according to an unmerited choice. It was a matter of God's elective grace to accomplish His promise to bring blessing to the nations.

It is rabbinic tradition that God answered Moses' question about the election
of Israel saying, "He replied to him: 'I did so because they are dearer to me than
all the nations. They are My treasure, I love them and have chosen them,' as it is
said: *And the Lord hath chosen thee to be his own treasure out of all peoples*"
(Deut. 14:2 emphasis mine).[30]

A Treasured People

God elected/chose Israel to be "His treasured possession" (*'am se'gulah*). This
does not refer to fixed assets, like real estate. It is property that can be moved
among locations. It has special value to an owner, like a favorite mug, a treasured
coin, or an heirloom which is used on special occasions. Israel was to be God's
very unique movable *treasure*.[31]

The nation of Israel, as a whole entity, was sanctified to be instrumental in
the accomplishment of God's program. The election of the nation, God's salvation plan, and His promises to the nation in the future were established on
the security of His own name. It was as if He drew up a contract and unilater-
ally signed it.

It follows that the individuals of the nation were collectively involved in the
purposes of God. What was the level of their individual participation in the divine plan? Was every Israelite guaranteed to personally enjoy the blessing of the
life-giving relationship in knowing Yahweh God?

There seems to be an answer in the apparent conditional "if" as it relates to obedience. Is Israel a holy nation only *if* she is obedient?

> "Now therefore, if you will indeed obey My voice and keep My covenant, then you shall be a special treasure to Me above all people; For all the earth *is* Mine. And you shall be to Me a kingdom of priests and a holy nation." (Exod. 19:5–6a)

Mentor and friend Walter C. Kaiser Jr., moves us toward illumination on the subject of apparent conditionality. Kaiser considered the results when the nation of Israel obeyed the voice of the Lord and saw a direct link between obedience and her experience of sanctification and fruitfulness of ministry. He rightly makes the distinction between the conditional experience of sanctification blessings and the unconditional standing of Israel's election as a chosen vessel of God.

> [Obedience] hardly could effect her election, salvation, or present and future inheritance of the ancient promise. She (Israel) must obey God's voice and heed His covenant, *not* "in order to" (*l*^e*ma'an* -purpose clause) live and have things go well for her, *but* "with the result that" (*l*^e*ma'an*-result clause) she will experience authentic living and things going well for her (Deut. 5:33).[32]

God's covenant plan would be carried out according to His elective purpose. National Israel's election to fulfill that salvific plan did not guarantee, at the same time, the personal election to salvation of every individual Israelite. Individuals in the nation could experience blessing from knowing Yahweh in their personal spiritual walk as the result of their personal obedience and a faith-based life.

A Holy Remnant

The Channel for the Blessing

The patriarchs provided a bloodline for Israel the nation. Only Jews could make more Jews. Throughout the millennia there was an unbroken chain of generations from Abraham to modern Jewish people.[33] A shared national experience, like the deliverance from Egypt,[34] was another point of continuity that connected the people through time and during seasons of dislocation from the land. Participation in the destiny of this special people, however, required something more than bloodline and common experiences.

From the very beginning, God intended to fulfill the redemption promise that He made to Adam and Eve in Genesis 3:15. Yahweh chose to bring forth children from the lineage of Abram for that salvific purpose. Through Abraham's seed would come the promised blessing for all the nations of the earth (Gen. 12:3).

Israel was God's elect instrument to accomplish His plan. Yahweh revealed to Abraham what He intended to do through his loins. Abraham first participated in the blessing when he responded by trusting God:

> Then He brought him outside and said, "Look now toward heaven, and count the stars—if you are able to number them." And He said to him, "So shall your descendants be." And he believed in the LORD, and He accounted it to him for righteousness. (Gen. 15:5–6)

The nation was created to be a channel for spiritual blessing to the nations, a delivery system for the Messiah. However, each individual Israelite needed faith to participate in God's blessing. Physical birth alone could provide only biological life. To experience more than warm breath, a descendant of Israel would need faith to be truly alive.

Participation in the Blessing

As the outward sign of inward participation in His covenant blessing, God called upon Abraham to undergo circumcision and to circumcise his children: "As for you, you shall keep My covenant, you and your descendants after you throughout their generations. This *is* My covenant which you shall keep, between me and You and your descendants after you" (Gen. 17:9–10a).

Circumcision was an act that demonstrated the faith of the parents. The male child would be a passive participant in the rite. The parents would thereby declare their faith in the God who would accomplish the delivery system through their children. Ron Allen has pointed out (in class lectures) that the actual cut was made in the biological organ that would in the future be instrumental in the continuation of the physical line of the people.

Each descendant of Abraham, Isaac, and Jacob would need to understand God's covenant relationship with their people and consider their own participation within that plan. Each individual Israelite would be responsible to establish his or her own relationship with the God who had promised salvific blessing through the nation.

Two parallel lines are evident in the relationship between God and the people of Israel. One line was a biological community from Abraham. This produced the people, who were set apart by God according to His elective purpose and through which salvation blessing would come to the nations of the earth. In the other line, individual members of the community could participate in the promised blessings by their obedient response of faith in the God of the covenant. The promises were sure. Participation in the promises was conditioned upon the obedient response of each individual Israelite.[35]

How was anyone expected to learn about the national destiny and participation in it? The ritual service of the sanctuary was, like a simple Sunday school lesson, a didactic tool through which the nation received spiritual instruction about the character of God. Through it, they were taught to relate to Him with faith.

> "I will dwell among the children of Israel and be their God. And they shall know that I am the LORD their God, who brought them up out of the land of Egypt, that I may dwell among them. I am the LORD their God." (Exod. 29:45–46)

Israelites, like the people of all the other nations, bear the heart defect of sin. Nevertheless, Yahweh could sanctify the nation according to His purpose. Still, circumcision was not sufficient to experience the blessings of God. Yahweh also called upon the people to circumcise their hearts as a demonstration of their faith in Him (Deut. 10:6; Jer. 4:4). Each individual within the nation, without respect to gender, would have to choose to put away faithlessness. They would be called to turn away from unbelief and turn their hearts to trust in Yahweh and His purpose.

Whenever the individual descendants of Israel would turn to the Lord with obedient hearts, they would experience the blessing of participation in the national relationship with God. So, the covenant had to be renewed on a personal level. This is the basis for the grace of God that was manifested as the new covenant (*haB'rit heHadashah*).[36] It was the opportunity to personally participate in the covenant blessing to Abraham through an ongoing inner restoration. It made personal renewal possible (Deut. 30:6; Jer. 31:31–34; Ezek. 18:31; 36:26).[37]

Individual participation in covenant and blessing was predicated upon faith and repentance in the heart of each Israelite. For example, at a time of transition when Israel was about to enter the land of promise, Joshua called the people to reconsecrate themselves.

The Lord had pledged to bring the generation of children from Egypt into the land stipulated in His covenant to Abraham. On the eve of fulfilling that promise, God told Israel's leaders to pile memorial stones in remembrance of their deliverer (Josh. 4:21, 24). Each could respond inwardly and personally to the facts of their recent history. Then, as a personal response and rededication, God called the people to circumcise their children (Josh. 5:2). Their obedience enabled spiritual participation in the destiny of the nation. Note that other nations learned from the lessons about God's character shown to Israel.[38]

With the advent of Messiah Jesus, the capstone of the nation's destiny was ready for fulfillment. So, when representatives of the Temple priesthood and the Sanhedrin came to investigate John the Baptist's teaching, he challenged them to produce a lifestyle of "fruit" in keeping with repentance. To participate in the redemptive plan, it would require more than a bloodline to Jacob. ". . . And do not begin to say to yourselves, 'We have Abraham as *our* father.' For I say to you that God is able to raise up children to Abraham from these stones" (Luke 3:8).

John, in true prophetic tradition, demanded nothing less than real "heart circumcision." This was necessary if an individual Israelite would experience personally the salvation blessing that was about to flow through the national channel to all humanity.

Throughout the history of the nation and until the Babylonian captivity, common people, political leaders, and religious heroes embraced false and abhorrent idolatry. However, obedience to Yahweh God was essential if one were to participate in the destiny of the nation. It is a common misconception in American society today, that the practice of Judaism is what defines a Jew. The fact is that by 1992 less than thirty-seven percent of American Jewry were members of a synagogue or were affiliated with any Jewish institutions.[39]

The founding of the modern State of Israel did not bring about a spiritual return of Jewish people to faith in God. Thomas Friedman observed that some Israelis hold the view "that because the sky in Israel is Jewish, once there you don't have to observe [religious practices] at all anymore." The American-born Israeli writer and humorist Ze'ev Chafets explained it:

> ". . . I don't need a synagogue. The whole country's my synagogue. The part of the synagogue that I always liked was the social hall, and the kitchen—you know, not the sanctuary. And so being here is a relief. I can be myself and be Jewish but without having to think about it all the time."[40]

A similar secular outlook is shared among the larger percentage of American Jews. According to a National Jewish Population Survey taken in 1990, seventy-two percent of American Jewish people regard themselves as a culture group, while a much smaller forty-seven percent regard themselves as members of a religious group.[41]

Currently Jewish religious leaders in North America and Israel are at odds about what form of Judaism is authoritative. Squabbles have erupted about the validity of Orthodox versus Conservative and Reform expressions of Judaism.[42]

Circumcised or Cut Off

Traditional religion, however, was not the issue in the relationship between God and the people of His covenant community. An Israelite was in jeopardy of losing the connection with God if he or she disregarded holiness requirements, like circumcision, or rejected memorial observances or the sanctity of the Temple when it still stood. Circumcision demonstrated the faith of Jewish parents. If an Israelite child grew up in unbelief, rejecting the covenant and God, that individual could be cut off from the people of God. "And the uncircumcised male child, who is not circumcised in the flesh of his foreskin, that person shall be cut off from his people; he has broken My covenant" (Gen. 17:14).

There are numerous other references in Torah to being cut off from Israel for failure to observe holiness requirements as a people set apart for God's purposes.[43] In the New Testament, the apostle Peter gave a warning to a crowd of Jewish people at Solomon's Colonnade in the Temple. He said that God called for repentance and conversion through the salvation of Messiah Y'shua (Jesus). Should his Israelite hearers reject that call, they would be separated from God for failing to heed Moses' words quoted from Deuteronomy 18.

> The LORD your God will raise up for you a Prophet like me from your brethren. Him you shall hear in all things, whatever He says to you. And it shall be that every soul who shall not hear that Prophet shall be utterly destroyed from among the people. (Acts 3:22–23)

So, a Jew could lose his status as part of Israel. Rabbinic tradition, government officials in the State of Israel, contemporary rabbis, and the Jewish "man in the street" all have expressed opinions about who can and cannot be considered a Jew, a member of the people Israel. However, it was only God who has authority to make such a judgment.

According to the tradition of the rabbis, very little can separate one from their status as the people of Israel. In their view, even sin could not negate Jewishness: "R. Abba b. Zabda said: 'Even though (the people) have sinned, they are still (called) Israel.' R. Abba said: 'Thus people say a myrtle, though it stands among reeds, is still a myrtle, and it is so called'" (Babylonian Talmud, *Sanhedrin* 44a.).[44]

According to the rabbis, the failure to qualify for *HaOlam HaBa*, "the world to come," does not negate Jewishness.

> All Israelites have a share in the world to come, for it is written, "Thy people shall be all righteous, they shall inherit the land forever; the branch of my planting, the work of my hands that I may be glorified. And these are they that have no share in the world to come. He that says there is no resurrection of the dead prescribed in the Law, and (he that says) that the Law is not from heaven and an Epicurean." (Mishnah *Sanhedrin* 10:1)

Yahweh ends the debate for it is He who has determinative authority. He alone called Israel out and set her apart to His purpose as His holy nation. He gave the descendants of Abraham, Isaac, and Jacob identity as a covenant people and defined their unique significance as a holy people, elected for His purposes.

The Remnant of Israel

And it shall come to pass in that day
That the remnant of Israel,
And such as have escaped of the house of Jacob,

Will never again depend on him who defeated them,
But will depend on the LORD, the Holy One of Israel, in truth.
The remnant will return, the remnant of Jacob, to the Mighty God.
For though your people, O Israel, be as the sand of the sea,
A remnant of them will return. (Isa. 10:20–22a)

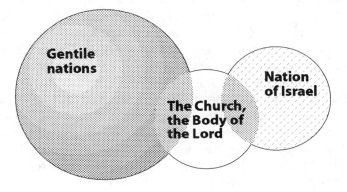

All physical descendants of Jacob may appear to be Israelites. However, God apparently makes a distinction between those who are outwardly Israel and those who are a spiritual elect, a remnant, within the community.

We have seen the significance of Israel in that she was chosen by God. The topic now turns to the purposes for which Israel was chosen from among the nations.

WHAT ARE THE PURPOSES OF ISRAEL?

Arise, shine;
For your light has come!
And the glory of the LORD is risen upon you.
For behold, the darkness shall cover the earth,
And deep darkness the people;
But the LORD will arise over you,
And His glory will be seen upon you.
The Gentiles shall come to your light,
And kings to the brightness of your rising. (Isa. 60:1–3)

The purpose of God for Israel as revealed in the Bible was that they would be a vehicle to shine forth the light of His revelation to the nations and the delivery system for God's Savior, the Messiah. Through Israel, God would introduce Himself to the human race and provide salvation from its sinful condition. There seem to be at least these two central purposes, therefore, for the sanctification of the descendants of Israel: revelation and salvation.

The Revelation of God

God has revealed three specific issues concerning Himself through Israel: (1) His existence; (2) His character; and (3) His plan to bring blessing to all peoples.

First, through Israel, God provided general revelation that He exists. The biblical basis for the origin of Israel demands that God exists and that He acted in history to set apart the nation. Like the starry host of heaven, the continued presence of the Jewish people gives testimony that the God of the patriarchs is real. If Yahweh did not exist, neither would the Jewish people. In Him is the explanation for their origin; in them is the evidence for His existence. He told Moses that He would be known as the God who is.

> And God said to Moses, "I AM WHO I AM." And He said, "Thus you shall say to the children of Israel, 'I AM has sent me to you.'" Moreover God said to Moses, "Thus you shall say to the children of Israel: 'The LORD God of your fathers, the God of Abraham, the God of Isaac, and the God of Jacob, has sent me to you.' This *is* My name forever, and this *is* My memorial to all generations." (Exod. 3:14–15)

Second, the character of God has been revealed in His relationship with His people Israel throughout history. Just as His "invisible attributes, His eternal power and divine nature" (Rom. 1:20) were revealed through creation, so too were these manifested in His faithful interaction with the nation of Israel.

> Now the LORD descended in the cloud and stood with him there, and proclaimed the name of the LORD. And the LORD passed before him and proclaimed, "The LORD, the LORD GOD, merciful and gracious, longsuffering and abounding in goodness and truth, keeping mercy for thousands, forgiving iniquity and transgression and sin, by no means clearing the *guilty*, visiting the iniquity of the fathers upon the children and the children's children to the third and the fourth generation." (Exod. 34:5–7)

God promised that all the nations of the earth would be blessed through the seed of Abraham, Isaac, Jacob, and their descendants (Gen. 12:3; 18:18; 22:18; 26:4; Ps. 72:17; Is. 61:9; Gal. 3:8). The revelation of His nature and the faithfulness of His character in relating to Israel were displayed for the nations to see. Like the testimony of creation in natural revelation, there was a unique revelation through national Israel. Yahweh was made known and His character was transparent through His people (Deut. 4:35; 6:4).

> ". . . for the LORD your God dried up the waters of the Jordan before you until you had crossed over, as the LORD your God did to the Red Sea, when He dried it up before us until we had crossed over, that all the

peoples of the earth may know the hand of the LORD, that it is mighty, that you may fear the LORD your God forever." (Josh. 4:23–4)

The great love of God was so clear to the people of Israel that the nations were called to praise Yahweh. "Praise the LORD, all you Gentiles! Laud Him, all you peoples!" (Ps. 117:1). His reputation for loyal loving kindness was at stake in His relationship with Israel. What if this "moveable treasure" were discarded at any time? What then would have been said of the character of God?

That was the concern of Moses at Sinai when many in Israel had sinned. It was Yahweh's name and reputation which stood at stake. Moses argued that God's trustworthiness, His reputation before the nations, was linked to Israel's destiny.

> "Why should the Egyptians speak, and say, 'He brought them out to harm them, to kill them in the mountains, and to consume them from the face of the earth'? Turn from your fierce wrath, and relent from this harm to Your people. Remember Abraham, Isaac and Israel, Your servants, to whom you swore by your own self, and said to them, 'I will multiply your descendants like the stars of heaven; and all this land that I have spoken of I give to your descendants, and they shall inherit it forever.'" (Exod. 32:12–13)

Third, in Israel the instrumentality of God's plan was revealed. This nation of priests would be used to teach spiritual concepts like sin, atonement sacrifice, and redemption. Throughout Israel's history, the message of God's delivering power was repeated annually at Passover: "I am the God who brought you out of Egypt" (Exod. 12:7).

King David understood that from Egypt to his own throne, God would fulfill His promise to Abraham through the line of Israel.

> "O LORD, for Your servant's sake, and according to Your own heart, You have done all this greatness, in making known all these great things. O LORD, *there is* none like You, nor *is there any* God besides You, according to all that we have heard with our ears.
>
> "And who is like your people Israel, the one nation on earth whom God went to redeem for Himself as a people—to make for Yourself a name by great and awesome deeds, by driving out nations from before Your people, whom you redeemed from Egypt?
>
> "For You have made Your people Israel Your very own people forever; and You, LORD, have become their God.
>
> "And now, LORD, the word which You have spoken concerning Your servant and concerning his house, let it be established forever, and do as You have said. So let it be established, that Your name be magnified forever, saying, 'The LORD of hosts, the God of Israel, is Israel's God.' And let the house of Your servant David be established before You." (1 Chron. 17:19–24)

From Abraham's chosen line, the Almighty declared that salvation blessing would come to the nations. Through the dynasty of David, the Holy One designated a unique individual to be the seed of blessing.[45] Finally, at the time of Jesus' birth, Simeon, a faithful man of Israel, testified that God had at long last produced the promised Savior. In this unique seed of Israel, Simeon saw the radiant *shekinah* of God shining through His people. In this One, he witnessed the light of the LORD's promised salvation, now revealed to the nations which had languished in darkness. He said,

> Lord, now You are letting Your servant depart in peace,
> According to Your word;
> For my eyes have seen Your salvation
> Which you have prepared before the face of all peoples,
> A light to *bring* revelation to the Gentiles,
> And the glory to Your people Israel. (Luke 2:29–32)

The Salvation of God Through the Nation of Israel

Messiah, the Savior, Came Through Israel

The purpose of God for Israel was to produce His light and life for the world. The light was His revelation to the nations, and the life was that of the deliverer who would come through the people Israel. As it was spoken by God through Isaiah the prophet, "And in that day there shall be a Root of Jesse, Who will stand as a banner to the people; For the Gentiles shall seek Him, and His resting place shall be glorious" (Isa. 11:10).

In the coming of Jesus from the rootstock of David, the descendant of Israel, those nations who walked in darkness will "have seen a great light" (Isa. 9:2). He would fulfill the longing for life that was given voice by the psalmist who wrote,

> How precious is your lovingkindness, O God! Therefore the children of men put their trust under the shadow of Your wings.
> They are abundantly satisfied with the fullness of Your house, And You give them drink from your river of Your pleasures.
> For with You is the fountain of life; In Your light we see light. (Ps. 36:7–9)

God, according to His faithfulness to Abraham, has preserved His testimony in the earth through the continued existence of His covenant people. He has revealed His blessing of new life in the coming of the Messiah.

In the passage above from Luke 2:29–32, Simeon testified to both the light and life. When he saw and finally held the infant Messiah, he declared, "a light for revelation to the Gentiles and for glory to your people Israel." Jesus is the glory of God shining through Israel; He is the light for the sin-darkened world.[46] Jesus confirmed to the Samaritan woman that He was the capstone of Israel's existence, "we [sons of Israel] worship what we do know, for salvation is from the Jews" (John 4:22). He was the very Savior expected through Israel according to her election: "In him was life, and that life was the light of men" (John 1:4).

The hope of life was to come through Israel, which was God's chosen delivery system for salvation. The blessing wasn't guaranteed to the nation; she was only the conduit for it. The wellsprings of salvation would be poured out to all the nations, including the elect among Israel.

The sons of Jacob were the cement for the channel of God's blessing. According to Solomon Schechter,[47] the rabbis wrote of God's desire to build creation upon a firm foundation. However, when He foresaw the pollution of the generations of the sons of men, He knew in advance what must be done to bring salvation and redemption. They spoke of the one to come through Israel as "the rock":

> But when he perceived that Abraham would one day arise, he said, "Behold, I have found the *Petra* [πετρα] on which to build and base the world." The patriarch Abraham is called the rock (Isaiah 51:1–2); and so Israel is called the rock (Num. 33:9).

We wonder whether this could have been the informing theology behind the Lord's reply to Simon Peter at Caesarea Philippi.

> Simon Peter answered and said, "You art the Christ [Messiah], the Son of the living God."
> Jesus answered and said to him, "Blessed are you, Simon Bar-Jonah, for flesh and blood has not revealed *this* to you, but My Father who is in heaven. And I also say to you that you are Peter, *Petros* [Πετρος], and on this rock [πετρα] I will build my church." (Matt. 16:16–18)

Is Israel Still Needed in God's Plans?

Since salvation has come through Jesus the Messiah, is it possible that Israel is no longer needed? Is it still valid to say that God is revealed in the existence of His ancient people? Isn't the revelation of God's existence now fulfilled through the body of Christ, the church? If so, does Israel have a future?

Does Israel, the Jewish people, still exist? Since the answer is yes, then we must conclude that the revelation of God's existence continues to shine through His covenant people, Israel. Does God also manifest Himself through the body of Christ? The answer is also yes. The instruction from Jesus was that "you are the light of the world" (Matt. 5:14). Then we may conclude that the revelation of salvation in the Messiah Jesus shines through the body of Christ, which is composed of a remnant from the Jewish people and from the nations. Yahweh continues to be revealed in Israel, both within and apart from the body of believers. Thus, there appears to be no warrant for suggesting that Israel the nation has been superseded by the existence of the body of Christ, the church.

Is the Church the Israel of God?

There is no broad basis upon which to say that the whole church is Israel. Moreover, the modern remnant of Israel is included within the church as Jewish Christians, "the Israel of God," of Galatians 6:16. We understand that from God's perspective, only the saved remnant from Jacob's line can be true Israel now. Others may do a more thorough job of developing why Paul wrote: "But it is not as though the word of God has failed. For they are not all Israel who are *descended* from Israel" (Rom. 9:6). The whole community of Jewish people alive today may be physical Israel, but only a small remnant are the Israel of faith. True Israel are those who have descended from physical Israel and who exhibit the obedience that comes from faith in Yahweh.

The Faithfulness of God to Israel

Indeed God is still revealed through the existence of the people of Israel, just as in times past. His electing grace was not dependent upon the belief of the people. Obedience on the part of Jewish individuals could only result in their participation in blessing, seen now as trust in Jesus. Nevertheless, God continues to demonstrate His covenant faithfulness through His current preservation of the whole nation.

The nation Israel was set apart so that God might prove Himself to be faithful. Yahweh fulfilled His promise through Abraham by the New Covenant relationship that came in the Messiah Jesus (Luke 22:20; 1 Cor. 11:25). When the prophet Jeremiah (31:31–34) spoke God's Word to announce the renewal of the covenant blessing to Abraham, He also issued its insurance policy. The blessing of the covenant was secure as the nation of Israel was protected. Thus, salvation and revelation were both guaranteed. God's purposes in Israel were sure.

> Thus says the LORD, Who gives the sun for a light by day, The ordinances of the moon and the stars for a light by night, Who disturbs the sea, And its waves roar (the LORD of hosts *is* His name):
>
> "If those ordinances depart from before Me," says the LORD, "Then the seed of Israel shall also cease from being a nation before Me forever."
>
> Thus says the LORD: "If heaven above can be measured, and the foundations of the earth searched out beneath, I will also cast off all the seed of Israel for all they have done," says the LORD. (Jer. 31:35–37)

The sun, moon, and stars still give their light, to the glory of Yahweh's handiwork. Since they exist, God will not forget His faithfulness to the physical descendants of Israel.

> O seed of Israel His servant, You children of Jacob, His chosen ones! He *is* the LORD our God; His judgments *are* in all the earth. Remember His covenant forever, the word which He commanded, for a thousand generations, *the covenant which* He made with Abraham, and His oath to Isaac, and confirmed it to Jacob for a statute, to Israel *for* an everlasting covenant. (1 Chron. 16:13–17)

SUMMARY

In the Word of the Lord, there is clarity for understanding the identity, significance, and purpose for the people of Israel. In the appearing of Jesus through the line of Israel, Yahweh accomplished His promised blessing, the salvation program for the nations. God has shown that He is faithful and His Word is true. He revealed that He would make life new, and He has done it. Moreover, He has preserved a banner to all the nations, even Israel His people. Humanity can be assured that all that remains of His promises will yet be accomplished. The appropriate response to such glory has been for the nations to now rejoice!

> O, Sing to the LORD a new song!
> For He has done marvelous things;
> His right hand and His holy arm have gained Him the victory.
> The LORD has made known His salvation;
> His righteousness He has revealed in the sight of the nations.
> He has remembered His mercy and His faithfulness to the house of Israel;
> all the ends of the earth have seen the salvation of our God. (Ps. 98:1–3)

EXCURSUS ON ISRAEL AND GENTILES

The origin of Israel begins among the Gentiles, the nations. Abraham was a descendant of Shem, who was living among the Chaldeans in the "sea lands" of Southern Babylonia. Wives for his heirs also came from related Semites who lived to the northwest in their path of migration. This "international" heritage was preserved in the Israelite celebration of Shavuot (the Feast of Weeks or Pentecost) where God's promise is lauded and the patriarch Jacob was honored with the words, "My father was a wandering Aramean" (Deut. 26:5).

Throughout history, Israelites have, by marriage, incorporated other people from among the nations who were Gentiles. Moses' wife, Zipporah, was a Midianite (Exod. 2:21 and Num. 12:1). Caleb, the hero of the Israelite conquest, was of the tribe of Judah, but bore an ancestral connection to the Kenizzite peoples of Edom (Num. 13:6; 32:12).

Marriage to Canaanites was forbidden by God (Exod. 34:12–17, Deut. 7:1–3). Violation of that command resulted in the spiritual destruction of Solomon (1 Kings 11:1–4). However, the Bible offers a record of non-Israelites who were fearers of Yahweh God, like Rahab, the prostitute from Jericho, and Uriah the Hittite, who was loyal to the king of Israel.

The most honored "foreigner" who turned to the Lord God of Israel was Ruth from the land of Moab. Like Abraham, she left her homeland and her people to follow the one true God, whom she calls by His specific name, Yahweh (Lord). She expressed her faith and her will with deep conviction.

> "Entreat me not to leave you, or to turn back from following after you;
> For wherever you go, I will go; and wherever you lodge, I will lodge;
> Your people *shall be* my people, and your God, my God. Where you die,
> I will die, and there will I be buried. The LORD do so to me, and more
> also, if *anything but* death parts you and me." (Ruth 1:16–17)

In New Testament times there were apparently many who were proselytes, Gentiles who joining themselves to the faith of the Jewish people (Acts 2:10, 6:5, and 13:43). Y'shua (Jesus) encountered some who caused Him to remark about their devotion to Yahweh, "Assuredly, I say to you, I have not found such great faith, not even in Israel" (Matt. 8:10; Luke 7:9).

Today, the question is how to regard those who join themselves to the God of Israel. On one hand, we acknowledge the physical connection through marriage. In practical terms these were not seen as Jews (i.e., Ruth *the Moabitess* or Uriah *the Hittite*) until the subsequent generations came along. Still, it is the bloodline that insures the continuation of Israel the people.

However, when one is joined to the God of Israel through the same faith evidenced by Abraham, something special has happened. They do not become Jews in the bloodline of Israel, but they do become spiritual children of Abraham. They are the recipients of the blessing that God promised through Abraham's seed to all who believe: "So then those who are of faith are blessed with believing Abraham" (Gal. 3:9).

In this unique way, proselytes from the nations have come to be regarded also as God's people through the blessing of the new covenant promise. Zion, Jerusalem, is the place that Yahweh called the center of His true worship. All who come to Him can be regarded as if they were born in Zion:

> His foundation *is* in the holy mountains.
> The LORD loves the gates of Zion more than all the dwellings of Jacob.
> Glorious things are spoken of you, O city of God! Selah
> "I will make mention of Rahab and Babylon to those who know Me;
> Behold, O Philistia and Tyre, with Ethiopia: 'This *one* was born in there.'"

And of Zion it will be said, "This *one* and that *one* were born in her;
And the Most High Himself shall establish her."
The LORD will record, when He registers the peoples:
"This *one* was born there."
Selah. (Ps. 87:1–6)[48]

DISCUSSION QUESTIONS

1. What have you learned about the elements that define Israel as a people?

2. How would God answer the question, Who is a Jew?

3. What is meant by the concept that Israel is a *chosen people?*

4. How could an individual Israelite be within the channel for blessing and a participant in the blessing?

5. What are the purposes for which God set Israel apart?

ENDNOTES

1. Barry Kosmin, "The Permeable Boundaries of Being Jewish in America," *Moment* (August 1992): 32.
2. Compare with Hos. 12:3, "In his strength he struggled with God" (NKJV).
3. Charles Pfeiffer, Howard Vos, and John Rea, *Wycliffe Bible Encyclopedia,* 2 vols. (Chicago: Moody Press, 1975), 863.
4. Ronald B. Allen, at the consultation in Jerusalem on which this book is based, has suggested the descriptive and vibrant term *Hebrew Scripture* as an alternative to the familiar *Old Testament,* which suggests something archaic rather than alive.
5. Edward Blaiklock and R. K. Harrison, eds. *The New International Dictionary of Biblical Archaeology* (Grand Rapids: Regency Reference Library, 1983), 254–55.
6. See Ronald B. Allen, *Praise: A Matter of Life and Breath* (Nashville: Nelson, 1980).
7. Walter C. Kaiser Jr., *Toward an Old Testament Theology* (Grand Rapids: Zondervan, 1978), 215. Kaiser notes the distinction between Israel the servant in many of the references in Isaiah 40–53 and the individual servant, who ministers to Israel and the nations, as the subject of the "four great servant songs" of Isa. 42:1–7; 49:1–6; 50:4–9; and 52:13–53:12.
8. See also Exod. 19:6.
9. *Israel* appears in the book of the Revelation three times: once it speaks of Israel in the Hebrew Scriptures (2:14) and twice of the twelve tribes of Israel (7:4 and 21:12).
10. Three times in Heb. 8:8, *Israel* refers to the northern kingdom mentioned in Jer. 31:31.
11. Matt. 15:31; Luke 1:68; Acts 13:17.
12. Matt. 27:42; Mark 15:32; John 1:49; 12:13.
13. Matt. 2:20, 21; Luke 4:25.
14. See Mark A. Elliot, "Israel," *Dictionary of Jesus and the Gospel,* ed. Joel B. Green and Scot McKnight (Downers Grove, Ill.: InterVarsity Press, 1982), 357.
15. See Reinhold Mayer, "Israel," *The New International Dictionary of New Testament*

Theology, ed. Colin Brown (Grand Rapids: Zondervan, 1976), 2:316: "Barnabas uses the word Israel mostly in connection with his exegesis of the Bible against Israel . . . but he does not yet dare take over the word for the church. Justin, on the other hand, asserts boldly: 'We are . . . the true spiritual Israel' (*Dial.* 11, 5; cf. 100, 4; 123, 9)," (*NIDNT,* 316). See H. Wayne House's discussion in chapter 4 of this book.

16. Saucy, in his explanation of progressive dispensationalism writes, "At least it must be acknowledged by all that the theological concept of the church as a 'new Israel' is never clearly, let alone predominantly, taught by Paul with that terminology." (Robert L. Saucy, *The Case for Progressive Dispensationalism* (Grand Rapids: Zondervan, 1993), 195.

17. Two of the disputed passages are Romans 9:6, which contains the phrase "not all who are descended from Israel are Israel," and Galatians 6:16, with the words "the Israel of God." Both most likely refer to the distinction of a faithful remnant of Jewish people within the nation of Israel. See Ray Pritz, chapter 3, and Harold Hoehner, chapter 6.

18. Judg. 20:2; 2 Sam. 14:13.

19. Even Marvin R. Wilson, Christian scholar, friend, and student of the Jewish people, reflected this same misidentification of the Jewish community when he called Judaism "the religion and culture of the Jewish people." *Our Father Abraham—Jewish Roots of the Christian Faith* (Grand Rapids: Eerdmans Publishing Co., 1989), 32.

20. Jacob Jocz, *The Jewish People and Jesus Christ* (Grand Rapids: Baker Book House, 1979; reprinted by permission from SPCK: 1949), 304.

21. This confusing, inseparable joining together of these two, nationality and religion, make it nearly impossible for contemporary Jewish people to understand the Christian message. The call to embrace Christ appears to be a challenge to reject the connection with the Jewish people, not just Judaism, and to embrace a foreign religion and people.

22. Elliott Abrams, *Faith or Fear* (Free Press, 1997), 256 pages as quoted in David Van Biema, "Sparse at Seder?" *Time* (April 28, 1997): 67.

23. Esth. 2:5; 3:4; 5:13; 6:10; 8:7; 9:29, 31; 10:3.

24. R. Laird Harris, Gleason L. Archer, and Bruce K. Waltke, eds., *Theological Wordbook of the Old Testament* (hereafter *TWOT*), vol. 1 (Chicago: Moody Press, 1980), 369, "Judah" article by Paul R. Gilchrist.

25. The plural "Jews" appears in the whole Bible more than 200 times, of which 64 are in the Hebrew Scriptures (in the books of Ezra, Nehemiah, Esther, Jeremiah and Daniel) and 81 are in the four Gospels alone. An excellent article by a rabbi and professor of classics at Yeshiva University addresses this charge. Louis Feldman, "Is The New Testament Anti-Semitic?" *Moment* (December 1990): 32–35, 50–52. Feldman helps his Jewish readers to appreciate the intramural nature of the discussion among Jewish people as it was being overheard in the New Testament.

26. David Horovitz, Leslie Susser, and Vince Beiser, "Who's Been A Jew," *The Jerusalem Report* (Dec. 12, 1996): 12–14.

27. Joseph H. Hertz, *Daily Prayer Book* (New York: Bloch Publishing Company, 1948), 799–801 from the *Amidah* for Festivals.

28. *Genesis Rabba,* Bereshit, I, 4 and *Seder Eliahu rabba und Seder Eliahu zuta (Tanna d'be Eliahu),* ed. Friedmann (Vienna: 1900), 160, as cited by Solomon Schechter, *Aspects of Rabbinic Theology* (Woodstock, Vt.: Jewish Lights Publishing, 1993), 59.

29. *Pesikhta Kahana* II, 17a; as cited by Claude G. Montefiore and Herbert Loewe, *A Rabbinic Anthology* (New York: Schocken Books, 1974), 77–78.

30. *Tanhuma Exodus,* כִּי תִשָּׂא ("When Thou Takest"), 8; The edition cited is *Midrash*

Tanhuma-Yelammedenu: An English Translation of Genesis and Exodus from the Printed Version of Tanhuma-Yelammedenu with an Introduction, Notes, and Indexes, by Samuel A. Berman (Hoboken, N.J.: Ktav, 1996), 579. Also found in Solomon Schechter, *Aspects of Rabbinic Theology* (Woodstock, Vt.: Jewish Lights Publishing, 1993), 61.

31. See Walter C Kaiser Jr., *Toward and Old Testament Theology* (Grand Rapids: Zondervan Publishing House, 1978), 105, for discussion of the "moveable" or portable treasure which was highly valued property, "set aside for a marked purpose."

32. Kaiser, op. cit., 110–11.

33. An interesting article in this discussion was written by Judy Siegel in the *Jerusalem Post International Edition* (January 1997), "Genetic link found among *kohanim*" on the work of Prof. Karl Sorecki of the Rambam Hospital in Haifa. He and others found a common genetic link in the chromosomes of Ashkenazi, Sephardi, and in some Oriental Jews, who trace lineage to the line of Aaron, the High Priest.

34. "I am the LORD your God, who brought you out of the land of Egypt." Kaiser mentions that this formula appears 125 times in the Hebrew Bible. Kaiser, op. cit., 34.

35. For an excellent discussion on circumcision as a "sign" not a condition of the covenant see Kaiser, op. cit., 83–84.

36. Many see this as the renewed covenant.

37. See the papers by Ralph Alexander and Robert Thomas for a fuller discussion of the new covenant.

38. E.g., Exod. 18:1 (Midianites); Josh. 2:10 (Canaanites of Jericho); Josh. 9:9 (Hivites).

39. Joshua O. Haberman, "The New Exodus Out of Judaism," *Moment*, (August , 1992), 35. Reporting from the *1990 Council of Jewish Federations, National Population Survey.*

40. Thomas Friedman, *From Beirut to Jerusalem* (New York: Farrar, Strauss, Grioux, 1989), 294–95.

41. Barry Kosmin, "The Permeable Boundaries of Being Jewish in America," *Moment* (August 1992): 33.

42. Larry Stammer reported on the controversy created by the Union of Orthodox Rabbis of the U.S. and Canada in "Orthodox Group to Declare Two Branches Are Not Jewish," *Los Angeles Times* (March 22, 1997), A31.

43. For eating leaven during the feast of unleavened bread—Exod. 12:15, 19; misuse of anointing oil—Exod. 30:33, 38; failure to observe the Sabbath—Exod. 31:14; ingestion of portions consecrated for worship or offering—Lev. 7:20, 21, 25, 27; unauthorized sacrifice—Lev. 17:4, 9, 14; general failure to regard holy things—Lev. 18:29; improper regard for fellowship offering—Lev. 19:8; worship of Molech—Lev. 20:5; violation of sexuality regulations—Lev. 20:17–18; improper regard for Yom Kippur—Lev. 23:29; failure to observe the Passover—Num. 9:13; defiant sin against the Lord—Num. 15:30, 31; the unclean person who enters the sanctuary—Lev. 19:13, 20.

44. This was basis on which rabbis explaining that a Jew who believes in Jesus remains a Jew, even if, in their eyes, messianic Jews are sinners.

45. 2 Sam. 7:11–16; 1 Chron. 17:11–19; Matt. 1:1, 17.

46. See Isa. 49:6, 60:3; John 8:12, 9:5; Acts 26:17–18, 23.

47. Schechter, 173. The following quote is reproduced from the *Yelammdenu* quoted by the Yalkut, *Num.* §766 cf. *Exod.R.*, 15:17.

48. See Ron Allen's notes, pages 968–96, for Psalm 87 in *The Nelson Study Bible.*

בית הכנסת ובית המדרש
צמח־צדק חב"ד
כנשיאות כ'ק אדמו'ר שלי'ט'א מליובאוויטש
TZEMACH - TZEDEK
CHABAD LUBAWITCH SYNAGOGUE
REOPENED AFTER SIX DAY WAR 5727(1967)
BY THE LUBAWITCH REBBE SHLITA
RENOVATED THROUGH THE GENEROSITY OF
JOEY & TOBY TANENBAUM TORONTO

The Chabad Lubawitch synagogue and study center in Jerusalem, opened to Jews once again after the Six-Day War in 1967.

CHAPTER THREE

THE REMNANT OF ISRAEL AND THE MESSIAH

Ray A. Pritz

A key to the understanding of Paul's argument in Romans 9–11 is the teaching concerning the remnant of Israel. In the first third of chapter 11 in particular, Paul uses the remnant as a central building block in his argument. In the following pages we will try to identify the basic elements of this doctrine as they were found in Paul's Bible and in his cultural heritage.

THE REMNANT BEFORE THE PROPHETIC BOOKS

The most important Hebrew roots for this concept are *sarad, palat, yathar,* and *sha'ar.* Of these, the terms which reckon in the more significant passages are *sha'ar* and *she'erith.* Probably the earliest occurrence of the idea comes in the story of the Flood. The main elements are familiar: There is a disaster (the degraded moral situation of mankind) and God's declared judgment (the flood). God Himself selects the one to be excluded from the judgment. With the saving of this one and his family comes a wider salvation, in this case the continuation of humanity.

It is immediately evident that God is the chief player. He is the one who selects those who will survive, He is the one who brings about the judgment, He is the one who saves the small remnant and through them saves humanity. These main elements remain more or less standard in the remnant doctrine throughout the Hebrew Scriptures (Tanach), although slight variations will be noted. Thus, in the case of Abraham, the element of disaster is not clearly delineated. Nonetheless, the saving of the race is narrowed down to one man and his wife, and again God is the initiator. This process of narrowing or selection continues also with Abraham's descendants. One of his sons is selected and in turn one of his grandsons.

The book of Genesis ends with a kind of microcosmic picture of salvation through the remnant in the story of Joseph. The disaster in this case is an impending famine which threatens to wipe out Jacob and his family. Long before the famine begins, however, God initiates a process whereby one of the family is put in a safe place so that he in turn can save the rest. Joseph recognizes what is happening even when his brothers do not: "God sent me before you to preserve for you a remnant [she' erith] in the earth, and to keep you alive by a great deliverance [pleta]" (Gen. 45:7).[1] It has long been noted, of course, that there are many parallels between the life of Joseph and the life of Jesus.[2] This story is perhaps the first time the Scriptures make a connection between the remnant idea and a messiah figure. It is by no means the last.

It would be a mistake to think that once God had narrowed His focus to the descendants of the twelve patriarchs, He would then abandon the concept of the righteous few who escape to carry forward His program. The remnant cycle continues throughout Scripture. It appears next in 1 Kings 19:9–18:

> There he went into a cave and spent the night.
> And the word of the LORD came to him: "What are you doing here, Elijah?"
> He replied, "I have been very zealous for the LORD God Almighty. The Israelites have rejected your covenant, broken down your altars, and put your prophets to death with the sword. I am the only one left, and now they are trying to kill me too."
> The LORD said, "Go out and stand on the mountain in the presence of the LORD, for the LORD is about to pass by."
> Then a great and powerful wind tore the mountains apart and shattered the rocks before the LORD, but the LORD was not in the wind. After the wind there was an earthquake, but the LORD was not in the earthquake. After the earthquake came a fire, but the LORD was not in the fire. And after the fire came a gentle whisper. When Elijah heard it, he pulled his cloak over his face and went out and stood at the mouth of the cave.
> Then a voice said to him, "What are you doing here, Elijah?"
> He replied, "I have been very zealous for the LORD God Almighty. The Israelites have rejected your covenant, broken down your altars, and put your prophets to death with the sword. I am the only one left, and now they are trying to kill me too."
> The LORD said to him, "Go back the way you came, and go to the Desert of Damascus. When you get there, anoint Hazael king over Aram. Also, anoint Jehu son of Nimshi king over Israel, and anoint Elisha son of Shaphat from Abel Meholah to succeed you as prophet. Jehu will put

to death any who escape the sword of Hazael, and Elisha will put to death any who escape the sword of Jehu. Yet I reserve *[vehish' arthi]* seven thousand in Israel—all whose knees have not bowed down to Baal and all whose mouths have not kissed him."

Clearly the disaster here is the spiritual corruption of the northern kingdom of Israel, as it is defined by Elijah himself (vv. 10, 14). The judgment is to be carried out by three men, two kings and a prophet, but God will see to it that a remnant of faithful Israelites is preserved (vv. 15–17).[3]

THE REMNANT IN THE PROPHETIC BOOKS

Some expression of the remnant theme can be found in most of the writing prophets. It will suffice us here to focus only on a few of the most prominent.

Probably the most important passage for gaining an understanding of the prophetic concept of the remnant is the six chapters of Isaiah 7–12. In fact, the attention of the prophet turns to the remnant already in the closing words of chapter 6, words which serve almost as an introduction to the remnant chapters:

He said, "Go and tell this people: 'Be ever hearing, but never understanding; be ever seeing, but never perceiving.' Make the heart of this people calloused; make their ears dull and close their eyes. Otherwise they might see with their eyes, hear with their ears, understand with their hearts, and turn and be healed."

Then I said, "For how long, O Lord?"

And he answered: "Until the cities lie ruined and without inhabitant, until the houses are left deserted and the fields ruined and ravaged, until the LORD has sent everyone far away and the land is utterly forsaken. And though a tenth remains in the land, it will again be laid waste. But as the terebinth and oak leave stumps when they are cut down, so the holy seed will be the stump in the land." (vv. 9–13)

The seed, the potential for the future life of the tree, is in the stump. The greater part of the tree has been cut down, but part has been left intact, and from that minor part life will spring forth and continue. In this dramatic picture, the nation is literally decimated, and even the tenth which remains is subjected to a further destruction. But there remains a "holy seed," which is the remnant.[4]

The major event facing Isaiah in the early years of his prophesying was the impending exile of his people. He foresaw that they would be uprooted from their land because of their sins (1:7ff.; 3:1ff.; 5:13). This would be a disaster indeed, and the appropriate salvation would be that they return to the land. However, Isaiah did not predict that the whole nation would return. He named his son Shear-Yashuv, which means "a remnant will return," indicating that only a portion would return (7:3). The name is later repeated as part of the prophecy in 10:20–22, to which we will return.

In 8:16–18 Isaiah indicates that he and his family in some way represent the remnant:

> Bind up the testimony and seal up the law among my disciples. I will wait for the LORD, who is hiding his face from the house of Jacob. I will put my trust in him. Here am I, and the children the LORD has given me. We are signs and symbols in Israel from the LORD Almighty, who dwells on Mount Zion.

The prophet sees himself and his children as signs *('othoth)*.[5] What he means by that may be derived from the fact that he gives a symbolic name to Shear-Yashuv. In fact, in these six chapters there are three children named, and their names reflect elements of the remnant cycle. Shear-Yashuv, as we have noted, hints at the exile and the fact that only a few will survive. In 8:3 we meet Maher-shalal-hash-baz, "hurry to the booty, speedily to the prey," an indication of the nature of the judgment. And in 7:14 there is a child who is to be named Immanuel, perhaps a reminder of the faithfulness of God and of the certainty that He will bring deliverance. Finally, Isaiah has stated that he himself is a sign for Israel.[6] His name, of course, means "the LORD will save."[7] From the names of the prophet and his sons emerges this picture: There will be judgment in the form of war and destruction; God promises salvation to the faithful and indeed will Himself bring that salvation, which will be the return of the remnant to the land.

What is to distinguish the remnant from the rest of the nation? From the earlier verses of chapter 8 it is clear that God is looking for those who are truly His, those who fear Him, treat Him as holy, trust Him. "The LORD Almighty is the one you are to regard as holy, he is the one you are to fear, he is the one you are to dread." "Bind up the testimony and seal up the law among my disciples. I will wait for the LORD, who is hiding his face from the house of Jacob. I will put my trust in him."[8] Similarly, 7:9 proclaims the key to being included in the remnant: "If you do not stand firm in your faith, you will not stand at all." It is the faithful whom God in His grace will choose; they will make up His remnant.

It should also be noted that, just as God is the initiator of the process of saving the remnant, so it is He who will sustain those who belong to it. While it is true and essential that they be dedicated and faithful, it is not they who determine the makeup of the remnant. It is God's initiative. This important aspect of remnant teaching is stated later in Isaiah. "Listen to me, O house of Jacob, all you who remain *[she' erith]* of the house of Israel, you whom I have upheld since you were conceived, and have carried since your birth. Even to your old age and gray hairs I am he, I am he who will sustain you. I have made you and I will carry you; I will sustain you and I will rescue you."[9]

THE REMNANT AND THE MESSIAH

While Isaiah 7–12 is replete with references to the remnant, it is no less characterized by its depiction of a coming redeemer figure. This section begins with the Immanuel promise in 7:14. At the heart of the section sits 9:2–7 with its dramatic conclusion:

> For to us a child is born, to us a son is given, and the government will be on his shoulders. And he will be called Wonderful Counselor, Mighty God, Everlasting Father, Prince of Peace. Of the increase of his government and peace there will be no end. He will reign on David's throne and over his kingdom, establishing and upholding it with justice and righteousness from that time on and for ever. The zeal of the LORD Almighty will accomplish this.

To whom is this "child/son" given? "Us" is surely a figure for the remnant within God's people. The closest antecedent for this first person plural is 8:18, where, as we saw, the prophet and his children are signs to the people and are representative of the remnant. The Messiah is given to the remnant. In this, as in other important matters, the remnant is the true Israel.

In fact, while it is true that the Messiah is to be given to the remnant, this can be stated in converse fashion: It is those who are truly God's remnant who will come to the Messiah. This is dramatically portrayed in the following chapter, which describes the punishment of Assyria for its haughtiness. After God has brought His judgment, only a small portion of Assyria will remain, "the remaining [sha' ar] trees of his forests will be so few that a child could write them down" (10:19). However, having mentioned the straggling remnant of Assyria, the prophetic focus turns immediately to a more significant remnant:

> In that day the remnant [sha' ar] of Israel, the survivors [pleta] of the house of Jacob, will no longer rely on him who struck them down but will truly rely on the LORD, the holy one of Israel. A remnant will return, a remnant of Jacob will return to the Mighty God [el-gibbor]. Though your people, O Israel, be like the sand by the sea, only a remnant will return.

To whom will this remnant return? To "el-gibbor," one of the exalted names of the Messiah in 9:6!

This double-hearted section of Isaiah draws to a close in chapter 11 with one of the most messianic passages in all of the Hebrew Bible. Indeed, Isaiah 11:1–10 is referred to in talmudic literature about a dozen times and is almost without exception interpreted messianically.[10] Before the paean of praise which makes up chapter 12, verse 16 concludes chapter 11 with these words: "There will be a highway for the remnant *[sha' ar]* of his people that is left from Assyria, as there was for Israel when they came up from Egypt."

In prophecies elsewhere in Isaiah and in other prophets, this direct connection between the remnant and the Messiah is reiterated. Thus, in Isaiah 4:2–3 we are introduced to another common title for the expected redeemer:

> In that day the Branch of the LORD will be beautiful and glorious, and the fruit of the land will be the pride and glory of the survivors *[pleta]* in Israel. Those who are left *[hanish' ar]* in Zion, who remain *[hanothar]* in Jerusalem, will be called holy, all who are recorded among the living in Jerusalem.

"Branch" is a frequent and powerful title for the Messiah and with the passage just quoted we may compare the well-known prophecy of Jeremiah 23:3–6:

> "I myself will gather the remnant *[she' erith]* of my flock out of all the countries where I have driven them and will bring them back to their pasture, where they will be fruitful and increase in number. I will place shepherds over them who will tend them, and they will no longer be afraid or terrified, nor will any be missing," declares the LORD.
>
> "The days are coming," declares the LORD, "when I will raise up to David a righteous branch, a King who will reign wisely and do what is just and right in the land. In his days Judah will be saved and Israel will live in safety. This is the name by which he will be called: The LORD Our Righteousness."

Here again we note the identification of the remnant with the coming of the Messiah on the one hand and the identification of the remnant and Israel on the other hand. In verse 4 it is the remnant who will "no longer be afraid or terrified," while in verse 6 it is Israel who will live in safety. It is God who will gather them, the branch of David who will bring their salvation. The remnant is the continuation of Israel, the true Israel.

Here we may take one step further and suggest that not only is the Messiah inseparably connected to the *saving* of the remnant, but He Himself embodies the *principle* of the remnant and is to be identified with it. In a number of Old Testament passages we find the close identification of the Messiah with His people. This is stated in simple fashion in Zechariah 6:12–13 where it is said of "the man whose name is Branch" that "he will branch out from his place," meaning that He will be one with His people.

In the seventh chapter of Daniel, from which Jesus took His title, the Son of Man, we again find this element of identity between the Messiah and His consecrated people. In verse 14 it is said of the "one like a son of man" that "he was given authority, glory and sovereign power; all peoples, nations and men of every language worshipped Him. His dominion is an everlasting dominion that will not pass away, and His kingdom is one that will never be destroyed." Toward the end of the chapter, however, the focus turns to the saints against whom the little horn is waging war. In a formulation strikingly similar to that in verse 14, it is said about the saints in verse 27: "Then the sovereignty, power and greatness of the kingdoms under the whole heaven will be handed over to the saints, the people of the Most High. His kingdom will be an everlasting kingdom, and all rulers will worship and obey him."[11]

In similar fashion the "servant of the LORD" in Isaiah 42, 49, and 53 is so closely identified with the people of Israel that Rashi[12] and later commentators were able to claim, albeit tendentiously in their polemic against the teachings of the church, that the passage was in fact speaking of the people of Israel.

One other passage, Micah 4–5, may be added to the picture of the messiah-remnant pairing:

> "In that day," declares the LORD, "I will gather the lame; I will assemble the exiles and those I have brought to grief. I will make the lame a remnant [she' erith], those driven away a strong nation. The LORD will rule over them in Mount Zion from that day and for ever."

Soon after this prophecy, in Micah 4:6–7, the focus turns to a ruler who will be born in Bethlehem (5:2–5). Israel will be abandoned until "the remnant [yether] of his brethren will return, together with (òì) the sons of Israel."[13] Having introduced the messianic figure, Micah returns to the idea of the remnant in 5:7–9:

> The remnant of Jacob will be in the midst of many peoples like dew from the LORD, like showers on the grass, which do not wait for man or linger for mankind. The remnant of Jacob will be among the nations, in the midst of many peoples, like a lion among the beasts of the forest, like a young lion among flocks of sheep, which mauls and mangles as it goes, and no one can rescue. Your hand will be lifted up in triumph over your enemies, and all your foes will be destroyed.

Once again, then, we see this interweaving of the preservation of the remnant with the appearance and operation of the messianic figure.[14]

This then was the background, the atmosphere in which Paul makes mention of the remnant. There is a promise of a remnant "in Israel." God is the one who gives it and sustains it. As long as the remnant remains, Israel remains. There is no indication that those who are outside of the nation of Israel have any part in it. However, neither are all physical Israelites automatically included. Within Israel one belongs to it by faithfulness, and so it is open to all who will be faithful. It is closely tied to the idea of one who will come as a savior of the nation, what we call Messiah. He is not the remnant, but He is inseparably identified with it.

THE REMNANT IN ROMANS 9–11

In sermons and commentaries one often encounters the claim that Romans 9–11 comprise a kind of excursus in the epistle to the Romans. Paul, it is said, has reached a climax in his development of "justification by faith" in chapter 8, and he could have continued with chapter 12 without any loss of continuity. In fact, it is asserted, the flow of his thought is interrupted by these three chapters, which he had to stick in here to clarify a misunderstanding which might have arisen for his readers in chapters 5 and 6. In order to understand Paul's application of the traditional remnant idea to his own circumstances, it is necessary to follow an important thread of thought through the chapters which precede 9–11.

If the theme of a Pauline epistle can be determined by the amount of relative time Paul spends speaking about something and the places he chooses to speak about them, then there can be little doubt that a most important theme of Romans is the fact that God has now included the Gentiles in His program of salvation. This revolutionary idea is found in every chapter, either directly or indirectly. Even before he gets to the "grace and peace" in the salutation, he is already declaring that the purpose of his apostleship is "to call people from among all the Gentiles to the obedience that comes from faith." So, too, as he closes the letter, Paul refers one last time to this mystery, "that all nations [Gentiles] might believe and obey him."

In the next paragraphs we will overview how Paul repeatedly emphasizes the new inclusiveness of God's salvation program as revealed in the gospel. One should note how frequently he uses the word *all* or some equivalent term.

After opening his epistle with words of greeting and the declaration that he desires to visit the Roman church, Paul's very first statement (v. 16) is that the gospel is intended for both Jews and Gentiles. This introduces the well-known phrase "to the Jew first, and also to the Greek," which is repeated twice within the next few verses (2:9–10). Indeed, the main theme of the second chapter is that God is impartial, that all are equally subject to His judgment.

This is expanded in chapter 3, where in verses 9–23 Paul develops the basis that all have sinned, regardless of ethnic background. This chapter concludes (vv. 26–30) with two very pointed rhetorical questions and Paul's response: "Is God the God of Jews only? Is He not the God of Gentiles too? Yes, of Gentiles too, since there is only one God, who will justify the circumcised by faith and the uncircumcised through that same faith."

In chapter 4 the focus is on Abraham, who is declared to be the father of all. The uniting factor is faith: "He is the father of all *who believe* but have not been circumcised" (v. 11); "and he is also the father of the circumcised who not only are circumcised *but who also walk in the footsteps of the faith* that our father

Abraham had before he was circumcised" (v. 12); "therefore, the promise comes *by faith*, so that it may be by grace and may be guaranteed to all Abraham's off-spring—not only to those who are of the law but also *to those who are of the faith of Abraham*. He is the father of us all" (v. 16).

Chapter 5 goes even further to strengthen Paul's contention that all are equal in terms of their means of access to God's salvation program. The first eleven verses are in the first person plural, in what linguists call an "inclusive we," one which includes both the writer and his readers: *We* have been justified by faith; the Holy Spirit has been given to *us*; *we* have been justified by His blood; *we* have received reconciliation. The second half of the chapter declares that all were in Adam, that "death came to all men, because all sinned" (v. 12); that "the result of one trespass was condemnation for all men, so also the result of one act of righteousness was justification that brings life for all men" (v. 18).

If there is an excursus in this epistle, it begins in chapter 6, not in chapter 9. In 6 and 7 Paul treats two questions which naturally arise from his emphasis on the equality of all in their need for and reception of the work of the Messiah. In 5:20 he has said that the law was added so that the trespass might increase, as a result of which grace increased all the more. Paul first answers the objection that an increase of grace is a good thing, and so perhaps we should sin more. Then in chapter 7 he expands on the real function of the law, as he has introduced it in 5:20.

Chapter 8, then, is the summary of what this justification and sanctification mean to *all* who are "in the Messiah." The division of Jew and Gentile is significantly absent in this chapter. The true children of God are "those who are led by the Spirit of God" (v. 14); "*we* are heirs of God and coheirs of the Messiah." There is no distinction.

This was revolutionary. At every turn Paul must have met objections from his fellow Jews and especially from his fellow Pharisees. Surely it was too radical to speak of opening up the floodgates to the uncircumcised Gentiles. And would that not negate—or at least dilute—the clear relationship which God had with the nation of Israel?

One can almost hear the shouts aimed at Paul. Wait a minute! You are saying that all are equally sinners, that all equally need salvation through the Messiah, that there is no difference in this most essential matter between a Jew who believes and a Gentile who believes, and—even more significantly—between a Jew who does not believe and an unbelieving Gentile. So has God finished with the Jews? After this long history of Israel, is there now to be no Israel?

Precisely because the theme of the inclusion of the Gentiles is so important in this letter, Paul dedicates three chapters to answering the objection that such a development would exclude the Israelites. These chapters are not an excursus but an integral part of the main argument. Here Paul undertakes to explain what this new reality means for the relationship of Jews and Gentiles, for the relationship of believing Jews to those who have rejected the Messiah.

Paul's answer is not what we might expect. He does not say "Israel continues just as it was"; neither does he say "Israel is finished completely." Instead, he builds on the concept of the remnant, which runs like a thread through these three chapters. After affirming his deep love for and identity with his people, Paul declares that God's promises to Israel have not failed. That is because "not all who are descended from Israel are Israel" (9:6).[15] Here, in fact, is a nutshell formulation of one aspect of the remnant concept: only part of those who are physically descended are really Israel, true heirs of the promise.

Since Paul recognizes that the initiative in this process is God's, he immediately finds it necessary to discuss the theological ramifications of God's sovereign choice (9:6–21). This discussion flows almost seamlessly back to his theme of the equality of Jews and Gentiles in the latest stage of God's messianic program. God has prepared in advance "objects of his mercy" (v. 23). From where will these objects of mercy come? Verse 24 is clear and consistent with what Paul has been saying throughout the letter: those toward whom God has chosen to show His mercy are "us, whom he also called, not only from the Jews but also from the Gentiles."

The apostle then reinforces the point yet again with quotations from Hosea and Isaiah. The Hosea quotations show that this chosen group will include some Gentiles (9:24–26: "I will call them 'my people' who are not my people"; "where it was said to them 'You are not my people,' they will be called 'sons of the living God'"), while the Isaiah passages (1:9 and 10:22–23, already discussed above) indicate that it will have some Jews, in fact the believing remnant of Israel (vv. 27–29).

Exactly what this group of the chosen or the saved is to be called is left somewhat vague. Paul still at this point uses the term Israel to include nonbelievers, while, as we have seen, "remnant" is reserved for the faithful element within Israel.

At the end of chapter 9 Paul returns to the two problems: What has happened to Israel, and what purpose does the Law serve? In a sweeping generalization he states that "the Gentiles" have attained a righteousness which is by faith while "Israel" has failed to attain that righteousness (v. 31). It is obvious from the rest of the epistle that Paul is not intending to claim that each and every individual Gentile has been made righteous; by the same token, he is far from saying that each Israelite has been excluded from that righteousness.

The opening verses of chapter 10 then discuss the significance of the promises made to Israel and the proper way of attaining righteousness. The conclusion of this section, in verses 12 and 13, has the familiar ring of a now oft-repeated refrain: "For there is no difference between Jew and Gentile—the same Lord is Lord of all and richly blesses all who call on Him, for 'Everyone who calls on the name of the Lord will be saved.'"[16] Inclusion in the select group is only by faith in Jesus. For the remainder of chapter 10, Paul summarizes by means of a series of quotations what he has been saying all along: the gospel has been preached to Jews and Gentiles alike; not all Israelites accepted it, while there were those among the nations who did.

THE REMNANT IN PAUL'S DAY

Clearly, by the time we come to Romans 11, the remnant idea has been thoroughly integrated into Paul's argument. It would be natural to expect that those who have been following his train of thought would begin to ask just what Paul understands the remnant to be now, at the time he is writing. He deals with this in the opening verses of chapter 11. Somewhat surprisingly, Paul asserts that it is sufficient for him to say that God's remnant promise to Israel is being fulfilled if there is even one faithful Israelite. Paul offers himself as proof that God has not rejected Israel (11:1).

For Paul, as for the prophets before him, the size of the remnant does not enter the discussion. Surely the prophets and Paul must have wished that the remnant would include a major portion of the nation, but that is never stated. Perhaps this is because the makeup of that group was to be determined sovereignly by God Himself, and it would have been meaningless to discuss its size in numbers or percentages. There may be a hint in Paul's choice of the example from Elijah. The number 7,000 there, while perhaps symbolic, certainly does not indicate a relatively large proportion of the kingdom of Israel. And Paul's stand is clear: if there is even one faithful Israelite, then God can be said to be faithful to His promises.

Paul, of course, does not see himself as the only faithful Israelite, and he affirms that "at the present time there is a remnant chosen by grace" (11:5). Who is this "remnant chosen by grace" for Paul? Clearly they are to be identified with the second of the three groups mentioned in verse 7: "What Israel sought so earnestly it did not obtain, but the elect did. The others were hardened." Israel is still inclusive, undoubtedly physical Israel. Then there are "the elect" and "the others." We note that here "Israel" is actually placed in contrast to "the elect." Israel did not obtain what it sought, but the elect did. Paul has already used himself as a representative member of this elect remnant; these are those who have believed in God's Messiah.

The remnant idea is in essence a statement of who makes up the "true" Israel. Although that phrase never occurs in the Bible, this is what the prophets were talking about. The same can be said of religious debate generally during the period of the Second Temple. Each group was convinced that it had the truth, that the path it was following was the one God required, and that others were in error. This attitude is normative for all revelatory religion. If you are truly convinced that your way is the revelation of God, then you are also saying that those who do not acknowledge your way are wrong. You may not go so far as to say that they are condemned, but you might, as the Old Testament prophets often did. Essenes felt they were the true Israel; so did the Pharisees. It should come as no surprise that Paul too would take such an uncompromising position. He stood in the tradition of the prophets and fit well into the religious mosaic of his time.

For Paul, then, he and others like him who had believed in Jesus the Messiah, in His atoning death and resurrection, were "the remnant at the present time." These were Jews who had been confronted with the claims of Jesus and had responded in faith. In the same way we can say that in our own day there is such a remnant of faith. While it is probably accurate to say that since New Testament times there have always been some Jews, physical Israelites who have recognized the visitation of God in His Messiah Jesus, this phenomenon has grown and flowered in our generation. Today in Israel, the United States, Argentina, Russia, and many other countries, there are increasing numbers who are ethnically Jewish and who have consummated their destiny as true Israelites by accepting God's grace for salvation in Jesus. The church has largely overlooked them or felt embarrassed by them while Judaism today sees them as traitors, trying by whatever means to delegitimize them.

But these are the faithful remnant. The church needs to recognize them as such and needs to walk hand in hand with them on its way to any dialogue with Jews who do not yet believe in Jesus.[17]

DISCUSSION QUESTIONS

1. What are the main elements of the remnant doctrine in the Old Testament? Whom does God allow to be included in the remnant?

2. In the Old Testament, what relationship does the remnant in Israel bear to the nation in its entirety?

3. In what ways does the remnant relate to the promised messianic figure? How are they identified with each other, and how are they distinguished?

4. Trace Paul's use of the remnant idea in Romans 9–11.

5. Whom does Paul see to be the remnant in his own day, and to whom might they correspond today?

ENDNOTES

1. Scripture quotations are taken from the NIV translation.
2. This was observed as early as Tertullian, *An Answer to the Jews* 10, and frequently since. See, most recently, E. Ben Avraham, "Mashiach ben Yosef" (Jerusalem: Netivyah, 1994).
3. Arnold Fruchtenbaum, *Israelology* (Tustin, Calif.: Ariel Ministries Press, 1994), 602–3, suggests that there is a symbolic meaning to the three noisy events, where only in the small voice (representing the remnant) is God truly to be found.

4. It is possible, even likely, that the holy seed primarily signifies a messianic savior figure. This, however, does not necessarily exclude the possibility that it can be applied to the remnant.

5. The element of God giving a sign *('oth)* first appears, in fact, in 7:14, where the birth of Immanuel is for a sign.

6. It is hard to avoid the similarity between this and Paul's assertion in Romans 11:1–2 that he himself is sufficient proof that God has preserved a remnant in Israel.

7. There is another child promised in 9:6–7. This one is unnamed, or perhaps we should say overnamed, having no less than four high-profile titles.

8. Isa. 8:12, 17.

9. Isa. 46:3–4. Compare also 2 Kings 19:30–31 with its declaration that "the zeal of the LORD Almighty will accomplish this."

10. See R. Pritz, *Nazarene Jewish Christianity* (Jerusalem: Magnes Press, 1988), 13–14, n. 13.

11. The last phrase could also be understood to refer to the "nation of the saints," where the possessive suffix on "kingdom" refers back to `am (people), and the last phrase would be translated "all rulers will serve and obey them." This is, in fact, the way it is translated by RSV/NRSV, Moffat, REB, and JPS (1985), among others.

12. "Rashi" is an acronym for Rabbi Shlomo ben Isaac, an 11th-century commentator.

13. This is the translation of C. F. Keil, *Commentary on the Old Testament,* vol. 10 (Grand Rapids: Eerdmans, 1984), 482. They comment: "the remnant of his brethren are those who are rescued from the judgment that has fallen upon Judah; *yether,* as in Zeph. ii. 9 and Zech. xiv. 2, denoting the remnant, in distinction from those who have perished . . . 'al bnei yisrael, not 'to the sons of Israel' [which] would not give any suitable meaning here, not only because 'the sons of Israel,' as distinguished from the brethren of the Messiah, could not possibly denote the true members of the nation of God. . ." (Ibid., 484–85). They substantiate at length this interpretation of 'al.

14. To this list we could add Jer. 31:27–37. Preceding the promise of the "new covenant" there is a picture of breaking and destroying which will happen to Israel, but the new covenant is followed by God's declaration that he will always preserve a seed for Israel.

15. Translations have found a variety of ways of rendering this verse, which has no verb in Greek. Among Jewish translators we find the following:
    Cassirer: "Not all who are descended from Israel belong to Israel."
    Stern: "For not everyone from Israel is truly part of Israel."
    Goble: "For not all those descended from Yisroel are truly redeemed Yisroel (of the eschatological Geulah)." The same variety can be seen in a selection of modern versions: NAB: "for not all Israelites are true Israelites"; TEV: "not all the people of Israel are the people of God"; NCV: "But only some of the people of Israel are truly God's people."

16. Paul's choice of Scripture here is highly significant. Joel 2:32 (3:5 in the Hebrew text) is a strong statement of the remnant promise: "And everyone who calls upon the name of the Lord will be saved; for on Mount Zion and in Jerusalem there will be deliverance *(pleta),* as the Lord has said, among the survivors *(sridim)* whom the Lord calls."

17. There is a certain irony in the need to make this point in our generation. While Paul saw fit to write at length to the Roman church on the surprising fact that the Gentiles had now been included in God's program, today it is necessary to inform the Gentile Christians that there are Jewish believers in the church who need to be given full recognition and consideration.

PART TWO

HISTORICAL ISSUES

"Ecclesia et Synagoga" from the Strasbourg Cathedral; photo of replica statues courtesy of the Museum of the Jewish Diaspora.

CHAPTER FOUR

THE CHURCH'S APPROPRIATION OF ISRAEL'S BLESSINGS

H. Wayne House

At the entrances of some cathedrals in Europe, one may observe female statues that are personifications of *Ecclesia* (the Church) and *Synagoga* (the
Synagogue). One notices that *Ecclesia* wears a crown, holding her head in a tri-
umphant pose. On the other hand, *Synagoga*—her head bowed, having lost her
crown, holding a broken staff, and wearing a blindfold—stands defeated and rejected.[1] These personifications symbolize the consensus of the church from the
middle of the second century A.D. to the present day, with few exceptions. Origen
expresses the move from the people of Israel to the church of Christ: "For what
nation is in exile from their own metropolis, and from the place sacred to the
worship of their fathers, save the Jews alone?"[2] This poses a problem often not
debated in the seeming "magic" of the restoration of Israel, namely, the dispersion of a nation among the nations.

Throughout most of the period of the New Testament, the recognition of Jesus
and the apostles as Jews and the importance of the Jerusalem church kept in check
any Gentile-Christian tendency toward the denigration of Israel or the Jewish-
Christian portion of the church. It was after all from this church that Gentile-
Christians had their beginnings. Massive changes occurred, however, in the last
several decades of the first century. The passing of the apostles and the destruction of the Jewish people and homeland in A.D. 70 and finally in A.D. 135 sig-
naled for many Gentile believers the end of the promises to Israel. She would
never rise from this ash heap to be restored to the grandeur and greatness prophesied by the prophets for her. Her rejection of God's Son, Jesus the Messiah, had

caused God to set her aside for another people, the church, who would receive all those blessings originally intended for His people. Israel, the church began to hold, had been replaced by the church. The blessings—the land, kingdom, and covenants—intended for the physical seed of Abraham had been turned over to his spiritual seed. Christian writers began to see the church as the fulfillment of the Old Testament promises to the people of Israel.

The church's position on the future of Israel was influenced by misunderstandings of "in-house" discussions of the biblical writers and the Jewish community, the anti-Christian response of some Jews to Christian sufferings, including the encouragement of the persecution, and the development of a non-literal hermeneutic. The church began to develop an anti-Jewish attitude and believe itself to be the true inheritor of the eschatological blessings prophesied concerning the people of Israel. This theology has come to be known as replacement theology. The intent of this chapter is to explore the reasons for the rise of this thinking from the time of the Zealot revolt (A.D. 66) and the triumphalism that occurred in the fourth century, after Constantine declared Christianity the official religion of the Roman Empire. Before examining these historical reasons, though, we will first look at what is meant by replacement theology and the nature of the promises to Israel which supposedly the church has become the recipient of.

REPLACEMENT THEOLOGY

Its Meaning

Many Christian scholars in our day advocate a view of Israel and the church known as replacement theology, or what Tuvya Zaretsky prefers to call supersessionism.[3] Walter Kaiser has defined it thus: "Replacement theology, then, declared that the church, Abraham's spiritual seed, has replaced national Israel in that it had transcended and fulfilled the terms of the covenant given to Israel, which covenant Israel had lost because of disobedience."[4] Because the church fulfills the covenant, it is expected that she receives the blessings that attend that covenant. Essentially the view claims that the church has replaced national Israel as the recipient of the blessings of God and that the church has fulfilled the terms of the covenants given to Israel, which they rejected.[5]

Its Origin

Those who would seek to support the idea that the church established by Christ has taken over the promises once given to the nation of Israel must find support in the writings of the New Testament and the understanding of such ideas at the earliest stages of the growth of Christianity. That this thinking has adherents, at least in some sense, in the second century and became essentially the only understanding of the church and Israel by the time of Constantine, cannot provide the required bricks from which to build replacement theology. One must also find solid evidence for such a view in the New Testament writings.

Unfortunately, the dilemma for replacement theology is that both in the New Testament and in the earliest periods of the ancient church, such a perspective is largely absent. One begins to find the concept of the church taking Israel's place in the prophecies of the Old Testament only after certain major events: (1) after the Jewish people ceased to be the primary source from which the theology of the New Testament sprang; (2) after those who had learned from the apostles had died and new problems faced the largely Gentile church; (3) after several non-Jewish Christian authors began to adopt the anti-Semitism of their pagan counterparts; and (4) after the hermeneutic found in the New Testament was replaced by Greek allegorism.

The move to replace Israel as the recipient of the eschatological blessings of the Old Testament did not occur all at once. One scholar, Jeffrey Siker, gives four stages in the development of this view:

1. Paul argues that the Gentiles, not only the Jews, are included (A.D. 30–60).
2. Other writers of the New Testament, such as Matthew, Hebrews and Luke-Acts, present the Gentiles as included but begin a discussion of the exclusion of the Jews (A.D. 60–90).
3. John, Ignatius, and Barnabas assume Gentile inclusion, but argue against Jewish inclusion (A.D. 90–120).
4. Several works, ending with Justin Martyr, do not believe Gentile inclusion to be an issue but do assume Jewish exclusion (A.D. 120–150).[6]

Siker has provided an interesting paradigm to see a possible progression of the substitution of Gentiles for Jews, but as Ray Pritz points out, the New Testament records are not as negative toward Jewish inclusion as Siker has postulated.[7] The New Testament writers certainly mention the hardness of Israel to their Messiah (Acts 2:23; 3:17; 7:51–53), but there is never total exclusion; there is a remnant within Israel found in the Gospels and the epistles who follow after the Messiah Jesus (Acts 3:24–26; 5:13–14; Rom. 11:25–27).

Others, such as Walter Kaiser, have argued that replacement theology probably had its origins in "an early political-ecclesiastical alliance forged between Eusebius Pamphilius and the Emperor Constantine."[8] He is probably correct if we should mean the formal development of the church's position, but the roots of this theology run deep in the preceding two centuries, namely, the second and third centuries A.D.

For replacement theology to be correct, one of two scenarios must be true regarding the various covenants that we observe in the Old Testament between Yahweh and Israel: The covenants must be bilateral agreements so that Israel's failure has caused them to be no longer in force or the covenants must be able to be spiritually interpreted so that the church assumes the covenants in some non-literal sense. Are either of these two positions truly reflective of the nature and intent of the covenants of the Old Testament? An examination of these biblical covenants will reveal the correct understanding.

ISRAEL'S BLESSINGS IN HOLY SCRIPTURE

The Blessings to Israel in the Hebrew Scriptures

The Seminal Covenants with Adam and Noah

The God of the Bible is a covenant-making God. We find from the very initiation of Scripture that God seeks to establish a relationship with His people, committing Himself to blessings and promises, as well as judgment for disobedience to the covenant.

Though Genesis 1:26–28 does not specifically use the Hebrew word for covenant, components of covenant are found in this passage, especially as one parallels these components with the covenant text of Genesis 9. In Genesis 1, God places man and woman in the garden with specific duties (v. 28) and blessings (vv. 29–30).

Genesis 9 is a renewal of the covenant that originated with Adam and Eve in view of the parallels with Genesis 1 and 2. Again, no word for making a covenant is present, but the word *qûm*, "to establish" is used of establishing a covenant elsewhere (cf. Gen. 6:18; 9:9, 11, 17; 17:7, 19, 21; Exod. 6:4).

Two important points must be emphasized about these two covenants. First, neither appears to be bilateral. They simply come from a sovereign God, maker and ruler of heaven and earth. Second, the covenants are with all of mankind, in stark contrast to the covenants with Abraham and his descendants.

The Central Covenant with Abraham

The future blessings to the people of Israel rest solidly on the covenant that Yahweh makes with Abraham in Genesis 12, 15, and 17. Whether these covenants are unilateral (unconditional) or bilateral (conditional) is pivotal to whether the physical descendants of Abraham through Isaac can truly have their blessings taken over by the church.

The future of Israel is tied to the Abrahamic covenant. The covenant with Abraham and his seed was not conditioned on their obedience, but the appropriation of any given generation was dependent on loyalty to Yahweh. For example, failure to obey the Sinaitic covenant, which was strongly tied to the Abrahamic covenant (Exod. 19:5 and 6:4 with Gen. 15), could bring loss of the blessings for disobedient Israel but not a revocation of the unconditional promises to the people of Israel.[9]

The Derivative Promises in the Covenants with Israel

Springing from the central covenant Israel had with Yahweh, were three consequent covenants: a land, a kingdom, and the blessings to all nations.[10] First, the people were promised a land, the land of the Canaanites and the land from Egypt to the Euphrates (Gen. 15:18; cf. also the Mosaic Covenant's land commitments in Deut. 11:24). Israel has never yet occupied all the promised land and will only do so when she finally turns to God in the future. Ellisen elucidates on the scope of the land of future Israel:

> In their final return, Israel will be divided by tribes in parallel strips of land running east and west (Ezek. 48:1–8). The boundaries will be the Mediterranean on the west, the Dead Sea . . . on the east, Damascus on the north, and Kadesh or the River of Egypt on the south. At the center will be the prince's portion (v. 21). This will include the city of Jerusalem, the temple area, and the suburbs for the priests.[11]

This everlasting covenant was in force dependent on obedience by Israel. The covenant of the land was an everlasting covenant but any generation which refused to comply with the covenant code of Moses would be cast out of the land (Deut. 29:25).[12]

Second, Yahweh promised that the throne of David would never be empty (Ps. 89:3–4). Though the kings of Israel faltered in their obedience to God and there were no kings on the throne during the intertestmental period, the promise is a guarantee that the line would not die out; Messiah would sit on the throne forever (2 Sam. 7:14–16; Jer. 23:1–8). Jesus *(Yeshúa)* became the greater Son of David to assurance of the continuance of David's royal line (Luke 1:32–33, 54–55).[13]

Third, the blessings to other nations and ultimately to the whole world was fulfilled in the coming of Jesus the Messiah as He extended His redemptive benefits beyond Israel.[14] Paul speaks of the grafting of the Gentiles into the natural branch (Rom. 11:16–24) but this should not be seen as a diminishing of the promises to Israel but the enhancement of the Gentile position.

Those who believe that the church has somehow taken over the blessings of Israel must explain the revoking of these apparently irrevocable callings of God on His people. The future blessings to Israel are directly connected to the unconditional covenants with Israel, namely, the Abrahamic, the "Palestinian" or land, and the Davidic, which were developed earlier. The Mosaic covenant was not an unconditional covenant and would be superseded by the New Covenant.

The Future of Israel According to the New Testament

In the Teachings of Jesus

Jesus came offering the kingdom to the people of Israel. He is declared in His

birth to be the Savior of His people (Matt. 1:21) and in His death King of the
Jews (Luke 23:38). He cried over the Jewish rejection of His offer to them (Matt.
23:37–39), and in His parables He spoke of the kingdom being taken from them
and given to another (Matt. 21:43–44). Prior to His ascension, however, when
the disciples asked about the offer of the kingdom, Jesus' response was not that
Israel had no future, but that this happening was in the authority of the Father so
that they were to concentrate on the task of the great commission given to them
(Acts 1:6–8).

In the Teachings of the Apostles prior to A.D. 70

The inclusion of the Gentiles in the redemptive plan of God is not viewed as a
replacement of God's promises to the Jewish people in the proclamation of the
apostles. Rather, for example, Peter anticipated the restoration of Israel (Acts
3:17–26) based on their acceptance of Jesus as their Messiah (a prophecy still to
be fulfilled from Zech. 12:10). Moreover, Paul envisioned the future salvation of
Israel to come upon the completion of God's work among the Gentiles (Rom
11:25–26).[15]

In the Teachings of the Revelation of John

The last book of the Bible, the Revelation of John, provides the final glimpse of
God's purposes for the Jewish people. This book is replete with Jewish allusions
from the Old Testament. The future sufferings of the Jewish people are foretold as
well as Israel's participation along with the church in the final blessings of God's
redemption during a millennial age.[16] The heavenly Jerusalem has the twelve tribes
represented and the reign of God's Messiah[17] over the people of Israel.[18]

The teaching of John in the Revelation was generally consistent with Jewish
thought during the first century, especially before A.D. 70, and was the basis of
the chiliasm (the belief in a thousand-year reign of Christ prior to the final
judgment) found in the earliest Christian writings of the second century. Post-
apostolic fathers who were acquainted with the apostle John or his disciples shared
a similar view of end-times events. This perspective, however, changed with the
introduction of nonliteral interpretation due to the increasing dependence on
allegorical thought introduced by non-Jewish writers.

The Old and New Testaments portray a future blessing for the Jewish people
which will have lasting results. There is no glossing over Israel's forsaking of God,
but are the promises to Abraham thereby set aside regarding his seed, the inheritance of the land of Israel, or the promises of an everlasting Davidic throne? These
promises appear to be taken literally by the prophets, in the teachings of the New
Testament writers as well as the early Fathers of the church. Only with the destruction of Israel by the Romans, the subsequent anti-Christian rhetoric and actions of
many Jews, and the rise of Greek philosophical interpretation of the biblical texts
does the church begin to view itself as the inheritor of Israel's promises.

As we have seen, the God of the Bible made a commitment that is irrevocable. The covenant included provisions of a land and kingdom for His people Israel, as well as many blessings to all other nations through her. The fact that Gentiles are benefited by the coming of Jesus (Gal. 3:15–18) in no way eliminates the remainder of His covenant to the children of Israel after the flesh. Such a view is in no way demanded by the New Testament text, and this would certainly be a violation of the plain reading of numerous Old Testament passages. God will fulfill all of His covenants, not just the parts that apply to the non-Jewish world.

ISRAEL'S BLESSINGS IN HISTORY

Jewish Christianity Before and After A.D. 70

The church, as Paul so strongly argues in Romans 11, finds it roots in Israel. Moreover, it is the Jewish people that continued the revelation of God and to whom God made great promises and performed great works as seen at the coming of the Spirit at Pentecost, the large response of Jews to Peter's sermon, the miracles of the apostles, and the deliverance of Peter from prison (Rom. 3:1–4; 9:4–5). For approximately ten years after the ascension of Christ, early Christians consisted entirely of Jewish converts. Only after Peter's preaching to the Jewish proselyte Cornelius in Joppa were Gentiles made heirs to the redemption (Acts 10:44–48; 11:18). It was not transparent that Gentiles were able to participate in this gospel since Peter had to make a formal defense before the apostles and elders in Jerusalem (Acts 11). Even this Gentile convert, Cornelius, was one who sought to adhere to the practices of the Jewish faith.[19] The first missionary journey of Paul in the middle 40s first offered the gospel of Christ to Gentiles in the fullest sense, and it was this non-Judaistic proclamation that brought the wrath of some from Jerusalem who sought to bring this new teaching of Paul to a halt. It was this Jewish element in the church from Jerusalem that precipitated the letter to the Galatians and subsequently the Jerusalem Council. The Jerusalem Council became necessary to bring peace between the different parties and to resolve the dispute as to whether Gentiles had to follow Jewish practices and laws to become disciples of Jesus. Only minimal requirements, ones whose violation would greatly offend Jewish believers, were imposed on the Gentile converts (Acts 15).

At this initial stage of the church it is evident that Peter, James, and John were the major figures within the Jewish church. The worship and fellowship was simple (Acts 2:44; 4:32–37), and the Christian community stayed in fellowship with Judaism. They visited the temple (Acts 3:1) and participated in Jewish practices. Jewish Christians were recognized by Jew and Roman alike as but another sect within Judaism (Acts 18:12–15).

Though the apostles clashed with the Jewish authorities, they continued their ministry and generally were well accepted by the people (Acts 2:47). Even when

Stephen, a Hellenistic Jew, was killed by the Jewish leaders because of his accusatory speech (Acts 6:8–7:60), the persecution seems to have been launched primarily against Greek-speaking Jews since the leaders in Jerusalem, at that time, apparently were not disturbed (Acts 8:1). When some of the early leaders were apprehended by Jewish authorities, Gamaliel the Elder, grandson of Hillel,[20] was a moderating influence, arguing that if their teaching was spurious, as many others had been, it would come to nothing, but if it was from God, the council would find themselves fighting against God (Acts 5:33–39).

Judaism was much more multifaceted than many have supposed. Christ's message was not entirely out of accord with the teaching of many Pharisees in His proclamations of moral theology. His rejection of certain teachings and practices of the Pharisees was consistent with the internal squabbles among the Pharisees and their concern about the corruption of the Temple. It was only His teaching on His Messiahship that confused the Jews since the majority were looking for a political-military Messiah.

Only as the church spread beyond Judea into more Gentile-controlled areas did the believers in Jesus receive a designation that became prominent in Gentile lands, that of "Christians" (Acts 11:19ff.). As we shall see, followers of Yeshua had many names, the most prominent being Nazarenes[21] and Ebionites.

Though Peter was the natural choice for leader in the beginnings of the church, eventually the family of Jesus began to play a more important role with James, the Lord's half-brother becoming the leader of the Jerusalem congregation.[22] Judea was without a procurator for a brief time after the departure of Festus. At this time (A.D. 62), James was called to the Sanhedrin on the orders of the high priest Annas II and stoned to death for having broken the law. This execution was greatly opposed by more moderate Jews and the Pharisees, who then brought charges against Annas II to King Agrippa II and the newly arrived procurator, Albinus. Annas was then deposed as high priest by Agrippa II.[23]

The Drifting of Jewish Christianity and Judaism After A.D. 70

The Rise of Judaism in Yavneh

The destruction of Jerusalem, its temple, and the halting of temple sacrifices caused major changes in Judaism. During this period Judaism moved toward a bloodless religion of ceremonies and ethics. The liturgy of Jewish worship was made uniform.[24] All other competing systems—the Sadducees, Herodians, Zealots, the Essenes—largely ceased to exist. The Pharisaic center at Yavneh served as the alternative to the temple cult of Jerusalem. Also, the synagogue, in order to save Judaism from extinction, sought to eradicate any competing systems within it, thus pushing Jewish Christians outside its walls. It was made plain that Christianity was not an accepted sect of Judaism as it was in its initiation.

The person who had the most impact on the new beginnings for Judaism was

Rabbi Yochanan ben Zakkai, who, according to one tradition, escaped from the Zealot-held city of Jerusalem in a coffin before its fall.[25] Whether this is true or not is not germane to this chapter. What is important is that his survival and move to Yavneh (Jamnia), with the encouragement of Rome, helped to solidify "Pharisaic Judaism's control over the life and doctrine of Jewish life in the Empire after the fall of Jerusalem."[26] With this solidification of religious expression, the Yavneh rabbis were not willing to share this status with Christians, and so caused the Roman government to understand that Christianity was not a part of Judaism. As Boer well said, "As Christianity spread, however, the Jews made it plain to the government that the followers of the Mosaic law and the followers of Christ were not one and the same."[27] This collaboration of ben Zakkai and Rome allowed these rabbis "the power of Rome to enforce their brand of Judaism on world Jewry, a fact that should not go unnoticed in light of the waves of persecutions the early church would have to face."[28]

Different Sects of Jewish Christianity

Jewish Christianity was not restricted to Christians in Palestine. The Therapeutae of Egypt, described by Philo, supposedly were converts of Mark. They are acknowledged by Epiphanius, who lived for some time among Egyptian monks, and the historian Sozomen called them "converted Jews, who continue to live after the Jewish fashion."[29]

Another Jewish Christian group that was clearly orthodox in theology but Jewish in many practices, was the Nazarenes. Supposedly the Church of Mesopotamia was founded by this community. The first mention we have of them is by Paul's opponent in Acts 24:5. Pritz says that the "name of the sect came from the title NAZORAIOS/NAZARENOS, evidently applied to Jesus from the beginning of his public ministry."[30] Bagatti says regarding the origin of the name: "In origin the name came from the contempt in which the Jews held the new faithful, naming them from a village without a history and without renown."[31] It may be, according to Pritz, that two different names were used for Christians in the earliest periods. "The Greek name, Christian, was first applied in Antioch, probably the earliest mission to non-Jews, and it is well known that 'Christian' was originally used by non-Christians to designate believers among the Gentiles, while 'Nazarenes' was already used in Palestine to describe Jewish adherents to the new messianic sect."[32]

Anti-Christian Sentiment in Post–A.D. 70 Pharisaism

One of the major reasons usually given for strong anti-Christian attitudes among the later Jewish population is that Jewish Christians fled Jerusalem in A.D. 66, shortly before the Romans laid siege to the city of Jerusalem. They are thought to have crossed the Jordan to the rocky mountains called Petra (Pella).[33] This abandonment of the Jewish plight in Jerusalem caused many to believe that the Jewish Christians were disloyal to Israel.[34]

Another reason for the hostility is much more pragmatic and personal; namely, the desire to maintain a hegemony over the religious life of the people. There was a danger, according to C. K. Barrett, that "Judaism would simply assimilate itself to other religions."[35] Whereas Judaism had been a cacophony of ideologies, rabbis at Yavneh sought to ensure that Judaism would sing one religious song. This was especially true with Jewish Christianity, for it was not even viewed as being a Jewish sect.

The former Benediction Concerning Heretics was revised to include Christians. Paul Johnson comments:

> The collapse of the Jewish-Christian church after 70 A.D. and the triumph of Hellenistic Christianity led the Jews, in turn, to castigate the Christians. Jewish daily prayers against heretics and opponents date from the Hellenistic reform programme of the second century B.C. . . . The prayer against heretics, originally known as "the Benediction to Him who humbles the arrogant," became part of the daily service, or Amidah, as the Twelfth Benediction. At one time it was specifically directed against the Sadducees. Under the rule of Raban Gamaliel II (c. A.D. 80–115), the Twelfth Benediction or *Birkat ha-Minim* ("Benediction concerning heretics") was recast to apply to Christians and this seems to have been the point at which the remaining Jewish followers of Christ were turned out of the synagogue. By the 132 [A.D.] uprising, Christians and Jews were seen as open opponents or even enemies. Indeed Christian communities in Palestine petitioned the Roman authorities to be given separate religious status to Jews, and the Christian writer Justin Martyr (c. 100–C. 165), who lived in Neapolis (Nablus), reported that the followers of Simon bar Kokhba massacred Christian as well as Greek communities. It is from this period that anti-Christian polemic begins to appear in Jewish Bible commentaries.[36]

The collapse mentioned by Johnson really only occurred after the Bar-Kokhba defeat in A.D. 135 and the subsequent limitation on Jews entering the city of Jerusalem (Jewish Christians were still found throughout Israel, though). At this time Gentile Christians were left in Jerusalem to develop a church absent for the first time from the Jews who gave life and growth to that church and provided its unbroken leadership. Johnson is correct that there was opposition against Christians at synagogue meetings, but as seen below these were largely addressed against the still vibrant Jewish Christian element within Israel.

There has been debate as to whether this curse on the "minim" refers to Jewish Christians, to Gentile Christians, both, or neither.[37] Certainly the term *heretics* may have been used earlier for other groups or sects but at this time probably came to include, though maybe not exclusively, Christians in general. Jocz believes it to be a reference to both Christian and Jew at different times: "The Minim were thus Christians, first Jewish Christians, then also Gentile Christians; later, when Christianity removed itself from the Jewish horizon, the appellation was given to any Jews of dissenting views."[38]

We have seen that in the aftermath of A.D. 70, alternative parties and rival ideologies to the Pharisees, namely, the Sadduccees, Herodians, Zealots, and Essenes, largely fell into oblivion. Only the vibrant Jewish-Christian movement posed a threat to the type of Judaism desired by those at Yavneh. In order to solidify their hold through the teaching and discipline of the synagogue, an attempt was made to remove Jewish Christians from the religious life of the Jewish community. This only caused a larger rift between Jewish Christianity and Rabbinic Judaism, one which grew larger with the influx of Gentiles into the formerly pervasive Jewish Christian movement, eventuating in the development of replacement theology in the second century A.D.

Reasons for the Development of Replacement Theology in Early Christianity

Confusion Between Orthodox Jewish Christianity and Heretical Jewish Groups

Candidly, as the church's membership became more and more Gentile and the influence of the Jewish community became less pronounced, the church's knowledge of Jewish Christianity became minuscule. Only a few of the theologians of the church seem to have serious contact with the Jewish Christian community. Origen and Eusebius preferred to call these Christians, the Nazarenes, by the term "believing Jews" and to use particular names for those they considered heretical, such as the Ebionites and Elkesaites. Bagatti says, "Since the Nazarenes did not differ much in faith from the gentile Christians, they were considered without more ado as faithful, albeit separated through national customs; all the other Judaeo-Christians were considered heretics."[39]

Epiphanius, who often appears hostile to Jewish Christianity, confuses Nazarenes and Ebionites. He seeks to distinguish Nazarenes who he believed lived in Pella, having left Jerusalem before the Roman siege, with other Jewish Christian groups. The Nazarenes according to Epiphanius, "have nothing to do with Christ; they observe the Sabbath but they have no animal sacrifices, nor do they accept the Patriarchs of the Old Testament."[40] Origen, also, seems to make this mistake:

> Let it be admitted, moreover, that there are some who accept Jesus, and who boast on that account of being Christians, and yet would regulate their lives, like the Jewish multitude, in accordance with the Jewish Law—and these are the twofold sect of the Ebionites, who either acknowledge with us that Jesus was born of a virgin, or deny this, and maintain that he was begotten like other human beings.[41]

Pritz rightly concludes, "If the more orthodox Jewish Christians (who can only be faulted for keeping the Law) are Nazarenes, then we have an early misuse of the name Ebionite to include all Jewish Christian Law-keepers."[42]

Rise of Anti-Semitism in the Early Church

One does not need to read far in the New Testament to find statements of condemnation of Jewish leadership. The general populace eventually rejected the offer of Jesus as the Messiah of Israel (Matt. 23:37–39; 27:20, 25). The gospel writers do not portray the Pharisees in favorable light (Matt. 23:27; Luke 11:44), though they were not largely in the final condemnation of Jesus (Matt. 27:22–27).[43] In reality, the Talmud itself identified good and bad Pharisees, the bad being little different from what Jesus described.

The gospel of the apostle John, more than any other gospel, is viewed as expressing hostility toward the Jews. Kaufmann Kohler, a well-known Reform Jewish scholar, called John's gospel "a Gospel of Christian love and Jew hatred."[44] That Kohler's assessment is incorrect is established in at least three ways. First, there are many passages in the Gospel of John that are equally "philo-semitic," to coin a term (John 4:22; 11:45–48). John has no animosity against Jewish people in general, it is clear. Second, the writer John, Jesus, and the disciples, after all, were Jews. As Feldman says,

> How could the New Testament condemn Jews as a group, when it clearly acknowledges Jesus as a Jew and also his predecessor John the Baptist, his twelve apostles and most if not all of his immediate followers? Even when Jesus prophesies the destruction, he refers to it as "my Father's house" (John 2:16). For Christianity, the daughter of Judaism, to be anti-Semitic would be a clear case of matricide.[45]

Last of all, the Jewish nature of the book and that John himself was a Jew has caused scholars difficulty in determining what he meant by the term "the Jews" which occurs sixteen times in his gospel.[46] The term must refer to Jewish people in a non-anti-Semitic manner, as Rabbi Louis Feldman has so poignantly demonstrated. The evidence seems to lean toward the term being used against "a group of Jew*ish leaders* who exercise great authority among their compatriots and are especially hostile to Jesus and his disciples."[47]

Luke, in Acts particularly, has been viewed as anti-Jewish since he placed little judgment on Rome but instead saw the Jewish leadership as being the major persecutor of "the Way." This may have been in part to present a good front to Roman authorities, but it nevertheless truly reflects the type of opposition that the sect of the Nazarenes, as well as Christians in missionary locales of Paul, encountered from Jewish leadership. He as well, however, softened the impact of his statements against the Jews (Luke 23:27–31, 48; 23:34; Acts 3:17), and distinguished between the Jewish people (Luke 19:47–48) and the Jewish leadership. He is by no means uniformly against the Jewish people as a whole in the speeches he includes in the Acts (Acts 7:52, 60; 28:24–25; cf. Acts 2:36; 4:10; 10:39 with 13:43 and 18:6 with 21:20).[48]

Even Paul, the apostle, viewed by many as the beginner of a new religion and a radical rabbi who left the teachings of Jesus[49] is, according to Feldman, remarkable for his lack of anti-Judaism.[50] In his first letter to the Corinthians there are three dominant personalities, all of them Jews. Moreover, Paul actually was proud of his Jewishness (cf. Phil. 3:5–6) and put himself under Jewish discipline (2 Cor. 11:24). In fact, the letters of Paul lead us to the reason for much of the confusion regarding tension among Jewish and non-Jewish Christians and Judaism, the presence of an intramural discussion in the New Testament.

Misunderstanding of "In-House" Discussion

If the writings of the New Testament are not really addressed against the entire Jewish people but only against certain rulers of the Jews who were hostile to Christ, the apostles, and early Christianity, then how did the fathers of the church so wrongly understand the situation in the New Testament? It is this writer's view that they eventually forgot the context of these writings and saw the teaching of the texts of the New Testament to be opposition to Jews in general, rather than for what it was, an in-house debate. Consequently, the greatest difficulty in properly understanding the supposed negative attitude of the New Testament writings to the Jewish community is that we are listening to a family squabble.

As we have already seen in the biblical passages, the gospel writers often cast the Jewish community in disparaging ways, either seeing them as an obstacle to genuine ethics (the Pharisees, Matt. 5:20; 23:26; Luke 7:39), perverters of true religion (the chief priests, Matt. 27:21, 41–43; Mark 15:10–13), connivers with those opposing Jesus (scribes and lawyers, Luke 10:25; 11:46; 20:19) and rejecters of the Word of God (Sadducees, Mark 12:24). The synoptic gospels give adequate testimony to these tendencies, but none is so harsh as John's gospel where he repeatedly uses the term "the Jews" negatively, and also in Acts where the Jews are depicted as constantly in opposition to the gospel. It may be that the reference to the "synagogue of Satan" and those "who say they are Jews but are not" in Revelation 2:9 is a participation in this controversy.[51]

The in-house discussion among the Jews, however, caused some at the end of the nineteenth century to disassociate Jesus from His Jewishness. H. St. Chamberlain, for example, contended that Jesus was not a Jew, that He had been born in Galilee where there was not a pure race of Jews, but that in fact He was Aryan, and that He then was eventually killed by the Jews. In the past, even when His Jewishness was recognized, His humanity has often been so downplayed that He has been severed from His Jewishness.[52]

Even the ancient church shared this misconception. Many of the church fathers believed that the New Testament authors and the early church were anti-Jewish. Such a view should be seen as preposterous in view of the fact that all of the authors (except Luke) were Jews and that our Lord was a Jew. Rather than the theology of these biblical writers being anti-Jewish, they were expressions of an in-house dispute which the writers and their hearers knew well. Such actions were very consistent with other such disputes in Judaism at the time and even in other cultures of the time.

One discovers very strong language against fellow Jews in much of the literature that is found among the Jews of the time,[53] at Qumran,[54] the Hebrew Bible,[55] and in the Talmud.[56] Moreover, among Jews there were many factions at war with each other. The authors of the Psalms of Solomon called other Jews "sinners." Pharisees, Sadducces, and Essenes were against each other. In A.D. 63 a supposed Jewish miracle worker from Galilee named Honi was stoned outside Jerusalem by Jews who could not get him to curse other Jews that they were against. That Jesus, Stephen, and James were killed by a certain group of Jews should not be viewed as unusual. Though Jesus speaks against different groups of the Jews, namely, the Pharisees and Sadducees, He was not against all Pharisees. Many of these Pharisees admired or even followed Him (Luke 11:37; 13:31). When the Gospel of John says that the death of Jesus was brought about by Jews, he does not mean all Jews and does not mean He was not a Jew.[57]

This phenomenon, as mentioned above, was not restricted to Judaism. In the Hellenistic world there are many examples of in-house fighting. For example, Dio of Prusa called the sophists "ignorant ones," "liars," and "flatterers," and Colotes, an Epicurean, called some philosophers "prostitutes."[58]

Moskowitz understands the dispute to be that the Jewish Christians didn't seek to replace the nationality of the Jewish people with a faith community but the replacement of the moral leadership of the nation with a faith community. "The remnant of Israel understood that even Gentiles were to be allowed into this new faith community, but that God was still going to use national Israel to accomplish His ultimate plan of redemption (Romans 11:11–12, 28–36)."[59] He then ruminates that it is

> . . . both ironic and sad to face that the Jewish Christians' understanding of their replacing the present leadership of Israel may have been one of the causes of the Gentile church adopting this doctrine which led her so far from favoring her twin sister Israel. This misunderstanding of the church's relationship to unbelieving Israel has led some of the great men of the church to postulate theories that have led to so much persecution of Israel.[60]

There are a number of instances, in the second through fourth centuries of opposition to the belief that the church supersedes Israel, receiving the blessings intended for the nation upon God's rejection and judgment of her. We will examine these presently. However, are there examples of this development in the earlier periods of the church's history? One may discover this replacement theology developing in two early books, the *Epistle of Barnabas* and the *Didache*. The former book represents early second century thought and the *Didache* represents how many Christians thought around the turn of the first century or early second century A.D.[61]

The *Didache* purports to represent the teachings of the twelve apostles (thus *didache*, "teaching"). The book was apparently written for Gentiles but it has strong Jewish flavor. It has several clear Jewish elements:[62]

1. The book starts with "the way of life" and then gives the Golden Rule in negative form, similar to how Hillel taught the rule.
2. The book emphasizes the Ten Commandments and then follows these commands with moral instruction:

   In Jewish literature, we not only have Halachah, but there is also a good deal of general moral instruction, exhortation to self-discipline, modesty, gentleness, patience, respect for old age, forgiveness, and family harmony. The *Didache* is very similar to three Rabbinic books of the same or later period: *Derech Eretz Rabbah*—what's good and bad, the way of life and death, lists of proper conduct; *De Zuta*—a long treatise on modesty with the last chapter on eschatology; *Perek haShalom*—we have the fear of sin, exhortation to modesty, perseverance, and the final eschatological chapter.[63]

3. The section on moral instruction ends with, "If you can bear the whole yoke of the Lord, you'll be perfect" (6:2). This is similar to the saying of the rabbis about the "yoke of Torah."
4. The statements in the *Didache* about pouring of water over the head in baptism is very similar to Pharisaic regulations for a *mikveh*.
5. In the section on fasting one may observe an interesting anti-rabbinic attitude: "You shall not fast on Monday and Thursday as the hypocrites do, but on Wednesday and Friday" (8:1). Monday and Thursday were fast days in the teaching of the rabbis (*Mishnah Taanith* 2:9). This difference indicates a definite attempt to distinguish the believers from rabbinic Judaism based on growing hostility between them.

Other features that reveal a Jewish influence is mentioned by Bagatti as being in the *Didache*

   . . . written when the descendants of David were at the head of the community, when it alludes to David on two occasions: "through the holy life of David thy servant" (IX, 2) and in saying: "to the Son of David," or to the "house of David" (X, 6).[64]

No early Christian document speaks so loudly and clearly of a supercessionist perspective than does the *Epistle of Barnabas*. Though portions of Clement and Ignatius have isolated comments, Barnabas easily exceeds them in teaching replacement. The author of Barnabas wrote his epistle probably somewhere between A.D. 117–138, a time of Jewish persecution of the church. This most likely explains the tone of this Christian letter. According to Kleist, Rome had a more lenient policy toward the Jewish people, beginning with Hadrian's reign in A.D. 117. This in turn caused many zealous Jews to aspire for independence, which led to the Bar Kochba revolt. During the interval, these aspirations led to heightened interest of Jewish Christians in Jewish religion and rituals. The author seeks to discourage the Jewish believers from defection.[65] This letter has many similarities in tone and intent with the canonical book of Hebrews (cf. Hebrews 10:1 with *Barnabas* 7:6), and there are also similarities with the *Didache*.

Barnabas says, ". . . do not imitate certain people by heaping sin after sin upon yourselves and saying: 'their covenant is ours also.' Ours indeed: but in the end they lost it."[66] He speaks elsewhere of Israel's loss of the covenant because of their sins: "Yes indeed! But let us see whether the covenant which He had sworn to the fathers to give their people was actually given. He has given it; but they, owing to their sins, proved unworthy of the favor."[67] Such teaching does not indicate anti-Semitism on the author's part but does serve as additional foundation to a later setting aside of Israel in favor of the church.

Anti-Semitism in the Second and Third Centuries

The predominantly Gentile church became increasingly anti-Semitic after the middle of the second century. One often observes harsh statements about the Jews. For example, the non-Jew Commodianus harshly states:

There is not an unbelieving people such as yours. O evil men! in so many places, and so often rebuked by the law of those who cry aloud. And the lofty One despises your Sabbaths, and altogether rejects your universal feasts according to the law, that ye should not make to Him the commanded sacrifices; who told you to throw a stone for your offense . . . ye with indurated heart insult Him [God].[68]

Impact of Pagan Anti-Semitism. Anti-Semitism is not difficult to find in the world surrounding Israel. To the Greeks who themselves had an extraordinarily high view of their culture and religions, the Jews appeared quaint if not antisocial. While the entire Mediterranean world was being Hellenized, the Jewish people to varying degrees were resistant to this assimilation. This is especially true in Israel, largely due to the rise of the bludgeoning policies of the Seleucids and Maccabees. It looked as if the Jewish people would be assimilated slowly, but the events leading to the Maccabean era largely reversed this trend, and the religious and nationalistic spirit of Israel led to temporary freedom and ongoing struggles with rulers stronger than itself. Johnson comments that "as Greek ideas on the oneness of humanity spread, the Jewish tendency to treat non-Jews as ritually unclean and forbid marriage to them was resented as being anti-humanitarian."[69] Moreover, the civilized world of the Greeks became an irresistible force that developed a multiracial and multinational society. Any people who opposed these changes were viewed as enemies of man.[70] Whereas the church saw its mission to infiltrate all nations with the truth of Jesus Christ, Judaism remained exclusive and elusive. The evaluation of the earlier pagan writer Hecataeus of Abdera is informative where in a history of Egypt he calls Moses the creator of a form of religion which was strange, narrow, exclusive, and antisocial.[71]

The church becomes primarily Gentile due the lack of Jewish influence in the church.[72] The revolt of Bar-Kokhba has indirect negative results to Jewish Christianity in Judah because Hadrian forbade Jews to come within sight of Jerusalem.[73] Until this decree, fifteen Jews had occupied the Jerusalem bishopric.[74] Now, because of Hadrian's decree, Jerusalem had its first Gentile bishop, Marcus, to head the church.[75]

Apparently, according to Bagatti, Jewish Christians returned to Jerusalem whereas non-Christian Jews were forbidden. Bagatti states, "This is explained by the fact that with the war a distinction was made between the Jews and the Judaeo-Christians, and that the decree of expulsion, promulgated by Hadrian, concerned only the Jews."[76] These Jewish Christians continued in prominence for several centuries. They are referred to in controversy over the date of the celebration of Easter. Eusebius speaks of Christians of Zion who preserved the throne of James.[77] In other places, Christianity had become for all intents and purposes a Gentile religion.

With the end of the Second Jewish War against Rome, Jewish influence and importance became marginalized. It had become so irrelevant to the majority of the church that by the fourth century, at the council at Nicea, eighteen members had come from Palestine. Every one was Gentile and not a single Jewish bishop attended. The council knew nothing of the Jewish-Christian community and took free hand in subjects like the dating of Easter without any opposition. Bagatti notes:

> Once the way was open, future councils followed the same track, ever widening the division among Christians. The point of view of the Judaeo-Christians, attached to their own tradition and devoid of Greek philosophical formation, was to remain firm on the *Testimonia* and therefore would not admit any extraneous word, *homoousios* included. The point of view of the Greek Fathers accustomed to the deductions of

philosophical reasoning, and unburdened by traditionalistic Jewish baggage, was this, that the Holy Spirit had inspired this word, even though it was not biblical, because it corresponded to the Christian truth of the nature of God; he was therefore a heretic who did not accept it.[78]

Another possibility for the lack of Jewish names on the roster of bishops at Nicea is that, though they were known, they were omitted due to anti-Semitic bias. We cannot know for sure the real reason.

Mutual Exclusivity of Christianity and Jewish Practices

There were numerous practices of the Jews which various councils and fathers forbade that would necessarily burden Jewish Christians who confessed the orthodox perspectives of Christ but followed their Jewish heritage.

The general sentiment expressed by many fathers and bishops of the church may be illustrated in the words of Ignatius from the beginning of the second century: "If any one celebrates the Passover along with the Jews, or receives the emblems of their feast, he is a partaker with those that killed the Lord and His apostles."[79]

This condemnation was not universal. Toward the end of the second century Origen sought to provide relief to Jewish followers of Jesus, bolstering his perspective with examples from Peter and Paul in the New Testament.[80]

Stereotype of Jews as Christ Killers

Several fathers speak harshly of the Jews as killers of Christ without differentiating between the rulership who were involved in the conspiracy against Jesus and the Jews as a group. They simply set aside that Jesus, the disciples, and most of the early Christians were Jewish. This anti-Semitism is not equivalent to replacement theology, but it certainly makes the abducting of Israel's blessing much easier to perform.

Ignatius speaks in his letter to the Magnesians of Jesus' enduring of the cross "at the hands of the Christ-killing Jews."[81]

The judgment against Israel was seen as God's judgment due to its grave sin against Jesus, as stated by Origen (c. 185–254) "And these calamities they [the Jews] have suffered, because they were a most wicked nation, which, although guilty of many other sins, yet has been punished so severely for none, as for those that were committed against our Jesus."[82]

For example, Melito (died c. 190), bishop of Sardis, said in his *Homily on the Passion*,

> He who hung the earth is hanging;
> he who fixed the heavens has been fixed;
> he who fastened the universe has been
>   fastened to a tree;

the Sovereign has been insulted;
the God has been murdered;
the King of Israel has been put to death by
an Israelite right hand.[83]

The anti-Semitism of the early church, based on the misunderstanding of an in-house debate, suspicion of Jewish theology and practices, the accusations of Jews as Christ-killers, and the reinforcement of anti-Semitism in the pagan community, was further reinforced by how the apologists and other Christians viewed the treatment of Jewish Christians by the synagogal community, the slaughter of Christians by Bar-Kokhba, and Jewish complicity in the martyrdom of Christians.

Reaction to Anti-Christian Sentiments

Cleansing the synagogues. The fathers of the church viewed the Benediction against the *minim* as Jewish hostility to the faith of Christianity. As mentioned earlier, there is debate as to whether the Benediction was specifically addressed against Christians since even before Christianity, a similar benediction had already been in use in the Jewish synagogues.[84] That the Jews were apt to exclude other groups besides Jewish Christians is not in doubt, but whether within those excluded were the Jewish Christians becomes the concern for this study.[85] In regards to these Jewish *minim,* they were to be more avoided than pagans and were to be hated. Note the benediction, "For the apostates let there be no hope, and may the reign of pride be quickly uprooted in our day; and may the Nazarenes and the *Minim* perish in an instant, and may they be cancelled from the book of the living, and may their name never appear amid the just."[86]

Not only did Pharisaic Jews seek to rid themselves of Jewish Christians by expulsion from the synagogue, they also sought to differentiate themselves from believers in Christ by introducing a double manner of wearing the phylacteries. This backfired on them because the Jewish Christians—who were *minim*—adopted the custom with a different meaning, seeing the sign of the cross, changing this Jewish practice to a Christological significance.[87]

The Jewish believers in Jesus caused the unbelieving Jews to make other changes by investing practices with Christological meaning. Bagatti illustrates this:

One was not to use in salutation the word "Adonai," because the *Minim* referred it to Christ. A second change was that of terminating prayer with the name of "God." In the *Mishna* (*Berak*, 9, 5)... we read: "At the close of every Benediction in the Temple they used to say, 'For everlasting'; but after the heretics had taught corruptly and said that there is but one world (eternity) it was ordained that one should salute his fellow [with the use of] the Name [of God]."[88]

Even the change to the Greek election of Aquila's translation of the Hebrew Scriptures in preference to the Septuagint was largely due to the appropriation of the latter by Christians. The opposition to the Jewish Christians by the post-A.D. 70 Pharisaic Jews is understandable. To these Jews Jesus was an impostor[89] while to the Jewish Christians (specifically the Nazarenes) He was the promised Messiah, even Deity. On the other hand, Gentile Christians would see this rejection and cursing of Jewish brothers, and even themselves, as hatred of Christians and Jesus Christ.[90]

Persecution of Jewish Christians by Bar-Kokhba. Justin, for whom Bar-Kokhba was recent history, mentions in his First Apology that during the revolt this extremist severely punished Christians if they did not blaspheme Yeshua:

> They are also in the possession of all Jews throughout the world; but they, though they read, do not understand what is said, but count us foes and enemies; and, like yourselves, they kill and punish us whenever they have the power, as you can well believe. For in the Jewish war which lately raged, Barchochebas, the leader of the revolt of the Jews, gave orders that Christians alone should be led to cruel punishments, unless they would deny Jesus Christ and utter blasphemy.[91]

Jewish collaboration in the persecution of Christians. Segments of the Jewish populace were against Christ and His followers from the beginning of the Christian era, whereas others were accepting or at least moderate in their response. There is some evidence of earlier hostility between Jews and followers of Christ under Claudius. Suetonius says that there was a disturbance among the Jews led by one Chrestus, probably a misunderstanding on his part regarding the followers of Christ.[92] This hostility was probably reaffirmed when the sect of Christians were blamed by Nero for torching Rome, for Jews were instigators against Christians.[93]

After A.D. 70, and especially after A.D. 135, the Jewish religion increasingly became the enemy of the gospel of Christ and the followers of Christ. The Roman empire began to persecute Christians in these days, and it appears that some non-Christian Jews were willing participants with Rome.

A famous example of this complicity with Rome is the martyrdom of Polycarp: "These things then happened with so great speed, quicker than it takes to tell, and the crowd came together immediately, and prepared wood and faggots from the work-shops and baths and the Jews were extremely zealous, as is their custom, in assisting at this."[94]

Several other statements made in the *Martyrdom* implicate certain Jews in rousing the animosity of the crowds,[95] protestation to the authorities to deny the Christians permission to bury Polycarp's body,[96] and causing the body of Polycarp to be burned.[97]

Another letter written about the same time is the anonymous letter to Diognetus. The author speaks of the difficulty of second century Christians and attaches to that the persecution activities from the Jews: "They are warred upon by the Jews as foreigners and are persecuted by the Greeks, and those who hate them cannot state the cause of their enmity."[98]

Hermeneutical Factors Affecting This Change

How the church interpreted the Hebrew Scriptures and how it saw itself in the prophetic passages of the Old Testament had a great impact on the appropriation of the blessings of the Jewish people. The struggle between the enormous impact of Greek philosophical thought and the church's interpretation of the Old Testament Scriptures caused the church to see itself as the new Israel, replacing the one they visibly saw destroyed in the biblical land in A.D. 70 and 135.

The Church's Use of the Jewish Scriptures

The church not only appropriated the special status of the Jewish people, it took over their Bible, the Septuagint (LXX). Gentile Christians, who generally could not read Hebrew, appropriated the Greek Old Testament, the Septuagint, for themselves. This translation had been done for the Hellenistic Jewish diaspora between the 3rd and 2nd centuries B.C. Justin speaks of the church's use of the Septuagint.[99] Not only the particular translation was at issue, but also whether the church had a legitimate right to the Bible used by the Jews at all:

> But if any of those who are wont to be forward in contradiction should say that these books do not belong to us, but to the Jews, and should assert that we in vain profess to have learnt our religion from them, let him know, as he may from those very things which are written in these books, that not to them, but to us, does the doctrine of them refer. That the books relating to our religion are to this day preserved among the Jews, has been a work of Divine Providence on our behalf; for lest, by producing them out of the Church, we should give occasion to those who wish to slander us to charge us with fraud, we demand that they be produced from the synagogue of the Jews, that from the very books still preserved among them it might clearly and evidently appear, that the laws which were written by holy men, for instruction pertains to us.[100]

It was not only the adoption of the Septuagint by the church but the way the church interpreted various statements from the Septuagint and referred them to Jesus as Messiah that caused consternation from many Jews and their eventual rejection of the Septuagint. Barrett says that the disapproval of the Septuagint may be seen in the type of debate that occurred between Justin and Trypho. When the LXX translates עלמה as παρθένος (virgin) in Isaiah 7:14, for example, this proves to be problematic for the Jewish interpreter. "Justin (*Trypho* 39) maintains that the Jews hate the Christians on account of their interpretation of scripture: "Now it is not surprising," I continued, "that you hate us who hold these opinions, and convict you of a continual hardness of heart."[101]

Rise of Greek Philosophical Interpretation

Though the church was greatly benefited by a common and readable translation of the Hebrew text and though it had good basis to argue from the Septuagint concerning the identity of Jesus as the Messiah prophesied in the Old Testament, it made a fateful move in adopting the Greek philosophical interpretation being popularized in Alexandria's neo-classical resurgence. By the end of the first century the allegorical method had gained considerable sway in the church. The more literal interpretation of the New Testament authors and post-apostolic fathers gave way to the influence of Greek philosophical interpretation found in Philo and later in *Hermes* and Justin Martyr. By the time of the brilliant Alexandrian theologian Origen, allegory was readily used to move beyond the literal sense of the text. In a criticism of Jewish interpretation that was literal, he says:

> Many, not understanding the Scriptures in a spiritual sense, but incorrectly, have fallen into heresies. . . . It seems necessary to explain this point . . . how certain persons, not reading them correctly, have given themselves over to erroneous opinions, inasmuch as the procedure to be followed, in order to attain an understanding of the holy writings, is unknown to many. The Jews, in fine, owing to the hardness of their heart, and from a desire to appear wise in their own eyes, have not believed in our Lord and Savior, judging that those statements which were uttered respecting Him ought to be understood literally. . . .[102]

Another example is fourth century historian Eusebius,

> An example of the allegorical method may be seen in how Eusebius explained away the millennial texts of the Scripture. In speaking of Isaiah 11:6–7 on the peace among animals during the future utopia, "He used the peace among animals to prove not the millenarianist thesis but that of the coming of Christ in the present church. Eusebius speaks of it twice . . . and St. Cyril . . . repeats: 'After the coming of this divine spirit into the ark of the church, the wolves, in the field of the spirits, feed beside the lambs, and the calf and the bull with the lion, as history shows us today, when the kings and princes of the earth allow themselves to be led and instructed by the bishops and by the priests of the church.' "[103]

From the early third century, then, with few exceptions, until the Reformation the allegorical method held sway. The Reformers removed this grotesque dealing with the text in most of the Scriptures except for matters of eschatology and the identification of the promises to Israel with the church.

The Theologians of the Church Seeing the Church as the Genuine Continuation of the Old Testament Faith

Church fathers saw Christians as the proper inheritors of the Old Testament faith and saw proof for this in the teachings of Christ when he said, "Therefore, I tell you, the kingdom of God will be taken away from you and given to a nation producing the *fruits* of it" (Matt. 21:43). For example, Origen in his debate against Celsus says, ". . . we have to say to him, that our Lord, seeing the conduct of the Jews not to be at all in keeping with the teaching of the prophets, inculcated by a parable that the kingdom of God would be taken from them, and given to the converts from heathenism."[104] So much did the church view itself as the true "Israel" that Justin Martyr (c. 100–165) said, "They [the Jewish Scriptures] are not yours but ours."[105] Justin indicates that the former gifts to the Jews were transferred to the church.[106]

Not only was the church the proper deposit for the Jewish Scriptures and the gifts of God but also for the covenants in the view of the Epistle of Barnabas (end of 1st and beginning of 2nd century), "Take heed to yourselves now, and be not made like unto some, heaping up your sins and saying that the covenant is both theirs [the Jews] and ours [Christians]. It is ours."[107] The church also inherited the blessings of Israel according to Barnabas.[108] Even the attempt on the part of Jewish Christians to continue Jewish practices was totally unacceptable, according to Ignatius (c. A.D. 36–108), "It is monstrous to talk of Jesus Christ and to practice Judaism. For Christianity did not base its faith on Judaism, but Judaism on Christianity."[109]

This view of the church being the true continuation of the Old Testament promises becomes a major theme in the apologetics and polemics of the second and third century. Certainly Ignatius overstates the case to say that Judaism is built on Christianity. That both Christianity and Judaism share a common root, however, is not only true to Paul in Romans 11 but conforms to the reality of the dynamics of the first century. Jhan Moskowitz speaks of these two faiths as "twin sisters."

It has been generally understood that Christianity is the daughter of Judaism. This is a poor understanding of the realities of that time. Both Christianity and normative, pharisaic Judaism are twin sisters. . . . Both look back to the Old Testament and claim themselves to be rightful heirs of her promises and authority.

It is in the conflicting claims of that birthright that we can see the emerging hostility of both camps. In the beginning, at a crucial time when her theology and ecclesiology were forming, the church did not have the power of the state to enforce her claims, and the synagogue could not afford to allow any heir to the faith other than themselves for fear of losing the inheritance altogether. Forged in the theology of the Martyr the church saw itself as the true daughter of the faith. Along with the growing number of Gentiles that now were entering the church, she no longer saw herself connected to an ancient national identity, but saw the unbelieving Israel as unworthy of the promise of God in her rejection of the Messiah.[110]

Christianity and Judaism initially, then, shared the same Scriptures, the same prophetic hope, and the same faith. The destruction of Jerusalem and the Jewish temple caused some Jews to develop along different lines than did the Jewish Christian community, the latter assuming the entrance of the blessings of Abraham through Jesus the Savior beyond the nation and the Jewish community. Christianity opened its arms to the world (Matt 28:18–20; Acts 1:8) while Judaism moved inwardly.

Perspectives on Jewish Theology

Jewish millennialism

Several of the Fathers who were generations removed from the apostles developed a firm hostility to teachings of the Jews on matters relating to the millennium and the restoration of Israel. This teaching gave way to a spiritualizing of the literal promises to Israel and the rejection of a future reign of the Jews, including the presence of the temple. Many of these fathers believed that the judgment on the Jews for rejecting—even killing—the Lord Jesus was permanent. This was compounded by the anti-Christian feelings of early second century Pharisaic Judaism. The idea that this obviously rejected people would once again enjoy God's blessings and the rebuilding of their temple seemed preposterous. Yet the promises of restoration in the Old Testament and the teachings of the Apocalypse had to be explained.

John's teaching had great influence on the Jewish community of Asia Minor as well as the post-apostolic fathers. Both of these groups tended toward literal interpretation of the future restoration of Israel and the millennium. Bagatti says,

Well known is the movement of Asia Minor with Ephesus as centre, where St. John had lived, and where he left a very personal imprint. His tomb . . . was a lighthouse, down the centuries, where devout people had manifested, with many graffiti, their attachment to the influence they had undergone. The movement depends in great part on the Judaeo-Christian ideas regarding millenarianism, the cult of angels, the celebration of

Easter on the 14th of Nisan, the use of Johannine phraseology, the continuation of architectonic motifs originating in Palestine *etc*. Yet if the imprint of these churches was near to the Judaeo-Christian current, it did not identify itself with it, because the churches were composed in great part of Gentile Christians and they did not adopt circumcision. The heterodox Judaeo-Christians currents were always treated as heretical and combated without let."[111]

Justin Martyr strongly supported a literal understanding of a millennial reign in answering Trypho on inconsistency between himself and those who claimed to be Christians but denied Christian doctrines:

> But I and others, who are right-minded Christians on all points, are as-sured that there will be a resurrection of the dead, and a thousand years in Jerusalem, which will then be built, adorned and enlarged, [as] the prophets Ezekiel and Isaiah and others declare. . . whose name was John, one of the apostles of Christ, who prophesied, by a revelation that was made to him, that those who believed in our Christ would dwell a thou-sand years in Jerusalem. . . .[112]

Some even, due to their rejection of millennialism, attempted to disavow the Apocalypse as being from John the apostle. For example, Bishop Dionysius at-tributed the Revelation to "the priest John, and not to the Apostle, especially be-cause 'many brethren were enthusiastic about it,' and more so, because they founded on it their extravagant doctrines."[113] Moreover, Eusebius repudiated millenarianism but not with the same extremism as Dionysius. Likewise, Origen, "who, in good faith, contented himself with deriding the simpletons 'who re-fused to work intellectually, preferring to dream in joy and peace; interpreting Scripture literally, after the manner of the Jews.'"[114]

Epiphanius (in 375–77) sought to disavow this Jewish Christian community since he held them to be heretics[115] and Gregory of Nyssa rejected the Christians of Zion after he was not accepted by some Christians in the city who held to "three resurrections, the millenarianism, the restoration of the Temple with bloody sacrifices," doctrines of Jewish Christians.[116] Similarly Jerome rarely passed up the opportunity to ridicule millenarianism and the idea of the reconstruction of the temple.[117]

Nicean View of Jewish Thought

Not only were Jews excluded from most of the deliberations and their per-spectives viewed as suspect or heterodox, but their thinking was also viewed as the fountain from which the heresies of the fourth centuries spewed regarding Christ.

The Christological doctrine which denies the divinity of Christ in the 3–4 century was not looked upon as an Ebionitistic formulation, but as developments from it; first the heresy of Paul of Samosata, and then that of Arius. The Jewish root of these deviations was very clear to the minds of the defenders in the Council of Nicaea, as we gather from St. Athanasius who accused Paul [of Samosata] of having a Jew as patron, namely, Zenobia . . . who for his doctrine merited to be called "a disciple of the Jews" (26, 381–2), and of the Arians he says that "all their stupid doctrine was Jewish" (26, 381–2). The same affirmation is made by Alexander of Alexandria . . . and by Lucifer of Cagliari . . . who calls the Arians—who made him to suffer atrocious persecution in Palestine— "the cursed disciples of the Jews."[118]

Skarsaune seeks to demonstrate, contrary to this perspective, that in reality the ideas about Christ propounded at Nicea came from Jewish theology, albeit clothed in Greek garb.[119] This form of thinking is certainly what one observes developing in the Jewish Christian community within Israel and the Diaspora as evidenced by the teachings found in the Pauline and Johannine corpus. Paul, in his letters, presents a strong case for the deity of Jesus Christ (cf. Phil. 2:5–11; Rom. 9:5; Titus 2:13) and the Trinity in his several benedictions (cf. 2 Cor. 13:14). John, as well, develops a profound statement in his gospel of the deity of the Son (1:1–3, 18; 8:58; 20:28) and personal relationship of the Father and the Son (14:15–18; 17:1–5).

The hope of Israel's restoration

Tertullian speaks of the ignorance of the Jews in putting Christ to death, their subsequent expulsion from their land, and the hope of future restoration.

For the Jews are pronounced "apostate son, begotten indeed and raised on high, but who have not understood the Lord, and who have quite forsaken the LORD, and have provoked unto anger the Holy One of Israel" . . . he has likewise had every more savory morsel torn from his throat, not to say the very land of promise . . . the Jew . . . is a beggar in alien territory.[120]

Having said this, he goes on to say, however, "for it will be fitting for the Christian to rejoice, and not to grieve, at the restoration of Israel, if it be true, (as it is), that the whole of our hope is intimately united with the remaining expectation of Israel."[121]

Origen, apart from his allegorical interpretations, has a fairly balanced presentation of judgment on the Jewish nation, on the one hand, and a recognition of their future restoration, on the other hand.

REPLACEMENT THEOLOGY AND THE TRIUMPH
OF CHRISTIANITY IN THE ROMAN EMPIRE

With the Jewish roots of Christianity virtually lost in the church's memory, the minimalization of the Jews with their destruction, the need for Christian apologists to justify the church's antiquity before the Roman government, and the theological orientation of the church altered by Greek philosophical interpretation, the stage was set for the church taking the blessings and identity of Israel to itself. The coup d'etat in the change to replacement theology was the triumph of Christianity in the Roman Empire. For example, Kaiser says that when Constantine gathered all the bishops together in the thirtieth year of his reign, he viewed it as a "foreshadowing of the eschatological Messianic banquet."[122] To Eusebius, then, it was no longer needful to distinguish between the church and the empire; they were viewed as "one fulfilled kingdom of God on earth."[123]

CONCLUSION

Israel is the chosen people of God. Unfortunately, they so often as a people have failed to participate in God's blessings due to their disobedience. The last major judgment of God against His people was with their rejection of the Messiah who came to them. Rather than believing the prophets of the Hebrew Scriptures or the living Torah of God (the Messiah), they rejected them and were driven in large part from their land and their temple worship. Due to this rejection and their consequent rejection of the message of the church, gradually the church turned hostile to the Jewish people and began to believe that the church became the recipients of the blessings of God irrevocably given to the physical lineage of Jacob. In so doing, the church began to reject Jewishness itself as well as the Jew.

Such response is dangerous to Christianity itself for it, along with Judaism, has its roots in the faith and Scriptures of Israel. Bagatti rightly perceives the actions of Eusebius toward the Jewish people in not losing the anchor of Israel for the faith of the church: "Evidently Eusebius foresaw the disastrous consequences which would have followed regarding the origin of Christianity, if he associated himself with the extremists who obstinately rejected the Christians of the Jewish race as nongenuine."[124] To reject Israel is to reject the tree from which the church has received its life and its future.

ENDNOTES

1. R. Steven Notley, "Anti-Jewish Tendencies in the Synoptic Gospels," *Jewish Perspectives* 51 (April–June 1996), 27.
2. Origen, *Origen against Celsus*, 2.8, from Alexander Roberts and James Donaldson, *Ante-Nicene Fathers*, vol. 4 (Peabody, Mass.: Hendrickson Publishers, Inc., 1995; originally published by Christian Literature Publishing Co., 1885). (Unless otherwise noted, all references of ante-Nicene Fathers are to this publication in ten volumes.) It is interesting that later in his debate with Celsus, Origen uses the staying

power in the land as a argument for the prophetic authority of the Bible. *Origen against Celsus* 3.2. Later in this work, though, he says with confidence that the Jewish people will never be restored to their "former condition" because of their great sin against Jesus. *Origen against Celsus* 4.22.

3. Tuvya Zaretsky, "The Church Has Replaced the Jewish People—A Perspective," *Mishkan* 21 (February 1994): 33. Most of this issue of *Mishkan* is dedicated to the matter of replacement theology.

4. Walter C. Kaiser Jr., "An Assessment of 'Replacement Theology:' The Relationship Between the Israel of the Abrahamic-Davidic Covenant and the Christian Church," *Mishkan* 21 (February 1994): 9.

5. Ibid.

6. Jeffrey Siker, *Disinheriting the Jews* (Louisville: Westminster, 1991), 28–76, 77–127, 128–143, 144–184, 190–91.

7. Ray Pritz, "Replacing the Jews in Early Christian Theology," *Mishkan* 21 (February 1994): 22.

8. Kaiser Jr., "An Assessment of 'Replacement Theology,'" 9.

9. David Larsen, *Jews, Gentiles & the Church* (Grand Rapids: Discovery House Publishers, 1995), 22.

10. Ibid., 26.

11. Stanley A. Ellisen, *Biography of a Great Planet* (Wheaton: Tyndale House Publishers, Inc., 1975), 216. Ellisen also lists the Persian Gulf as a possibility but few would hold to this. For a chart providing key biblical texts for the land promises, see Larsen, *Jews, Gentiles & the Church*, 26.

12. Larsen, *Jews, Gentiles & the Church*, 34. David Larsen explains this dynamic: "Abraham and his immediate descendants did not in God's purpose possess the promised land (but Abraham indeed purchased the burial-place for Sarah as described in Genesis 23). Later the chosen people were dispersed in captivity because of their disobedience. 'Any member of the line of David may by sin forfeit his own share in the promise, but he may not forget that which belongs to his successors to eternity.' The promissory covenants of the Old Testament guarantee both the physical posterity and property of God's ancient people in perpetuity. Temporary dispossession does not mean loss of the inheritance. The fulfillment of the land-promise becomes critical for anyone contemplating the fidelity of God to any or all of His promises." Larsen, *Jews, Gentiles & the Church*, 22.

13. See H. Wayne House, "David's Role in Prophecy," *Dictionary of Premillennial Theology*, gen. ed. Mal Couch (Grand Rapids: Kregel Publications, 1997), 85–86.

14. Paul Johnson sees Jesus within the Hillel camp, for most part, taking the thinking of Hillel to logical conclusion: "Jesus' rigorism in taking Hillel's teaching to its logical conclusion led him to cease to be an orthodox sage in any sense which had meaning and, indeed, cease to be a Jew. He created a religion which was *sui generis*, and it is accurately called Christianity. He incorporated in his ethical Judaism an impressive composite of the eschatology he found in Isaiah, Daniel and Enoch, as well as what he found useful in the Essenes and the Baptist, so that he was able to present a clear perspective of death, judgment and the afterlife. And he offered this new theology to everyone within reach of his mission: pious Jews, the *am ha-area*, the Samaritans, the unclean, the gentiles even." Paul Johnson, *A History of the Jews* (New York: Harper & Row, Publishers, 1987), 120.

15. See Larsen, *Jews, Gentiles & the Church*, 52–54 for a discussion of the future of Israel based on Romans 11.

16. See Larsen for a discussion on the various ages to come, the millennial age, and the

great likelihood of an intermediate kingdom. Larsen, *Jews, Gentiles & the Church*, 55–56.

17. Ibid.
18. Some believe the present reign of Christ in His Father's throne is the fulfillment of Jesus to sit on David's throne. Sitting on the Father's throne in heaven in no way fulfills the literal reign predicted in the Old Testament nor is it in agreement with Jesus' own words. In Matthew 25:31–32, Jesus indicates that this reign on David's throne to rule the nations occurs only in His second coming: "But when the Son of Man comes in His glory, and all the angels with Him, then He will sit on His glorious throne. And all the nations will be gathered before Him. . . ." See H. Wayne House and Thomas Ice, *Dominion Theology: Blessing or Curse?* (Portland, Oreg.: Multnomah Press, 1988), 26.
19. The conversion of the Ethiopian eunuch under Philip (Acts 8:26–40) is an aberration from this; the gospel to the God-fearer Cornelius, as evidenced by Acts 11 is the public, decisive offer of gospel to the Gentile world.
20. Johnson, *A History of the Jews,* 125.
21. The Nazarenes were one of two major Jewish groups who were viewed as sects within Judaism; they considered themselves to be equal to Christians of Gentile stock. They wished, as one of their exponents, Hegesippus, says, "to appear as true Christians distinct from the heretics, even though of their own stock." Fr. Bellarmino Bagatti, *The Church from the Circumcision: History and Archaeology of the Judaeo-Christians,* Studium Biblicum Franciscanum, no. 2 (Jerusalem: Franciscan Printing Press, 1984).
22. James and then Simeon became leaders, the first being a half-brother of Jesus, and Simeon was elected because of being cousin of Christ. Ibid., 9.
23. Josephus, *Antiquities of the Jews*, 20.19.1, as found in *The Complete Works of Josephus,* trans. William Whiston (Grand Rapids: Kregel Publications, 1960). Also see Henk Jagersma, *A History of Israel from Alexander the Great to Bar Kochba* (Philadelphia: Fortress Press, 1986), 136.
24. It was thought earlier that the Hebrew canon was completed at Jamnia but recent studies have demonstrated that the canon was finished no later than the second century B.C. and possibly as early as the fourth century B.C. Jack P. Lewis, "What Do We Mean by Jabneh?" *Journal of Bible and Religion* 32 (1964): 125–32 and Sid Z. Leiman, *The Canonization of Hebrew Scripture: The Talmudic and Midrashic Evidence* (Hamdon, Conn.: Transactions of the Connecticut Academy of Arts and Sciences, Archon Books, 1976).
25. Ray Pritz, *Nazarene Jewish Christianity, Studia Post-Biblica* (Jerusalem-Leiden: The Magnes Press, The Hebrew University, E. J. Brill, 1988), 126.
26. Jhan Moskowitz, "Some Possible Causes for the Rise of Anti-Jewish Sentiments in the Early Church" (unpublished paper), 2.
27. Harry R. Boer, *A Short History of the Early Church* (Grand Rapids: Eerdmans Publishing Company, 1976), 44.
28. Ibid. Jews were often involved in stirring up trouble against Christians and so brought on themselves severe response at times from Christian apologists.
29. Bagatti, *The Church from the Circumcision*, 28.
30. Pritz, *Nazarene Jewish Christianity*, 11.
31. Bagatti, *The Church from the Circumcision*, 31. See the discussion on several possible derivations of the name in Pritz, *Nazarene Jewish Christianity*, 11–12.
32. Pritz, *Nazarene Jewish Christianity*, 13.
33. Bagatti identifies this withdrawal to Pella with a passage from the Ascension of Isaiah: "And many of the faithful and of the saints who saw him crucified in whom they

had hoped, Jesus Christ our Lord, and of those also who had believed in him (without seeing him) during these days will remain his servants in a small number, fleeing from desert to desert, awaiting his coming." *Ascension of Isaiah,* 4:13, as cited by Bagatti, *The Church from the Circumcision,* 8.

34. Jagersma indicates that the flight to Pella has been the standard position of the past and still is among most scholars but also speaks of recent scholarly questioning of this fact. He says, "in recent times it has been increasingly challenged. Among other things, scholars point out the great distance between Pella and Jerusalem (about sixty miles), involving a journey through a region controlled by the Romans, and that in 66 Pella was plundered by Jewish partisans, which certainly would not have encouraged the Jewish Christians to settle there. It therefore seems most likely that the members of the earliest community in Jerusalem shared the fate of their fellow-citizens in the siege and after its capture by Titus in 70. All this does not exclude the possibility that individual members of the Jerusalem community like Johanan ben Zakkai . . . could have fled before or during the siege." Jagersma, *A History of Israel,* 136–37.

35. C. K. Barrett, *The Gospel of John & Judaism,* trans. D. M. Smith (Philadelphia: Fortress Press, 1975), 69.

36. Johnson, *A History of the Jews,* 146–47. D. Moody Smith comments on this benediction designed against Jewish Christians: "Presumably its purpose was to smoke out Christ-confessors within the synagogue, who could not pronounce this benediction, or malediction, against themselves. This reformulation of the Twelfth Benediction took place in the Rabbinic Academy at Jamnia. According to tradition, it was done by a sage called Samuel the Small under the auspices of Rabbi Gamaliel II, and it has been dated in the ninth decade of the first century." D. Moody Smith, "Judaism and the Gospel of John," in *Jews and Christians, Exploring the Past, Present, and Future,* ed. James H. Charlesworth, vol. 1 of *Shared Ground Among Jews and Christians, a Series of Explorations* (New York: Crossroad, 1990), 85.

37. See the study by Pritz, *Nazarene Jewish Christianity,* 102–7, especially the identification of the Nazarenes within the *minim*; also Bagatti, *The Church from the Circumcision,* 95, 98–106.

38. Jacob Jocz, *The Jewish People and Jesus Christ* (Grand Rapids: Baker Book House, 1949), 180.

39. Bagatti, *The Church from the Circumcision,* 31.

40. Ibid., 34–35.

41. *Origen against Celsus,* 5.61.

42. Pritz, *Nazarene Jewish Christianity,* 21.

43. See Notley, "Anti-Jewish Tendencies," 20–34 for the view of the synoptic Gospels being anti-Semitic.

44. Quoted in Louis Feldman, "Is the New Testament Anti-Semitic?" *Moment,* vol. 15, no. 6 (December 1990): 35.

45. Ibid., 33–34.

46. See the review of options given by Smith, "Judaism and the Gospel of John," 79–83.

47. Ibid., 82.

48. Feldman, "Is the New Testament Anti-Semitic?" 35.

49. Ibid., 50. Feldman speaks of Rabbi Lewis Browne who "remarked that Jesus was not the founder but the foundling of Christianity, or, as the jingle would have it, 'A man named Saul, later called Paul, came and spoiled it all.'"

50. Ibid.

51. On the other hand, the use of sunagwghv (synagogue) may simply refer to an "assembly" of believers, into whose midst some come claiming to be Jews but are not really.

52. James H. Charlesworth, "Exploring Opportunities for Rethinking Relations among Jews and Christians," *Jews and Christians: Exploring the Past, Present, and Future, Shared Ground Among Jews and Christians, A Series of Explorations,* vol. 1, gen. ed. James H. Charlesworth (New York: Crossroad Publishing Company, 1990), 43.

53. An important form of rhetoric at the time was taught by Jews such as Theodorus and Caecilius of Calacte and vituperative rhetoric was well used at this time. Feldman, "Is the New Testament Anti-Semitic?" 52.

54. The Dead Sea Scrolls, in the *Manual of Discipline,* urge the readers to hate the children of darkness. *Manual of Discipline* 1.10, 11a. Also see *Hymns* 4.10, 20. See Feldman, "Is the New Testament Anti-Semitic?" 52.

55. See Ezekiel 16:48; 23:37; Isaiah 56:8–11; 57:3.

56. *Pesachim* 57a.

57. James H. Charlesworth, "Christians and Jews in the First Six Centuries," in *Christianity and Rabbinic Judaism,* ed. Hershel Shanks (Washington, D.C.: Biblical Archaeology Society, 1992), 309.

58. Ibid.

59. Moskowitz, "Some Possible Causes for the Rise of Anti-Jewish Sentiments," 12.

60. Ibid.

61. The dating of the *Didache* has been the subject of much debate. Part of the problem resides in the probable development of the *Didache* in several recensions over several decades. Kirsopp Lake views the "Two Ways" to reflect most likely the early first century while the remainder may be late first century or early second century. Kirsopp Lake, "The *Didache,* or Teaching of the Twelve Apostles," *The Apostolic Fathers,* vol. 1 in *The Loeb Classical Library* (Cambridge, Mass.: Harvard University Press, 1965), 306–7; the *International Standard Bible Encylopaedia* places the date between A.D. 80–120 (*The International Standard Bible Encyclopedia,* vol. III, gen. ed. James Orr [Grand Rapids: Wm. B. Eerdmans Publishing Co. 1946], 1898) whereas the Enchiridion Patristicum places it between A.D. 80–100. M. J. Rouët de Journel, Enchiridion Patristicum (Barcione: Herder, 1969), 1. The earliest suggestion (at least of some portions of the *Didache*) is that of Geoff Trowbridge with a date between A.D. 60–100. www.qtm.net/~trowbridge/*Didache*.htm, 1.

62. I have largely followed the presentation of Moskowitz on evidence of Jewish influence in the *Didache.*

63. Moskowitz, "Some Possible Causes for the Rise of Anti-Jewish Sentiments," 13–14.

64. Bellarmino Bagatti, *The Church from the Gentiles in Palestine,* trans. Eugene Hoade (Jerusalem: Franciscan Printing Press, 1971; reprinted 1984), 26.

65. James Kleist, *Ancient Christian Writers, The Works of the Fathers in Translation* (New York: Newman Press, 1946), 31–32. That this letter, even as Romans, was not written to an audience entirely composed of Jews is clear from passages such as Romans 11:6–14.

66. *Epistle of Barnabas* 4:6–9, in *The Apostolic Fathers,* vol. 1 *The Loeb Classical Library,* 351, 353.

67. *Epistle of Barnabas* 4.1, in *The Apostolic Fathers,* vol. 1 in *The Loeb Classical Library,* 391.

68. *The Instruction of Commodianus,* 210.

69. Johnson, *A History of the Jews,* 134.

70. Ibid.
71. Ibid.
72. Eusebius 4.6.4. *The Church History of Eusebius*, trans. Arthur Cushman McGiffert, in *Nicene and Post-Nicene Fathers,* ed. Philip Schaff and Henry Wall, second series, vol. 1 (Peabody, Mass.: Hendrickson Publishers, 1995). Unless otherwise noted, all references to Eusebius are from this publication. Bagatti, *The Church from the Circumcision,* 87.
73. Eusebius, in abridging the account of Ariston of Pella, says, "After these things a decree and a disposition of Hadrian forbade the whole people to put a foot in the region adjoining Jerusalem; and so for the Jews, alas! it was forbidden to contemplate even from afar their homeland. So does Ariston of Pella tell us." Bagatti, *The Church from the Gentiles in Palestine,* 8.
74. Eusebius 4.5.1–4: ". . . until the siege of the Jews, which took place under Adrian, there were fifteen bishops in succession there, all of whom are said to have been of Hebrew descent, and to have received the knowledge of Christ in purity, so that they were approved by those who were able to judge of such matters, and were deemed worthy of the episcopate. For their whole church consisted then of believing Hebrews who continued from the days of the apostles until the siege which took place at this time; in which siege the Jews, having again rebelled against the Romans, were conquered after several battles. But since the bishops of the circumcision ceased at this time, it is proper to give here a list of their names from the beginning. The first, then was James, the so-called brother of the Lord; the second, Symeon; the third, Justus; the fourth, Zacchaeus; the fifth, Tobias; the sixth, Benjamin; the seventh, John; the eighth, Matthias; the ninth, Philip; the tenth, Seneca; the eleventh, Justus; the twelfth, Levi; the thirteenth, Ephres; the fourteenth, Joseph; and finally, the fifteenth, Judas."
75. Eusebius, *The Church History* 4.6.4. See Yigael Yadin, *Bar-Kokhba* (London: Weidenfeld and Nicolson, 1971), 22, for a treatment of the banishment of the Jews from Jerusalem.
76. Bagatti, *The Church from the Circumcision,* 10.
77. Ibid.
78. Ibid., 87. For the view that the Nicene council was heavily influenced by Jewish theological ideas see, Oscar Skarsaune, "The Christological Dogma of Nicaea— Greek or Jewish?" *Mishkan* 1 (January 1984), 40–49. Also see Oscar Skarsaune, *Incarnation: Myth or Fact?* trans. Trygve R. Skarsten (St. Louis: Concordia Publishing House, 1946). Also see various influences that Jewish Christianity had on Gentile Christian writers in Bagatti, *The Church from the Circumcision,* 82–86.
79. Ignatius, *Epistle of Ignatius to the Philippians,* 14.
80. Origen, *Origen against Celsus,* 428–29.
81. Ignatius, *Epistle of Ignatius to the Magnesians,* 11. Elsewhere he says the Jews are "murders of the Lord," *Epistle of Ignatius to the Trallians,* 11., and a "murderer of Christ." *Epistle of Ignatius to the Philippians,* 13.
82. Origen, *Origen against Celsus,* 2.8.
83. Melito, *Homily on the Passion,* lines 711–16.
84. Pritz clarifies the broader use of the term *minim*: "A survey of the term reveals *minim* who clearly lived before Christianity, *minim* who reject the resurrection from the dead and therefore cannot be Christians, etc. However, one will also see many places where the *minim* clearly are Christians and most likely *Jewish* Christians. Generally, it is safe to say that *minim* are Jews who reckon themselves to be Jews but who are excluded by the rabbis." Pritz, *Nazarene Jewish Christianity,* 103.

85. See the text accompanying footnote 38.

86. Bagatti, *The Church from the Circumcision,* 102.

87. Ibid., 101.

88. Ibid.

89. These Jews, still smarting from the Roman defeat and the loss of their temple probably had great difficulty with Jesus who spoke of the destruction of the temple and
who also was not a liberating Messiah they had anticipated. The Talmud does seem
to indicate that they viewed Jesus to be in the line of David but never received official anointing as was true of former kings and priests. See *Sanhedrin* 43a in the
Babylonian Talmud where it is recorded "(Rabbi) Ulla said, 'Would you believe that
any defence would have been so zealously sought for him? He was a deceiver, and
the All-merciful says: 'You shall not spare him, neither shall you conceal him.' It
was different with Jesus, for he was near to the kingship." Cf. chart in H. Wayne
House, *Chronological and Background Charts of the New Testament* (Grand Rapids: Zondervan Publishing House, 1981), 77.

90. Though the widespread treatment of Jewish Christians was hostile, there were those
among the Jews who were more moderate. "Of Rabbi Judah b. Levi (third century)
. . . we read 'that he was tolerant also of the Judaeo-Christians, albeit often they
annoyed him; that he refused to curse one of them, saying rather the words of Psalm
149:9: 'The mercy of God embraces all his creatures.'" Bagatti, *The Church from
the Circumcision,* 108.

91. Justin Martyr, *First Apology,* 31. This was also noted by Eusebius in *Ecclesiastical
History,* 4.8. Translation by Kirsopp Lake, *The Loeb Classical Library* (London:
Heinemann Ltd. and Harvard University Press, 1926), 322–33: "only Christians
whom Bar Chocheba, the leader of the rebellion of the Jews, commanded to be pun-
ished severely, if they did not deny Jesus as the Messiah and blaspheme him." See
Barrett, 10.

92. Suetonius, *Claudius,* 25

93. Suetonius, *Nero,* 16.

94. *Martyrdom of Polycarp,* 13:1 trans. Kirsopp Lake in *The Apostolic Fathers,* Loeb
Series, vol. 2 (Cambridge, Mass.: Harvard University Press, 1913), 329.

95. *Martyrdom of Polycarp,* 12:2.

96. *Martyrdom of Polycarp,* 17:2–3.

97. *Martyrdom of Polycarp,* 18:1.

98. *The Epistle to Diognetus,* 5:17. A contrary opinion on all of this was forcefully argued by James Parkes in an appendix to *The Conflict of the Church and the Synagogue* (New York: Hermon Press, 1974).

99. Justin Martyr, *Dialogue with Trypho,* 137.

100. Justin Martyr, *Justin's Hortatory Address to the Greeks,* 13.

101. Barrett, 51; Justin Martyr, *Dialogue with Trypho,* 39: οὐδὲν θαυμαστὸν εἰ καὶ
ἡμας μισειϛτε τοῦ ταῦτα νοοὺντας καὶ ἐλέγχοντας ὑμῶν τὴν ἀεὶ σκληροκαρδίαν
γνώμης.

102. Origen, *de Principiis,* 4.1.8. (Latin). Origen provides examples of what he understood as the proper method of interpretation in that the Jews were physical shadows
of the spiritual people of God. He speaks of "spiritual Israelites," the church, of whom
the physical Jews were the type. Ibid.

103. Bagatti, *The Church from the Circumcision,* 90.

104. Origen, *Origen against Celsus,* 2.5.

105. Justin Martyr, *Dialogue with Trypho,* 29.2.

106. Ibid.

107. *Epistle of Barnabas*, 4.6–7, trans. Kirsopp Lake, *Loeb Classical Library* (Cambridge, Mass.: Harvard University Press, 1965).
108. *Epistle of Barnabas,* 13.
109. Ignatius, *Epistle to the Magnesians*, 10.2–3, trans. Kirsopp Lake, *Loeb Classical Library* (Cambridge, Mass.: Harvard University Press, 1965).
110. Moskowitz, "Some Possible Causes for the Rise of Anti-Jewish Sentiments," 7–8.
111. Bagatti, *The Church from the Circumcision,* 26. The millennial idea was not confined to Asia Minor but existed in Egypt (fifth to sixth centuries). Bagatti, 28. Origen, likewise, speaks of Jews as persecutors of Christians, placing Christians in the same category as the Hebrew prophets and the Lord persecuted by the Jews. Origen, *Origen to Africanus*, 389.
112. Justin Martyr, *Dialogue with Trypho*, 240.
113. Bagatti, *The Church from the Circumcision*, 89.
114. Ibid., 90.
115. Ibid., 11. Epiphanius greatly erred in this assessment as the fathers Justin, Tertullian, Origen, and Eusebius indicate and the research of Pritz on the Nazarenes, in contrast to other Jewish sects, demonstrates.
116. Ibid.
117. See Ibid., 90–91 for a description of Jerome's arguments.
118. Ibid., 90.
119. Skarsaune, "The Christological Dogma," 40–49.
120. Tertullian, *On Modesty*, 4.54.
121. Ibid.
122. Walter C. Kaiser Jr., *An Assessment of "Replacement The*ology," *Mishkan* 21 (February 1994): 9.
123. Ibid.
124. Bagatti, *The Church from the Circumcision,* 84.

The menorah outside the Knesset building.

CHAPTER FIVE

HISTORICAL AND POLITICAL FACTORS IN THE TWENTIETH CENTURY AFFECTING THE IDENTITY OF ISRAEL

Louis Goldberg

By far, the greatest event in modern history affecting Jewish people was the Holocaust, the death of six million people, which affected almost one-third of the total population of world Jewry of some 18,000,000.[1] That it happened in this particular century is a factor that cannot be overlooked. While an explanation of why these people perished is difficult to ascertain, one needs to take into account that just a scant three years after Hitler took his life during the last gasping moments of the Third Reich, the State of Israel was born in the Middle East. Short of Messiah's coming, only the presence of an independent State of Israel could assuage some of the hurt and agony Jewish people felt and continue to feel.

While these events are important regarding the twentieth century for both Jewish people and the church, what occurred in the background of the nineteenth century is also significant for Zionism's interest in a homeland in the Middle East for Jewish people, as well as for the church's interest in reaching out to them. The major thrusts of this chapter are, first, to explore further the prophetic significance of events leading to the rise of Israel as a state and, second, to show the interest by various groups of Christians who began and sustained a ministry in Israel. Third, I want to demonstrate how the effect of the Holocaust caused various Christians to give up on evangelism of Jewish people, feeling it is no longer a viable objective. Instead, believers are to demonstrate a love for, and have an unquestioned political support of Israel. I will also go a step further and assess with serious misgivings a few of, the statements, articles, and books now appearing by many in Christendom who have softened their theological position on key doctrines considered offensive to Jewish people. In the last two areas, the implications of these beliefs can seriously affect a biblical view of missions to the Jewish people.

THE PROPHETIC MESSAGE

God's work in the regathering of His people in modern times is centered in a prophecy uttered some twenty-seven hundred years ago by one of the eighth century B.C. prophets:

> For the Israelites will live many days without king or prince, without sacrifice or sacred stones, without ephod or idol. Afterward the Israelites will return and seek the Lord their God and David their King. They will come trembling to the Lord and to His blessings in the last days. (Hos. 3:4–5)[2]

Hard Realities

No king has ruled the Israel of the North since the Assyrians destroyed Samaria in 722/721 B.C., but did Hosea mean to also apply his message to the southern kingdom? And yet, Judah has also been without a king of the Solomonic line since the Babylonian exile. Because of Jeremiah's curse on Jehoiachin (Coniah) in the early 500s B.C. (Jer. 22:30), the high priests of Israel, while serving as the priestly representatives, also provided, for the most part, the leadership over the nation during the second Commonwealth of Israel from 536 B.C. to A.D. 70.[3] The throne of David through the line of David has officially remained empty from 586 B.C. through today.

Hosea also condemned the Israelite pagan worship of his day—the illicit sacrifices to the pagan gods on the stone pillars associated with the Canaanite cult. The ephod had some legitimate use in the early history of Israel as special jackets which the priests wore or for inquiring direction from the Lord as when David did (1 Sam. 30:7–8). These objects, however, also became objects of worship, as with Gideon (Judg. 8:24–25) and in Hosea's day as well. With the rise of the prophets, the use of the ephod was phased out and any magic or superstitious attachment to it was condemned. Similarly, the *teraphim*, or household gods, were also denounced as objects of worship. The Israel of the North had departed from the legitimate worship of the Lord at the temple in Jerusalem, but now Hosea declared that the substitute worship they had in their kingdom would also be taken from them.[4]

Furthermore, although Judah came back from exile in Babylon and was permitted to have their second temple, they lost it as well in A.D. 70, and Jewish people have had no legitimate Levitical sacrifices nor has there been an altar on which to place a sacrifice. They have not had a Levitical high priest since A.D. 70. And, since the Council's decisions at Yavneh in A.D. 70–90, Judaism is a religion with no substitute atonement. The prophet's message could also have had a connotation of a greater loss than that which the northern kingdom experienced.

Hope

Many in Christendom have stopped after verse 4, declaring that since the coming of Yeshua (Jesus),[5] no place exists for Israel as a people to occupy a piece of land with a special unique blessing upon them. They assert that Jewish people can receive Yeshua the Messiah on a personal level and God can accept them as part of the body of the Messiah, the church, regarded by many as the "New Israel." But does the prophet declare that national Israel is finished as such?

In noting the Massoretic or Hebrew text (MT), the major break in the sentence of Hosea 3:5, ". . . Afterward the Israelites . . . and David their king, . . ." occurs after "king." Does it mean a simultaneous action of Israel returning to the land and also seeking the Lord their God and David their king? Minor breaks do occur as well after "will return" and after "seek the Lord their God." It is therefore possible to understand the passage in the light of historical development. First, the Lord will recover His people from a worldwide dispersion, and then, over a period of time in the land, many will seek the Lord and David their king; then, at the time of the Lord's return, "all Israel" will become believers in that cataclysmic event.[6]

So, if words have any meaning ("Afterward the Israelites will return") it would seem that the prophet spoke meaningfully that after a nighttime of wandering, pain, suffering, separation for the most part from a homeland, and even at this writing where peace is so elusive for the Israelis and Arabs, God has a plan for Israel being in the land. One day, Israelis will not only return to the Lord, but they also will seek the Lord and He will permit the opportunities for them to find Him and know Him.

But Why a Return to the Land of Israel?

For Jewish people, as a rule, the land of Israel was like a beacon. For centuries, they affirmed their hope of a return to this land during the Passover, praying over the plate of three masot (three pieces of unleavened bread) and concluding in the last line of the prayer, *"This year, we are here, but next year, in the land of Israel."*[7] Every holiday on the Jewish calendar makes sense only in connection with the agricultural cycle in the land of Israel. Passover is also a reminder of the barley harvest in the spring (Lev. 23:10–12); *Shavuot*, or Pentecost, in late spring, was the time of the wheat harvest (Lev. 23:16–21). *Sukkot* came in the fall, after the general harvest of the land (Deut. 16:13–15). God has a way of reminding Jewish people that *'Eretz Yisrael* (Land of Israel) is a special place. Even though Jewish people may forget, God doesn't. The Abrahamic covenant not only guarantees the presence of these people (Gen. 17:7), but the Lord had also promised that the land of Israel belongs to the descendants of Abraham, Isaac, and Jacob (Gen. 15:18; 26:3; 35:12). And, it is to this very land Israel has been returning, as will be seen over the next several pages, as a matter of historical record and as the prophet Ezekiel also declared (37:21–25).

Many believers have the tendency to think only in terms of God's working in the cataclysmic event: Messiah will come, Israel will be "born again in a day," and then the kingdom will commence. However, the providence of God works quietly in and through the events of human history, as in the establishment of modern Israel through a people still in unbelief concerning the reality and identity of the Messiah. We assert that it is no quirk in history that for over a hundred years Jewish people have been returning to the land of Israel. And the process is not over yet. We should note the significant movements, dates, and circumstances for Israel in the modern scene as to how God has worked in His mercy.

PROVIDENTIAL CIRCUMSTANCES

To understand how and why 600,000 Israeli Jewish people were present in the land in 1948, we need to go back to the 1800s to consider the beginning of modern Israel.[8]

The New Jerusalem

A few people moved out of the Old City of Jerusalem on its western side to the other side of the valley of Gehenna in 1869 to build a very small settlement, which became the vision for New or West Jerusalem.

Agricultural School

The first agricultural school in Israel in modern times, the Mikveh Israel, was established in 1869–1870 by the Alliance Israelite Universelle[9] that encouraged Jewish people in a back-to-the-land movement. Resources were put in place for future immigrants to transform the then arid desert and wasted homeland, making it fertile and productive. As a result, Israelis today are some of the best agronomists in the world.

The Suez Canal

Of extreme importance regarding the beginning of modern Israel was the opening of the Suez Canal, which by 1875 was a joint British–French venture. From the days of Marco Polo in the 1200s up to the 1800s, the Middle East was the backwash of the Western nations while they carved out their empires elsewhere. A few missionaries were present in this forlorn region, but not much else was going on. The beginning of the flow of commerce and the movement of troops through the Suez Canal once more focused attention on the Middle East and by 1900, Great Britain, France, and Germany began to stake out their areas of interest across this region.

Persecutions

The persecution of Jewish people became the major reason for their desire to move, particularly from Eastern Europe where they had suffered the most from pogroms (extreme pressure and persecution) for centuries. In particular, beginning in 1881 under Alexander II, harsh measures were taken against Russian Jews which lasted until the March revolution of 1917.[10] The pogroms that came as a result of Russian policy shattered their lingering illusions of equality and achievement under the czarist rule. Through a policy of discrimination, the objective was to remove Jews from key economic and public positions.[11] Between 1880 and 1914, about 2,000,000 Jewish people emigrated from eastern Europe, principally Russia, to the United States, but the persecutions also served to push a good number toward the land of Israel.[12]

Pogroms also existed in Lithuania as well as in Rumania, causing Jewish people to flee to places of refuge, such as the United States, but a steady movement also went to the land of Israel.

The Jewish Essayists

From the early 1840s to 1890s, a number of Jewish writers crafted essays, outlining the rationale of a Jewish presence on the soil of the ancient homeland. Rabbi Yehudah Alkalai was one of the earliest writers (1843), changing the theme from messianic prophecy to a Jewish nationalism. His essays "Darkhei Noam" and "Shelom Yerushalaim" allude to the need for establishing Jewish colonies in the holy land as a necessary prelude to the redemption. Self effort toward this climactic physical and spiritual achievement was justified by the "proof texts" of messianic fulfillment. Citing the Kabala, he asserted that the struggle by devoted Jewish common people everywhere would prefigure the coming of the Messiah.[13] He propagated the idea of Jewish national unity through an overall organization of world Jewry with modernized Hebrew as its common language.[14]

Rabbi Zvi Hirsch Kalischer in 1862 introduced in his "Seeking Zion," the idea of

> . . . an active human element into the concept of redemption of the Jewish people. . . . Pointing to the struggles of European nations to achieve independence, . . . he chastised his fellow Jews for being the only people without such an aspiration. . . . Redemption would come in two stages, . . . the natural one, return to Israel and labor—in the country, and the supernatural to follow. . . .[15]

Again, these theories of redemption were derived from a reinterpretation of the messianic tradition in light of recent political experiences in Europe.

Moses Hess likewise, after a period as a social revolutionary and philosopher, returned to the religious culture of his people, and in his writings in the 1860s, he based his Zionist ideas on the concept of a national religious spirit which once permeated the life of Jewish people. Hess believed the only way this original spirit could be rescued was by the reconstruction of a national life in the ancient homeland.[16]

The most dominating figure to encourage emigration to the homeland prior to Herzl was Leon Pinsker. In his "Auto-Emancipation" in 1881, he declared that emancipation is the treasured acquisition of Occidental or Western Jewry and that it represented equality, not only before the Law but also with ensuing social privileges.[17] Winer also points out how Pinsker's essay encouraged his people in a plan of self-help to create a national homeland.[18]

As a result, Zionist study circles and clubs began to formulate in hundreds of the cities and towns of the Pale, primarily in the 1860s and 1870s, calling themselves "Chovevei Zion" or "The Lovers of Zion." Their common ingredient was the creed, "There is no salvation for the people of Israel unless they establish a government on their own in the Land of Israel."[19] Also, the movement called BILU was founded immediately after the pogroms of 1881, a name derived from the initial letters of the verse, Beit Yaakov Lehu Venelcha—"O house of Jacob, come, let us go."[20]

With the beginning of the first migration in the early 1870s and 1880s, the rationale already existed for Jewish people to move to Israel and begin the task of national redemption. The seeds for modern Israel were thus laid in the 1800s.

Aliyah (Emigration) to Israel

In 1880, the total number of Jewish people in Palestine numbered 20–25,000, two-thirds of whom were in Jerusalem, constituting half of its population.[21] Smaller communities also existed in three other "holy cities," Safed (4,000), Tiberias (2,500), and Hebron (800).[22]

The example of the first emigration wave became the shining light that beckoned to other Jewish people to do likewise in succeeding generations. In the first move, Jewish people came from Eastern Europe in the early 1880s and within a year or two, a number of agricultural settlements were established. Edmund De Rothschild of Paris sponsored these settlers who sunk roots down into the land, creating settlements that would encourage other countrymen to return.[23] Towns and small cities today have already celebrated their centennials in the 1980s; thus, modern Israel did not begin in 1948. The budding of the fig tree mentioned by Yeshua (Matt. 24:32, 33) has already gone on now for some 125 years. By 1900, the Jewish population totaled nearly 50,000, of which 10,000 were comprised of new settlers from Eastern Europe.

The second emigration was largely the instigation of Herzl who brought to a culmination the desired response for emigration by the former essayists. His challenge for emigration to Israel had a strong impact on his fellow Jews when he declared that their future was to be in a homeland of their own.[24] Commencing in 1904, some 40,000 new settlers had come by 1914, bringing the Jewish population to 85,000. After World War I, the third aliyah during 1919–23 consisted of pioneers with strong Zionist convictions, prepared for the rigors of building a new country in the land. Some 35,000 immigrants came in this wave, again, most from Eastern Europe. The fourth aliyah, 1924–28, was from the middle class in Poland, numbering 34,000[25] while the fifth aliyah, beginning in 1929 and running through to 1936, consisted largely of immigrants from Austria and Germany, totaling some 164,267. By 1936, the Jewish population was close to 400,000, thirty percent of the total population, and Jerusalem's Jewish population in 1936 was sixty percent of the city's total.

England's White Paper of 1939 severely limited Jewish emigration to the land, establishing a quota of 25,000 Jews per year for five years, and with an extra 25,000 as a gesture of grace.[26] Any who exceeded these figures in trying to enter Israel were classified by the British as illegal immigrants, even though they were fleeing for their lives from Hitler's Europe. By 1942, the war had cut off all escape for Jewish people, and six million died in the concentration camps. Most of the several hundred thousand Jewish people who were left in Europe after World War II wanted to get on to the Land of Israel, but the White Paper remained in force until the United Nations took the action that led to the statehood of Israel and the Palestinians, if they wanted it.

What has been demonstrated through the historical movement of people, based on Hosea's statement, "Afterward the Israelites will return"? Unlike any Jewish emigration to the land before, the population in Israel in 1948 numbered some 600,000 Israeli Jews, and, sanctioned by the United Nations, the Israelis constituted themselves as a state.

FURTHER IMMIGRATIONS

Immigrations to Israel did not end in 1948 and, in fact, with a state now in existence, Jewish people are free to enter as citizens. If any Jew chooses to live abroad, that is his or her decision, but technically, no longer can it be said that these people are living in exile.

With the signing of cease-fires in 1949 with the Arab nations who had attacked Israel, emigration picked up, and by 1951, some 750,000 people entered the state, from Europe, North Africa, as well as from the Middle East, Syria, Iraq, Iran, and even from Yemen. The last source makes for an almost unbelievable tale as Yemini Jews had returned to the land in stages, but finally, the rest came after being cut off from the outside world for centuries.[27]

Immigration tapered off for a while, but after the Six-Day War, about 100,000

Jewish people from the Soviet Union and 50,000 from North America emigrated
to Israel in the 1967–1974 period. In return for trade privileges with the United
States, the Soviet authorities relaxed their emigration policies to allow for such
an influx of Jewish people. When the Soviet system collapsed in 1990, Jewish
people again took advantage of the window of opportunity, and by 1995 some
500,000 people had emigrated to their homeland. The numbers have waned now
but Israeli authorities want to bring out possibly a million more before any severe
limitations will close down all possibilities of leaving. At this writing, according
to figures provided by the immigration offices of *Aliyah* in Jerusalem, Israel now
has 4,500,000 Jewish people, more than New York City and its environs. If the
emigration trend continues over the next twenty years, more Jewish people will
be living in Israel than in the United States, which now has the largest
concentration of Jews, numbering some 5,500,000.

AN ASSESSMENT OF THE EMIGRATION
MOVEMENT IN MODERN ISRAEL

This writer has always sought to be very cautious with Scripture when interpreting events as they occur, particularly as it is implied from Hosea 3:5 and other
pertinent passages. While the formation of the State of Israel in 1948 was an
achievement, God had already been working in history to accomplish His purposes in bringing His people back to the land. However, this writer would not
attach any special prophetic significance to the 1948 date. The desire is to resist
the attempt to establish a starting point for the fulfillment of prophecy. If one
does, then the tendency is that some will speculate on the length of a generation,
trying to pinpoint the coming of the Messiah (Matt. 24:32–34). All Yeshua said
in that passage was that when the fig tree puts forth its leaves, the time of redemption is near.

All this writer will say is that the presence of Jewish people in their land is
providential, parallel perhaps to the ancient regathering from Egypt to Sinai and
then Israel. The present time does appear to reflect a work of God, and the prophecies of recovery, such as Hosea 3:5, seem to have a validity.

THE MEANS OF REACHING OUT TO
JEWISH PEOPLE IN THE LAND OF ISRAEL

Hosea also made a statement regarding the spiritual status of the returnees:
"[The Israelites] will seek the Lord their God . . . they will come trembling to the
Lord and to His blessings in the last days" (Hos. 3:5).

While it is true that in the day Messiah returns an entire people of Israel will
know the Lord, in the meanwhile God has been and is gracious to raise up the
witness, working providentially through the multitude of circumstances to reach
His people, back to even before the modern emigration movement. God did not
bring His people back to the land merely to sit and enjoy themselves. He will

use the various means possible in order to reach His people with the message of Yeshua, and some of the distinctives of spiritual outreach are now mentioned.[28]

The Earliest Protestant Witness[29]

The Church's Ministry among the Jews (CMJ), an Anglican ministry in England,[30] has had an outgoing work in Palestine since 1809, carrying on an effort of distributing Bibles and tracts and running schools and industries of various kinds to help Jewish people. The first bishop, Michael Alexander, a Jewish believer, was consecrated in 1841 in England and sent to Jerusalem, and while he had a fruitful ministry, he died in 1845. The first Protestant church in the Middle East was built in the Old City and consecrated in 1849.

Across the years until the State of Israel was formed in 1948, schools and hospitals were founded in various cities and a number of charitable works were carried on to help poor and needy folk. The CMJ was concerned with how to break down barriers between Christians and Jewish people, especially because of the Holocaust, and Stella Carmel in Isfiyah, outside of Haifa to the east, became a conference center that brought Jews and Christians together to address this problem.

A school still exists in West Jerusalem, providing an education in English, but which also maintains a biblical witness. Immanuel House in Jaffa now serves as a school, a hostel, and of late, is also the home for a messianic congregation, Beit Immanuel. Other messianic congregations are hosted at Stella Carmel and in Jerusalem in the Old City in Christ Church.

The Templers and Other Interests

The Templers was a German Protestant sect with roots in the Pietist movement within the Lutheran church.[31] Put out of the Lutheran church in 1858 because of their millennial views, they then formed themselves into the *Tempelgesellschaft,* or "Temple Society." Their chief aim was to be present and realize "the apocalyptic visions of the prophets of Israel in the Holy Land." Some moved to Israel in 1866 and established colonies, working as farmers on land they eventually bought. Colonies existed at the foot of Mt. Carmel in what today is Tel Aviv, as well as in Jerusalem.

Was there a reason why these believers moved to Israel at this particular juncture in time, some prophetic sign of the soon return of Yeshua? It is difficult to say. By the third generation, hardly any belief existed among them, and in the 1930s, many fell prey to German National Socialism; during World War II, the British repatriated what were left of them to Germany in exchange for "Palestinians who had fallen into German hands."

Other Significant Responses

Again, the essays by the Jewish writers, the occurrence of the First Aliyah in the 1870s and 1880s, as well as the convening of the Zionist congresses, beginning in 1897, all had an influence upon some British evangelicals known as "lovers of the Bible."[32] As early as 1902, some of these believers, as officials in or involved with the British government, had a keen interest in the Zionist movement and contacts were ongoing with Theodor Herzl which formed "part of the background to the Balfour Declaration."[33] At the outbreak of World War I, Chaim Weizmann, already a prominent figure in the World Zionist Movement, was also able to find a sympathetic ear among many of these British leaders.[34] These men were eventually able to persuade others in and out of the government to push for what came to be known as the Balfour Declaration, which in 1917 called for the "establishment in Palestine of a national home for the Jewish people." On a personal basis, the influence of these evangelicals also lent special credence to the testimony of Scripture that Israel is the place for Jewish people in the Middle East and that Yeshua is the Messiah and King who will one day rule from Jerusalem over the nations.

WORLD WAR II AND AFTERWARD

We shall skip over many of the basic attitudes of the church, which were either pro-Jewish or anti-Jewish prior to the World War II and shortly afterwards. Possibly three major events were to change attitudes within the church after World War II: (1) the Holocaust, already alluded to at the beginning of this chapter; (2) the formation of the State of Israel in 1948 where finally, after many centuries, Jewish people had a country of their own;[35] and (3) the discovery of the Qumran literature. The Dead Sea Scrolls reopened the entire question of Old Testament study, theology, and the Massoretic text of the Old Testament.[36] All combine to focus a heightened interest upon Jewish people in general and the land of Israel in particular.

Many denominations felt they now had to reassess the entire Jewish question, anti-Jewishness, the meaning of the land of Israel, and possibly consider the millennial issue as it relates to the presence of a free Jewish state. Generally, these assessments may be stated as follows: 1) Some groups feel that because of what has happened to Jewish people in the Holocaust, Christians have no right any more to evangelize them but rather should demonstrate Christian love. Dialogue is the only means to share with Jewish people; 2) Others, however, feel that Jewish evangelism cannot be dropped, but the entire issue of church-Jewish relations must once again be explored. This second area will be examined first, while the first concern will be considered later.

Protestant Statements Which Do Encourage Jewish Evangelism

The International Missionary Conference
When the World Missionary Conference met in Edinburgh in 1910, it reported that forty-five American missions were employing one hundred and forty-seven

missionaries to reach Jewish people. According to missiologist William Bjoraker, "The cultural and religious aspects of Judaism were seldom distinguished; Judaism was viewed as a false and obsolete religion. The cultural and ethnic dimensions were also to be renounced when a Jew came to Christ."[37] Besides translations of the New Testament into Hebrew, Yiddish, and Russian, there was little else being done to contextualize the gospel to reach Jewish people in the early twentieth century.

Massive Jewish immigration at the end of the nineteenth century and into the beginning of the twentieth century brought almost two million Jews to America. Shortly after World War I, a renewal of world Jewish missionary effort shifted from Great Britain to the United States. In 1923 the International Missionary Council (IMC) met in Oxford, England, where it was decided to promote further conferences to encourage missionary work among Jewish people. In 1927, the first two subsequent meetings were convened by the IMC in Warsaw and in Budapest, with John R. Mott presiding. A third was held in Atlantic City, New Jersey, in 1931. These were the first international conferences focusing on the subject of Jewish evangelism.

In 1928, the IMC met in general conference in Jerusalem where they received a resolution out of the three previous Jewish mission conferences to establish the "International Committee on the Christian Approach to the Jew" (ICCAJ). The first act of that conference meeting in Atlantic City in 1931 was to issue a statement declaring, "Not to offer the gospel to the Jew would be discrimination against the Jews."[38] In the first half of the twentieth century, international evangelicalism favored the evangelization of Jewish people.

The International Conferences in the Later Half of the Twentieth Century

Shortly after World War II, a Christian reassessment of Jewish mission was quickly underway. The first assembly of the World Council of Churches (WCC), meeting in Amsterdam in 1948, issued a final report with a section titled "The Approach to Adherence of Other Faiths." It contained the statement, "If we hold that Christ died for all men, and that His gospel is to be preached to all nations, the proclamation of the gospel stands out as an absolute obligation from which the church must not try to escape."[39] Six years later, when the second assembly of the WCC convened in Evanston, Illinois, all references to the Jews or to the State of Israel were deleted from the report. By the third assembly, in 1961, the WCC convening in New Delhi, India, avoided the whole subject of Jewish evangelism except for a pronouncement against anti-Semitism. It was at that time that the International Missionary Council, which had been functioning from 1921–1961, was absorbed into the World Council of Churches. The former Committee on the Christian Approach to the Jews was replaced by what came to be known as the Consultation on the Church and the Jewish People. The former emphasis on evangelism was replaced by concerns for understanding, reconciliation, and cooperation.

According to Arthur F. Glasser, Dean Emeritus of the Fuller School of World Mission, a study group was convened in 1969 that involved scholars from the U.S. National Council of Churches' Faith and Order Commission and the Secretariat for Catholic-Jewish Relations of the National Conference of Catholic Bishops. In 1973 this study group produced a *Statement to Our Fellow Christians* which deliberately omitted any reference to Christian witness to the Jewish people.

Lausanne Congress on World Evangelism

At the end of the twentieth century, very encouraging developments have again moved world evangelicalism toward Jewish evangelism. In 1974 the Lausanne Congress on World Evangelization came forward, encouraging mission effort to unreached people groups. One result of the 1980 conference of the LCWE meeting in Thailand was the establishment of the Lausanne Consultation on Jewish Evangelism. The mission focus of the former IMC and the ICCAJ of fifty years earlier was resurrected.

In April of 1989, a group of international scholars met at Willowbank, Bermuda. Convened as the Willowbank Consultation of the Christian Gospel and the Jewish People, they released the *Willowbank Declaration* that was widely regarded as a watershed statement on the evangelical approach to Jewish missions. The document states that "To refuse to bring the gospel to the Jewish people would be the highest form of anti-Semitism."[40] Similar language was adopted later that year at the LCWE in Manila. In 1991 the World Evangelical Fellowship covened a Task Force of the Theological Commission in Chicago that also encouraged evangelization of the Jewish people as a necessity of the Christian mission. Thus, by the end of the twentieth century, evangelicalism has come full circle and once again is encouraging Jewish evangelism.

First Assembly of the World Council of Churches

The meeting by the World Council of Churches in Amsterdam, Holland in 1948 developed a number of statements regarding evangelism, and a few state:

> . . . the converted Jew calls for particular tenderness and full acceptance just because his coming into the church carries with it often a deeply wounding break with family and friends. . . . To the member churches of the World Council we recommend that they seek to recover the universality of our Lord's commission by including the Jewish people in their evangelistic work.[41]

While this statement was adopted by a majority of the body, not every member church would agree to this call. This writer has had numerous discussions with leaders who are members of church bodies of the World Council of Churches but who disagree with proselytizing Jewish people, and their numbers have increased with the years. This agency's interest eventually waned, especially in its support for the State of Israel and also Jewish evangelism.[42]

The Department of World Mission of the Lutheran World Federation and the Church and the Jewish People, in Denmark, in 1964

The statement regarding mission and dialogue declares: "The 'witness to the Jewish people is inherent in the content of the gospel,' . . . and recommends that it be 'pursued in the normal activity of the Christian Congregation.'"[43] Again, not every last member and pastor of individual churches would adhere to the statement, but it gives sanction to the efforts of individual bodies of Lutheran missionary societies who carry on a ministry in Israel.

Report of the Consultation, held under the auspices of the Lutheran World Federation, Oslo, Norway, 1975

Under the statement of Christian witness and the Jewish people:

> . . . Christians, however, . . . cannot abandon the New Testament proclamation even though they must recognize that the proclamation continues to put contemporary Judaism under the same original challenge. Yet . . . in . . . compassion and solidarity . . .[44]

The Acts of the Synod of Christian Reformed Board of Home Missions Report— "Guidelines and Principles for the Mission to the Jews"—states:

> The church must recognize that the provocation to "jealousy" and "emulation" in Romans 11 stand out as God's provisions for pressing the claims of the gospel upon the Jew, and that this provocation does not imply a specific method other than confronting the Jews with a personal collective witness to the grace of God in Christ by the church.[45]

The Lausanne Consultation for Jewish Evangelism (LCJE)

In 1980, at the second world evangelism congress, under the auspices of the Lausanne Consultation for World Evangelism (the first was held in Lausanne, Switzerland, in 1974), a number of delegates met in Pattya, Thailand, representing numerous task forces who addressed themselves to the ongoing effort of evangelization of the people groups present in the world. Their deliberations were to sharpen their evangelism interests under The Lausanne Covenant, which had been drawn up in 1974.[46]

One of the task forces was comprised of Jewish and Gentile believers who were vitally interested in Jewish evangelism, and following the 1980 conference, and as already noted, this group organized to become the Lausanne Consultation for Jewish Evangelism. The LCJE is an association of agencies, congregations and individuals who are committed to Jewish evangelism worldwide, and to cooperating and networking with others who share that commitment. An executive committee, comprised of people from various countries, provides direction for the movement, but there is also regional representation on various continents, each with its own coordinator selected by members of the organization in the separate countries. Regional groups meet once a year, where individuals read papers pertinent to theological and evangelistic concerns, while the entire international organization meets every three or four years.

At the Manila conference of the Lausanne Committee for World Evangelism in 1989, one of the statements within the Manila Manifesto included the following words in connection with the uniqueness of Christ which had a direct bearing on Jewish evangelism:

> It is sometimes held that in virtue of God's covenant with Abraham, Jewish people do not need to acknowledge Jesus as their Messiah. We affirm that they need him as much as anyone else, that it would be a form of anti-Semitism, as well as being disloyal to Christ, to depart from the New Testament pattern of taking the gospel "to the Jew first. . . ." We therefore reject the thesis that Jews have their own covenant which renders faith in Jesus unconditional.[47]

Statements on Anti-Jewishness and the State and Land of Israel

In every document by both Roman Catholics and Protestants, statements exist repudiating anti-Jewishness. In particular, the Metropolitan New York Synod of the Lutheran Church adopted a statement on the writings of Martin Luther, in September 1971, that "repudiates the anti-Semitic writings of Dr. Martin Luther."[48] Since then, the entire Missouri Synod of the Lutheran Church voted likewise to reject these very same statements in its Convention Resolution 3–09, in St. Louis in 1983. "We deplore and disassociate ourselves from Luther's negative statements about the Jewish people. . . ."

When it comes to a word concerning the State of Israel and the concept of the land of Israel, many denominations had little or nothing to say, or when they do, the sentiments are ambivalent. No clear-cut statement exists regarding a millennial stance for the land by the church for the most part, i.e., Reformed churches, the majority of Lutheran churches (although individual Lutheran churches do espouse a millennial concept), Presbyterian churches (although again, some do hold to a covenant premillennial position), as well as many Baptist and other churches. Some Lutherans speak of a "theology of the land," perhaps reflecting some interest in a place for the people of Israel in its land, but when thinking in terms of Arab refugees, the concept of "the theology of the poor" is a concern, an expression which arises out of a sociological recognition for the poor and needy.

The closest any Reformed document came regarding the land of Israel is the statement by the Synod of the Reformed Church, Holland, in 1970, on "Israel: People, Land and State," which suggests: "As matters are at the moment, we see a free state as the only possibility which safeguards the existence of the people and which offers them the chance to be truly themselves. . . ."[49]

This solution arises out of a political and sociological point of view of what best helps Israeli Jewish and Arab peoples in their land areas.

VARIOUS MISSION GROUPS IN THE LAND

A number of missionary societies work in the land of Israel, but no exhaustive list can be provided. Of those involved in ministry, no question is here raised as to their theological and missiological convictions, and to the best of their ability, they seek to accomplish their goals.

The Church of Scotland entered the land after the CMJ in 1885, to establish a hospital, and subsequently, they have churches, hospices, and schools in various cities. [50] The Christian Missionary Alliance[51] has been in the country since 1890, working among Arab as well as Jewish peoples, maintaining schools and churches. Since 1948, the Alliance missionaries have attempted build up a ministry in Jerusalem at its Alliance church building. With the coming of a new missionary couple to take the Jewish work in BeerSheva, they then moved to Jerusalem, joined the Messianic Assembly, a messianic congregation; the husband became an elder in the congregation while the wife works with children, developing a wide range of materials for children and youth, not only locally but for all the messianic congregations. At the moment, the BeerSheva congregation, somewhat of a messianic congregation model, is growing and attempting to start a congregation in Arad.

The Norwegian Lutheran Mission to Israel Society[52] has supported English and German missions among Jewish people in Palestine, but primarily its main ministry since 1948 "has been congregational work in Haifa and Tel Aviv." Their theological statement and stated objectives are thorough, with the goal "to help establish congregations which predominantly consist of Christian Jews . . . and that they integrate into their worship, services and holidays those elements of the Jewish traditions which they find appropriate." The statement well defines (1) issues of church and Israel, avoiding any word that the church is "the new Israel"; (2) Israel and the Law, which allows using elements of Torah which can be supported by Scripture; and (3) recognizing that Jewish believers should recontextualize their beliefs and lifestyle, which will reflect more of how Yeshua and Jewish believers would have lived and shared their message.

Another group owned by the Norwegian Church Ministries to Israel, is the Caspari Center, a theological study center combining "messianic Jewish and Gentile Christian resources in order to contribute to the messianic Jewish movement, to the Christian church and to scholarly work on Judeo Christianity."[53] Among a number of projects, the Center seeks to provide Bible and theological education for messianic congregations and believers in Israel.

Mishkan is a "semi-annual journal dedicated to biblical and theological thinking on issues related to Jewish evangelism, Hebrew–Christian/messianic–Jewish identity and Jewish–Christian relations" and is a "forum for discussion." The journal "is published by the United Christian Council in Israel in cooperation with the Caspari Center." The editorial policy is "openly evangelical, committed to the New Testament proclamation that the gospel of salvation through faith in Jesus (Yeshua) the Messiah is 'to the Jew first.'"[54]

The Finnish Missionary Society began work in 1924 in Jerusalem with a boarding school and a church and parish ministry; today it operates a Christian missionary school in conjunction with the Norwegian Lutheran mission. The Swedish Lutherans have had a theological institute since 1951, and Danish groups are also present.[55] The Southern Baptist Convention is also involved, beginning in 1911, and has a church and book shop in Jerusalem as well as an agricultural settlement and church in Petah Tikvah and a library and printing press in Tel Aviv.[56] Pentecostal communities[57] and Holiness communities[58] are present, as well as a number of interdenominational communities,[59] including the Jerusalem University College (originally the American Institute for Holy Land Studies), which began in 1959 to provide undergraduate and graduate studies on-site for evangelicals from a number of countries. Finally, Osterbye includes in his survey the various Adventist communities (American Messianic Fellowship, Chosen People Ministries) as well as Jehovah's Witnesses, and also minor and supporting societies, such as the Bethel Hostel in Haifa, founded in 1948 as a school.[60]

The Messianic Congregations[61] are comprised of congregations of Jewish believers primarily, some under the auspices of the various societies mentioned above, but the majority of them are indigenous, made up of believers from the land of Israel. A few are self-supporting while the rest depend upon some financial support from abroad, but they are self-contained, governed by the elders from within each congregation. Some are of a brethren-type form while others follow the older Hebrew Christian model, using some of the traditional practices while a few adopt more of these practices. This new movement grew slowly after the War of Independence in 1948, and when this writer was first present in Israel in 1968, some three or four of these congregations existed. By the latter 1980s, more and more of the young people became disenchanted with the older liberalism as the basis for Zionism and began looking for belief systems that would best serve their needs. A few returned to religious Judaism, others are open to the New Age movement, but some have accepted the gospel message. God raised up these leaders and congregations, and today some fifty-five to sixty exist.[62] At the youth conference in December, 1996, Victor Smadja, leading elder in the Messianic

Assembly in Jerusalem and long-time sponsor of the youth conferences, wrote of young Russian believers who "came from new fellowships in different parts of Israel of whom we had never heard before."[63]

Ever since the founding of the state, Zeev Kofsman, leader of such a congregation, fought a difficult battle with the government to obtain *amuta* status, the formal permission to be recognized as a congregation–society by the government of Israel. Finally, permission was granted in 1958, and one of the objectives "allows for joint divine service to members of our community, to encourage each other in his common faith."[64] Since then, others likewise have this recognition.

These congregations follow good basic biblical doctrine. The elders meet from time to time to discuss mutual concerns and difficulties they encounter. Most of the leaders from this group sponsor an evangelism committee, which plans various kinds of outreach in the big cities, on the beaches, or at youth music conferences. Plans are also being made today to provide for a more formal theological training for the young people in the congregations. Many of the young people, with the *ḥuṣpah* (assertiveness) of the average Israeli, have taken to evangelism, distributing literature and seeking conversations with people.

Three or four congregations own their own buildings and have an attendance of between one and two hundred. The rest either rent their facilities or are house congregations. A few are in the beginning stages with only a few people, others have from between ten and twenty and up to sixty to seventy-five attendees. This witness appears to be the wave of the future, and should all the expatriate missionary personnel leave, a viable church does exist which can carry on the work.

Are these congregations all they could be? Not yet. The body of Messiah in Israel is still in its infancy stage. Many leaders do not have formal theological training and can tend to be quite individualistic. Congregations can often differ over minor issues. Some leaders and people are still moved by fear when faced by the necessity to evangelize their peers, and a few fear the fierce repercussions by the religious Jewish bodies in the country. Certainly problems abound among these congregations if one looks close enough.

Sometimes the messianic leaders tend to have difficulties with the missionary societies (1) in areas of contextualization of theology where the missionary finds it difficult to recontextualize so as to find an expression of a basic theology from within the Jewish roots of the early Jewish believers; (2) when holding to practices whereby the Jewish believer loses his or her identity when joining the mission churches; and (3) in the area of "self leadership," whereby mission leaders from abroad find it difficult to accept and allow even trained Jewish believers to become leaders of the missions or the denominational congregation.[65] While some of the missionary societies mentioned above have made progress with some of the concerns raised by Victor Smadja, it yet appears that the societies have a way to go to address these very serious considerations.

A JARRING NOTE

Comment on a number of positions which raises questions for evangelicals who seek to be faithful to a biblical theology and missiology will be reserved until these statements have been presented.

Church Statements Where Jewish Evangelism Is No Longer Encouraged

Statement by the Vatican Authority

In the reflections and suggestions for the application of the directives of Nostra Aetate, which was the Vatican II statement on the Jews, The Declaration on the Relationship to the Church of Non-Christian Religions), the following is recommended for dialogue:

> Relations between Christians and Jews have for the most part been no more than a monologue. A true dialogue must now be established. . . . The condition of dialogue was respect for the other as he is, for his faith and religious convictions. All intent of proselytizing and conversion is excluded. . . .[66]

In October 1974, Pope Paul VI set up a Commission for Religious Relation with the Jews and the Vatican Commission, which stated in January 1975, that no evangelism is to be encouraged: "Catholics . . . must take care to live and spread their Christian faith while maintaining the strictest respect for religious liberty. . . ."[67]

The National Catholic Commission for Relations between Christians and Jews in Belgium stated in 1973: "The Jewish people is a true relative of the church, not her rival or a minority to be assimilated. . . . Christians and Jews fulfill their specific roles and stimulate each other regarding the salvation of the nations (Romans 9–11)."[68]

As a summation of many of the Roman Catholic statements, the church must realize her Jewish roots; Catholics must not make Jewish people culpable for the death of Yeshua, but rather, all mankind is responsible for His death; Catholics and Jewish people are regarded as fraternal brothers and consequently, no Jewish evangelism is actively promulgated.

Protestant Denominations

Reference is made again to the statement by the World Council of Church's statement on "including the Jewish people in their evangelistic effort."[69] But forty years later, in 1988, the leaders of the World Council of Churches had an altogether different viewpoint, affirming,

> The church today knows Christianity to be a distinctly different religion from Judaism. . . . The next step may be to proscribe all proselytism of Jews on the theological ground that it is rejection of Israel's valid covenant with God.[70]

The latter is a reference to the Two Covenant Theory, whereby Israel has a valid avenue to God through the Mosaic Covenant, mentioned further on in this chapter.[71]

Another specific statement contained in "Stepping Stones to Further Jewish–Christian Relations," the general conference of the United Methodist Church issued a statement in Atlanta, Georgia, in 1972, where no clear-cut word is issued for any active evangelism.[72]

Bridges for Peace

Clarence Wagner and other leaders of *Bridges for Peace*, an organization founded in 1976, would classify themselves as evangelicals, comprised of many Christians from different denominations and "dedicated to the building of sincere relationships between the Christian and Jewish communities, while encouraging greater concern for the land and people of Israel, . . . [to seeing] Christians and Jews working side by side for better understanding and a more secure Israel" and "faithful to Israel and to the Jewish community."[73] The group publishes a paper, *Dispatch from Jerusalem,* and also engages in social aid, food, and money for hurting immigrants, as well as welcome gifts for those arriving in Israel.

But while these folk are avowedly evangelicals, do they share a biblical witness? This writer one day sat at a street-side table for lunch in downtown Jerusalem and at the next table, two women were discussing the seminar they were attending under the sponsorship of Bridges. An Israeli walked by, heard the discussion, and asked these ladies why they are in Jerusalem. Their response was they had come to the land of Israel to show their love for Jewish people; the Israeli persisted and wanted to know the real reason why they were in the land, and again they declared their love for Jewish people, the land, and that God was bringing Jewish people home from all over the world. They wanted to see this latter phenomenon first-hand! Never at any time did these two ladies share any gospel at all, saying afterward they were told not to share their faith.

Similar organizations exist in North America and Europe, all sharing their love for Jewish people but with no offer of a message of salvation.

The International Christian Embassy of Jerusalem

A group of evangelicals came together in Jerusalem in 1980 to form the Christian Embassy. The desire was, with so many countries who refused to have their embassies in Jerusalem, the capital, to be in "supportive fellowship" with the people of Israel in general and with the leadership in Israel in particular.

The leaders of the Embassy claim that by their stand as Christian Zionists, they give Christians everywhere the "channel through which they can express their love for Israel."[74] But do they represent the majority of believers, and, what is their specific position on evangelism?

In response, Sevener offered his assessment,[75] and the magazine *Mishkan*[76] later devoted an entire issue to the question of the Embassy. Because the latter refused to offer any official response, the observations had to be one-sided except for one article by David Friedman, pastor of Beth-El Messianic Congregation in Kfar Saba, Israel. He explained that the Embassy serves its purpose by reminding Christians everywhere that "reconciliation between Jews and gentiles and of God's love to Israel" is necessary and that Israel needs support and prayer because it "is of the highest value to God and to the Jewish people."[77]

In the assessment, no one raised any question regarding specific beliefs of the Embassy leaders. Many, including this writer, feel that on the *personal level*, each leader takes the occasion to witness to individuals when the occasion arises. But the focus of questions was repeatedly on the public issue of evangelism. This the Embassy consistently avoided, and nothing is said publicly regarding the message of Messiah Yeshua's atonement which is the only basis that gives real meaning to a love for Israel. This writer understands that for the Embassy to exist in Jerusalem, assurances had to be given to the government of Israel that they would not evangelize or proselytize. So, officially, the lips of the leaders of the Embassy are sealed.

Their claim to represent Christians everywhere is unfounded. They take no issue with decisions by the Israeli government. They do not seek for links with the messianic congregations in Israel, except on two occasions in a strong defense of messianic Jews when they were under attack. These and other facets raise questions as to what the Embassy stands for.

The Archbishop of Canterbury

Of interest was the action taken by the new archbishop of Canterbury, an evangelical, when he took office in 1992 and declared in a letter (5 March 1992) that he could no longer maintain his patronage of the CMJ, stating, "There is potential for much trouble here . . . if we ignore the need to nurture trust across the boundaries of the faith communities. . . . Such trust need not be an obstacle to evangelism, and there is no inconsistency in being committed to both causes. . . ."[78] The leadership of the CMJ felt that, while recognizing the archbishop had the right to make whatever choices he wished, they were free to continue the ministry as had been done since the early 1800s, following a biblical theology and missiology.[79]

Statements (or the Lack of Them) by Individual Believers

A number of assessments by evangelicals in their writings are available, but only a few will be enumerated. Some evangelical students have completed graduate studies in Jewish schools of higher learning, and such training is commendable. But in not a few cases, positions taken by some of these scholars ever since their training have led to serious questions concerning a biblical theology. This writer knows of one such professor who now denies any messianic message of fulfillment in key passages, i.e., Psalm 22, Isaiah 7:14, as well as others. Only a fulfillment at the time of writing is viewed as the correct interpretation. A recent book by Young,[80] who studied under Professor Flusser of the Hebrew University, provides us with a valuable study of many of Yeshua's lessons set in the midst of His Jewish roots. But one difficulty surfaces: the tendency not to say anything or overlook facets Yeshua taught that mark Him as unique, for which no parallel exists in Jewish sources. Young asserts that the events at the baptism of Yeshua demonstrate the deity of Yeshua, but that Peter's great confession demonstrates who Messiah is (Matt. 16:16); Yeshua commends him for his statement: You are the "Messiah of God." No comment is suggested that this disciple also declared that Yeshua is the Son of God. In discussing whether Yeshua is human or divine, great emphasis is placed on Him as the Son of Man, who is someone supernatural, but Young does not say He is also Deity.

The Jewish Position and an Assessment of Christian Zionism

The Jewish Position

This writer has to affirm, as Paul said almost two thousand years ago, that "from the standpoint of the gospel they are enemies for your sake, but from the standpoint of God's choice they are beloved for the sake of the fathers" (Rom. 11:28). Concerning the first phrase of the passage, most of Israel are still in unbelief with regard to Israel's Messiah, and a good many do not even assert ultimate authority for the Hebrew Scriptures, to say nothing of the New Covenant. Jewish religious leaders strive with all their energies today to deflect all attempts of evangelism, declaring that the people of Israel have God's favor and are still under the Mosaic Covenant. The religious ideology developed by Franz Rosenzweig in his *Star of Redemption* has become the apologetic by which religious leaders claim that Jewish people are those upon whom God's star is still shining while Yeshua is the one through whom the Gentiles can also have relation to this star.[81]

However, the last phrase of Paul's word in Romans 11:28 causes us to pause and reflect on the mercies of God in caring for His people Israel. With respect to the presence of Israelis in their land already prior to World War II, one example of God's mercies is paramount: at least these people, most of whom came from Europe, did not fall prey to the gas chambers in the concentration camps. God's mercies because of the fathers only points out that He has a covenant with the descendants of Abraham, through Isaac and Jacob, and has promised to make sure that there will always be a presence of their descendants as long as there is a history of mankind (Gen. 17:7). But if Jewish people were able to come from Europe, God's purpose is also to see to it they will hear the message of Yeshua; in that sense, His mercies are evident. But the nation must still face up to Paul's concern mentioned in the first part of Romans 11:28: Without the Messiah Yeshua, there is no salvation; without His leadership, there never will be a lasting peace.

The Christian Zionist Position

This writer does not question whether those already mentioned above are believers or say that in their hearts they no longer acknowledge the supremacy of Yeshua in His Deity. Rather, it is in what they do not say that constitutes a serious challenge to a sound theology and missiology. If the claims for the Deity of Yeshua or His death for us as the only means for salvation are not fully shared with our Jewish friends because these doctrines are considered offensive, what message does that communicate? Three basic replies are noted: (1) A moral question is raised because the believer is withholding information that he knows needs to be conveyed to all peoples, including Jewish people; (2) The example to a younger generation is the possibility to waffle on basic doctrines, if in sharing them a violent reaction will occur among the hearers. But while we seek for good relations with our Jewish friends and desire peace with them, this writer takes seriously what is really in their best interests. From God's view, our task is to reconcile people to God through the Messiah Yeshua because only in Him are we made into a new creation (2 Cor. 5:17–20). If we fail in our responsibilities as believers, we will have to answer to God not only for not sharing with people, but also for demonstrating to the next generation that it is not necessary to do so; (3) The time could well come that a future generation will not consider it necessary to believe in these basic biblical doctrines. At that point, no message will be present to share, and a biblical faith will have become bankrupt.

The first step away from the biblical position is a crucial one. The last step will shipwreck the faith of believers, and at the worst, pseudo-Christians can become the worst anti-Jewish people. The believer has to have a keen sense of what is that first step and avoid it!

GOD WILL HAVE HIS WAY

In spite of what man says and does, God's purpose from Hosea 3:5, as already noted, is to yet bring Israel to Himself, and He has worked and is working providentially to see to it that His people hear the Word. Besides the work of genuine believers, we also consider these facets.

Old Testament Study

Ever since the ministers of education sat down in 1948 to outline what will be the curriculum in the Israeli schools, Taanach (Old Testament) was considered a necessary requirement. With this textbook of Israel's background of history, culture, and religious observances, every student from first to twelfth grade spends four to six hours a week in this study, in either secular or religious state schools. In many situations, students are imbued with a critical approach to the miraculous element of the Word, and very little attempt is made to inculcate the dimension of faith. But we also have the assurance of what the prophet Isaiah once said: The Word of God will never return empty. It will accomplish what God desires, and it will succeed in the matter for which He sends it (Isa. 55:11).

The New Testament

Many students take courses in New Testament in the university; some do so because they seem to have a genuine interest for its background as well as for the figure of Yeshua while others are required to read it for important background study in courses in art, music, or other disciplines. But why should Israelis have any interest in Yeshua and what he taught? Israel is a small country, and Bethlehem, Jerusalem, Galilee, in particular, the Sea of Galilee (Kinneret), all are reminders Yeshua was there. The average Israeli is not like the proverbial ostrich, sticking his head in the sand and pretending Yeshua never existed. After all, He has his part in this country. This writer can testify to the fact that Bible study is indeed important. Many times one finds it easy to point Israelis to passages to which they have already been exposed. Many people are open to talking about spiritual things and among many younger Israelis a curious interest exists in Yeshua.

Messianic Congregations

This subject has already been discussed above but is included here to indicate a phenomenon for which God is also responsible. Paul once wrote that he was personally unknown to the congregations in Judea (Gal. 1:22), but the ministry has come full circle today.

Messianic Jewish Publishers

Two publishers produce evangelical literature in modern Hebrew, Keren Ahvah in Jerusalem under Victor Smadja and HaGefen in Rishon LeTsion under Baruch MaOz. Many of the books are translated from English and other Western languages into Hebrew. The former press began operating in 1968. Over two hundred titles are available today, which in itself is a major means for reaching Israelis with the gospel message. It is difficult to evangelize without literature, and these publishers meet a genuine need. In addition, Keren Ahvah publishes Hebrew and Russian Bibles, the latter particularly for the newly arrived Russian peoples. While these two publishers need outside help to produce the materials, they provide the leadership in the operation of the work and distribution of the materials.

CONCLUSION

A consideration of Israel today in its land must take into account many of the geopolitical factors concerning the establishment of the State of Israel, particularly the background of the modern period in the nineteenth century affecting Jewish people and their plight in Europe. Nor can the message of biblical prophecy be ignored, either, with the presence of so many Jewish people in the land of Israel, from a mere handful of 25,000 in 1880 to some 4,500,000 by 1996.

With so many Jewish people in the land, missionaries came from a number of societies, seeking to reach out with the life-giving message of Yeshua. Their witness continues for the most part to this day as each worker seeks to faithfully communicate the message once given in this very land of its origins.

However, also present today are Christians who mute the message of the gospel and share instead their concerns that, because of the Holocaust and past dislike and hatred by so-called Christians, Israelis must be shown love and the state must know that Christians do support Israel and have a concern for her well-being. As a result, evangelism is muted and basic doctrines are toned down or not shared at all. If the Messiah is not Lord, then all we have left is a human Yeshua, much like other great religious leaders in the past who are now buried and gone. If all we share with Israelis is our love, then we have lost the basic meaning of true love. It is the love of Yeshua and only His atonement that changes people. This is the love that needs to be shared with our Jewish people and Israelis alike. A mere human love only loves people into a lost eternity! We have to be faithful to a God-honoring theology and missiology. If we withhold, or waffle, on the basic doctrines of the Messiah's Deity and sole redemption, we will come to a generation where pseudo-Christians no longer have a viable message.

But God will not be mocked. His intention according to Hosea 3:5 is that a people must hear the Word, that eventually an entire nation will come trembling to Him and "to his blessings in the last days." For that reason, He has worked through the educational system whereby several generations already have and are studying the Word, Old and New Testaments alike. Messianic congregations are present, of and by the people of Israel themselves, that are centered in the religious and cultural mindset of a people already present. His Spirit strives today with a younger generation who are looking for basic meaning to life; some are going back to a religious Judaism; others are turning to the occult and New Age beliefs. Some are also considering the message of the Word of God and have believed and have become a part of the messianic congregations. Believers are publishing Bibles and producing books best suited to reach the Israeli.

Gentile believers from abroad, working through the various societies, can cooperate with the Jewish believers and will be accepted, but the Israeli phenomenon of a viable witness is present and needs to be encouraged in every way.

How close are we to His coming? We must not speculate; prophecy does have some bearing, but we must work with the leadership of the Holy Spirit. While one eye is cocked, looking upward to His coming, the other eye is upon the task that Israelis hear the Word and have opportunity to respond to the Messiah of Israel. We also sow the seed of the Word, because we can never know how God will use it in dire days ahead when a people will be pressured and their only remedy is to turn to the One who alone can give peace to mind and heart.

DISCUSSION QUESTIONS

1. Why does the land of Israel serve as a beacon that Jewish people not forget their land, and also encourage them to return to it?

2. Name some of the factors which contributed to the *Aliyot* (immigration) of Jewish people to the land of Israel, and what bearing do they have in not assigning prophetsic significance to the 1948 date when Israel became a state?

3. Put into your own words the specific statements by various church groups which specially mention the function for Jewish evangelism.

4. What are the alternative actions suggested by some denominations and agencies as substitutes for Jewish evangelism?

5. What are the consequences when believers do not share Yeshua as the atonement for sin with their Jewish friends?

6. Name facets present today whereby God is providentially working to bring Israel to Himself.

ENDNOTES

1. S. Ettinger, "Demographic Changes and Economic Activity of the Nineteenth and Beginning of the Twentieth Century" in *History of the Jewish People,* ed. H. H. Ben Sasson (Cambridge, Mass.: Harvard University Press, 1976), 1063–66. Information was gleaned from several figures provided for population on continents where Jewish people lived in the eve of World War II.
2. All Scripture references are from the New International Version (NIV), unless noted otherwise.
3. As the Maccabean rulers became more and more ungodly, where even brothers contended sharply for leadership, Rome saw an opportunity to intervene in Judean politics in 63 B.C. and from then on, she ruled through the Idumean Antipater and the Maccabean Hyrcanus II. However, as even this arrangement became more and more contentious with other family members, the Romans finally appointed Herod, son of Antipater, ruler over Judea in 37 B.C., which then became a Roman province. Judea had lost its independence. See Charles F. Pfeiffer, *Old Testament History* (Grand Rapids: Baker Book House, 1973), 583–87.
4. See Francis I. Andersen & David N. Freedman, *Hosea, A New Translation with Introduction and Commentary in the Anchor Bible*, eds. William F. Albright & David

N. Freedman (Garden City, N.Y.: Doubleday, 1980), 305–6 for a full discussion of Hos. 3:4.

5. Yeshua as the Hebrew name for Jesus will be used throughout this chapter.
6. Stuart, *Hosea-Jonah, Word Biblical Commentary*, vol. 31, eds. David A. Hubbard and Glenn W. Barker (Waco, Tex.: Word Books, 1987), 67–68.
7. *The Passover Haggadah*, ed. Nahum N. Glatzer (New York: Schocken Books, 1953, 1969, 1979), 21.
8. Louis Goldberg, *Turbulence Over the Middle East* (Neptune, N.J.: Loizeaux, 1982), 69–74, where references are made to a number of the circumstances through which God had worked to impress it upon His people to return to the land. For a more detailed treatment, see Howard M. Sachar, *A History of Israel from the Rise of Zionism to Our Time* (New York: Alfred A. Knopf, 1996 rev. ed., from the earlier edition of 1976), 4ff.
9. Sachar, 25.
10. Ibid., 12–13.
11. Yehuda Slutsky, "Pogroms," in *Encyclopedia Judaica*, vol. 13 (New York: Macmillan, 1971), 695.
12. Ettinger, "Demographic Changes," 861–62.
13. Ibid., 6.
14. Jacob Katz, "Zionism," in *Encyclopedia Judaica*, vol. 16, ed. Cecil Roth (Jerusalem: Keter Publishing House, 1972), 1034.
15. Getzel Kressel, "Zevi Hirsch Kalischer," in *Encyclopedia Judaica*, vol. 10, 708. See also Geoffrey Wheatcroft, *The Controversy of Zion* (London: Michelin House, 1996), 41.
16. Katz, "Zionism," 1035.
17. Gershom Winer, *The Founding Fathers of Israel* (New York: Bloch Publishing Co., 1971), 53.
18. Ibid., 84–85.
19. Sacher, 16.
20. Abraham Revusky, *Jews on Palestine* (New York: Vanguard, 1935), 8.
21. Zvi Singer, "Modern Aliyah," under "State of Israel (Aliyah and Absorption)," in *Encyclopedia Judaica*, vol. 9, 515–46.
22. James Parkes, *A History of Palestine* (London: Victor Gollancz, 1949), 22, who provides figures for Jewish population in Israel in 1880.
23. Getzel Kressel, "Edmond James de Rothschild," in *Encyclopedia Judaica*, vol. 14, 342–46.
24. Theodore Herzl, *The Jewish State* (Garden City, N.Y.: Doubleday, 1959), tr. from the earlier German in 1896. He also called for delegates from Western and Eastern Europe to assemble at the first Zionist congress to be held in Basle, Switzerland, in 1897 to consider the move back to the land. At this gathering of Jewish leaders and people, Herzl declared that if the delegates could will it, then within five years, but certainly within fifty years, a State of Israel would be in existence. He was right to within a year! See also Sachar, 38–47.
25. No doubt, this group would have preferred to move to the United States, but in 1923, the United States Congress enacted quotas so as to stop the unlimited immigration, looking with favor on immigrants from Western and Northern Europe but restricting severely any who desired to come from Eastern Europe.
26. Ettinger, "Demographic Changes," 1015–16.
27. Yehudah Ratzaby, "Yemen, Settlement in Erez Israel," in *Encyclopedia Judaica*, vol. 16, 752–53.

28. The best most recent survey on the various ministries is by Per Osterbye, *The Church in Israel: A Report on the Work and Position of the Christian Churches in Israel, with Special Reference to the Protestant Churches and Communities* (Lund: C. W. K. Gleerup Bokforlag, 1970). The bibliography is invaluable.

29. The Turkish Empire was extended to include what today is Israel by the beginning of the 1500s. Already present were the Orthodox and Catholic churches, the Armenian and Coptic churches, as well as traditional Jewish groups. Each had freedom under what is called the millet system to practice their own religious expression. Proselyting was forbidden and hardly anything was done by any of the churches to reach Jewish peoples. What is interesting, two French brothers, Theodore and Alphonse Ratisbonne had come to Catholicism, and then both "established the Congregation of Notre Dame de Zion for women, for the purpose of bringing about a better understanding between Jews and Christians and to convert Jews," while the latter went to Jerusalem in 1855 and founded Ecce Homo convent for the Sisters of Zion in the old city of Jerusalem, which also had a testimony to Jewish people; see Editorial Staff, "Ratisbonne Brothers," in *Encyclopedia Judaica*, vol. 13, 1570–72.

30. Information gleaned from Walter Barker, *A Fountain Opened* (London: Olive Press, 1983), 24–33, as well as from a number of articles from the CMJ magazine, *Shalom*, 1996. Originally, the work was known as "London Society for Promoting Christianity among Jews," but became CMJ in 1962.

31. Abraham J. Brawer and Ann Ussishkin in "Templers (*Tempelgesellschaft*)," in *Encyclopedia Judaica*, 994–96, not to be confused with the Knights Templar.

32. Lord Balfour met with Herzl in 1902, wanting to know why most Zionists had turned down England's offer of Uganda as a place to settle Jewish people. Several generations of the Wingate family were friends with officials in the government and in particular, Charles Ord Wingate took a keen interest in the defense of the Jewish settlements in the land of Israel during 1930–1939. C. P. Snow, editor of the *Manchester Guardian*, was a friend of Chaim Weizmann. Eventually Weizmann met David Lloyd George in 1916, who was to become the Prime Minister, and of him it was said he had been exposed to Bible stories as a child and was familiar with the importance of Israel. Both Barbara Tuchman, *The Bible and the Sword* (New York: Ballantine Books, 1983, repr. from earlier edition of 1956, New York: New York University Press, 1956), 310–18 and Sachar, 96–105 especially emphasize this "Anglo-Zionist Alliance," vol. 15, f.n. 33 for further discussion on this subject.

33. Leonard J. Stein, "Balfour Declaration," in *Encyclopedia Judaica*, vol. 4, 131–35.

34. Samuel A. Miller, "Chaim Weizmann," in *Encyclopedia Judaica*, vol. 16, 423–38.

35. In 167 B.C., after Antiochus Epiphanes had instituted severe measures against the practice of the Jewish religion, Judea revolted, led by Mattathias and his five sons. The rest of the country rallied behind this leadership and in 164 B.C., they were able to wrest religious freedom from the Seleucids, which is celebrated as Hanukkah when the temple was rededicated for service. These Maccabeean leaders lead their people to fight on for political freedom, achieved fully by 128 B.C. But later leaders of this family vied for the leadership among themselves and Rome stepped in to adjudicate in 63 B.C., ruling through Antipater the Idumean and Hyrcanus II. When this family continued to fight among themselves, Rome assumed control of the country in 37 B.C., ruling through Herod. See Philip Goodman, *The Hanukkah Anthology* (Philadephia: The Jewish Publication Society, 1976) and Charles Pfeiffer, *Old Testament History* (Grand Rapids: Baker Book House, 1973), 574–92.

36. By 1941, scholarship among most evangelicals considered the Septuagint more authoritative than the Massoretic text because manuscript and papari texts in Greek

predated the oldest Massoretic texts. The Dead Sea Scroll texts now predated the existing Greek texts and no wonder so much interest was generated in the entire gamut of Old Testament studies.

37. William Bjoraker, "The Beginning of Modern Jewish Missions in the English Speaking World," *Mishkan* 16 (January 1992): 65.
38. Bjoraker, 69.
39. Arthur F. Glasser, "Ecumenism: Signs of Hope?" *Mishkan* 12 (January 1990): 39.
40. For a copy of the Willowbank Declaration, contact Tuvya Zaretsky, Jews for Jesus; 10962 Le Conte Avenue, Los Angeles, CA 90024.
41. *Stepping Stones to Further Jewish Christian Relations, An Unabridged Collection of Christian Documents*, compiled by Helga Croner (London: Stimulus Books, 1977), 71.
43. Ibid., 85.
44. Ibid., 129.
45. *Acts of the Synod of Christian Reformed Board of Home Missions*, 1971, 59.
46. Reprinted in the LCJE Bulletin, June 1995, 8–12, in connection with the Fifth International Conference of the LCJE which met from 18–23 June 1995 in Jerusalem, Israel. Page 1 of this issue also mentions the purposes of the LCJE in its involvement with Jewish evangelism.
47. Susan Perlman, "From Manila to Holland," in LCJE Bulletin, 5 August 1991, 22. The statement is interesting inasmuch as it was adopted by the larger constituency involved with world evangelism but it does serve to undergird the efforts of the LCJE.
48. *Stepping Stones*, 109.
49. *Stepping Stones*, 102, 104.
50. Per Osterbye, 182–84.
51. Gleaned from an interview with John Harvey, Regional Director for Europe and the Middle East for the Christian and Missionary Alliance, and from Robert L. Niklaus, "Israel, Connecting the Incompatibles" in *To All Peoples, Missions World Book* (Camp Hill, Pa.: Christian Publications, 1996), 214–21.
52. Information gleaned from an article, "To the Jew First," which is a statement about "Christian Ministry to the Jewish People from the National Board of Directors, the Norwegian Mission to Israel (February 1986). Per Oesterbye, 187.
53. From a statement of "What we are . . . Our overall goals . . . and Our purpose," published by the Caspari Center, Jerusalem.
54. These statements are found in every issue of *Mishkan* on the inside of the cover.
55. Osterbye, 188–89.
56. Ibid., 190.
57. Ibid., 192f.
58. Ibid., 197f.
59. Ibid., 200f.
60. Ibid., 206–16.
61. The information concerning these congregations comes from this writer after years of working with believers and leaders from 1968 to the present day. He has spent entire summers, sabbaticals, and other occasions there during the year, preaching and teaching among them, and well as sharing in the youth conferences.
62. Gleaned from a personal conversation with Baruch MaOz, who is spiritual leader of congregation *Hesed veEmet* (Love and Truth) and messianic publisher of *HaGefen*. He has the file of names and addresses of these congregations.
63. The quarterly, *Report from Jerusalem*, published by Keren Ahvah Meshihit (Messianic Brotherhood Fund), December 1996, Victor Smadja, editor.

64. Translated from a letter dated 25 February 1958, from the District Commissioner's office, State of Israel.
65. Victor Smadja, "How Expatriate and Indigenous Cooperation Could be Improved," an address given by Victor Smadja at the 21st Annual Conference of the United Christian Council in Israel, 9 November 1977.
66. *Stepping Stones*, 7.
67. *Stepping Stones*, 12.
68. Ibid., 58.
69. Note again Helga Croner, *Op.Cit.*, 71.
70. *The Theology of the Churches and the Jewish People*—Statements by the World Council of Churches and its member churches (Geneva: WCC Publications, 1988), 5, 185, 186. However, note again Susan Perlman, "From Manila to Holland," *Op.Cit.*, en. 47.
71. Franz Rosenzweig, *Star of Redemption*, tr. W. Hallo, 2nd. of 1930 (New York: Holt, Rinehart & Winston, 1970). See also Maurice G. Bowler, "Rosenzweig on Judaism and Christianity," and Louis Goldberg, "Are There Two Ways of Atonement," in *Mishkan* 11 (June 1989).
72. *Stepping Stones*, 114–17.
73. Taken from this organization's Internet site on the World Wide Web at: http://www.serve.com/Bridges/index.html.
74. *International Christian Embassy Statement*, Jerusalem, ICEJ, 4.
75. Harold A. Sevener, "The Christian Embassy, A Viewpoint of a Jewish Mission," in *Mishkan*, 7, February 1986.
76. *Mishkan*, 12, January 1990, which contains a number of articles by Baruch Maoz and John S. Ross, and responses by Arnold Fruchtenbaum and Tuvya Zaretzky, speaking on the critical assessment of the Embassy, while David Friedman offers his personal positive statement.
77. David Friedman, "Why a Christian Embassy," in ibid.
78. Letter by George Carey, archbishop of Caterbury, Lambeth Palace, London, 5 March 1992 to the leaders of the CMJ.
79. CMJ press statement, in commenting on the letter by the archbishop.
80. Brad Young, *Jesus the Jewish Theologian* (Peabody, Mass.: Hendrickson, 1995).
81. Note again documentation, en. 71.

PART THREE

BIBLICAL ISSUES

A doorway in the Jewish Quarter of the Old City.

CHAPTER SIX

ISRAEL IN ROMANS 9–11

Harold W. Hoehner

The identity of Israel has been debated through the centuries. Various opinions have been given regarding the identity of Israel in Paul's letter to the
Romans, especially in chapters 9–11. There are some who want to identify the
church as the replacement of Israel.[1] They claim that since the Jews were responsible for the death of Jesus, God was finished with Israel and the church has replaced her. Others redefine Israel as those who have a share in the world to come.
Hence, it does not refer to Israel after the flesh but Israel after the Spirit whether
they be Jews or Gentiles, not as an ethnic group but a supernatural entity.[2] Still
others would see the church as a subset of Israel.[3] However, more interpreters,
especially after the Holocaust, see Israel as a national entity that is distinct from
the church.[4] With the abhorrence of Christian triumphalism over against the Jews,
Pawlikowski suggests that revelation remains open and ongoing and that we must,
in the light of Holocaust, realize that "the revelation at Sinai stands on equal foot-
ing with the revelation in Jesus." Thus the mission of the church is to share insights of Christ's incarnation but not to proselytize Jews.[5] This also fits in well
with the pluralistic thinking of the present.[6] This is also called the "two-covenant"
view (more discussion below). There is, therefore, a variety of views regarding
Israel's identity in the New Testament.[7]

Certainly Israel plays a prominent place in the New Testament. It is mentioned
sixty-eight times, forty-five times in the Gospels and Acts, seventeen times by
Paul, three times in Hebrews, and three times in Revelation. Of the seventeen
times it is mentioned by Paul, it occurs eleven times in Romans, all of them in
Romans 9–11, five times in chapter 9 (vv. 6*bis,* 27*bis,* 31), twice in chapter 10
(vv. 19, 21), and four times in chapter 11 (vv. 2, 7, 25–26). The term *Jews* is used

195 times in the New Testament, 167 times in the Gospels and Acts, twenty-six times in Paul, and twice in Revelation. Of the twenty-six times Paul uses the term, it appears eleven times in Romans (1:16; 2:9–10, 17, 28–29; 3:1, 9, 29; 9:24; 10:12).

THE SETTING OF ROMANS 9–11

On the one hand, some consider Romans 9–11 only as an appendix or post-script after the completion of the doctrine of salvation in chapters 1–8,[8] whereas, on the other hand, some think this is the climax of the epistle.[9] Most commentators avoid these extremes and consider that Paul has completed the main argument of the epistle with chapter 8 and that chapters 9–11 are an important extension of his argument. Although Israel was considered the chosen people through whom the Messiah came, Paul needs to explain why most of her people rejected Messiah and God's provision of righteousness that resulted in their rejection by God. How can God reject His chosen people? Also, it has been previously stated that Paul had ministered first to the Jews and then to the Gentiles (1:16; 2:9), and yet it was the Gentiles who responded and the Jews who rejected the message. In fact, Paul had so harshly criticized the Jew that there was a question asked regarding what advantage the Jew really had (3:1). Nevertheless, Paul left this question dangling in order to finish the argument regarding God's righteousness obtained on the basis of God's grace and by means of faith. In chapters 9–11 he returns to the Jewish dilemma concerning why the majority are rejected by God. Furthermore, chapters 9–11 are critical to Paul's argument because he argued in chapters 1–8 that it is on the basis of God's grace by means of faith that anyone can obtain a right standing (justification) before God resulting in eternal life. The question then arises, Will God keep His promise of eternal life if He has not kept His covenant promise to Israel?

THE ARGUMENT OF ROMANS 9–11

The argument in Romans 9–11 is very important to the entire letter. Up to this point Paul has argued cogently that one has a right standing before God by simply trusting God's work in Jesus Christ on the cross at Calvary. As God's covenanted nation, why has Israel rejected God's Messiah who was born from among them to be her deliverer while many Gentiles have accepted this Messiah for salvation and deliverance?

Israel's Rejection Considered—Romans 9:1–29

Paul's argument can be divided into three parts. First, Paul expresses his grief over Israel's rejection of God's salvation (vv. 1–5). He laments that his kinsman of the flesh, namely, Israelites, who had all the privileges and from whom Christ was born, have rejected God. This grief over fellow Israelites indicates that Israel and the church are not the same entity.

Second, Paul demonstrates that God's rejection of Israel is not inconsistent with His promises (vv. 6–13). In verse 6 he states that God's Word has not failed "for not all those who are from Israel are Israel."[10] He then substantiates by two rounds of proof that God has not failed in His promises. The first round of proof is that though all are Abraham's children (τέκνα), not all are Abraham's seed (σπέρμα)—only those who are called (vv. 7–9). This is demonstrated by the fact that both Isaac and Ishmael were Abraham's children (τέκνα), but only Isaac was Abraham's seed (σπέρμα). Since Paul's detractors might have argued that this is readily understandable because Ishmael was born of Hagar whereas Isaac was born of Sarah, Paul tightens his argument by a second round of proof. He argues that though the twins Esau and Jacob originated from one act of conception on the part of Isaac and Rebekah, only Jacob, not Esau, was considered seed (vv. 10–13). It could be visualized in this way:

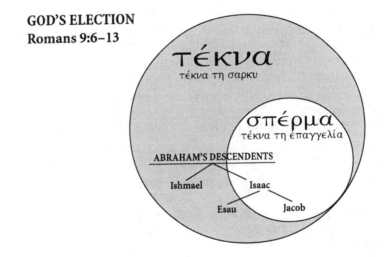

GOD'S ELECTION
Romans 9:6–13

TÉKVA
τέκνα τη σαρκυ

σπέρμα
τέκνα τη έπαγγελία

ABRAHAM'S DESCENDENTS

Ishmael   Isaac

Esau   Jacob

This argument is irrefutable because from one conception there are two children, yet one is not seed whereas the other is. If there had been two children from two conceptions by the same parents, it could be argued that one or both of the parents may have been out of fellowship when Esau was conceived or born but in fellowship when Jacob was conceived or born. Paul argues that of the twins only Jacob was considered seed. Hence, Ishmael and Esau were children and grandchildren of Abraham as were Isaac and Jacob respectively, but only the latter two were considered seed (σπέρμα) or the children of promise. Therefore, birth to the right family was not enough; there must also be an election according to grace. God never promised that every child born to Abraham would be considered seed; thus not all those who are descendants of Abraham are Israel. Only those who are related to Abraham physically *and* spiritually are the true Israel.

Third, Paul asserts that the rejection of Israel is not inconsistent with God's justice (vv. 14–29). According to Paul, God is not unjust in His actions (vv. 14–18) for He has mercy and compassion on whomever He wills, rather than on those who will (inward desire) and those who run (outward activity). He illustrates this in the lives of Moses and Pharaoh. In light of this it could be asked if God is actually just since He extends mercy. Strict justice has no mercy. Paul continues his argument by showing God's patience with the vessels of wrath which were destined for destruction in order to make known the wealth of His glory on the vessels of mercy which He had prepared beforehand for glory from among Israel and even among some Gentiles (vv. 19–29).[11] Thus, God has a right to show mercy to whomever He wills and wrath to whomever He wills.

Israel's Rejection Culpable—Romans 9:30–10:21

Having dealt with the rejection of Israel from the viewpoint of divine justice and power, now Paul is going to show rejection from the side of human responsibility. He demonstrates this in three parts, showing how Israel did not obtain righteousness by faith. First, Israel repudiated righteousness by faith (9:30–10:4). Paul argues that the Gentiles, who did not seek righteousness, obtained it but it was a righteousness by faith. On the other hand, Israel pursued righteousness but did not attain it because they pursued it by works and not by faith, stumbling right over the one who could provide it (vv. 30–33). Before continuing with the argument, Paul expresses to the believers in Rome his desire and prayer that Israelites might be saved (10:1). This is the only verse in the New Testament that expresses a prayer for the unsaved (cf. also 1 Tim. 2:1–4). Here the unsaved are those Israelites who have repudiated righteousness by faith. It is another indication that Israel is not the church. It also demonstrates the fact that there are two Israels, namely, Israel according to the flesh, every descendant of Abraham, and Israel which is the seed. Paul desires that every Israelite be saved. He then picks up his argument that the righteousness Israel pursued was their own and not God's, which is obtained by faith (10:2–4).

Second, Israel rejected God because she ignored the Old Testament teaching of righteousness by faith (10:5–13). Instead, there was an attempt to attain a righteous standing before God through keeping the Law of Moses, which required full obedience in every aspect. On the contrary, God's righteousness is obtained by faith in God's provision of Christ's death and resurrection. This is true for anyone, Jew or Gentile, who calls on the name of the Lord. Paul demonstrates that this is not a new concept, but rather, it originated in Old Testament times, and he demonstrates this by quoting Old Testament passages (Lev. 18:5; Deut. 30:12–14; Isa. 28:16; Joel 2:32).

Third, Israel refused the opportunity to accept righteousness by faith (10:14–21). In order to believe the message of salvation, one must hear the good news. However, the majority of Israel did hear the Good News but rejected it (vv. 14–17). Paul asks two questions that might exonerate Israel's lack of response. First, possibly Israel did not hear the message. However, Paul replies that the message went throughout the world (v. 18). Second, is it possible that Israel did not understand the message? Paul responds by saying that this is absurd since even Gentiles, who never had the privilege of a long history of revelation and association with God, understood the message (vv. 19–20). Gentiles, who never sought it, found it and would now provoke Israel to jealousy. Paul concludes that the real reason for Israel's refusal of God's righteousness is due to their disobedience and obstinacy.

Therefore, in both the Old and New Testament times Israel rejected God's righteousness. It was thought that righteousness could be attained by means of the works of the Law rather than by faith. Hence, Israel was responsible for rejecting God.

Israel's Rejection Not Complete nor Final—Romans 11:1–32

In chapter 9 Israel's rejection by God was considered, and Paul concluded that God is free to reject Israel since He is the creator and never promised that every Israelite would inherit the promises (9:6–13). Nor is it inconsistent with His justice (9:14–29). Further, in 9:30–10:21 Paul shows that Israel was culpable in neglecting God's method of salvation by faith, which she had ample opportunity to accept. Now the logical question is, Has God really cast away Israel completely and forever? Paul is going to discuss this in three parts: (1) the rejection of Israel is not complete (11:1–10); (2) the rejection of Israel is not final (11:11–24); and (3) the restoration of Israel is certain (11:25–32). Paul ends the chapter with a paean of praise (11:33–36).

The Rejection of Israel Is Not Complete (11:1–10)

The Example of Paul (11:1). Paul demonstrates that the rejection of Israel is not complete but only partial. The conjunction "therefore, then" (οὖν) refers broadly to the consequence arising out of the discussion of God's rejection of Israel in 9:6–29, of Israel's rejection of God in 9:30–10:21 and, more particularly, from the immediately preceding verse where Israel was labeled as a disobedient and obstinate people. The natural question is raised, namely, God has not rejected His people, has He? With the expected negative answer, Paul answers "absolutely not" (μὴ γένοιτο).

To substantiate his answer Paul uses himself as an example, an Israelite, a descendant of Abraham of the tribe of Benjamin. He was not only from Abraham (as was Ishmael) and Isaac (as was Esau) but also from Jacob or Israel. Furthermore, Paul was from the seed (σπέρμα) of Abraham and not merely a child (τέκνον) of Abraham and, more particularly, of the tribe of Benjamin suggesting no purer Israelite. Some indicators of this are as follows:

1. Benjamin (with Joseph) was a son of Jacob's favorite wife, Rachel (Gen. 35:17–18)—so not only a son of Israel but also out of Israel's favorite wife.

Also, Benjamin was the only son of Jacob who was born in Israel, the promised land.

2. He was favored over Joseph for the tribe of Benjamin went to the promised land—Joseph did not.
3. The first ruler of the undivided monarch was the Benjaminite Saul, Paul's Hebrew namesake.
4. After the split of the kingdom, Benjamin, at least in part, went with Judah while Joseph's two sons (Ephraem and Manassah) were the strongholds of the north.
5. Jerusalem—political and religious capital—was in the territory of Benjamin.
6. After the seventy-year captivity, it was Judah and Benjamin who returned.
7. In the book of Esther, it was Mordecai, a Benjaminite, who protected the Jews against Haman. Hence, a Benjaminite was the most authentic Israelite.

In conclusion, Paul himself is proof that God has not rejected all His people. But is he the only one? No. Paul gives another example.

The Calling of the Remnant (11:2–10). In verse 2 Paul states, "God has not rejected His people whom He foreknew." Paul changes from a question in verse 1 to a statement of denial in these next verses. He simply states firmly that God has not rejected His people and adds the words "whom He foreknew" (ὅν προέγνω). "The fact that God has foreknown his people, i.e., has chosen them, makes it impossible that he should now reject them."[12] Although the term *foreknow* (προγινώσκω) can refer to knowing in advance, in the New Testament it refers to God's "election or foreordination of His people (Rom. 8:29; 11:2) or Christ (1 Peter 1:20)."[13] But who are His people in this context? Is "His people" a reference to the nation Israel in a general sense, or does it refer to the elect within the nation of Israel in a restrictive sense? Many think it refers to the nation as a whole.[14] The reasons for this view are: (1) the whole context is about the status of the nation as a whole in 9:30–10:21 and about whom Paul asks in 11:1; (2) 11:28 speaks of the nation Israel as the enemy of the gospel and yet God's choice; (3) it is stated that in the future all Israel will be saved (11:26); and (4) the nation is seen corporately in the rest of chapter 11.

Others propose that Paul is referring to a remnant within Israel[15] because (1) the context states that not all Israel is Israel (9:6–8); (2) 11:1 speaks of the example of Paul as one Israelite who is part of the remnant; (3) 11:2–4 refers to Elijah and the 7,000 who did not bow down to Baal; (4) 11:5 and 7 speaks of a remnant according to the election of grace known as His people in contrast to the rest of Israel who were hardened; and (5) the concept of "foreknowledge" is consistent with 8:29 where those whom God foreknew are ultimately glorified. Hence, His people whom He foreknew are the remnant as opposed to the nation as a whole.[16] With some hesitation, this latter view is preferred.

In summary, not only is Paul one of God's chosen, but God also selected Elijah and 7,000 within Israel who did not bow their knee to Baal (vv. 2b–4). Also, in Paul's day there was the remnant according to the election of grace (vv. 5–7a). The rest of those in Israel were hardened, and this Paul substantiates from Deuteronomy 29:4, Isaiah 29:10 and Psalm 69:22–23 [LXX 68:23–24] (vv. 7b–10).

The Rejection of Israel Is Not Final (11:11–24)

Having developed in verses 1–10 that Israel's rejection was not complete but only partial, Paul next discusses in verses 11–24 the fact that Israel's rejection was not final, only temporary.

Blessings from Israel's Rejection and Acceptance (11:11–15). With discussion of not only the immediately preceding verses but also of chapters 9–10, the question naturally arises, "Is Israel's stumbling so extensive that she will fall completely or irrevocably?" In other words, when Israel rejected Jesus, their Messiah, did that make it impossible for her to rise again after the fall? Paul emphatically answers this negatively by saying, "absolutely not" (μὴ γένοιτο). God uses their transgression to the good, namely, first for the Gentiles, and then for Israel. The transgression referred to here is the same thing as the "fall" in verse 11. The purpose of salvation for the Gentiles is to provoke Israel to jealousy. It is similar to offering a toy to a child who then refuses it. However, when the toy is offered to another child, the first child then wants it. The role of the Gentiles is to provoke Israel to jealousy—not a cause for the Gentiles to boast. So God's aim for the Jews is not their fall but their recovery. Gentiles are saved not only for their sake but for the sake of Israel. Gentile salvation is a means to an end. Now if Israel's transgression means riches for the rest of the world and their defeat or loss means riches of salvation for Gentiles, how much more will their fullness mean? The pronoun *their* must have reference to Israel because it is used twice before in this verse, and it is clearly referring to Israel in both instances. The "fullness" (πλήρωμα) normally has the qualitative sense of the full restoration of Israel's blessings[17] but in the present context most think it has quantitative sense of the full number of the Jewish remnant.[18] Moo observes, "Paul would then be suggesting that the present 'defeat' of Israel, in which Israel is numerically reduced to a small remnant, will be reversed by the addition of far greater numbers of true believers: this will be Israel's destined 'fullness.'"[19] Therefore, if Israel's transgression brings the riches of God's salvation through Christ to the Gentiles, so much greater will be blessings to the whole world, both to Jews and Gentiles, when Israel's full number is attained. This is not a new concept but an elaboration of an Old Testament concept that Israel is to be the blesser of the nations (Gen. 12:3; 18:18; 22:18; 26:4; 28:14; Acts 3:25; Gal. 3:8).

Next, in verses 13–15, Paul, aware of the Gentile audience, states that he glories in the ministry to the Gentiles because the greater number of Gentiles won to

Christ would make provision for Israel's jealousy with the hope that some would be saved. He explains (γάρ) that if Israel's rejection means reconciliation of the world, Israel's acceptance means life from the dead. There are two items that need further clarification. First, who is the subject of the actions of rejection and acceptance? A few understand the pronoun *them* (αὐτῶν) as a subjective genitive, that is, their (Jews) rejection or acceptance,[20] but more see the pronoun function as an objective genitive, that is, God's rejection or acceptance of them.[21] Both are true, for Israel did reject the Messiah/Christ and also God rejected Israel, and when Israel accepts Christ's provision of salvation then God will again accept them. The first interpretation is preferred. Israel's rejection means present reconciliation of the world and their acceptance of Messiah/Christ will mean life from the dead. The second problem is regarding the meaning of "life from the dead" (ζωὴ ἐκ νεκρῶν). Most understand it literally, as referring to a general resurrection of the dead at the end of time or when Christ returns to usher in the messianic age.[22] However, these words are never used of general resurrection but rather the words *resurrection of the dead* (ἀνάστασις τῶν νεκρῶν) are used (Rom. 1:4; 1 Cor. 15:12–13, 21, 42). Others understand this figuratively, referring to the unprecedented blessing for the entire world, that is, the messianic rule and blessings.[23] This understanding is preferred. This concept of messianic rule and blessing is not new, for Psalm 67:1–2 says:

> May God be gracious to us and bless us and make his face to shine upon us, *(Selah)* that your way may be known upon the earth, your saving power among all nations. (NRSV)

The point is that Israel is the means to worldwide salvation and blessing. So when Israel is blessed, the whole world will be blessed. Their rejection is only temporary, and when that period of time is over, there will be unprecedented blessings.

Restoration of Israel Guaranteed by the Patriarch's Earnest (11:16). This is a transitional verse and the point it makes is that if the part is holy, the whole is also holy. The part conveys holiness to the whole. The first half of the verse states that if the firstfruit is holy so is the lump. This probably has reference to the time when the people of Israel entered the promised land and were to offer to the Lord the first portion of the dough (Num. 15:17–21). The point Paul makes is that the first portion of the dough affects the whole lump of dough. Likewise, Israel's acceptance of messianic blessing will bring blessing not only to Israel but also to the whole world (v. 15). Also, the remnant will affect the whole nation (vv. 25–26). The imagery of the root in connection with the branches in the last half of the verse is obviously continued in the simile of the olive tree in verses 17–24. If the root is holy so also the branches. The root probably has reference to Abraham and/or the patriarchs for verse 28 speaks of Israel being "beloved for the fathers' sake."

Instruction from the Simile of the Olive Tree (11:17–24)

Admonition against Gentile Pride (11:17–22). First to be observed is that some of the branches which were cut off is an understatement for the great majority of the nation. This continues the thought of 9:6 that not all Israel is Israel. The un-cut branches would be the true Israel or the remnant. In place of the cut-off branches a wild olive branch is grafted in among the remaining branches to become a partaker of the rich root of the olive tree. Who is represented by the wild olive branch? There has been much speculation over this. Many suggest that it refers to Gentile Christians[24] but it is more likely that it refers to Gentiles[25] or possibly to Gentile Christendom.[26] This parallels well with the natural branches. The natural branches represent Israel, those remaining on the tree are the believing remnant, the seed, and those cut off are unbelieving Jews who lost their covenant relationship and are not seed but only children of Abraham by physical lineage. The engrafted wild branches represent Gentiles, and by implication the believing will remain on the tree and the unbelieving will be cut off. In Galatians the believing Gentiles are Abraham's seed through Christ (Gal. 3:26–29).

The point of the whole passage is that the wild engrafted Gentiles should not become proud about their favored situation and the plight of the Jews. The Gentiles who have opportunity to participate in God's blessing of salvation could lose that privilege in the same way Israel did. The Gentiles were engrafted only because of Israel's unbelief. Gentiles, as with Israel, will remain only because of faith. If God did not spare the natural branches there is no reason to spare the unnatural branches, namely, the Gentiles. Here again is a warning for the Gentiles not to become haughty against Israel. Unfortunately, Paul's warning went unheeded because segments of the Christendom became proud and anti-Semitic, standing in danger of being cut off.

Anticipation of Israel's Future Restoration (11:23–24). If Israelites do not continue in their unbelief, God will regraft them for God is able to do so. Certainly if God is able to graft in unnatural branches, He is easily able to graft the natural branches back into their own olive tree. The unbelieving Jews were cut off because of unbelief, and one must presume that regrafting will be by faith. The condition of being a "branch" is faith (11:23).[27]

In conclusion, again we see that the reason the Gentiles were given the opportunity is not for self-indulgence but to provoke Israel to jealousy so that she will come back and be grafted into her own tree. Also, this simile points to the fact that rejection of Israel is only temporary and not permanent.

The Restoration of Israel Is Certain (11:25–32). This marks the climax of Paul's argumentation. He has shown that God's rejection of Israel was not inconsistent with His promises or His justice (9:1–29) and has shown that Israel was responsible for she had always rejected righteousness by faith up to the time of Paul's preaching (9:30–10:21). The rejection of Israel is neither complete nor final (11:1–24). Paul now proceeds to discuss God's restoration of Israel (11:25–32).

Israel's Hardness Is Partial and Temporary (11:25). Gentiles are again warned not to be conceited because Israel's hardening is partial and will continue until the fullness of the Gentiles should come in.[28] Some take the Greek phrase "in part" (μέρος) adverbially, modifying "hardening," meaning that Israel has been partially hardened (NEB, NASB, NIV)[29] while others see it adjectively modifying "Israel" meaning in the numerical sense that part of Israel has been hardened (RSV, NKJV, NJB, NRSV).[30] The latter view is preferred because the context mentions two kinds of Israelites—elect and hardened (11:5, 7, 11).

Furthermore, this is in contrast to "all Israel will be saved" in the next verse. Part of Israel has been hardened, and this will continue until "the fullness of the Gentiles should come in." The temporariness of the Israel's hardness is expressed by the words "until that time when" (ἄχρι οὖ) the fullness of the Gentiles should come in. The expression "fullness of the Gentiles" is difficult to understand. As mentioned above, the term *fullness* (πλήρωμα) normally has the qualitative sense of the fullness of blessing for the Gentiles, but in the present context (as also in v. 12) it is best to consider it in the quantitative sense, the completion of the Gentile mission when the last Gentile is saved before the messianic age. In verse 12 Paul speaks of the full number of the Jewish remnant; here he mentions the full number of Gentiles.

Israel's Future Restoration (11:26–27)

Its consequence. The word introducing verse 26, "so" or "thus" (οὕτως), has been rendered in different ways. Some take it as temporal "and then" (καὶ τότε),[31] but, as Fitzmyer states, this is not attested in Greek usage.[32] Others think this word indicates manner ("in this way") which can be interpreted in two ways. First, some think it refers back to the preceding verses, namely, part of Israel was hardened and the Gentiles come into messianic blessings to provoke Israel to jealousy. It is "in this way" all Israel will be saved.[33] However, it is difficult to understand how the preceding "that" (ὅτι) clause (Israel's hardening and Gentiles' salvation) is the manner of how all Israel will be saved.[34] Second, others think it is looking forward by connecting it to "just as it written" (καθὼ γέγραπται), and so "in this way" all Israel will be saved just as it was written in Isaiah (59:20–21; 27:9).[35] But nowhere else does Paul tie οὕτως with καθώς and the latter does not express the manner of the former.[36] Finally, it would seem best to consider that it introduces a logical consequence or inference, that is, the logical consequence of Israel's hardening until the fullness of the Gentiles comes in so that all Israel will be saved.[37] This is the normal usage of οὕτως as seen in Romans 5:12. Although οὕτως is not temporal in meaning, it is temporally conditioned because the salvation of all Israel occurs after Israel's hardening and the entrance of the fullness of the Gentiles mentioned in verse 25.[38] The temporal aspect is reinforced by the change of tenses from the perfect and aorist in verse 25 to the future in verse 26. So the logical consequence will occur in the future.

Its scope. What is meant by "all Israel will be saved"? This is the heart of the mystery mentioned in verse 25. The mystery concerns both the hardening of a part of Israel and the salvation of all of Israel. But when it speaks of "all" Israel, many different interpretations surface.[39] There are three main views. First, some interpreters thinks this refers to all the elect Jews and Gentiles.[40] However, the whole context of Romans 9–11, especially 11:11–32, never indicates the inclusion of the Gentiles as a part of Israel.[41] In fact, in verse 25 there is a contrast between Israel and the Gentiles, and to consider the Gentiles as a part of Israel in verse 26 makes no sense.

Second, some think it refers to the whole elect remnant of Israel throughout history.[42] This is an unlikely view. Granted, all the elect of Israel will be saved, but that is a given in contrast to those who were hardened, and it is not relevant to the apostle's interest in this section. How would this known factor make it a special kind of revelation implied by "this mystery" (v. 25)?[43] Moreover, it would be anticlimactic for "all Israel" to refer only to all the elect after Paul has argued that something greater will occur after Israel's temporary hardening. The earlier references to Israel's fullness (v. 12), acceptance (v. 15), and regrafting (vv. 23–24) would anticipate more than a truism known in all generations.[44] Israel here would not be the same as Israel in the preceding verse.

Third, most think that "all Israel" refers to the whole nation of Israel. However, those who accept this view understand it in two ways. On the one hand, most think this does not mean every individual Israelite but the nation as a whole collectively.[45] Certainly there are instances in the Bible where "all" does not mean every individual. For example, with regards to John the Baptist's ministry, it is stated that all Judea (Matt. 3:5) and all the people of Jerusalem (Mark 1:5) went out to see him. No one would consider that means every individual (cf. also 1 Sam. 25:1; 1 Kings 12:1; 2 Chron. 12:1; Dan. 9:11). This is a viable solution, but it seems that if Paul meant the nation as a whole, he could have been more precise by saying, "whole of Israel" (ὅλος ᾽Ισραήλ).

On the other hand, others think that Paul is referring to the whole nation of Israel, including every individual member.[46] This seems to make the best sense. First, this makes sense in the context in contrast to the full number (of individuals) of Gentiles in the preceding verse. Second, the removal of some of the branches (v. 17) and the regrafting (vv. 23–24) seem to imply every branch. Third, the firstfruit (v. 16) will affect every part of the lump. Also, in the same verse it states, "if the root is holy, so also the branches" which implies every branch is affected. Fourth, as mentioned earlier, the "part of Israel" that has been hardened, mentioned in the preceding verse, had a numerical sense, and thus it makes good sense to have the "all" in the present verse as referring to the numerical idea of every individual. Fifth, the whole nation is made up of every individual member.

Hence, though "all Israel" could have reference to the nation collectively, it seems best to think it refers to the whole nation, including every individual member.

There is one more thing to be considered regarding "all Israel." Some see it in a diachronic sense, namely, that "all Israel" refers to the nation as it has existed throughout history and that will have a share in the world to come (*Sanhedrin* 10:1) after the resurrection.[47] Others take it in a synchronic sense where "all Israel" refers to the nation only as it exists at a moment in history, particularly at the end time as a part of the eschatological program.[48] The second alternative is preferred. Moo states, "No occurrence of the phrase 'all Israel' has a clearly diachronic meaning."[49] Furthermore, the context speaks of Israel's rejection of Messiah and her hardening which was to continue until the time when the fullness of Gentiles should come in. Then, in sharp contrast, at a particular moment in history, "all Israel" will experience salvation. The use of the future tense in this verse in contrast to the perfect and aorist tenses in the preceding verse substantiates this concept.

Its time. As mentioned in the previous paragraph, the time of this national salvation is in the future. It is the second phase in Israel's salvation history outlined in this context. The first phase was their rejection of Messiah and their hardening, both of which were occurring at the time Paul wrote this letter. This state will continue until the fullness of the Gentiles should come in. The second phase is when "all Israel shall be saved." This is also depicted as "their fullness" in verse 12, "their acceptance" in verse 15, "the natural branches shall be engrafted in their own olive tree" in verse 24, and that they will "have received mercy" in verse 30.[50]

There is a stark contrast between their rejection and their acceptance. Certainly Paul's description of Israel's state in his day was one of rejection and, as stated, he envisioned their acceptance as occurring future to his time. This is confirmed in verses 26b–27 where Paul cites Isaiah 59:20–21 and 27:9 which speak of the deliverer coming out of Zion and removing the ungodliness of Jacob and forgiving their sins. Isaiah 59 speaks of the ungodliness of Israel and promises that a redeemer will come to Zion to remove their ungodliness. Isaiah depicts the redeemer as God, and Paul identifies the redeemer as Christ.[51] Isaiah speaks of God's covenant with Israel that awaits its consummation at the time of the redeemer's appearance in Zion. Also, Isaiah 27 speaks of Jacob's/Israel's punishment of dispersion but also her preservation (vv. 7–8), unlike her enemies, and promises that her iniquities will be forgiven (v. 9) and she will be regathered to her own city, Jerusalem, to worship the Lord (vv. 6, 12–13). Both of these passages speak of the forgiveness of Israel's sin and the prominence of Jerusalem in that day of salvation.

That time of salvation for Israel is often depicted by the Old Testament prophets as the messianic age. Hence, the promise that "all Israel will be saved" will be fulfilled at the commencement of the age to come, the age which was future to

Paul's day and is also future to our time.[52] More specifically, this time of forgiveness is mentioned in Zechariah 12:10 as a time when Israel will look on Him whom they pierced and will mourn for Him.[53] At this time there will be the outpouring of the Spirit of grace and of supplication on the house of David and on the inhabitants of Jerusalem. This great deliverance of Israel will occur at the second coming of Jesus Christ to earth.[54] It is also a time of judgment of Israel where there will be the purging of unbelievers (Ezek. 20:33–38; Zech. 13:8–9). The only remaining Israelites are those who have believed. Hence, every Israelite will be saved.

Its manner. Paul states that "all Israel will be saved," but he does not state how this will happen. It is thought by some that though the Gentiles are saved by faith in Christ, Israel will be saved in a "special way" by faith. It is a two-covenant theory. Stendahl notes that there is no mention of Jesus Christ in Romans 10:18–11:36, including the doxology (11:33–36), the only doxology of Paul without any Christological element. Hence, Israel will be saved by faith but not in Christ.[55] Mussner states, "The *parousia* Christ will save all Israel without a preceding 'conversion' of the Jews to the gospel."[56] Gaston proposes that if Paul conceived of Christ's involvement with Israel's salvation, it was in such a way that Christ is the agent of that "special way" of Israel's salvation. Those who hold this view contend that Gentiles will not be eschatologically absorbed into Israel or that the Jews will be eschatologically absorbed into the church, but that "God's righteousness for salvation [is] for both, without changing one into the other."[57] In the same vein, Gager relates that "Paul never explicitly equates Israel's salvation with conversion to Christianity."[58] When Paul states in Romans 3:30 that God "will justify the circumcised on the ground of their faith and the uncircumcised because of their faith," it means that faith is "the proper response to God's righteousness, whether for Israel in the Torah or for Gentiles in Christ."[59] This idea of a special way for Israel has become more prominent since the Holocaust, and it fits well with the pluralistic thinking of the present day.[60]

Although the Christological language is absent in Romans 10:18–11:36, in light of the entire argument of Romans, it is not plausible to consider that Paul thought Israel would be saved apart from Christ. Even Segal (who calls himself a believing Jew and a twentieth-century humanist) thinks that Stendahl, Gaston, and Gager attempt to read two separate paths of salvation—Christ for the Gentiles and the Torah for the Jews—which is not supported by Paul. For Paul both Jews and Gentiles are saved only through Christ.[61] The central argument of Romans 1–8 is that faith in Christ means forgiveness of sin and a right standing before God by means of imputation of God's righteousness. There is salvation by no other way.

In Romans 9–11 Paul develops the argument by posing the question that if justification is by faith in Christ, why did most of Israel reject God's Messiah and righteousness? Certainly, in 10:9–10 Paul is relating to the Jews that they need to confess that Jesus is the Lord and that they are to believe that God raised Jesus from the dead in order to be saved. Hence, salvation of the Jews is only in Jesus Christ. Paul continues his argument by stating that anyone, Jew or Gentile, who calls on the name of the Lord will be saved (vv. 11–13). This belief in the Lord Jesus Christ is the result of hearing the Word of Christ (vv. 14–17), this Word which has gone throughout the world and which Israel refused to obey (vv. 18–21).

Romans 11 continues in the same vein, that is, Israel's rejection of God's righteousness through Christ. Israel's transgression of rejection brought salvation to the Gentiles (v. 11) and that salvation is by faith in Christ. Gentile salvation is to provoke Israel to jealousy, that she too would come to faith in Christ. In fact, Paul glories in his ministry to the Gentiles in the hope that it will result in the salvation of some of his fellow Jews (vv. 13–14). How would these Jews be saved? Surely Paul means that they would be saved by placing their faith in Christ and His work on the cross.[62] Räisänen states, "If Israel was not supposed to believe in Jesus as the Messiah at all, it becomes unclear why Paul should speak of its ἀπιστία [unbelief], as in Rom. 11:20–23, or of its disobedience (Rom. 11:31)."[63] With regards to the olive tree, many of Israel were cut off because of unbelief (v. 17), and presumably they will be regrafted by faith (vv. 23–24). Certainly the Gentiles will remain in the tree only if they have faith (v. 22). Both are in the same tree with the same faith in the same object, namely, Christ.[64] Finally, Paul states that after Israel's hardening, the fullness of the Gentiles would come in, and then "all Israel will be saved" (vv. 25–26). Again, how will they be saved? In answer to this, Paul cites Isaiah 59:20–21 and 27:9 to show that the deliverer will come out of Zion and take away their sins. Who is the deliverer mentioned in Isaiah? In Isaiah the deliverer is God, but Paul applies it to Christ.

Therefore, Israel's salvation is only through Christ. This fits with the first eight chapters of Romans. There is no hint that salvation is by any other means for Israel. Furthermore, Paul's anguish over his kinfolk (9:1–2; 10:1) is unexplainable if their salvation were not through Christ.[65] Thus, it is incumbent on the church to preach salvation through Christ not only to the Gentiles but also to the Jews.

Israel's Present Alienation in Light of Future Restoration (11:28–32). These verses mark the conclusion of Paul's discussion in chapter 11, as well as chapters 9–11. Israel's disobedience brings mercy or salvation to the Gentiles which, in the end, will bring Israel into God's mercy or salvation. This is reiterating what Paul had said earlier that when Gentiles obtain salvation, it will provoke Israel to jealousy (11:11–15). In reality both Jews and Gentiles have been disobedient and both receive God's mercy. It is to show that salvation is of grace and not of works whether one is a Jew or Gentile. This demonstrates that Paul was not anti-Semitic for both Jews and Gentiles were disobedient and both Jews and Gentiles need God's mercy.[66]

Response of Praise (11:33–36)

Paul concludes the difficult chapters 9–11 with a hymn of praise to God. Paul attempted to answer some very complex issues regarding Israel in the plan of God. Some of the issues cannot be resolved with finality because we are not able to comprehend the mind of God. Rest assured that God is righteous in His dealings with Israel. God is to be praised!

CONCLUSION

Israel has always had a preeminent place in God's program. Old Testament Scripture depicts God's concern and care for Israel. Israel figures largely in the New Testament as well. In the Gospels Jesus' ministry is centered in Israel. Jesus told the Canaanite woman that He was sent only to the lost sheep of the house of Israel (Matt. 15:24) and told his disciples not to go to the Gentiles but rather to go to the lost sheep of the house of Israel (Matt. 10:5–6). However, the nation of Israel rejected Him (John 1:11) and in conjunction with the Roman government crucified Him (Acts 2:22–23). In the early part of Acts (chaps. 2–7) the message of Christ was preached to the people in Israel, and many responded by placing their faith in Christ. Then Paul, a devout Jew and a persecutor of the church, came face to face with Christ and realized that he was actually persecuting Christ and became a believer in Christ (Acts 9). In his missionary journeys Paul went first to the synagogue and preached that Jews as well as Gentiles need to put their trust in Jesus Christ for the forgiveness of sins (cf. Acts 13:16–41; 16:30–34). Before Herod Agrippa II Paul continued to press home the fact that one needs to have faith in Christ in order to be saved (Acts 26). When Paul was sent to Rome, he had an audience with the Jews and tried to convince them that salvation was through Jesus (Acts 28:23–28). Therefore, Israel has always been prominent in the plan of God.

The prominence of Israel in the book of Romans is also evident. Certainly in Romans 9–11 Israel is the center of discussion. Paul discusses God's rejection of the people of Israel and their rejection of God. However, this rejection is not complete nor permanent. In the future "all Israel" will be saved. This will occur when Christ returns and judges the nations, including Israel, and will save those who call on Him. Israel will mourn after the One whom they pierced (Zech. 12:10). How will Israel be saved? Consistent with the preaching in the book of Acts, Israel will be saved through Christ.[67]

Having discussed the message of salvation in the past (depicted in the book of Acts) and for the future (Rom. 11:26), what is the message for the present day? Paul was concerned about Israel's rejection and prayed for her salvation (Rom. 10:1). He continues by saying to the Jews that they cannot be saved by the Law but by confessing with their mouths that Jesus is Lord, by believing that God raised Him from the dead and they will be saved. The message is the same for both Jews and Gentiles—for there is no distinction and whoever calls on Him will be saved (Rom. 10:1–13). Therefore, the message to everyone, Jews and Gentiles, is that one needs to put his or her faith in Christ in order to be saved. Hence, the mission of the church is to proclaim the message of salvation both to the Jews and Gentiles.[68]

DISCUSSION QUESTIONS

1. How have interpreters identified Israel in relationship to the church?

2. What is the purpose of God granting salvation to the Gentiles (Rom. 11:11–14)?

3. Who is represented by the wild olive branches that are grafted in to the olive tree (vv. 17, 22, 24)?

4. To what does "the fulness of the Gentiles" refer (v. 25)?

5. What does "all Israel" mean? Does Israel refer to an ethnic group? If so, does the "all" refer to every individual (v. 26)?

6. When will all Israel be saved (v. 26)?

7. What is the salvation of Israel? Is it different from the salvation of the Gentiles (vv. 26–27, 31)?

ENDNOTES

1. C. K. Barrett, *A Commentary on the Epistle to the Romans,* Harper's New Testament Commentaries, ed. Henry Chadwick (New York: New York, 1957), 191–92, 217–18; Karl Barth, *The Epistle to the Romans,* 6th ed., trans. Edwyn C. Hoskyns (London: Oxford University Press, 1933), where he titles chap. 9 "The Tribulation of the Church," 330; chap. 10 "The Guilt of the Church," 362; and chap. 11 "The Hope of the Church," 391. However, Barth in his theology is clear that the church is not a replacement of Israel, cf. Karl Barth, *Church Dogmatics,* trans. G. T. Thompson, G. W. Bromiley, et al., ed. G. W. Bromiley and T. F. Torrance, vol. 2/2 (Edinburgh: T. & T. Clark, 1957), 290–91. For much information on Barth, I am indebted to Stephen R. Haynes, *Prospects for Post-Holocaust Theology,* American Academy of Religion Academy Series, ed. Susan Thistlethwaite, no. 77 (Atlanta: Scholars Press, 1991), 47–102.

2. Bruce Chilton and Jacob Neusner, *Judaism in the New Testament: Practices and Beliefs* (London/New York: Routledge, 1995), 58–97, 191–94, esp. 71–86; Frank Thielman, "Unexpected Mercy: Echoes of a Biblical Motif in Romans 9–11," *SJT* 47, no. 2 (1994): 169–81, esp. 170, 178–81.

3. James D. G. Dunn, *Romans 9–16,* Word Biblical Commentary, ed. David A. Hubbard and Glenn W. Barker; New Testament ed. Ralph P. Martin, vol. 38B (Dallas: Word Books, 1988), 520; James D. G. Dunn, "How New Was Paul's Gospel? The Problem

of Continuity and Discontinuity," in *Gospel in Paul: Studies on Corinthians, Galatians, and Romans for Richard L. Longenecker,* ed. L. Ann Jervis and Peter Richardson, Journal for the Study of the New Testament Supplement Series, ed. Stanley E. Porter, vol. 108 (Sheffield: Sheffield Academic Press, 1994), 373–74; J. Christiaan Beker, "The New Testament View of Judaism," in *Jews and Christians: Exploring the Past, Present, and Future,* ed. James H. Charlesworth, Frank X. Blisard, and Jeffrey S. Siker (New York: Crossroad Publishing Company, 1990), 60–75. For other scenarios of the church and Israel, see Robert T. Osborn, "The Christian Blasphemy," *Journal of the American Academy of Religion* 53 (September 1985): 344–50.

4. Cf. C. E. B. Cranfield, *The Epistle to the Romans, The International Critical Commentary,* ed. J. A. Emerton and C. E. B. Cranfield, vol. 2 (Edinburgh: T. & T. Clark, Limited, 1979), 448; Douglas J. Moo, *The Epistle to the Romans, The New International Commentary on the New Testament,* ed. Gordon D. Fee (Grand Rapids: William B. Eerdmans Publishing Company, 1996), 548–53. Cf. Stephen R. Haynes, "'Recovering the Real Paul:' Theology and Exegesis in Romans 9–11," *Ex Auditu* 4 (1988): 70–84; cf. also Marten H. Woudstra, "Israel and the Church: A Case for Continuity," in *Continuity and Discontinuity: Perspectives on the Relationship between the Old and New Testaments. Essays in Honor of S. Lewis Johnson, Jr.,* ed. John S. Feinberg (Wheaton, Ill.: Crossway Books, 1988), 221–38; Robert L. Saucy, "Israel and the Church: A Case for Discontinuity," in *Continuity and Discontinuity: Perspectives on the Relationship between the Old and New Testaments. Essays in Honor of S. Lewis Johnson, Jr.,* ed. John S. Feinberg (Wheaton, Ill.: Crossway Books, 1988), 239–59.

5. John T. Pawlikowski, *Christ in the Light of the Christian-Jewish Dialogue,* Studies in Judaism and Christianity, ed. Lawrence Boadt et al. (Ramsey, N.J.: Paulist Press, 1982), 137, 122, 148–52. For a critique of Pawlikowski, see Donald Alfred Hagner, *The Jewish Reclamation of Jesus: An Analysis and Critique of the Modern Jewish Study of Jesus* (Grand Rapids: Zondervan Publishing House, 1984), 297–303.

6. There is much on the Christian and Jewish dialogue, e.g., Peter von der Osten-Sacken, *Christian-Jewish Dialogue: Theological Foundations,* trans. Margaret Kohl (Philadelphia: Fortress Press, 1986); James H. Charlesworth, Frank X. Blisard, and Jeffrey S. Siker, eds., *Jews and Christians: Exploring the Past, Present, and Future,* Shared Ground among Jews and Christians: A Series of Explorations, vol. 1 (New York: Crossroad Publishing Company, 1990); David Burrell and Yehezkel Landau, eds., *Voices from Jerusalem: Jews and Christians Reflect on the Holy Land,* Studies in Judaism and Christianity: Exploration of Issues in the Contemporary Dialogue Between Christians and Jews, ed. Helga Croner et al. (New York: Paulist Press, 1992); Eugene J. Fisher, ed., *Visions of the Other: Jewish and Christian Theologians Assess the Dialogue,* Studies in Judaism and Christianity: Exploration of Issues in the Contemporary Dialogue Between Christians and Jews, ed. Helga Croner et al. (New York: Paulist Press, 1994).

7. For a discussion of the views on the relationship between Israel and the church, see Bertold Klappert, *Israel und die Kirche: Erwägungen zur Israellehre Karl Barths,* Theologische Existenz Heute, ed. Trutz Rendtorff and Karl Gerhard Steck, vol. 207 (Munich: Chr. Kaiser Verlag, 1980), 11–37.

8. D. M. Lloyd-Jones, *Romans: An Exposition of Chapter 8:17–39: The Final Perseverance of the Saints* (Grand Rapids: Zondervan Publishing House, 1975), 367–68.

9. Krister Stendahl, *Paul Among Jews and Gentiles and Other Essays* (Philadelphia: Fortress Press, 1976), 4.

10. Translation of biblical texts are mine unless indicated.

11. For Paul's use of Hosea in relation to the church, see W. Edward Glenny, "The 'People of God' in Romans 9:25–26," *BibSac* 152 (January–March 1995): 42–59.
12. Johannes Munck, *Christ & Israel: An Interpretation of Romans 9–11,* trans. Ingeborg Nixon (Philadelphia: Fortress Press, 1967), 107.
13. Rudolf Bultmann, "προγινώσκω, πρόγνωσι," in *Theological Dictionary of the New Testament,* ed. Gerhard Kittel, trans. Geoffrey W. Bromiley, vol. 1 (Grand Rapids: Wm. B. Eerdmans Publishing Co., 1964), 715.
14. Henry Alford, *The Greek New Testament: With a Critically Revised Text: A Digest of Various Readings: Marginal References to Verbal and Idiomatic Usage: Prolegomena: and a Critical and Exegetical Commentary,* 5th ed., vol. 2 (London: Rivingtons, 1871), 424–25; William Sanday and Arthur C. Headlam, *A Critical and Exegetical Commentary on the Epistle to the Romans,* 5th ed., *International Critical Commentary,* ed. S. R. Driver, A. Plummer, and C. A. Briggs (Edinburgh: T. & T. Clark, 1902), 310; James Denney, "St. Paul's Epistle to the Romans," in *The Expositor's Greek Testament,* 3rd ed., ed. W. Robertson Nicoll, vol. 2 (London: Hodder and Stoughton, 1903), 676; John Murray, *The Epistle to the Romans: The English Text with Introduction, Exposition and Notes, The New International Commentary on the New Testament,* ed. F. F. Bruce, vol. 2 (Grand Rapids: Wm. B. Eerdmans Publishing Co., 1965), 67–68; C. E. B. Cranfield, *The Epistle to the Romans, The International Critical Commentary,* ed. J. A. Emerton and C. E. B. Cranfield, 2 vols. (Edinburgh: T. & T. Clark, Limited, 1975–79), 545; Dunn, 38B:636; Moo, 674–75; cf. also Scott Hafemann, "The Salvation of Israel in Romans 11:25–32: A Response to Krister Stendahl," *Ex Audit* 4 (1988): 50.
15. [Jean] Calvin, T*he Epistles of Paul the Apostle to the Romans and to the Thessalonians,* trans. Ross Mackenzie, *Calvin's Commentaries,* ed. David W. Torrance and Thomas F. Torrance, vol. 8 (Grand Rapids: William B. Eerdmans Publishing Company; Edinburgh/London: Oliver & Boyd, 1960), 239–40; Robert Haldane, *Exposition of the Epistle to the Romans: with Remarks on the Commentaries of Dr. Macknight, Professor Moses Stuart, and Professor Tholuck,* 9th ed. (Edinburgh: William Oliphant and Co.; London: Hamilton, Adams, and Co., 1874), 523–24; Charles Hodge, *A Commentary on the Epistle to the Romans,* rev. ed. (New York: Hodder & Stoughton; George H. Doran Company, 1883; reprint, Grand Rapids: Wm. B. Eerdmans Publishing Company, 1954), 353–54; Matthew Black, *Romans,* New Century Bible Commentary, ed. Matthew Black (Grand Rapids: Wm. B. Eerdmans Publishing Company, 1973), 141; Peter Stuhlmacher, *Paul's Letter to the Romans: A Commentary,* trans. Scott J. Hafemann (Louisville, Ky.: Westminster/John Knox Press, 1994), 161–64; Terence L. Donaldson, "'Riches for the Gentiles' (Rom 11:12): Israel's Rejection and Paul's Gentile Mission," *JBL* 112 (spring 1993): 89.
16. For further discussion on the remnant, see Pritz, "Who Is the *Remnant of Israel?*" in this volume.
17. Hodge, 363; Murray, 2:78–79.
18. Sanday and Headlam, 322; Barrett, 214; Cranfield, 2:558; Ernst Käsemann, *Commentary on Romans,* trans. and ed. Geoffrey W. Bromiley (Grand Rapids: William B. Eerdmans Publishing Company, 1980), 305; William Hendriksen, *Exposition of Paul's Epistle to the Romans, New Testament Commentary,* vol. 2 (Grand Rapids: Baker Book House, 1981), 367 n. 308, 368; Joseph A. Fitzmyer, *Romans,* The Anchor Bible, ed. William Foxwell Albright and David Noel Freedman, vol. 33 (Garden City, N.Y.: Doubleday & Company, 1993), 611; Moo, 689–90.
19. Moo, 690.
20. Fitzmyer, 612; Donaldson, *JBL* 112 (spring 1993): 93 n. 50.

21. F. Godet, *Commentary on St. Paul's Epistle to the Romans,* trans. A. Cusin, rev. and ed. Talbot W. Chambers (New York: Funk & Wagnells Company, 1883; reprint, *Commentary on the Epistle to the Romans,* Grand Rapids: Zondervan Publishing House, 1956), 401; Murray, 2:81; Cranfield, 2:562; Dunn, 38B:670; Leon Morris, *The Epistle to the Romans* (Grand Rapids: William B. Eerdmans Publishing Company; Leicester, England: Inter-Varsity Press, 1988), 411; Moo, 693 n. 55; Munck, *Christ & Israel,* 126.

22. Sanday and Headlam, 325; Barrett, 215; Cranfield, 2:563; Dunn, 38B:658; Moo, 694–95.

23. Calvin, 248; Godet, 403–4; Murray, 2:82–84; Fitzmyer, 613.

24. Hodge, 368; Godet, 405–6; Sanday and Headlam, 327; Barrett, 217; Cranfield, 2:568–72; Käsemann, 309; Hendriksen, 2:371; Dunn, 38B:661; Morris, 412; Fitzmyer, 614; Stuhlmacher, 168–69; Moo, 701–2; Philip E. Hughes, "The Olive Tree of Romans xi," *EvQ* 20 (January 15, 1948): 33–45; Munck, *Christ & Israel,* 127–28. The difficulty with this view is that v. 22 states that they could be cut off if they do not remain in the kindness of God. Hence, the Gentile believers could lose their salvation. However, it is suggested that those who are cut off were never a part of the tree (Moo, 707 n. 57) or that Paul is not making reference to individual believers but Gentiles as a people (Calvin, 252–53; Hodge, 370; Godet, 408).

25. J. Dwight Pentecost, *Things to Come: A Study of Biblical Eschatology* (Findlay, Ohio: Dunham Publishing Company, 1958), 468; John F. Walvoord, *The Millennial Kingdom* (Findlay, Ohio: Dunham Publishing Company, 1959), 166–67; John F. Walvoord, *The Prophecy Knowledge Handbook* (Dallas: Dallas Seminary Press, 1990), 452–53; cf., Dale Richard Younce, "An Exegetical Interpretation of the Figure of the Olive Tree of Romans Eleven" (Th.M. thesis, Dallas Theological Seminary, 1963), 7–37, 47–52. This view thinks that it refers to the Gentile people who have a place of blessing with the opportunity of having a relationship to God by faith. This opportunity can be taken away by cutting out the branches as was the case for Israel (v. 22). Hence, the original branches that remain are believing Israelites (9:6) and the remaining Gentile branches are believing Gentiles. Support for this view is the fact that "Gentiles" is mentioned in the context (vv. 11–13) and not believing Gentiles. However, a difficulty with this view is that Paul is addressing Gentile believers in Rome.

26. Possibly many commentators who suggest that this refers to Gentile Christians could be included in this category of Gentile Christendom. Christendom includes believers as well as those who profess Christianity. Hence, those who are "cut off" (v. 22) had a profession of faith but not the reality of conversion. These have never been a part of the tree (Moo, 707 n. 57). The strength of this view is that those who are "cut off" do not lose salvation because they never had it. The weakness of this view is that the text does not speak specifically of Christendom.

27. E. P. Sanders, *Paul, the Law, and the Jewish People* (Philadelphia: Fortress Press, 1983), 195.

28. Wallace states that the subjunctive when used after a temporal adverb or improper preposition (as here) "indicates future contingency from the perspective of the time of the main verb [γέγονεν]." See Daniel B. Wallace, *Greek Grammar Beyond the Basics: An Exegetical Syntax of the New Testament* (Grand Rapids: Zondervan Publishing House, 1996), 479.

29. Sanday and Headlam, 334; Dunn, 38B:679.

30. Barrett, 223; Black, 147; Käsemann, 313; Cranfield, 2:574; Morris, 420; Fitzmyer, 621; Moo, 717 n. 28; Richard Batey, "So All Israel Shall Be Saved," *Int* 20 (April 1966): 221.

31. E.g., Barrett, 223; Käsemann, 313.
32. Fitzmyer, 622.
33. E.g., Cranfield, 2:576; Dunn, 38B:681; Moo, 720.
34. Judith M. Gundry Volf, *Paul and Perseverance: Staying in and Falling Away,* Wissenschaftliche Untersuchungen zum Neuen Testament, ed. Martin Hengel and Otfried Hofius, vol. 37 (Tübingen: J. C. B. Mohr [Paul Siebeck], 1990), 180.
35. Walter Bauer, *A Greek-English Lexicon of the New Testament and Other Christian Literature,* 2nd ed., rev. and augmented by F. Wilbur Gingrich and Frederick W. Danker from Walter Bauer's 5th ed., 1958 (Chicago/London: The University of Chicago Press, 1979), 598; Hendrikus Berkhof, *Christ the Meaning of History,* trans. Lambertus Buurman (Richmond, Va.: John Knox Press; London: SCM Press Ltd., 1966), 145–46; Stuhlmacher, 172; Lloyd Gaston, *Paul and the Torah* (Vancouver: University of British Columbia Press, 1987), 143; reprinted Lloyd Gaston, "Israel's Misstep in the Eyes of Paul," in *The Romans Debate,* rev. and expanded ed., ed. Karl P. Donfried (Peabody, Mass.: Hendrickson Publishers, Inc., 1991), 319.
36. Moo, 720; Gundry Volf, *Paul and Perseverance,* 180.
37. E.g., Alford, 435; Denney, 2:683; Murray, 2:96; Fitzmyer, 623; Munck, *Christ & Israel,* 136; Seyoon Kim, *The Origin of Paul's Gospel,* 2nd ed. rev. and enlarged, Wissenschaftliche Untersuchungen zum Neuen Testament, ed. Martin Hengel and Otfried Hofius, vol. 4 (Tübingen: J. C. B. Mohr (Paul Siebeck), 1984), 84; Morris, 420; Otfried Hofius, "'All Israel Will Be Saved': Divine Salvation and Israel's Deliverance in Romans 9–11 [trans. Judith Gundry Volf]," *Princeton Seminary Bulletin,* Supplementary Issue 1 (1990): 35 ; Gundry Volf, *Paul and Perseverance,* 180–81; Richard H. Bell, *Provoked to Jealousy: The Origin and Purpose of the Jealousy Motif in Romans 9–11,* Wissenschaftliche Untersuchungen zum Neuen Testament, ed. Martin Hengel and Otfried Hofius, vol. 63 (Tübingen: J. C. B. Mohr [Paul Siebeck], 1994), 136.
38. Moo, 720; Gundry Volf, *Paul and Perseverance,* 180–81.
39. For a good discussion of the interpretation of this verse, see Bruce W. Longenecker, "Different Answers to Different Issues: Israel, the Gentiles and Salvation History in Romans 9–11," *JSNT* 36 (June 1989): 95–123.
40. Calvin, 255; Barth, *The Epistle to the Romans,* 416; R. C. H. Lenski, *The Interpretation of St. Paul's Epistle to the Romans* (Columbus, Ohio: Lutheran Book Concern, 1936; reprint, Minneapolis: Augsburg Publishing House, 1961), 725–27; Anders Nygren, *Commentary on Romans,* trans. Carl Rasmussen (Philadelphia: Fortress Press, 1949), 399–400; Hughes, *EvQ* 20 (January 15, 1948): 44–45; Bruce Chilton, "Romans 9–11 as Scriptural Interpretation and Dialogue with Judaism," *Ex Auditu* 4 (1988): 27, 31. Fitzmyer (624) mentions that church fathers such as Irenaeus, Clement of Alexandria, Theodore of Mopsuestia, Theodoret understood it as referring to the elect Jews and Gentiles. Cf. also, Marcus Barth, "One God, One Christ, One People," *Ex Auditu* 4 (1988): 11–19.
41. Murray, 2:96; Fitzmyer, 624.
42. John Albert Bengel, *Gnomon of the New Testament,* 2nd ed., trans. rev., and ed. by Andrew R. Fausset, trans. James Bryce, vol. 3 (Edinburgh: T. & T. Clark, 1859), 154–55; Hendriksen, 2:381–82; Berkhof, *Christ the Meaning of History,* 146; Charles M. Horne, "The Meaning of the Phrase 'And Thus All Israel Will Be Saved' (Romans 11:26)," *JETS* 21 (December 1978): 333–34; Anthony A. Hoekema, *The Bible and the Future* (Grand Rapids: William B. Eerdmans Publishing Company, 1979), 140–47. Fitzmyer (624) mentions that church fathers such as Origen and Augustine as well as most of the commentators from the fifth to the twelfth centuries held this view. Cf. Marcel Dubois, "Jews, Judaism and Israel in the Theology of Saint Augustine—

How He Links the Jewish People and the Land of Zion," in *People, Land and State of Israel: Jewish and Christian Perspectives,* ed. Malcolm Lowe, *Immanuel* 22–23 (1989): 162–214, esp. 182–85.

43. Murray, 2:97.
44. Murray, 2:97; Cranfield, 2:576–77; Gundry Volf, *Paul and Perseverance,* 182.
45. Godet, 411; Sanday and Headlam, 335; Munck, *Christ & Israel,* 136; Barrett, 223–24; Käsemann, 313; Murray, 2:98; Cranfield, 2:577; Dunn, 38A:681; Gundry Volf, *Paul and Perseverance,* 182–84; Fitzmyer, 623.
46. Heinrich August Wilhelm Meyer, *Critical and Exegetical Handbook to the Epistle to the Romans,* 2nd ed., trans. John C. Moore and Edwin Johnson, trans. rev. and ed. William P. Dickson, Critical and Exegetical Commentary on the New Testament, vol. 2 (Edinburgh: T. & T. Clark, 1884), 234–35; Karl Ludwig Schmidt, *Die Judenfrage im Lichte der Kapitel 9–11 des Römerbriefes,* Theologische Studien, ed. Karl Barth, vol. 13 (Zollikon-Zürich: Evangelischer Verlag, 1943), 37–41; Bell, *Provoked to Jealousy,* 136–45. Cranfield (2:576 n. 5) also cites Aquinas as holding this view.
47. Hofius, *Princeton Seminary Bulletin,* Supplementary Issue 1 (1990): 35–36; Bell, *Provoked to Jealousy,* 140–41; Sanday and Headlam, 335–36.
48. Cranfield, 2:577; Dunn, 38B: 681–82; Gundry Volf, *Paul and Perseverance,* 185; Moo, 723.
49. Moo, 723.
50. Ibid.
51. Bell, *Provoked to Jealousy,* 141–42; Christopher D. Stanley, "'The Redeemer Will Come ἐκ Σιών: Romans 11:26–27 Revisited," in *Paul and the Scriptures of Israel,* ed. Craig A. Evans and James A. Sanders, Journal for the Study of the New Testament Supplement Series, ed. Stanley E. Porter, vol. 83 (Sheffield: JSOT Press, 1993), 136–42.
52. Wright thinks this is not referring to the second coming of Christ. Rather he suggests that Paul is talking about the inclusion of the Gentiles in to the people of God in the present age which is composed of both Jews and Gentiles. See N. T. Wright, *The Climax of the Covenant: Christ and the Law in Pauline Theology* (Minneapolis: Fortress Press, 1992), 249–51; N. T. Wright, "Romans and the Theology of Paul," in *Society of Biblical Literature 1992 Seminar Papers,* ed. Eugene H. Lovering, Jr., Society of Biblical Literature Seminar Papers Series, no. 31 (Atlanta: Scholars Press, 1992), 207. However, in Rom. 11:26 Wright needs to redefine Israel as the people of God which Murray correctly states, "that it is exegetically impossible to give to 'Israel' in this verse any other denotation than that which belongs to the term throughout this chapter" (Murray, 2:96).
53. From apocalyptic and rabbinic sources, Allison demonstrates that there will be repentance when the day of the Lord is ushered in, Dale C. Allison, Jr., "Romans 11:11–15: A Suggestion," *Perspectives in Religious Studies* 12 (spring 1985): 23–30.
54. Vanlaningham thinks that may well occur several years before Christ returns in order to allow time for Israel's conversion. See Michael G. Vanlaningham, "Romans 11:25–27 and the Future of Israel in Paul's Thought," *The Master's Seminary Journal* 3 (fall 1992): 164–70, esp. 170.
55. Krister Stendahl, *Paul among the Jews and Gentiles and Other Essays,* 4. See also an article titled "Christ's Lordship and Religious Pluralism" in Krister Stendahl, *Meanings: The Bible as Document and as Guide* (Philadelphia: Fortress Press, 1984), 233–44, esp. 243–44; cf. also 205–31. In fact, Stendahl suggests that Paul was not converted to Christianity but had a call to minister to the Gentiles. This goes against

that Jews needed to be converted to Christianity, but if he were living today, he would
have modified his view towards the two-covenant theory. See E. P. Sanders, "Paul's
Attitude toward the Jewish People," *Union Seminary Quarterly Review* 33 (spring
& summer 1978): 185; E. P. Sanders, *Paul, the Law, and the Jewish People* (Philadelphia: Fortress Press, 1983), 197.

56. Franz Mussner, *Tractate on the Jews: The Significance of Judaism for Christian Faith*,
trans. Leonard Swidler (Philadelphia: Fortress Press, 1984), 34, cf. 28–36, 146.

57. Gaston, *Paul and the Torah*, 148; reprinted Gaston, "Israel's Misstep in the Eyes of
Paul," in *The Romans Debate*, 324.

58. John H. Gager, *The Origins of Anti-Semitism: Attitudes Toward Judaism in Pagan
and Christian Antiquity* (New York: Oxford University Press, 1983), 261.

59. Gager, *The Origins of Anti-Semitism*, 262. Cf. also Paul M. van Buren, *A Theology
of the Jewish-Christian Reality*, part I, *Discerning the Way* (San Francisco: Harper
& Row, Publishers, 1980), 27–67, 184–201; Bertold Klappert, "Traktat für Israel
(Römer 9–11): Die paulinische Verhältnisbestimmung von Israel und Kirche als
Kriterium neutestamentlicher Sachaussagen über die Juden," in *Jüdische Existenz
und die Erneuerung der christlichen Theologie: Versuch der Bilanz der christlich-
jüdischen Dialogs für die Systematische Theologie*, ed. Martin Stöhr, Abhandlungen
zum christlich-jüdischen Dialog, ed. Helmut Gollwitzer et al., vol. 11 (Munich: Chr.
Kaiser, 1981), 58–137; Paul M. van Buren, *A Christian Theology of the People of
Israel*, part II: *A Theology of the Jewish-Christian Reality* (New York: Seabury Press,
1983), 1–42, 268–83, 320–52; Pinchas Lapide, "The Rabbi from Tarsus," in *Paul:
Rabbi and Apostle*, written by Pinchas Lapide and Peter Stuhlmacher, trans. Lawrence
W. Denef (Minneapolis: Augsburg Publishing House, 1984), 51; Paul M. van Buren,
"The Church and Israel: Romans 9–11," *Princeton Seminary Bulletin*, Supplemen-
tary Issue 1 (1990): 8, 11, 14–17; Sidney G. Hall III, *Christian Anti-Semitism and
Paul's Theology* (Minneapolis: Fortress Press, 1993), 85–130.

60. For a discussion of avoiding the extremes of replacement theology and two-covenant
theology, see Halvor Ronning, "The Land of Israel—A Christian Zionist View," in
People, Land and State of Israel: Jewish and Christian Perspectives, ed. Malcolm
Lowe, *Immanuel* 22–23 (1989): 120–32; cf. also Geert H. Cohen Stuart, "The Atti-
tude of the Netherlands Reformed Church to Israel: People, Land and State," in
People, Land and State of Israel: Jewish and Christian Perspectives, ed. Malcolm
Lowe, *Immanuel* 22–23 (1989): 146–61.

61. Alan F. Segal, "Paul's Experience and Romans 9–11," *Princeton Seminary Bulletin*,
Supplementary Issue 1 (1990): 56–70, esp. 61–67, 69; Alan F. Segal, *Paul the Con-
vert: The Apostolate and Apostasy of Saul the Pharisee* (New Haven/London: Yale
University Press, 1990), 276–84; cf. Peter Stuhlmacher, "Paul: Apostate or Apostle?"
in *Paul: Rabbi and Apostle*, written by Pinchas Lapide and Peter Stuhlmacher, trans.
Lawrence W. Denef (Minneapolis: Augsburg Publishing House, 1984), 25–26; Gerd
Theissen, "Judentum und Christentum bei Paulus: Sozialgeschichtliche Überlegungen
zu einem beginnenden Schisma," in *Paulus und das antike Judentum: Tübingen-
Durham-Symposium im Gedenken an den 50. Todestag Adolf Schlatters (†19. Mai
1938)*, ed. Martin Hengel and Ulrich Heckel, Wissenschaftliche Untersuchungen zum
Neuen Testament, ed. Martin Hengel and Otfried Hofius, vol. 58 (Tübingen: J. C.
B. Mohr [Paul Siebeck], 1991), 339 n. 17; Karl Kertelge, "Biblische Theologie im
Römerbrief," in *New Directions in Biblical Theology: Papers of the Aarhus Conference, 16–19 September 1992*, ed. Sigfred Pedersen, Supplements to Novum Testamentum, ed. A. J. Malherbe, D. P. Moessner, et al., vol. 76 (Leiden: E. J. Brill, 1994),
56.

62. Hagner, *The Jewish Reclamation of Jesus*, 301; Sanders, *Paul, the Law, and the Jewish People,* 192–99; Wright, *The Climax of the Covenant*, 252–57.

63. Heikki Räisänen, "Paul, God, and Israel: Romans 9–11 in Recent Research," in *The Social World of Formative Christianity and Judaism: Essays in Tribute to Howard Clark Kee*, ed. Jacob Neusner, Peder Borgen, Ernest S. Frerichs, and Richard Horsley (Philadelphia: Fortress Press, 1988), 190.

64. Cf. Hafemann, *Ex Auditu* 4 (1988): 54.

65. Bernhard W. Anderson, "The Bible as the Shared Story of a People," in *The Old and New Testaments: Their Relationship and the "Intertestamental" Literature*, ed. James H. Charlesworth and Walter P. Weaver (Valley Forge, Pa.: Trinity Press International, 1993), 35.

66. Traugott Holtz, "The Judgment on the Jews and the Salvation of All Israel: 1 Thess. 2:15–16 and Rom. 11:25–26," in *The Thessalonian Correspondence*, ed. Raymond F. Collins, Bibliotheca Ephemeridum Theologicarum Louvaniensium, vol. 87 (Leuven: Leuven University Press, 1990), 292.

67. Hofius (*Princeton Seminary Bulletin*, Supplementary Issue 1 [1990]: 36–37) suggests that "all Israel will be saved" refers specifically to the time of Christ's return when Israel will hear the gospel directly from the mouth of Christ. Hence, Israel will not be saved by the preaching of the gospel by the church. Rather Israel will have a direct encounter with Christ at that time, similar to Paul's encounter with Christ on the Damascus road. He opposes the "special way" and suggests a "special day" and by "special means." However, this seems to be special pleading.

68. Günter Wagner, "The Future of Israel: Reflections on Romans 9–11," in *Eschatology and the New Testament: Essays in Honor of George Raymond Beasley-Murray*, ed. W. Hulitt Gloer (Peabody, Mass.: Hendrickson Publishers, Inc., 1988), 110.

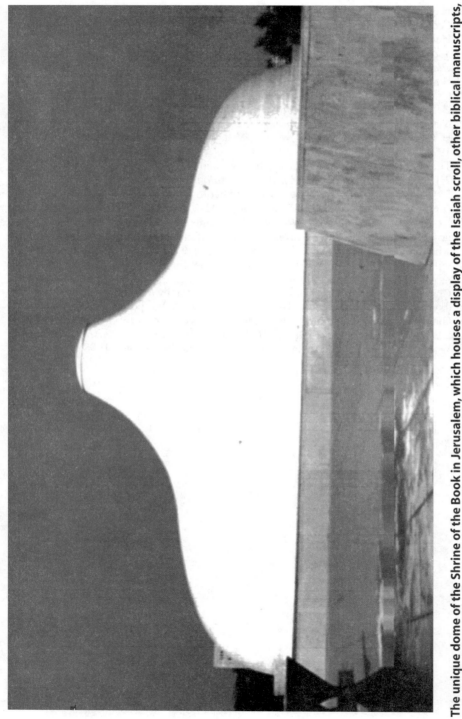

The unique dome of the Shrine of the Book in Jerusalem, which houses a display of the Isaiah scroll, other biblical manuscripts, and the Dead Sea Scrolls.

CHAPTER SEVEN

A NEW COVENANT—AN ETERNAL PEOPLE (JEREMIAH 31)

Ralph H. Alexander

The questions of Israel's right to the land, the rule of Jerusalem, and the definition and place of the Jewish people have been before the world for centuries. Yet the Hebrew prophets, like Jeremiah, have spoken clearly to these issues. Jeremiah 31 declares that (1) the nation of Israel will most definitely be restored to the land promised to her forefathers, (2) the Jewish people will be as permanent as God's laws of nature—an eternal people, and (3) Jerusalem will be holy to God for eternity.

God will also provide for Israel a New Covenant, better than the Mosaic Law, whereby sins may be forgiven once and for all by the Messiah, Yeshua, and whereby they will be enabled to live according to the righteous principles of the Law.

What a marvelous message of hope and encouragement!

THE SETTING OF JEREMIAH 31 (30:1–31:1)

The setting of Jeremiah's message of hope[1] in chapters 30–31 is not stated with certainty, but the context, especially 32:1–2, may imply that Jeremiah was writing these encouraging words at the very time the Babylonians were besieging Jerusalem prior to its fall in 586 B.C. If so, this message would have been a tremendous encouragement to the nation of Judah in Jeremiah's day, and this manifesto of hope continues to be a blessing to the nation of Israel and to all believers unto this day and into the future. The importance of this prophetic proclamation led Yahweh to request that Jeremiah write all the words of this singular message in a book so that both his contemporaries, as well as those in Israel at later times, might not forget the message but be able to ponder its wonderful truths (30:2).

As part of this larger unified message of hope, it is necessary to understand the context and argument of chapter 30 in order to understand the argument of chapter 31. Jeremiah 30:1–3 sets forth the central theme of these two chapters: the restoration of a unified Israel and Judah to the land which Yahweh gave to their forefathers to possess.[2] This restoration would be perceived as imminent by both Israel and Judah.[3] The northern kingdom of Israel had gone into Assyrian captivity in 722 B.C., and Judah's captivity in Babylon was soon to come. The restoration in view, therefore, would most likely be understood by Jeremiah's contemporaries as the return of both Israel and Judah from their respective exiles. Though many of the concepts throughout both chapters are encouraging and apply to Judah's return from Babylon in the latter part of the sixth century B.C., the restoration of both parts of the nation in a unified way, as recounted in these chapters, would not occur until the end times, or the "latter days" (cf. 30:24–31:1; 31:27, 29, 31, 33, 38).

To understand the necessity for such a restoration and to grasp its miraculous and encouraging nature, God reviewed through Jeremiah the status of Israel and Judah prior to Yahweh's gracious restoring of their fortunes. Because of the iniquities of both nations, Yahweh will bring upon them a future day of great trouble and sorrow[4]—a time of panic, no peace, and overwhelming fright such as Jacob has never known.[5] No day has ever existed like it (30:5–7a), which is another argument for placing the final application of this passage at the end time. The encouraging announcement, however, is that Jacob will be delivered from this horrible day (30:7b–9) as Yahweh breaks the bondage of Jacob's captors. With that release the combined nation of Israel and Judah will no longer serve foreign oppressors but, instead, will serve Yahweh their God and David their king, the Messiah,[6] whom Yahweh will raise up for them.

Such a marvelous promise from Yahweh calls for Jacob to be encouraged rather than to fear and be dismayed. Though Yahweh will have disciplined Jacob, it is also Yahweh who will destroy all the nations where He has scattered Jacob's descendants. The result will be that Israel and Judah will be delivered from these distant captive lands in order to live undisturbed and securely in the land of Israel (30:10–11).[7] Israel's punishment for her many sins had left her like one with an incurably diseased wound. Her detestable condition caused all of her previous "lovers" (nations),[8] who had cared for her in the past, to now forget her. There was no one to plead her case (30:12–15a). While this punishment has come from Yahweh, He reassures Jacob that it is He who will also bring retribution in kind upon Israel's adversaries: those who devoured Jacob will be devoured; those who took the nation into captivity will be taken into exile; and those who plundered and spoiled it will be plundered and spoiled (30:16). Yahweh will heal Jacob's wound so that the nation will no longer be declared an outcast (30:17).

So, declared Jeremiah, Yahweh's restoration of Jacob from captivity is imminent! Out of Yahweh's compassion He will rebuild Jacob's dwelling places in the land. Certainly Jacob's descendants will be full of joy and thanksgiving (30:18–19a). When they return to the land Yahweh will multiply the people as He previously had and honor them once again with significance (vv. 19b–20).[9] The prince and ruler of the people will come forth boldly from their midst as Yahweh's Messiah (30:21).[10] Jacob will once again live in covenant relationship with Yahweh as His people, and Yahweh will once again be their God (30:22)! The final restoration will be at the end of days when Yahweh's wrath will have accomplished its intended purpose against the wicked so that this restoration might take place. At that time Jacob will discern clearly the full import of this message (30:23–24).

THE CERTAINTY OF ISRAEL'S FUTURE RESTORATION (31:1)

Jeremiah 31:1 continues the emphasis on the restoration of Israel with significant stress on its time, and the fact that it is the authoritative message of Yahweh. "In that time" refers directly to the phrase "in the end of days"[11] of 30:24. The events in chapter 31 will occur specifically during that period of "the end of days." This phrase clearly points to a time at the end of "Jacob's day of trouble" when God will restore His people Israel to their land one last time—an event that appears to be still future since no day like "Jacob's great day of trouble" (30:7) has yet occurred. In addition to the events of Jeremiah transpiring at the end of time, the prophecy likewise emphasizes a time when "all the families" (or tribes) of restored Israel will enter into a final covenant relationship with Yahweh.[12] The Hebrew emphasizes that the covenant relationship in 30:22 is upon Yahweh (notice the emphatic אָנֹכִי, 'ānokî, "I," in the context of a ruler being raised up in the relationship). The stress in 31:1 is upon the people (notice the emphatic הֵמָּה, hēmmâ, "they") and covenant relationship. While the covenant relationship emphasis of Jeremiah 30:22 is more upon a theocratic government that will once again be instituted with Yahweh as Israel's ruler and suzerain, 31:1 tends to stress the necessity for restoration so that the people of Israel might be able to enter again, once and for all, into covenant relationship with Yahweh as their ruler. So the prophecies of Jeremiah 31 focus on the end of days when the covenant relationship with Yahweh is renewed with the entire nation, culminating in their experience of God's promised blessings forever.

The promises in Jeremiah 31 are not just wishes. Twelve times in Jeremiah 30 and twenty times in chapter 31 the authority of this message is stressed with phrases like "an utterance of Yahweh" and "thus says Yahweh." With such an emphasis throughout the two chapters, it becomes quite clear that Yahweh wants it known that these promises of hope and encouragement are definitely from Him, and they will most surely be realized according to His authority.

Following these introductory emphases in Jeremiah 30 and 31:1, Jeremiah structures the remainder of his message in chapter 31 into three parts. God reassures each nation of the divided kingdom of Israel concerning its respective part in the restoration: first, the northern kingdom of Israel in verses 2–22, then Judah in verses 23–26, then concluding the rest of the chapter with Yahweh's promises of blessing upon a united Israel in the final return to the land (27–40).

THE RESTORATION OF ISRAEL (31:2–22)

It may seem unusual that God reassures the northern kingdom of Israel about their part in the restoration. However, while many prophecies of restoration stress the return of Judah from Babylon, there are fewer announcements about Israel's return from her Assyrian exile. Yet the northern kingdom was the larger part of divided Israel, and she must be included in the final restoration of the latter days. Jeremiah 31:2–22 is one of the Scriptures that argues this most strongly. Though the name *Jacob* is employed twice within verses 2–22, the dominant names for the nation in these verses are "Israel," "Samaria," or "Ephraim"—all of which argue for this section being given over primarily to the discussion of the northern kingdom.[13] The name *Judah* is not used in these verses. However, in verses 23–26 the message of restoration focuses on the land of Judah with "Judah" as the dominant name employed.[14] This section, therefore, seems to specifically rehearse the return of Judah. Jeremiah 31:27 begins the final section of Jeremiah's message by speaking of the house of Israel and the house of Judah together and announcing Yahweh's promises of blessing upon the entire nation of Israel throughout the balance of the chapter.

Restoration Grace (31:2–6)

Israel's promised restoration is likened to a second wilderness wandering in which Israel, a nation which has survived the sword of her oppressors, will find grace when she finally takes the initiative to gain rest for herself (v. 2).[15] The imagery of the desert not only brings back memories of Israel's first wilderness experience of discipline in the Sinai but also carries the connotations of desolateness. The northern kingdom certainly experienced the abandonment and discipline of the desert of God's judgment, and were it not for God's marvelous grace of restoration, that kingdom would not ultimately survive. It is necessary, however, that Israel, the subject of the infinitive absolute הָלוֹךְ, *hālok*, ("go" or "went"), take the initiative[16] to decide to go and seek rest for herself (v. 2b). A prerequisite for restoration is that the people return to Yahweh.

In the past[17] Yahweh has revealed Himself to Israel[18] as a loving God whose "everlasting love" will never end (v. 3). That love has been specifically expressed to God's people in the term חֶסֶד (*hesed*), *lovingkindness*, a strong word for God's love manifested especially toward Israel through the benefactions of God's covenants with her. *Hesed* is as close to the concept of *grace* as any term in Hebrew Scriptures.[19] Israel is privileged to be in a covenant relationship with Yahweh,

and because of this relationship, she experiences the manifold grace and blessings of God—especially when she is obedient to His covenants. It was God's
grace that brought Israel out of Egypt in her early history (Deut. 7:8) and into
the land of Canaan (Neh. 9:19). It was Yahweh's great parental compassion for
Israel that caused Him to yearn for her to return to Him when she sinned against
Him (Hos. 11:1–11). Now Yahweh once again continues[20] this same everlasting
grace and covenant compassion toward Ephraim by demonstrating His love again
and again in the restoration.

First, God's love will be manifested by rebuilding the "virgin Israel" (v. 4a).
Two images are employed here. *Virgin* implies purity before union in relationship. Describing Israel with this term implies that Israel will be cleansed and
purified prior to her restoration back into a covenant relationship with Yahweh
(cf. Jer. 18:11–17; 31:21; Lam. 1:15; 2:13). In Jeremiah's commission he was
instructed to announce punishment with the words *uproot, tear down, destroy,*
and *overthrow.* He was also to proclaim restoration with the words *build* and *plant*
(Jer. 1:10; cf. Deut. 28:63 and Jer. 31:28). So God's love in the restoration will
"again" "build" Israel, implying the physical as well as spiritual rebuilding of
the country which will occur.[21] Building activity, of course, assumes a stable future which will be guaranteed by the restoration.

Second, Yahweh's love will "again" enable Israel to make merry and celebrate
with dancing because Yahweh will decorate the "virgin" Israel with tambourines
(or cymbals/timbres) so that she might celebrate her victories, especially in the
restoration (v. 4b).[22] Yahweh gives Israel something to be merry about, and she
will respond by festively celebrating what Yahweh has done in her restoration.

Third, the stable future of Israel in the restoration will once "again" provide a
basis for agricultural prosperity (v. 5). In the restoration farmers will "plant" (cf.
Jer. 1:10) vineyards on the hills of Samaria so that they will become commonplace once more.[23] All of this building, planting, and celebrating implies that there
will be a day in the "latter days" (cf. 30:24 and 31:1 supra.) when watchmen will
cry out their announcements in Mount Ephraim, calling the Israelites to arise in
order that they might go up to Zion (v. 6).[24] This means that the Israelites from
the previous northern kingdom will return once more to worship Yahweh their
God at the temple mount in Jerusalem. At that time it will be safe to return to
Zion; moreover Yahweh will desire Israel's worship of Him in the renewed covenant relationship.

Restoration Joy and Praise (31:7–14)

In light of these manifestations of Yahweh's everlasting grace for Israel in her
restoration, Yahweh exhorts Israel to celebrate with shrill cries and shouts of gladness[25] because Jacob will become the head of the nations as God's chosen people
(v. 7).[26] Some may feel that this statement implies pride, but it is simply a declaration of the importance of what Israel was chosen to be when God created her

(cf. Exod. 19:5–6 in light of Gen. 12:2–3). Yahweh calls Israel with imperatives to cause others to hear about His coming deliverance and restoration of her by giving praise and declaring: "O Yahweh, cause to deliver our people, the remnant of Israel!" (v. 7b). Though the nation of Israel has suffered decline in exile, there is still a remnant whom Yahweh will return to the land. With only a remnant, how can Yahweh be so bold as to call upon Israel to make proclamations such as these? He answers in verses 8–9 with a series of verbs emphasizing restoration.[27] Yahweh wants all to know that He is about to bring Israel back from the land of the north (Assyria) and gather her from the farthest reaches of the earth, that is, from all other places where she has been scattered (v. 8a). All Israelites will be included, even those handicapped such as the blind, lame, pregnant women, and those giving birth. No one will be left behind for any reason. When Yahweh restores Israel to her land, she will no longer be a remnant, but she will be a great assembly of people (v. 8b). She will be "the head of the nations." When Israel returns, the people will do so with hearts of contrition, crying most likely for their previous sins while at the same time weeping with joy because of Yahweh's grace in bringing them back (v. 9a). They will make supplication to Him for such marvelous grace at that time.[28] Consequentially Yahweh will gently bring them along straight and smooth paths with streams of water, caring for them so that they will not stumble (v. 9b). Such care and concern in the return journey to the promised land will be a manifestation of Yahweh's fatherly love of Ephraim (Israel), His firstborn (v. 9c; cf. the definitive statement in 1 Chron. 5:1–2).

Therefore, Yahweh exhorts the Israelites to declare this wonderful news among the nations, even as far as the distant islands (vv. 10–11).[29] The message is clear and simple: Yahweh, the one who scattered Israel among the nations in exile, will gather her, and will now guard and protect His "flock" as a shepherd (v. 10b). In the ancient Near East a nation was closely tied to its god. What happened to a given people reflected on the character and nature of their god. Yahweh, Israel's God, had allowed Himself to look weak and uncaring by scattering His people in judgment. In reality He was being just and righteous. Now, however, Yahweh will show Himself strong and caring by regathering Israel and caring for her once again as a good shepherd cares for His flock (cf. Ezek. 34:5–6, 11–16; Jer. 23:9–10; John 10). All the nations will see and recognize that Yahweh is God and that He surely cares for His people. He will protect them from future oppressors.

This regathering and shepherding is not arbitrary. It is based rather upon Yahweh's ransom and redemption of Israel from the hand of nations stronger than she (v. 11).[30] In the future Israel will be in a weakened state because of her many years in exile, so unless Yahweh supernaturally redeems her from these stronger oppressors, Israel will never be delivered and restored to her land.[31] Likewise, only with Yahweh's strength will Israel be protected from these foreigners. Therefore, the truth of Israel's marvelous restoration needs to be proclaimed to the nations because Yahweh's love has redeemed and ransomed her out of the grip of stronger nations. This will be a strong witness to the nations of Yahweh's love for Israel.

The joy of the restoration event appears unrestrainable. It arises in these chapters because the truth of God's restoration of His people is such marvelous and wonderful news! So Yahweh again calls Israel to come and rejoice in the temple over the refreshment that Yahweh's goodness will provide in the promised land (vv. 12–14). This invitation implies the future unification of the nation since Israel is being called to go and give victory cries *on the height of Zion*. Zion is in Jerusalem. The temple is located on this mountain. Yahweh wants Israel to come to the temple area and radiate Yahweh's goodness manifested especially in the prosperity of the land (v. 12a). Grain, fresh wine, oil, young lambs, and calves will refresh the people's souls like a well-watered garden (v. 12b). The experience of such bountiful blessings will cause the people to beam[32] about Yahweh's goodness since they will never again become faint from hunger (v. 12c).[33]

Every age level will be happy—the young virgins, the young men, and the elders—everyone together (v. 13a). Their mourning will turn into rejoicing as Yahweh's comfort and encouragement results in happiness rather than their exilic grief and sorrow (v. 13b).[34] The priests will once again be "saturated" with abundance (14a). The text actually states that the priests will be saturated with fat, which implies that the people will once again obediently bring their offerings to the priests (cf. Lev. 1:8; 3:3–4, 9–10, 14–16; 4:8–10, 19–20, 26, 31, 35).[35] This means that the Israelites will be obeying the Mosaic covenant by offering appropriate sacrifices in those future days. Not only will they be obedient, but they will also be able to offer sacrifices because of Yahweh's blessings upon both their flocks and herds. No wonder God's people will be satisfied with Yahweh's goodness toward them (v. 14b; cf. v. 12a), and no wonder that they will be rejoicing with exceeding gladness!

Present Mourning Turns to Future Joy (31:15–22)

On the contrary, a somber note of present reality is struck in verses 15–20. Yes, the future will be a time of great rejoicing over God's goodness demonstrated in the restoration with all of its blessings and benefits. But what about the present? Look at Israel's current condition, which only brings sorrow and misery. Jeremiah pictures Israel's situation in his day as Rachel weeping over her children at Ramah (v. 15), refusing to be comforted. Ramah, approximately five miles north of Jerusalem, was the location where the Judean exiles were gathered before their deportation in 586 B.C. (cf. Jer. 40:1; Josh. 18:25; Josephus, *Antiquities*, 8, 12, 3).[36] Though the emphasis in this section of Jeremiah 31 is on Israel's restoration, the imagery of this event at Ramah, which was directly related to the exile of Judeans, only demonstrates that the restoration of Israel and Judah cannot be completely separated. Rachel was the mother of Joseph and

Benjamin. Joseph's two sons were Ephraim and Manasseh, so the stress is still upon the northern kingdom as Ephraim is also emphasized in the following verses of 18–20. Jeremiah is painting a picture of the bitter weeping of the mothers of Israel as their sons went into Assyrian captivity in 722 B.C. Rachel, in the imagery, is weeping intensely for her children, the descendants of Israel. She is refusing to be comforted since they no longer exist as a nation. That was the condition of the nation in Jeremiah's day.

In response, Yahweh reassures Rachel, or Israel in the present case, to restrain her crying (v. 16a): Don't weep! But why shouldn't she? Yahweh replies by declaring that Rachel (and Israel) should have hope because her "work," implied in the context to be her weeping and concern for the Israelite exiles, will be rewarded when the exiles return from the land of their enemies (v. 16b).[37] The current misery will be changed and alleviated in the future restoration when Rachel's children return to the borders of their own land. There is hope for the future (v. 17)! What a wonderful encouragement! In the promises of God there is always hope for Israel's future. This promise is underscored with God's stamp of certainty— "an utterance of Yahweh."

The family imagery moves to one of a father and son. Yahweh is portrayed as the father and Ephraim (Israel) as the son. God has heard Ephraim's grievous repentance and confession (vv. 18–19). Ephraim bemoans his condition for Yahweh has disciplined him as if he were an untrained calf. Such severe correction has come because of the nation's turning from Yahweh and His commandments. In Ephraim's repentance, he requests help from God. He rightly recognizes that without the help of God no one can turn from his sins. So he asks that Yahweh would cause him to turn from his sin for the purpose that he might turn.[38] Since Yahweh is Ephraim's God, Ephraim knows that God can enable him to turn (v. 18). As Ephraim returns to Yahweh, he will also repent (v. 19a). Repentance is possible only when one fully recognizes sin, confesses it to God, and then makes the decision to turn from it. Yahweh will make Ephraim's sin known to him, and when He does, Ephraim will repent. But knowledge of one's past sins, when acknowledged in confession, not only leads to repentance but also leads to remorse, shame, and humiliation (v. 19b).[39] In Ephraim's case, he began to bear "the reproach of my youth," that is, all the sins of the northern kingdom that caused exile by Assyria. He had been a reproach among the nations and in turn caused Yahweh to be dishonored among the nations. The burden of such reproach laid heavy upon Ephraim (the northern kingdom of Israel), bringing genuine remorse, shame, and humiliation.

Whenever one returns to God in contrition with confession, repentance, and genuine remorse, Yahweh always responds positively according to His character and word (v. 20). On the one hand Ephraim (Israel) will repent concerning his past sins as a kingdom; on the other Yahweh reminds us rhetorically that Ephraim is His precious son, a delightful boy (v. 20a; Hos. 11:1). What a marvelous

A stone carving of the Ark of the Covenant being carried on a wheeled vehicle, discovered in Capernaum on the north side of the Sea of Galilee.

Overlooking the Sea of Galilee.

Fishing boats moored along the Sea of Galilee.

The upper Jordan River north of the Sea of Galilee.

Looking toward the Sea of Galilee from the traditional site of the Sermon on the Mount.

Stormy waves on the Sea of Galilee.

A grinding stone from Capernaum.

A species of lily, the Crown Daisy, from Mount Gilboa.

Overlooking the site of ancient Pergama.

Waterfalls in northern Galilee at the headwaters of the Jordan River.

Cana of Galilee.

A coastal view of modern Tel Aviv.

Modern sailboats at harbor in Tel Aviv.

The Roman aqueduct at Caesarea, which carried water from Mount Carmel.

A hillside in the area of Nazareth.

A view of Bethlehem.

Working the fields with a horse-drawn plow.

Grain harvest near Shiloh.

The valley of Elah, site of the confrontation between David and Goliath.

A Bedouin encampment in the area of Dibon, east of the Dead Sea.

Herding sheep in the Negev.

The modern site of ancient Bethany.

Lachish, to the west of Hebron, an Amorite city prior to Joshua's conquest and later fortified by Rehoboam.

The Temple Mount, looking east toward the Mount of Olives.

The Temple Mount, from the southeast.

Along the Via Delorosa in Jerusalem.

The Pool of Siloam, reservoir for the water tunnel constructed by Hezekiah to bring water from the Gihon spring.

Israeli soldiers in the Old City.

Praying at the Western Wall. A partition screen separates men and women in accordance with Orthodox practice.

The interior of the Dome of the Rock, which covers the threshing floor purchased by King David.

Steps going down to the pool of Bethesda, by the Sheep Gate on the northeast of the Temple Mount.

The tombs of Zecharia (right) and Beit-hezir (left), monuments built by priestly and aristocratic families at the foot of Mount Zion in the Kidron Valley dating from the first century B.C. to the first century A.D.

The road from Jerusalem to Jericho.

A camel market at Beer-Sheba in the Negev.

Masada on the western shore of the Dead Sea, the last stronghold to fall to the Romans in A.D. 73, where almost one thousand Jewish inhabitants chose to take their own lives rather than surrender.

A floor mosaic from an inner chamber at Masada.

Looking eastward from Masada toward the Dead Sea.

One of the enormous cisterns which supplied Masada with water.

A pool of water at En Gedi on the western side of the Dead Sea.

The caves of Qumran where the Dead Sea Scrolls were discovered in 1947.

The mountains of the Sinai Peninsula, an area occupied by Israel in the Six-Day War of 1967 but returned to Eygpt in 1982 in accordance with the Camp David Accords.

demonstration of Yahweh's gracious and forgiving perspective! Father-son relationships cannot be destroyed—not even by sin. Yahweh explains that though He has often spoken against Ephraim, Yahweh has continually remembered him.[40] He cannot forget His own son (v. 20b; Hos. 11:2–9). He loves him! Yahweh's inner being, like a father, has a tremendous deep-felt compassion and sympathy for Israel (v. 20c).[41] He will forgive! Therefore, God's great love for Israel, "His son," will cause Yahweh to restore the father-son relationship in the future and with it restore Israel to the land of promise. Once again this truth is accentuated by the strong phrase of authority, *an utterance of Yahweh!*

Therefore, because of Yahweh's fatherly compassion toward Israel's repentance, there is no reason to weep and mourn now. Rather, Yahweh calls Israel to turn back to a relationship with Yahweh and return to the land of Israel with joy and purity (vv. 21–22). Yahweh challenges Israel to set up clear signposts that will clearly point her way back to the land (v. 21a).[42] Israel is to make a decision and decisively set her heart to follow that highway, the very way she went into captivity (v. 21b; Isa. 11:16; cf. Jer. 6:16).[43] "Return, O virgin of Israel," commands Yahweh. "Return to these your cities" (v. 21c). Once again Yahweh reminds Israel that like a virgin she must be pure and therefore cleansed (as though she never sinned) before she may return to her true lover, Yahweh (cf. Jer. 31:4 comments; 18:11–17). This imagery is augmented by the phrase, "How long will you go hither and thither, O apostate daughter" (v. 22a). Israel was, and is, like an apostate daughter rather than a virgin bride. She cannot return to Yahweh in an unfaithful condition. Therefore she must become cleansed so she will be like a pure virgin again in order to enter into an intimate covenant relationship with Yahweh in the latter days. When she does, a new thing will occur. Israel will be as a female who will surround a man (22b).[44] While this latter phrase has been interpreted in many different ways,[45] some commentators feel the meaning is totally obscure.[46] While dogmatism cannot be maintained in the interpretation of this phrase, one should seek, it seems, to interpret the phrase in light of the context. The context is employing female imagery for the nation of Israel's return to Yahweh with the use of words like *virgin* and *apostate daughter*. These terms convey a move from impurity and waywardness as a daughter to purity and faithfulness as a virgin in order to return to an intimate covenant relationship with Yahweh. The phrase "a female will surround a man," therefore, may portray the sense of Israel, as a female, surrounding, or protecting,[47] this New Covenant relationship she will have with her strong warrior man—a figure perhaps for Yahweh.[48] This desire to protect her relationship with Yahweh, now that she once again is restored to it, will definitely be a *new thing* in Israel's history.

Therefore, the northern kingdom of Israel should prepare herself to return to Yahweh in purity and joy as He likewise restores her to the promised land and an intimate covenant relationship with Him. Yahweh's love for her is everlasting, demonstrated in both the imagery of a lover for His bride as well as a father for

His son. Out of His great compassion for Israel, Yahweh will restore her to Himself and to the land and pour out upon her the covenant blessings and benefits. Naturally this will be a time of great joy and rejoicing on Israel's part. It will be a brand new occurrence in Israel's history.

THE RESTORATION OF JUDAH (31:23–26)

The mighty Lord of Armies, who will restore the northern kingdom of Israel to Himself, will likewise do the same for the kingdom of Judah. In Jeremiah's day Judah was on the brink of being taken captive to Babylon. Jeremiah had announced this discipline over and over again. But now he proclaims future hope and blessing upon Judah as he did upon Israel. When Yahweh restores Judah from their captivity in the end of days, a word of blessing will be spoken again throughout the cities of Judah (v. 23a): "Yahweh will bless you, O righteous abode, O holy mountain!" (v. 23b). The phrase *holy mountain* is frequently used of the temple mount in Jerusalem (cf. Ps. 2:6; 43:3; Isa. 66:20). When Yahweh restores Judah to her land, the temple mountain (or Zion), the place where Yahweh is worshipped, will once again become a righteous dwelling for Yahweh (cf. Isa. 1:21).[49] Here Judah will return and worship Yahweh together with Israel (cf. v. 12), and Yahweh's presence, in turn, will bless Jerusalem and the temple so that they will once again be righteous and holy in those days.

Judah and all her cities, along with her farmers and ranchers, will once again dwell together on their own land just like Israel will in Samaria (v. 24; cf. v. 5). When Yahweh restores Judah to her land, He likewise will cause these captives of seventy years in Babylon, who are tired and faint from hunger, to be refreshed ("drink one's fill") and filled (v. 25). He will make the land so productive that there will be abundance of drink and food so that everyone will be satiated. Judah will enjoy the fruits of God's blessings upon the land in those days. She will be completely rejuvenated by them.

Jeremiah then awakes from his "prophetic sleep" (vision) and sees that his sleep was beautiful and pleasant to him (v. 26; cf. Zech. 4:1). These visions that Jeremiah has seen have been wonderful encouragements of restoration hope for Israel and Judah. Nothing could be more gratifying and magnificent to Jeremiah at this moment in Judah's history. But his excitement will only increase because Jeremiah will now have the exhilaration of declaring the marvelous blessings Yahweh will bestow upon this restored and united Israel in the end times.

RESTORATION BLESSINGS (31:27–40)

With the restoration fully proclaimed, its supernatural accomplishment explained, its character portrayed, and the response of both Israel and Judah described, Yahweh now proceeds to enumerate the blessings He will shower upon His restored people in the land following the restoration of the end of days (vv. 27–40). The recipients of these blessings will be both the "house of Israel" *and* "the house of Judah," the future united kingdom of Israel (27b; cf. Hos. 1:11; Ezek. 37:15–28).[50] These blessings will be poured out in the future, though those end days are presented once again as imminent (v. 27a).[51] By verifying each of these blessings with an authoritative prophetic confirmation, *an utterance of Yahweh*, Yahweh certifies His divine promise to perform each blessing.[52]

Repopulation of the Land (31:27–30)

Yahweh's first blessing will be to repopulate the land (v. 27c). The land will have been deprived of its Israelite and Judean population because of the Assyrian and Babylonian captivities as well as future dispersions of the Jews. Yahweh will "sow" the restored united kingdom with both the seed of mankind as well as the seed of animals (cf. Ezek. 36:8–12 and Hos. 2:23). A great assembly of people will return, as argued in verse 8. This will be an elaboration of the concept of "plant" foretold by Jeremiah (1:10; cf. v. 28). It is part of the rebuilding of the nation that God will accomplish in the restoration.

As Yahweh had been faithful to fulfill Jeremiah's commission (given in 1:10) to discipline His people, so He will be just as faithful and watchful to bless them by planting them and building them once again in the land through restoration (v. 28).[53] God's greatest delight is to rebuild and replant His people in the promised land, not to discipline them through tearing them down and uprooting them.

When the covenant people are restored and replanted in Canaan, they will recognize that the chastisement they have experienced was not just because their "fathers" had sinned, but they also sinned. In the end of days everyone will realize that they are individually responsible for their own sin. An old proverb declared, "Fathers eat grapes and their sons' teeth become blunt."[54] This proverb was used to convey the idea that a son suffers for the actions of his father. The son is supposedly receiving the blunt teeth though his father ate the grapes. This was not fair. The people of Israel applied this saying to their present discipline. They reasoned that they were being chastened because their forefathers had sinned. Yahweh was not fair and just. Yahweh is clarifying in these verses that the use of this proverb and the improper meaning drawn from it is invalid (vv. 29–30; cf. a similar discussion in Ezekiel 18). Just as the wrongs of a father do not bring penal consequences to his son, so the iniquity of a man causes only himself to die, not his son. Though Yahweh will restore His people to the land, they will still be individually (and corporately) accountable for their own acts, especially their sins against God. Others cannot be blamed. This principle will be true in the latter days, as it was in the time of Jeremiah and Ezekiel and is today.[55]

New Covenant Blessing (31:31–34)

One of the greatest blessings ever promised in the Scriptures—the New Covenant—is declared in Jeremiah 31:31–34. This promised covenant will be made (literally "cut")[56] by Yahweh with a united Israel in the "coming days"[57] of the end times (v. 31; cf. Ezek. 36:24–28; 37:15–28). The combined houses of Israel and Judah will be the recipients of the New Covenant, partners with Yahweh in this agreement. However, since Israel's vocation is to be "a blessing to the world" (Gen. 12:3) by being "a kingdom of priests and a holy nation" (Exod. 19:6), the future blessings of the New Covenant will be experienced by all who will trust in the sacrifice of Jesus, the mediator of the New Covenant (Heb. 8:6; 9:11–15, 28; 10:14).

Yahweh makes it clear that this is a new covenant not like the old covenant that Yahweh made with their fathers when He brought Israel out of Egypt. That former covenant was the Mosaic covenant, given on Mount Sinai as the constitution of the nation of Israel when God created the nation. That covenant was "holy, righteous, and good," as Paul declares in Romans 7:12. Following the Mosaic covenant enabled the children of Israel to live as God meant, and thereby become a holy nation (Exod. 19:6). This covenant was for their own good (Deut. 10:13), and its observance demonstrated their love for Yahweh (Deut. 10:12). The Mosaic covenant seems to have followed the pattern of the international suzerain-vassal treaty of Moses' day, portraying Yahweh as the great suzerain, or king, and Israel as His vassal.[58] Yahweh was the Lord and Master of His people in a genuine theocracy. The weakness of the Mosaic covenant lay with the vassal, the people of Israel. They could make the choice to obey or disobey the stipulations of the covenant. Unfortunately, throughout most of Israel's history, they chose to rebel against God's way given in the Mosaic covenant. Jeremiah emphasizes that *they*, not Yahweh, broke Yahweh's covenant.[59] Even though Yahweh was "a husband," or perhaps more clearly, "a master" or "suzerain"[60] over them, they still, even as His vassals, chose to disobey Him.[61]

The text makes a contrast between Yahweh ("I") and Israel ("they").[62] *Yahweh* was their lord, but *they* broke the covenant (cf. Deut. 31:16–20; Lev. 26:14–15; Isa. 24:5; Jer. 11:10; Ezek. 44:7). As the stipulations of the New Covenant imply, the old covenant did not inherently provide internal power and motivation to live according to the righteous demands of that law. The inherent weakness of that old covenant lay in the weakness of sinful people who sought to follow the good principles but regularly found themselves unsuccessful due to their own sinful nature and lack of internal power to implement God's ways (cf. Paul's struggle in Rom. 7:7–25). As a consequence of their continual failure, both Israel and Judah found themselves in bondage to foreign nations in Jeremiah's day (cf. the consequences enumerated in the Mosaic covenant for continual disobedience to its demands in Deut. 28:36–41, 58–68). Therefore, the only ultimate hope for Israel (and for us all) was for Yahweh to institute a new and better covenant.

Having pointed out the need for a New Covenant, Yahweh described the essential characteristics of the New Covenant in verses 33–34. First, the New Covenant is future. It will be enacted "after those days," that is, the days after Israel is restored, the future time of "the end of days" as set forth in Jeremiah 30:24 and 31:1, 31 (v. 33a). Second, in the New Covenant Yahweh's law (another term for the old covenant) will be internalized so that God's people might be better able to keep the righteous stipulations (v. 33b).[63] The internalization process will be done by Yahweh Himself as He "writes" His torah upon their hearts. In doing so, He will place the righteous principles of the Mosaic covenant in their "inner part" (v. 33c). This "writing" of the law upon the heart is in contrast to the writing of the Mosaic covenant upon tablets of stone, as Paul so vividly argues in 2 Corinthians 3:2–3 (cf. Heb. 8:10; 10:16; and Rom. 2:15 with Exod. 34:27; Deut. 4:13; 5:22; 10:1–2; 31:9; 32:15). Under the New Covenant, God's law will be internalized so that its enactment will come from within rather than from without. It also needs to be observed that the internalization process is corporate, that is, "in *their* midst or inner part" and "*their* heart." The torah will be placed within God's people, Israel, and, of course, then within each individual Israelite who believes. The Holy Spirit is also internalized under the New Covenant according to Ezekiel 36:26–27, and it is the indwelling Holy Spirit who internalizes the Mosaic covenant in the heart (Ezek. 36:27). Through the inward endowment of the Holy Spirit (cf. Rom. 8:9; 1 Cor. 2:11–15), believers under the New Covenant will be empowered to follow the righteous requirements of the law (Rom. 8:4). This clarifies that the old covenant was not a bad covenant for as Paul states, it was holy, righteous, and good (Rom. 7:12). The Israelites were simply unable to keep that covenant because of their sinful nature. The point Jeremiah and the author of Hebrews (Heb. 8:6) make is that the New Covenant is a better covenant because of the internalization of God's righteous ways, Christ's death once and for all for sin (see v. 34), and the enablement of the Holy Spirit from within. Second Corinthians 3 argues that the indwelling of the Holy Spirit in all who believe (when the New Covenant is instituted) will empower these people of God to reflect God's glory and minister for Him by living according to God's righteous principles as set forth in the Mosaic covenant (cf. Exod. 19:5–6 and 1 Peter 2:5, 9). The New Covenant incorporates the righteous principles of the Mosaic covenant by internalizing them.[64]

When 2 Corinthians 3, Acts 2, and Hebrews 7:22; 8:6–13; 9:15; 12:24 are compared with the prophecies of Joel 2:28–29, Jeremiah 31:33–34, and Ezekiel 36:26–27, it becomes evident that the New Covenant was instituted with the death of Christ on the cross and the outpouring of the Holy Spirit in Acts 2. The full appropriation of this New Covenant by the nation of Israel is still future, as argued by Jeremiah 31. But for both Israelite and Gentile believers since the time of Christ's sacrifice for sin, the New Covenant has become the covenant under which they live in covenant relationship with the Lord. This covenant relationship, described in Jeremiah 31:1, is enabled by the institution of the New Covenant as expressed at the end of verse 33 with the familiar covenant formula, "I will become their God, and they will become my people" (cf. comments above on v. 1).[65] Israel's restored covenant relationship with Yahweh at the "end of days" is part of the promised blessing of the New Covenant.

Under the New Covenant all will know Yahweh from the least to the greatest (v. 34a; cf. chapter 6 by Harold Hoehner in this volume). To know often implies a personal relationship with Yahweh in Old Testament Scriptures (cf. Deut. 4:35, 39; Jer. 24:5–7; Ezek. 34:25–31). The people of God (in this case, Israel) will no longer need to teach one another (their neighbor or brother) by exhorting them to know Yahweh because all of them will know Yahweh ("me"; cf. Rom. 11:26).[66] The second כִּי (ki, *for*) of verse 34, which introduces the last phrase, is the key to understanding what is meant by "know Yahweh." One of the greatest truths of the New Covenant is that Yahweh will forgive their iniquity (Israel and all else who believe) and remember their sin no more.[67] All sin will be forgiven once and for all, and this will be accomplished by the sacrificial death of Christ on the cross as He mediates and institutes the New Covenant (cf. Heb. 9:11–15, 25–26). Because of Christ's forgiveness on the cross, it is possible for all people to know God under the New Covenant. Forgiveness has no favorites. It is available for all ages, whether they are considered great on the societal scale or are the least among mankind. Among the people of God, forgiveness will have been accomplished once and for all so all who believe will then know God and need no longer exhort each other to know Him. The particle כִּי (ki, *because*) states the reason why all will know Yahweh.[68] It is only because He will have forgiven their iniquity and will remember their sin no more.

Matthew 26:27–28 and Luke 22:20 both declare that in the observance of the Lord's table the cup is the blood of the New Covenant. Christ is the mediator of the New Covenant (Heb. 8:6), and His shed blood was necessary for the covenant to be enacted.[69] Likewise both Romans 11:11–27 and Ephesians 2:11–13 tell us that Gentiles are included in the benefits of the New Covenant where sin is forgiven once and for all. In light of these passages it is clear that all believers in Christ since His salvific work, Jew or Gentile, are also participants and partners in the New Covenant and live under its guidance, just as the nation of Israel will do in the future when they turn to Yahweh and are restored to their land.[70] The New Covenant has been instituted at the cross and Pentecost (as noted above). It will be appropriated by Israel as a nation at the time of their future restoration to the land as described in these chapters of Jeremiah.

An Eternal People (31:35–37)

Just as the New Covenant is eternal and permanent because it is conditioned only upon God, likewise the existence of Israel as a nation is eternal and permanent (vv. 35–37). As an additional encouragement Yahweh promises that the New Covenant will be made with an eternal people. God uses the physical ordinances of His creation as the basis of His argument for permanence (v. 35). He points out that in the creation of Genesis 1, He established the sun, moon, and stars to provide permanent light by day and night, respectively. Likewise, the Yahweh of armies,[71] the great and powerful God that He is, stirs the sea so that waves roar. These ordinances are permanent and never change.[72] Therefore, if[73] one is able to cause any of these ordinances to cease,[74] then, and only then, would the descendants of Israel cease from being a nation before Yahweh for all days, that is, for eternity (v. 36). Obviously the sun, moon, and stars, along with the power of God to create waves, will not cease unless God ceases—a clear impossibility. Therefore, the eternal perpetuity of the nation of Israel is certain! Many peoples and nations, even to the present, have attempted to eliminate the nation of Israel, but all in vain. None have been successful, and no one ever will be because God clearly promises here that Israel will never cease to exist as a nation.

In order to reinforce this truth, Yahweh employs another illustration and comparison. If anyone can measure the heavens above or search out the earth's foundations below, then Yahweh[75] will reject all of Israel's descendants because of all that they have done (v. 37).[76] Israel has certainly done many things contrary to Yahweh's commands. They have rebelled over and over again against Him and deserve to be eternally punished and banished forever. But Yahweh's love and blessing upon them is sure. They will exist forever, and He cannot reject them any more than a human is able to measure the heavens or search out the foundations of the earth. Those two tasks are humanly impossible. Likewise, by analogy, it is divinely impossible for Yahweh to reject His chosen people, Israel. This people with whom Yahweh will enter the New Covenant will exist forever as a nation. This is accentuated once again by the repeated divine phrase of authority—*the utterance of Yahweh!*

Jerusalem's Permanent Holiness (31:38–40)

The final blessing that will come to restored Israel when they enter into the covenant relationship with Yahweh in the end of days is the permanence of Jerusalem as holy to Yahweh (vv. 38–40). Jerusalem will be rebuilt. Though the name Jerusalem *per se* is not used in the text, הָעִיר (ha'ir, *the city*) definitely refers to Jerusalem in light of the description which follows (v. 38a). The city that is described is Jerusalem. Jeremiah begins at the northeast corner of the city as it was known in his day and follows the wall of the city in an apparent counter-clockwise direction. The tower of Hananel is at the northeast corner (v. 38b; cf. Neh. 3:1; 12:39; Zech. 14:10). The description moves next to the corner gate (cf. 2 Kings 14:13; 2 Chron. 26:9). Though the specific location of the corner gate is not certain, the destruction of the wall mentioned in 2 Kings 14:13 was most likely the northern wall of the city, which was the most vulnerable. John Bright feels that the corner mentioned was the northwest corner.[77] The "measuring line" stretches out unto the hill of Gareb and then to Goah (v. 39), both unknown landmarks biblically, though the topography would tend to place a hill more to the northwest.[78] The next topographical marker is the valley of carcasses and fat ashes (v. 40a), which most likely refers to the

Hinnom valley on the west side of Jerusalem, known as the valley where garbage
and trash of all kinds were burned (cf. 2 Kings 23:10). This would, of course,
continue the counter-clockwise movement around the city that is furthered by
descriptions of the terraces (or fields) one would pass as the measuring line moves
toward the Kidron valley on the east and to the Horse gate. The Kidron valley is
certainly well known as the natural eastern boundary of Jerusalem. Nehemiah 3:28,
together with the rest of the description of the rebuilt wall of Nehemiah's day (Neh.
3:15–32; cf. 2 Chron. 23:15), clearly places the Horse gate on the eastern wall of
the city as well. So, though somewhat sketchy, the general counter-clockwise
description of Jerusalem's wall is given so that the reader might know plainly that
Jerusalem is the city described in this passage. The most salient truths about
Jerusalem, however, are given at the end of verse 40. Jerusalem at the end of days
will once again be holy to Yahweh (cf. Ezek. 45:1; 48:35)! Once again Yahweh's
people Israel will dwell in the land of blessing in a covenant relationship with
Yahweh. Jerusalem will be their place of worship once more, and thereby it will
be holy to Yahweh (cf. Isa. 44:26). In addition, its permanence is declared even as
the perpetuity of Israel as a people was stressed (cf. vv. 35–37). Jerusalem will
never be plucked up nor torn down again—forever (cf. v. 28). This does not mean
that Jerusalem would not experience destruction and war throughout history, which
has occurred from the time of the Babylonian captivity until the present. The point
is that Jerusalem will never again be destroyed after God's people are restored to
the land at the end of days. Jerusalem and Israel will exist as Yahweh's special place
and people forever.

CONCLUSION

Jeremiah 31 presents a wonderful message of hope to the people of Israel and
Judah at the time of Jeremiah. Though both nations will experience captivity and
suffering due to their rebellion against Yahweh's righteous ordinances, both nations will be restored by Yahweh Himself to the land of blessing at the end of
days. Yahweh's everlasting love will ultimately draw them back to Himself and
make all the provisions whereby they might be restored. In turn this will mean
repentance on the part of Israel and Judah with resulting cleansing in order to
prepare them to reenter a covenant relationship with Yahweh. Once Yahweh restores them to Himself and to the land, He will shower them with His many blessings. The land will once again be fruitful and prosperous, and Yahweh will
repopulate the land with His people. They will genuinely be rebuilt and replanted
in the land. Yahweh will enter into a New Covenant with them, a covenant which
is better than the Mosaic covenant. The principle of the Mosaic covenant will be
internalized by Yahweh through His Holy Spirit so that they might fulfill the righteous requirements of the law as God meant them to do. This, in turn, will enable them to be a kingdom of priests and a holy nation that is a blessing to the
world in accordance with Yahweh's purposes for them. In the New Covenant

Yahweh will make provisions for the forgiveness of iniquity once and for all. All sin will be remembered no more because the mediator of the New Covenant, the Messiah, will sacrifice Himself for all sin (cf. Isa. 52:13–53:12). God's people will then know Yahweh in the covenant relationship for which they were created. Yahweh will also bless His people with eternal existence and with a permanent place of worship, holy Jerusalem—forever.

God definitely has a purpose for His people Israel that is clearly set forth in Jeremiah 31. What a blessed and wonderful God He is!

DISCUSSION QUESTIONS

1. Why were Israel and Judah in a condition that required restoration?

2. How and when will the restoration of Israel and Judah occur?

3. How is God's grace manifested toward Israel in Jeremiah 31?

4. Set forth the characteristics of the New Covenant and explain how and when the benefits of this covenant relate to the nation Israel and also to believers today.

5. How does Jeremiah declare the nation of Israel to be an eternal people?

ENDNOTES

1. The "Book of Hope" (Jer. 30–31) has been structured in different ways. Two profitable and beautiful outlines may be found in Charles Augustus Briggs, *Messianic Prophecy* (New York: Charles Scribner's Sons, 1895), 246–57, and Bernard Anderson, "The New Covenant and the Old Testament" in *Old Testament and Christian Faith*, ed. Bernard W. Anderson (New York: Harper and Row, 1963), 229, 230, especially n. 11.
2. Cf. the original promise is in Gen. 12:7, repeated in Gen. 15:7–19, 28:13, and Israel first begins to experience the initial possession of the land in the conquest of Canaan described in Joshua.
3. "Behold the days are about to come . . ." (Jer. 30:3) is reflecting the use of the future instans participle. Likewise, the prophets frequently present the future "Day of the Lord" as "near," that is, they perceive it as an event which could occur at any time.
4. For a discussion of various interpretations see Charles L. Feinberg, "Jeremiah," *The Expositor's Bible Commentary*, vol. 6, Frank E. Gaebelein ed. (Grand Rapids: Zondervan Publishing House, 1986), 560.
5. "Jacob" is the name which Jeremiah consistently uses in chapter 30 for the combined nations of Israel and Judah, cf. vv. 4, 7, 10, 18.
6. Cf. Hos. 3.5; Ezek. 34:23ff., 37:24–25.
7. שָׁקַט often has the concept of *respite from war*, as in Josh. 11:22; 14:15; Judg. 3:11, 30; 5:31; and 8:28. Also cf. Jer. 46:27–28.

8. Cf. Ezek. 16 and 23 and Hos. 1 where both Israel and Judah are portrayed as adulterous women seeking foreign nations as lovers instead of Yahweh their God.

9. Cf. discussion in William L. Holladay, "Jeremiah 2," *Hermeneia: A Critical and Historical Commentary on the Bible,* ed. Paul D. Hanson (Minneapolis: Fortress Press, 1989), 177–78.

10. Cf. Mic. 5:2. Cf. Feinberg's discussion of this messianic prediction in some detail in "Jeremiah," 564.

11. בְּאַחֲרִית הַיָּמִים is best translated "the end of days" (cf. NASB "latter days"). The phrase is used twelve times in the Old Testament with clear indications of the still future end times. Balaam prophecies a future ruler and king, a star from Jacob, the Messiah who will come (Num. 24:14ff.); Moses speaks of the future restoration when Israel obediently seeks God with their whole heart and soul (Deut. 4:30); Isaiah 2:2 and Micah 4:1 use the phrase of the time when the mountain of Yahweh's temple will become the chief among mountains; Ezek. 38:16 describes Gog's invasion of the land of Israel just prior to the millennial age (see discussion in Ralph H. Alexander, "Ezekiel," *The Expositor's Bible Commentary*, vol. 6, Frank E. Gaebelein, ed. [Grand Rapids: Zondervan Publishing House, 1986], 932); Israel seeks their God and David their king as they return to their land in the end of days according to Hos. 3:5; and Daniel's vision of the "end of days" is clarified as a vision of days yet future (Dan. 10:14). This phrase clearly points to a future time at the end of days following the great day of Jacob's trouble—a day not yet realized.

12. The importance of covenant relationship with Yahweh as Israel's God began with the promises to Abraham (Gen. 17:8) and then to Israel through Moses in passages like Exod. 6:7, 29:45, and Lev. 26:12. Yahweh would dwell among Israel in an intimate way as their God while they would be His people. Israel's vocation was to be a special treasure to Yahweh and to represent Him to the world and the world to Him as a kingdom of priests and a holy nation (Exod. 19:5–6; cf. Deut. 7:6; 14:2, 21; 26:18–19). This meant that Israel was to obey their God so that they might represent Him correctly as His people (Deut. 27:9). In Israel's history they frequently failed to do this, so their covenant relationship was broken when they broke the Mosaic covenant in disobedience. The renewal of covenant relationship implies that Israel once again obeys Yahweh and follows His ways. This will occur only when Israel returns and seeks Yahweh in faith and obedience followed by Yahweh's restoration of His people to Himself and to their land of blessing as promised in the Abrahamic Covenant. The prophets continually proclaim this important truth of future covenant renewal (cf. Jer. 7:23; 11:4; 13:11; 24:7; 31:33; 32:8; Ezek. 11:20; 14:11; 34:24; 37:23, 27; Zech. 2:15; 8:8).

13. Vv. 2, 4–7, 9–10, 18, 20–21.

14. Vv. 23–24.

15. Though the nouns and pronouns are masculine, the normal English gender for a nation is feminine.

16. Hiphil infinitive construct of רנע.

17. There are two interpretations of the word מֵרָחוֹק as reflected in various translations: a temporal concept as "in the past" or "long ago" (NIV, NEB, NJV) and a spatial perspective in "from afar" (RSV, JB, NASB). Together with the use of עוֹד in vv. 4–5 (with the meaning of *again*) (cf. R. Laird Harris, ed., *Theological Wordbook of the Old Testament*, vol. 2 [Chicago: Moody Press, 1980], 648, which states that the term has a "sense of repetition and permanence" and here can have the nuance of a past or present event in the sense of "again") and the context that demonstrates the renewed manifestations of Yahweh's previous love, the temporal meaning seems to fit more appropriately. (Cf. Holladay, 180, for his argument for a temporal usage.)

18. The MT reads לִי *to me*. This would refer to Jeremiah as the recipient of the "appearance" which may well be the case. Contextually it would seem perhaps better to see the appearance as to Israel in which case the masculine singular pronominal suffix should be used. The LXX reads αὐτῷ (*to him*) which reflects a Hebrew reading of לֹו (*to him*). A waw and a yod may be easily confused in scribal activity, in which case the word might be read לֹו *to him* implying Israel. The NIV interestingly translates *to us* which has no textual base.

19. Cf. Ronald B. Allen, "Affirming Right of Way on Ancient Paths," in *BibSac* (January–March, 1996).

20. מָשַׁךְ means to *draw out*, or, in this passage, *continue*.

21. עֹוד has the meaning of *again* in vv. 4 and 5 (see n. 17).

22. Women dancing with tambourines or cymbals was one way of celebrating military victories (cf. Exod. 15:20; Judg. 11:34; 1 Sam. 8:6).

23. חִלְּלוּ in the Piel means *profane* or *commonplace*. The sense here is that vineyards will become so plentiful that they will once again be commonplace in Samaria. There is no reason to try to alter the text to the root הלל for *praise*. Undoubtedly the farmers will be praising God for the good vineyards, but the MT meaning of "commonplace" makes good sense in the context. Cf. John Bright, "Jeremiah: A New Translation with Introduction and Commentary," *The Anchor Bible*, vol. 21 (Garden City, N.Y.: Doubleday & Company, Inc., 1985), 281.

24. The particle of existence, יֵשׁ, *there is,* means that the day will exist. Time is determined from the context.

25. The two verbs רָנּוּ (*cry victoriously*) and צַהֲלוּ (*cry shrilly*) express great joy, excitement, and praise.

26. Holladay implies that this is the only instance of רֹאשׁ (*head*) in the meaning of *chief* of the nations in the Old Testament (Holladay, 184). In the context this usage appears to fit well.

27. מֵבִיא (*bring*), קַבֵּץ (*gather*), שׁוּב (*return*), יָבֵל: (*bear along*), הָלַךְ; (*go*).

28. The Heb. בְּתַחֲנוּנִים (*supplication for favor*) clearly conveys making supplication specifically for favor/grace.

29. Three verbs are employed to emphasize the proclamation: שִׁמְעוּ, הַגִּידוּ אִמְרוּ, respectively stressing the importance to *listen, to cause* (hiphil) *to declare,* and *to say.*

30. Isa. 48:20, 21 elaborates on Yahweh's redemption of Judah from Babylon, a similar redemption to that of Israel mentioned in our verses here. Israel's redeemer (גֹּאֵל) is the Holy One of Israel (cf. Is. 41:14; 44:6, 22–23; 49:25–26; Jer. 50:34; Ps. 25:22 [פָּדָה, *redeem*]; 107:1–3). This redemption and ransoming is not an issue of spiritual deliverance from sin, though there will certainly be confession of sin and returning to Yahweh (cf. v. 9). Rather this is a physical redemption and ransom of Israel from foreign lands—a redemption which is only possible by the almighty God!

31. Certainly the recent wave of immigration into Israel from Europe following the Nazi Holocaust is a clear demonstration of this truth.

32. נָהֲרוּ means to *be radiant*. Yahweh's goodness will cause the Israelites to beam because they are so joyous over His provisions of blessing, just as God's goodness should have its similar effect in our lives.

33. Cf. Holladay, 186, for the meaning of דָּאֲבָה (*be anxious, concerned*). Cf. the usage in v. 25.

34. The verbs רִוֵּיתִי (*saturate*) שִׂמַּחְתִּים (*be happy*) נִחַמְתִּים (*comfort*) הָפַכְתִּי (*turn*) are all perfects used as prophetic perfects in this context.

35. MT is וְרִוֵּתִי נֶפֶשׁ הַכֹּהֲנִים דָּשֶׁן (*I will satisfy the priests with abundance*).

36. For a more complete discussion of the locations of Ramah and Rachel's association with the town, cf. Feinberg, 571–72, n. 15.

37. The context implies future. The actual word employed, יֵשׁ (*there is*), implies existence.

38. The cohortative form וְאָשׁוּבָה (*I will surely return*) with the waw following an imperative, הֲשִׁיבֵנִי (*restore me*), introduces a telic clause.

39. "Slapping the thigh," סָפַקְתִּי עַל־יָרֵךְ, is a gesture of remorse in the ancient Near East (cf. Ezek. 21:17).

40. The preposition, בְּ, is translated as either *against* or *of* by interpreters of this text. Both are legitimate translations. Context is the determining factor. Since the context is one of discipline upon Israel and her ultimate repentance that results from that punishment, it seems to this author best to render the preposition as *against*. Others, however, think otherwise (cf. the translation of "of" in Bright, 282).

41. The concept of compassion is strongly expressed in this last phrase of v. 20. מֵעַי (*my inner parts*) refers to Yahweh's inner being from which issues groaning or murmurs of compassion. Francis Brown, S. R. Driver, and Charles A. Briggs, *Hebrew and English Lexicon of the Old Testament* (Oxford: At the Clarendon Press, 1968), 242, declares that the verb הָמוּ (*murmur*) when used together with מֵעַי conveys the "thrill of deep felt compassion or sympathy." In addition, the use of the infinitive absolute in רַחֵם אֲרַחֲמֶנּוּ (*I will have great compassion for him*) places emphasis upon Yahweh's compassion for Ephraim.

42. The two terms employed in the text are צִיֻּנִים and תַּמְרוּרִים which mean *guide, signpost, monument* and *high tree or guidepost* respectively. In the context these two terms are synonymous with the apparent sense of sign-posts.

43. The phrase דֶּרֶךְ הָלָכְתִּי could be translated *a way you went* or *a way you go*, implying respectively either the way the Israelites went into captivity or the way they will return. The latter seems a bit redundant. It seems better to render the phrase as *the way you went*, meaning the way the Israelites used when they went into exile, rather than *the way you go* which implies the way they are returning during the restoration.

44. This particle here seems to imply an explanation. It is introducing an answer to Yahweh's rhetorical challenge: "How long will you continue to go here and there, O faithless daughter?"

45. For summaries of various interpretations see Feinberg, 571, and Holladay, 192–95.

46. Cf. Bright, 282.

47. שבב may have the meanings *to move around protectively* and *to shelter* according to Ludwig Koehler and Walter Baumgartner, *The Hebrew and Aramaic Lexicon of the Old Testament*, vol. 3 (Leiden: E.J. Brill, 1996), 739.

48. Ronald B. Allen, in personal conversation, suggests that with the use of clearly sexual terminology (בתולה, *virgin;* נקבה, *female*) for the woman instead of the normal אישה (*woman*) perhaps סבב (*surround*) might be understood as an imagery of sexual embrace, finally consummating the marriage union of Yahweh and Israel (cf. New Testament imagery).

49. The phrase נְוֵה־צֶדֶק (*abode of righteousness*) is used in Jer. 50:7 in reference to Yahweh Himself. Bright, 282, sees the reference in our passage as a title of Yahweh (as well as translating the phrase holy mountain as "the holy One"—another title of Yahweh), and on this basis he concludes that "the temple mountain seems to be intended." The phrases make perfect sense as references to the temple mountain alone, though the Jer. 50:7 usage for Yahweh does lend weight to the fact the temple mount is where Yahweh is visually represented among Israel and therefore worshiped.

50. Cf. Ezek. 37:15-28 and the commentary in Alexander, *Ezekiel*, 926–28.

51. The phrase הִנֵּה יָמִים בָּאִים (*behold days are coming*) is a future instans participial phrase expressing an event which is viewed as about to happen. The "days" are the same "days" mentioned in Jer. 30:24 and 31:1—the future end of days. It must be remembered that the prophets' primary concern is not the exact time of the prophesied events, but the general time that the promised restoration, in this case, will occur. The future is anything after the present, whether far or near. Jeremiah is presenting the end of days as imminent as if they were almost ready to occur. That is how certain the restoration is viewed.

52. Jer. 31:27–28, 31–34, 36–38.

53. The root שָׁקַד expresses "alertness" (*TWOT*, vol. 2, 952) or "watchfulness" to either benefit or injure (*BDB*, 1052; cf. Jer. 44:27 and Dan. 9:14). Cf. the noun שָׁקֵד *almond tree*, in Jeremiah's call in Jer. 1:10–12.

54. The proverb is based upon the problem that eating grapes with seeds often wore down the teeth, making them blunt.

55. בַּיָּמִים הָהֵם (*in those days*), refers to the same time period as v. 27 and 30:24 and 31:1— the end of days.

56. כָּרַתִּי is a prophetic perfect indicating the future certainty of this action as if it were already complete.

57. Note that the phrase הִנֵּה יָמִים בָּאִים (*behold days are coming*) is the same chronological notice as that found in v. 27. Note the discussion on p. 171 and in note 11.

58. Cf. Meredith Kline, *The Treaty of the Great King* (Grand Rapids: Wm. B. Eerdmans Publishing Company, 1963).

59. The pronominal afformative on בְּרִיתִי (*my covenant*) is a resumptive pronoun reinforcing the fact that this was "*my* covenant," the *my* referring to Yahweh. This would also certainly imply that the covenant was good.

60. The use of the verb בָּעַלְתִּי (*I was a husband*) emphasizes the concepts of "master" and "lordship," or "suzerain." Yahweh was their suzerain, the senior partner in the covenant (cf. the discussion in Holladay, 198). In addition the preposition בְ in בָּם (*over them*) has the meaning of *over* or in *charge of* in the passage (see David A. Clines, *Dictionary of Classical Hebrew*, vol. 1 [Sheffield: Sheffield Press, 1993], 287).

61. הֵפֵרוּ is a hiphil form of פרר (violate, frustrate, or break), which stresses the initiative of the subject, which in this case is *they*, or Israel.

62. Emphasis is made by the use of the independent personal pronouns in addition to the inherent subject within the verbal forms. These pronouns are placed in parallel contrast to one another.

63. It is literally "my" torah in reference to Yahweh in the context.

64. It is the righteous spiritual principles of the Law that are incorporated into the New Covenant. Exod. 25:8, 40 state that the portions of the Mosaic Covenant in Exod. 25–40 and Lev. 1–27 are "patterns" or "models" and when the reality of the patterns comes (in Christ), the patterns are made obsolete. Num. 35:31 demonstrates that capital offense crimes may be "released" or "ransomed" (כפר) by a substitute, except for the crime of murder. Therefore, "patterns" and "penalties" (all) are not observed in the New Covenant. In addition, 2 Tim. 3:15–16 shows that Scripture (Hebrew Scripture in context) still teaches New Covenant believers concerning the nature of God, the condition of man, salvation, etc.—training in righteousness. These are righteous principles.

65. The verb הָיָה (*to be*) followed by the preposition לְ conveys the idea of "become." When the New Covenant is inaugurated, Yahweh will become Israel's (and all the people of God) God, and they will become His people.

66. MT אוֹתִי (*me*) contextually refers to Yahweh.

67. The verb סלח (*forgive*) is used solely of God pardoning and forgiving the sinner (*TWOT,* vol. 2, 626).
68. לֹא (*not*) plus the imperfect אֶזְכָּר (*I will remember*) is a strong objective negative prohibition which implies "never," or the negation of an ongoing iterative action. Coupled with the particle עוֹד, "again," it means that Yahweh will never again remember their sin.
69. Blood covenants in the OT were always enacted with the killing of animals and the shedding of blood. The understanding was that the partners of the covenant were strongly bound by the agreement to the extent that if one of the partners broke the covenant, what had happened to the animals would happen to them: death. So it was a very binding agreement with the only exception being its termination by the death of one of the partners who broke the covenant. In the case of the New Covenant only God is bound by the covenant for its existence. Therefore the covenant is instituted by his shed blood, and the agreement is permanent because God will always be faithful to keep his promises of the New Covenant.
70. Israel benefits both from spiritual and physical blessings of the New Covenant when she is restored to her land in the end days. Parallel New Covenant passages like Ezek. 16:60–63; 36:24–28; 37:24–28 show that Israel will receive spiritual cleansing and forgiveness (cf. 1 Peter 1:10–12) but also the temple, universal peace, and gathering to the land, whereas church believers under the New Covenant receive only the spiritual benefits as seen in passages like Matt. 26:27, 28, Luke 22:20, Rom. 11:11–27, Eph. 2:11–13, and Heb. 8–9. Cf. Walter C. Kaiser Jr., "The Old Promise and the New Covenant," *Journal of the Evangelical Theological Society* (winter 1972), 11–23.
71. יהוה צְבָאוֹת שְׁמוֹ (*Yahweh of armies is his name*) emphasizes Yahweh's might and power. The stress that this is His name is given in this context to underscore His power and sovereign authority to sustain His creation and its physical ordinances.
72. חֻקֹּת and חֻקִּים in vv. 35 and 36 respectively refer to *ordinances*, whether physical or spiritual. In this case they indicate God's physical ordinances established in creation.
73. Holladay, 171, rightly argues that the use of a "protasis-apodosis sequence in which an impossible (or inconceivable) circumstance negatively reinforces the assurance" strongly undergirds the reassurance that "the nation of Israel will endure under Yahweh."
74. יָמֻשׁוּ has the sense of *withdraw* or *cease*. The hypothetical rhetorical question asks if these ordinances might be withdrawn or cease, neither of which is possible.
75. The rhetorical denial of rejection by Yahweh is emphasized by the additional independent personal pronoun, אֲנִי (*I*).
76. In this context עַל (*because*) has a causal nuance.
77. Bright, 283.
78. Cf. map 74 in Barry J. Beitzel, *The Moody Atlas of Bible Lands* (Chicago: Moody Press, 1985), 159.

Looking over the fertile Valley of Megiddo in northwest Israel.

CHAPTER EIGHT

THE LAND OF ISRAEL AND THE FUTURE RETURN (ZECHARIAH 10:6–12)

Walter C. Kaiser Jr.

Christian theologians are once again reclaiming the fact that "the land is central, if not *the central theme* of biblical faith," and therefore, as W. D. Davies warned, "it will no longer do to talk about Yahweh and his people, but we must speak about Yahweh and his people *and his land.*"[1] Likewise, Gerhard von Rad summarized the situation by saying, "Of all the promises made to the patriarchs it was that of the land that was the most prominent and decisive."[2] In fact, few issues are as important as that of the promise of the land to the patriarchs and the nation of Israel: the Hebrew word *'erets* is the fourth most frequent substantive in the Hebrew Bible.[3]

In this sense, then, the message of the Bible is very earthy. In one of the most striking enactments of the covenant made with the patriarch Abraham (in which God passed between the pieces of the divided animals in Genesis 15 and thereby took upon Himself an oath of a state of extinction, similar to the animals that now formed an aisle through which He moved), God promised on His life, "To your seed I give this land" (Gen. 15:18, my translation).[4] Later, when Abraham was ninety-nine years old, God again restated this promise in Genesis 17:8 to be a *perpetual* covenant. The promise-plan of God founded in the covenant was forever bound to our kind of history and geography. The boundaries of the land given to Israel were described in the contexts of the covenant promise to be centered in what is today known as the State of Israel, celebrating in 1998 fifty years as a revived political entity after being absent from this soil, in some cases, since 721 B.C., but in any event certainly since A.D. 70.

So strong is this sentiment in modern Jewish thought that its hallmark was found in the prayer at Passover: "Next year in Jerusalem." This same hope is expressed at every Jewish wedding ceremony, where a glass is broken in remembrance of the destruction of the Temple. The psalmist cries, "If I forget you, O Jerusalem, may my right hand forget its skill. May my tongue cling to the roof of my mouth if I do not remember you, if I do not consider Jerusalem my highest joy" (Ps. 137:5). In fact, Jewish prayers three times a day and at the Sabbath service and festivals bring to mind the centrality of Zion by saying,

> Father of Mercies
>   Do good in thy favor unto Zion;
> Build Thou the walls of Jerusalem.
> For in Thee alone do we trust,
>   O King, high and exalted God, Lord of worlds.[5]

Truly the land was at the heart and soul of biblical and Jewish thinking. Rabbi Heschel evaluated the situation by observing,

> The love of the land was due to an imperative, not to an instinct, not to a sentiment. There is a covenant, an engagement of the people to the land. . . . To abandon the land would be to make mockery of all our longings, prayer, and commitments. To abandon the land would be to repudiate the Bible.[6]

Despite all this evidence, the question still remains: Is this focus on the land really as central to the message of the first testament of the Bible as it has been made out to be? And is the promise of the land, if it is present in that part of the canon and is so germane to the thinking of the Tanakh (or Old Testament) as many claim it to be, an irrevocable promise or a conditional possession dependent on obedience and faithfulness? Why is it that the first six books of the Tanakh never refer to this possession as "the land of *Israel*," but it is always "the land of *Canaan*," "land of the *Canaanites*," or "of the *Amorites*"? These questions must be addressed before we ask the more difficult question as to whether the emphasis of the older testament is that of the New Testament as well.[7]

THE PROMISE OF THE LAND

The promise of the land to the patriarchs and their descendants began in Genesis 12:1–7. In some twenty passages in Genesis and Exodus alone God promised that He would give the land that had belonged to the Amorites, Hittites, Perizzites, Canaanites, and Jebusites to Abraham and his offspring.[8] It is clear that the land was a major concern and part of the covenant of God.

But an even more important point must be made. The promise of the coming Seed (eventually to be known as the Messiah) and the offer of the good news (i.e., that in Abraham's seed all the nations of the earth would be blessed) was inextricably tied to the promise of the land. Already we have seen how God obligated Himself to give the land as a gift to Abraham in that unilateral covenant in which only God, not Abraham, walked between the pieces of animals in Genesis 15:18. Added to this one-sided obligation found in Genesis 15 was the promise of the land as a perpetual inheritance when the sign of the covenant, circumcision, was performed in Genesis 17:8. And what God had repeatedly promised to Abraham, he reiterated in the same basic promise to his son Isaac in Genesis 26:3 and to his grandson Jacob in Genesis 28:4 and 28:13. Later, Joseph would allude to this same treasured thought in Genesis 50:24. He said, "I am about to die. But God will surely come to your aid, and take you up out of this land to the land that he promised on oath to Abraham, Isaac, and Jacob."

The irrevocability of the promise doctrine, or plan of God, was not only stressed in passages like Genesis 17, but the same point continued to be made in the New Testament as well. According to the writer of Hebrews (6:13, 17–18), that is why God swore by Himself when He made the promise: to show how immutable His purpose was. Therefore, God interposed with two immutable things wherein it is impossible for God to lie: *viz.*, His word in Genesis 12 and His oath in Genesis 22. That is why the gifts and calling of God which He extended to Israel are irrevocable (Rom. 11:29). They simply cannot be disannulled (Gal. 3:15–18).

Just as Abraham was assured of an eternal promise, so King David was given the same promise when the promised content of the covenant was given to him in 2 Samuel 7 (with its parallels in 1 Chron. 17 and Ps. 89). The Davidic line and their kingdom would enjoy this irrevocable divine purpose. The word *eternal* appears three times in Nathan's message from God, five times in utterances of David in the presence of Yahweh, and six times in Psalm 89 (2 Sam. 7:13, 16, 24–26, 29; Ps. 89:29, 36–37).

There is an important point that is to be made in the fact that all three parts of the covenant (i.e., the seed, the land, and the gospel) were bound together as *one* promise with a promise that this one promise was *eternal*. Most Christians will grant that the seed and gospel aspects of this promise are eternal, but somehow they think it is possible to dissect the eternal promise of the land from the other two eternal aspects! But to use a theological scalpel to cut out one part is to expose the rest of this same covenant to diminution and a time limitation.

Promises with Conditions

Some will object that ordinarily Yahweh's promises to mortals are conditioned on obedience. Was not the promise of possessing the land contingent on Israel's living by God's righteous standards? It would appear from texts like Deuteronomy 4:25–27 that to break the law was to lose the land. It warned:

After you have had children and grandchildren and have lived in the land a long time—if you then become corrupt and make any kind of idol, doing evil in the eyes of the LORD your God and provoking him to anger, . . . you will quickly perish from the land that you are crossing the Jordan to possess. You will not live there long but will certainly be destroyed. . . . Only a few of you will survive among the nations to which the LORD will drive you.

Deuteronomy 4:40 also warned:

Keep his decrees and commands, which I am giving to you today, so that it may go well with you and your children after you and that you may live in the land the LORD your God gives you for all time.

Even Leviticus 18:24–30 and 20:22–26 warned that if there was no obedience and following of the statutes, decrees, and ordinances of Yahweh, then the very land itself would "vomit [them] out" for their lack of holiness before God. There is no doubt about the seriousness of Israel's failure in this regard.

The Unconditional Promise

However, there are passages that pledge an unconditional gift of the promise and the land to Israel. Leviticus 26:44–46 affirmed:

Yet in spite of this, when they are in the land of their enemies [in exile], I will not reject them or abhor them so as to destroy them completely, breaking my covenant with them. I am the LORD their God. But for their sake I will remember the covenant with their ancestors whom I brought out of Egypt in the sight of the nations to be their God. I am the LORD.

So how does one solve this seeming verbal paradox? It can be solved rather easily, as Willis J. Beecher did in 1904 Stone Lectures at Princeton. He explained,

So far as its benefits accrue to any particular person or generation in Israel, it is conditioned on their obedience. But in its character as expressing God's purpose of blessing for the human race, we should not expect it to depend on the obedience or disobedience of a few.[9]

Elsewhere I have explained this same tension by saying in terms similar to Beecher's:

The conditionality was not attached to the promise but only to the participants who would benefit from these abiding promises. . . . The promise remained permanent, but the participation in the blessings depended on the individual's spiritual condition.[10]

THE PROPHETS AND THE PROMISE OF A RETURN TO THE LAND

The "headwaters" of the "return" passages, as Elmer Martens assessed it in one of the first studies of land theology in the prophets, are to be found in Jeremiah and Ezekiel.[11] Both Jeremiah and Ezekiel had experienced firsthand the loss of the land; yet together they uttered twenty-five explicit statements about the return of Israel to the land and five additional texts that contained indirect announcements of this return.[12]

Jeremiah's characteristic formula for the restoration of Israel to the land is this: "Restore the fortunes (or captivity)" [šabtî 'et šᵉbût]. Twelve of its twenty-six occurrences in the Old Testament are found in Jeremiah (e.g., Jer. 29:14; 30:3; 32:44). Ezekiel, on the other hand, usually casts his message about the return in a three-part formula (e.g., Ezek. 11:17; 20:41–42; 36:24; 37:21): (a) "I will bring you from the people"; (b) "I will gather you from the lands"; and (c) "I will bring you into the land of Israel."

One of the most striking passages in the prophets is one where Yahweh promises that His pledge to restore Israel's fortunes will be as dependable as His covenant with day and night (Jer. 33:20, 25–26).

But despite this overwhelming array of texts to the contrary from almost every one of the prophets, many still insist on saying that this promise to restore Israel to her promised land was fulfilled when Zerubbabel, Ezra, and Nehemiah led their respective returns from Babylon back to the old land of Canaan. However, there is a serious deficiency to this line of reasoning. How then shall we explain the prophecy in Zechariah 10:8–12 that announces in 518 B.C. a still future return, which would not only emanate from Babylon, but from around the world? It is to this text, then, that we turn for an examination of timing and the substance of this promise.

THE RETURN PROMISED IN ZECHARIAH 10:6–12

The section opens with Yahweh promising that He will "strengthen the house of Judah and save the house of Joseph" (Zech. 10:6). The parallelism between the two lines cannot be missed, for they cannot be separated without violating what Zechariah was affirming. Naturally, the writer does not mean Joseph alone any more than he meant Judah alone, but the "house of Joseph" represented the ten tribes of the northern kingdom while the "house of Judah" represented the two southern tribes.[13] Such an enlargement of the promised return beyond the boundaries of the two southern tribes to include all of the northern ten tribes clearly extended the vision of what was involved in the return far beyond the return of the Judahites from Babylon.

God promised that He would "restore" all Israel "because [he would] have

compassion on them" (v. 6d). The form of this verb for "restore" (*wehosebotim*)
apparently represents something of a conflation between the causative form of
the verb *šûb,* "to return," and *yašab,* "to settle, dwell, reinstate." Most Hebrew
manuscripts have a hybrid or mongrel form, though a few Hebrew manuscripts
preserve a form based on *yašab,* as does the Greek Septuagint. The similarity of
the two roots in Hebrew and the closeness of the meaning of each ("to bring back"
the exiles and "to resettle" them) provided some basis for the confusion in the
Hebrew text. However, there could be no denying the fact that God intended to
return all the twelve tribes back to their homeland once again. Later, in verse 10,
the proper form of the causative stem of the verb *šûb,* "to cause to return," appears in the Hebrew text, as it does in the Vulgate, Peshitta, and Targums. As
David Baron said,

> . . . the most satisfactory explanation of the Hebrew word is that it is a
> blending of two verbs which have the respective meanings of "I will make
> them dwell," and "I will bring them back"—both ideas, as already the
> Jewish commentator [David] Kimchi [c. A.D. 1160–c. 1235] points out,
> being expressed in the one word, namely, "He will cause them to return
> to their own land, and will cause them to dwell there in peace and
> security."[14]

   The reason for this restoration of the whole nation, long since divided, back
to their land is stated in verse 6d: "because I will have compassion on them."
What makes this statement stand out is that this word *compassion* is found in the
midst of masculine military imagery in verses 3–7. It derives from the noun *rehem,*
"womb," and depicts the maternal care one has for one's own children. Thus, the
female imagery poignantly depicts God's tender care for His people. The text
adds immediately: "They will be as though I had not rejected [*zānâh,* "to spurn,
exclude, reject"] them" (v. 6e). Surprisingly, God is most often the subject of
both the verb "to be compassionate" and "to spurn." So thorough will be this
restoration that it will be as if the exile had never taken place.
   In order to match what God had promised Judah in verse 5 (i.e., that "they
will be like mighty men"), Ephraim too will be empowered to "become like
mighty men" in verse 7. The resulting joy will be so effusive that it will be "as if
[it came] from wine." Nor will it cease with that generation for "their children
will see it and be joyful" (v. 7c), "their hearts will rejoice in the LORD" (v. 7d).
   The pastoral imagery is resumed in verse 8 and again announced in the first
person of God's intention to restore His people. He will "whistle" or "pipe" for
His people in a signal that will call them together from among the nations to
accomplish His purpose among them. Most of the twenty usages of the Hebrew
verb *šaraq,* "to hiss, whistle, pipe," are used in negative and derisive contexts,
such as Jerusalem is a city to be "hissed at" (Jer. 19:8; Lam. 2:15–16). However,

in Judges 5:16 it is the piping of the shepherd that assembles his herd before he moves on that parallels our usage here. God will whistle or pipe the familiar tune that the flock of Israel recognizes as He assembles His scattered sheep from among the nations. The same thought is found in the prophet Isaiah:

> He lifts up a banner [ensign to] for the distant nations,
>> he whistles for those [his people, v. 25]
>> at the ends of the earth.
> Here they come,
>> swiftly and speedily! (Isa. 5:26).

It is not an infrequent scene in the Near East to see how the sheep of several shepherds will freely mingle with each others' herds at a watering hole or at a spot where the shepherds have stopped to rest or talk. But when each shepherd sounds a distinctive whistle or takes out a reed pipe and starts to play, the scattered sheep that may have wandered off far distances will suddenly regroup and form into a flock before the shepherd moves on again ahead of them playing his reed pipe. So God "will pipe for them and gather them" (v. 8a).

Not only will they be regathered, but they "will be as numerous as before" (v. 8c). Such multiplication echoes the language and theology of Genesis 1:22, 28; 9:1, 7; and 35:11. But as numerous as before what? Presumably before the exile! Recent ethnoarchaeological studies estimated that the Persian period after the exile was marked by a real decline in the population in the land of Israel. There was a preponderance of rural areas, tiny villages, often with not more than eleven to thirty families per village, and barely eleven percent of the settlements had more than sixty families per village. Accordingly, the population of the post-exilic period was shockingly small.[15] This does not appear to be what was promised in this text; thus we have another reason for doubting that the return referred to here was the return from the Babylonian captivity.

Interestingly enough, the Lord acknowledges in verse 9 that the exile was His doing (cf. Deut. 28:63–64). The Hebrew root of this word zāra' means "to plant, to sow, to scatter the seed." Some emend the text from the root zāra' to zārâh, "to winnow, to throw up the grain so as to scatter it." But there is no need to make even this slight emendation of the text for both are examples of agricultural metaphors. Moreover, in order to sow, one had to scatter the seed by hand over the fields in order to plant the crop. This figure is more suited to the dispersion of the tribes, for they were not simply scattered as chaff is winnowed. They were really planted, and they grew in all the places to which they had been taken by one empire after another in the ancient Near East. It would seem that Zechariah was dependent on two former prophets who had declared the same truth in the same agrarian figure of speech:

> I will plant [sow] her for myself in the land;
>   I will show my love to the One I called "Not my loved one."
> I will say to those called "Not my people," "You are my people";
>   and they will say, "You are my God" (Hos. 2:23).

Again in Jeremiah 31:27 the prophet announced:

> "The days are coming," declares the LORD, "when I will plant [sow] the
> house of Israel and the house of Judah with the offspring of men and
> animals."

It is important to notice again that it would not be the return and restoration of
the house of Judah, as was the case in the return from the Babylonian Exile, but
it would include the house of Israel/Joseph as well. And not only will the parents
and children come back to their land once again, but they "will live" (v. 9c). This
is more than a mere survival; it is the gift of a life of blessing for the whole nation. "And they will return" (v. 9d) is the ultimate destiny of the people whom
God has called, gathered, and redeemed (v. 7). This theme had been set forth by
the prophet Ezekiel in his amazing description of the valley of dry bones in Ezekiel
37:11–14.

> Then he said to me, "Son of man, these bones are the whole house of
> Israel. They say, 'Our bones are dried up and our hope is gone; we are
> cut off.' Therefore prophesy and say to them: 'This is what the Sover-
> eign LORD says: "O my people, I am going to open your graves and bring
> you up from them; I will bring you back to the land of Israel. Then you,
> my people, will know that I am the LORD, when I open your graves and
> bring you up from them. I will put my Spirit in you and you will live,
> and I will settle you in your own land. Then you will know that I the
> LORD have spoken, and I have done it, declares the LORD.'"

Such passages that speak of the nation turning to the Lord while they are still
in their foreign countries of the Diaspora may appear to seriously conflict with
the many prophecies that depict a restoration of the nation of Israel in the time
that they are still in a state of unbelief, with their conversion in the land coming
only when Christ visibly appears the second time. But as David Baron explained:

> But there is no real conflict or contradiction between these various Scrip-
> tures, the solution of the apparent difficulty being in the fact that while a
> large representative section of the nation will be in Palestine in a condi-
> tion of unbelief when the Lord appears, and will be converted there, the
> remaining part of the nation will still be in the dispersion, and upon them

the spirit of grace and supplication will come in the "far countries" where they shall be found.[16]

God will gather Israel and Judah from two powers: Egypt and Assyria (v. 10). Do these nations stand here as representing all Israel's hostile powers both past, present, and future? It is clear that "Assyria" repeatedly is used of the powers that came one after another to take Assyria's place in the history of the ancient Near East. Places where this phenomenon takes place are Jeremiah 2:18, Lamentations 5:6, and Micah 7:12. Later in Ezra 6:22 "Assyria" and in Ezra 5:13 and Nehemiah 13:6 "Babylonia" is used for "Persia." Accordingly, "Egypt," "Assyria," and "Babylon" were used at times to designate the existing world power, or its seat, without directly referencing their original or literal signification. Thus Egypt could refer to the lands to the south, as Assyria could allude to the nations to the north. On the other hand, there may be no need to use these names as a metonymy for their dynamic equivalents. The prophecy that merges into the distant future will be literally fulfilled, even as Isaiah instructed:

> In that day the LORD will reach out his hand a second time to reclaim the remnant that is left of his people from Assyria, from lower Egypt, from Upper Egypt, from Cush [Ethiopia], from Elam, from Babylonia, from Hamath and from the islands of the sea. He will raise a banner for the nations and gather the exiles of Israel; he will assemble the scattered people of Judah from the four corners of the earth (Isa. 11:11–12).

The dispersed people of Israel will be gathered from "the four corners of the earth" in order to be brought back "to Gilead and Lebanon," resulting in the situation that "there will not be room enough for them" (Zech. 10:10). Gilead, of course, designates the territory east of the Jordan, but it is doubtful that all of Transjordania, where the two and half tribes settled during the days of Moses and the conquest, was intended. The best estimate of what is intended can be seen better when the boundaries of the land, as promised to the patriarchs, is investigated more thoroughly later in this chapter.

The promise that the returnees would inherit the land of Lebanon is more difficult, for the name "Lebanon" usually designated the chain of mountains that began in northern Israel and continued northward for another one hundred miles. As Carol Meyers and Eric Meyers commented,

> The Lebanon was reckoned as part of Israel (Deut. 1:7; 3:25; 11:24; Josh. 1:4; 13:5, 6; 1 Kings 9:19). If the coastal areas to the west of the Lebanon range are meant to be included in the designation "Lebanon," then the Phoenician cities there controlled territory that perhaps was considered part of Israel's allotment. . . . Together with Gilead, Lebanon thus

represents Israelite territory to be populated under optimal conditions, i.e., the eschatological restoration of all Israel.[17]

So large will be the ingathering of the formerly divided nation that there will not be room enough for them even with these expanded boundaries. The prophet Isaiah foresaw the same problem:

> The children born during your bereavement will yet say in your hearing, "This place is too small for us; give us more space to live in." Then you will say in your heart, "Who bore me these? I was bereaved and barren; I was exiled and rejected. Who brought these up? I was left all alone, but these—where have they come from?" (Isa. 49:20–21).

The Boundaries of the Land

The borders of the land promised to Abraham were to run "from the River Egypt" (*minnehar miṣrayim*) to the Great River, the River Euphrates (*hannahar haggādol nehar perāt*). (Gen. 15:18). Even though some have incorrectly judged the "River Egypt" to be the Nile River, it is more accurately placed at the Wadi el-'Arish, which reaches the Mediterranean Sea at the town of El-'Arish, some ninety miles east and north of the Suez Canal and almost fifty miles southwest of Gaza (Num. 34:2, 5; Ezek. 47:14, 19; 48:28). Amos 6:14 likewise pointed to the southern border as the "brook of the Arabah" (*naḥal hā 'arābâh*). In other words, exactly where the southern boundary for Israel was set after the Six Day War in 1967 is where the biblical text had placed it all along. The western boundary was the Mediterranean Sea and the eastern border was the eastern shore of the Sea of Galilee, the Jordan River, and the Dead Sea. Never was Transjordania included as a permanent part of their possession in the land.

The northern boundary is the most difficult of all to fix. It was the "Great River" that was to mark off that boundary, which appears to be glossed in Genesis 15:18, Deuteronomy 1:7, and Joshua 1:4 as the "River Euphrates." But is this correct? It would appear that the name "Great River" is more accurately located in the valley which currently runs between the northern boundary of Lebanon and the southern boundary of Syria. That river is called in modern Arabic *Nahr el-Kebir*, "the Great River."[18] Contributing to the difficulty of this identification is the frequent reference in these lists to a "Labwah Hamath" (Num. 34:8; Josh. 13:3–5; 1 Kings 8:65; 2 Kings 14:5; 1 Chron. 13:5; Amos 6:18; Ezek. 47:15; 48:1–28). Benjamin Mazar identified "Labwah Hamath" or "towards Hamath" as the modern city of Labwah in Lebanon. This city, in a forest just to the south of Kadesh and northeast of Baalbek, was of sufficient stature to be mentioned in Amenhotep II's stele as Rameses II's favorite hunting grounds and in Tiglath Pileser III's text along with Hamath.[19] Even so, the precise details of the northern boundary remain extremely tentative. Nevertheless, the data at hand favor a settlement of the revived and restored nation far to the north of Dan, including such old Canaanite settlements as Sidon and the whole of the Phoenician coastal section from north of Beirut, down to the Philistine Gaza Strip (Gen. 10:15, 19).

In the event that any hindrance should present itself, as it did in the exodus from Egypt, even though "they will pass through the sea of trouble, the surging sea will be subdued and all the depths of the river [the Nile] will dry up" (Zech. 10:1). The word used for "river, stream" here (Hebrew *ye'or*) normally refers to the Nile River and is a loan word from Egyptian. The use of the plural "depths" with *ye'or* would seem to form a phrase representing the varied waterways in general (e.g., Isa. 33:21; Job 28:10) or even the Tigris (as in Dan. 12:5–7; 10:4). But inasmuch as the language is meant to be paradigmatic of a future exodus of God's people with obvious allusions to what God did at the Red Sea, it is not necessary to limit it to the Nile River. But wherever these obstacles present themselves, they will evaporate and dry up before the hand of the Lord. And all oppressors, as again indicated by the phrase "Assyria . . . and Egypt," will be subdued and removed. The fact that the order of the two nations is Assyria and then Egypt (rather than the historical order of Egypt and Assyria) goes far to demonstrating that they are symbols of all the oppressors of Yahweh's people.

This section ends with Yahweh making Israel "mighty" (the fourth occurrence of the root רבב in chapter 10) and the nation "walk[ing]" "in his name" (Zech. 10:12).

OBJECTIONS

Hermeneutical Objections

It is widely held that the most obvious corollary to the Christocentric hermeneutic is the *theologia crucis* that the New Testament must always be our guide to interpreting the Old Testament.[20] But why would a rule be imposed on the revelation of God that demands that the Old Testament passages may not become the basis for giving primary direction on any doctrines or truths that have relevancy for New Testament times? This is only to argue in the end for a canon within a canon. Or put in theological terms, this is to use the *analogia fidei* ("analogy of faith")[21] as an exegetical device rather than as the tool it was designed to be: the process of collecting all the texts on a particular doctrine in the formation of the contents of systematic theology. To extrapolate meanings back to the Old Testament from the New Testament is not the science of exegesis but rather that of eisegesis, that is, a "reading into" the text (of the Old Testament) what is not there. This assertion is heavily contested in our day, but the borrowing of freight from the New Testament and then imposing it on the Old Testament is at best reductionistic, not to mention that it tends to slip into a Marcionite view of the Old Testament, that is, that it has no relevancy for the contemporary believer.

Several New Testament texts are typically used to show that earthly promise of the land finds new spiritual applications in the progress of doctrine. For example, 1 Peter 1:4 speaks of "an inheritance" that cannot perish or fade and Hebrews 4:1–3 speaks of a "rest" that is entered into by faith. But these texts fail to make the point that a spiritual interpretation must now be substituted for a literal fulfillment. Already within the Old Testament both aspects of the literal and spiritual fulfillments were present and part of this prediction that had both a now and not-yet aspect to their realization.[22]

Philological Objections

The repeated emphasis on the fact that the land was promised to the patriarchs and Israel "forever," or as an "everlasting" promise is another point of contention. It is said that the Hebrew word *'ôlām*, "everlasting," did not mean that which was permanent without historical limitations, but that it only meant what was relatively permanent beyond the foreseeable future.[23] But as Allan A. MacRae pointed out, only twenty of the over three hundred usages of *'olam* referred to the past; the overwhelming majority of usages denoted indefinite continuance into the very distant future.[24] So said James Barr as well: "We might therefore best state the 'basic meaning' as a kind of range between 'remotest time' and 'perpetuity.'"[25] It must be remembered, however, that the same designation was used of the Lord, *'El 'ôlām*, the "Eternal God" (Gen. 21:33).

When these explanations are placed alongside synonymous parallel expressions, such as "the fixed laws of heaven and earth" (Jer. 33:25), "from the four corners of the earth" (Isa. 11:11–12), or as long as heaven and earth endure (Jer. 33:20), it is clear that the promise of the land did not end with pre-Christian times but continued on in perpetuity as long as the heaven and the earth lasted.

One counter argument to this emphasis on the "everlasting" or "eternal" aspect of the covenant is to claim, as Colin Chapman does, "that the insistence on a literal fulfillment [of the land promise] could be a double-edged weapon. God promised the Aaronic priesthood would continue 'forever' (1 Chron. 23:13). Has he fulfilled that promise literally?" demanded Chapman.[26] Chapman likewise complained that no descendant of David has occupied the Davidic throne "forever" either.

But the response to both is the same: both the priesthood of Aaron and the throneship of David have, as a matter of fact, lasted "forever," for our Lord Jesus has fulfilled both literally. His is the *priesthood* and His is the *throne* of David forever!

Conditional Arguments

It is acknowledged by even the most adamant opponents of a future restoration to the land that there are at least four prophetic predictions that promise, either implicitly or explicitly, a restoration of the people of Israel to their land forever/permanently: Isaiah 61:7–8; Jeremiah 32:37–41; Ezekiel

37:24–26; and Amos 9:15. But this gracious concession is immediately countered with the fact that the fulfillment of these promises is made dependent on Israel's meeting certain conditions in the very same contexts where these permanent promises are given. Isaiah condemned injustice and unbelief (Isa. 59:1–15), Jeremiah and Ezekiel demanded faith and obedience (Jer. 32:23–24, 29–35; Ezek. 37:23–24), and Amos saw that righteousness and mercy were necessary (Amos 5:12–24; 8:4–12). In fact, it is usually contended that this conditionality was traced in detail in Leviticus 26 and Deuteronomy 28. Without these prerequisites, it was impossible for God to fulfill His promise of the land, it was held. Moreover, the claim is often made that all of God's prophecies are conditional, as Jeremiah 18:7–10 demonstrates.

But these objectors fail to note that there is a difference between conditional and unconditional prophecies. Among the few unconditional prophecies are the covenant of the seasons made with Noah in Genesis 8, the covenant made with Abraham, Isaac, Jacob and later with David (Gen. 12, 15, 17; 2 Sam. 7), the promise of the New Heavens and the New Earth (Isa. 65 and 66), and the New Covenant (Jer. 31:31–34). These all depend on God Himself for their fulfillment. There may be a failure to *participate* in these benefits because of the absence of faith, but that will not stop the Almighty from eventually doing what He had promised. Every other prophecy is conditional and follows the word found in Jeremiah 18:7–10. These all have an alternative prospect, depending on how the nations or individuals respond. Jeremiah teaches us that when God has predicted blessing for a nation, it will not follow if that nation refuses to obey Him and walk in His ways. However, if God has decreed judgment on a nation, and that nation reverses its practice of evil and unrighteousness, then God will reverse His predicted judgment on that same people (Jer. 18:7–10). The same alternative prospect is true for individuals (1 Kings 21:27–29).

The conditionality of some, or even most, is no more detrimental to the eventual fulfillment of the promise than is the conditionality expressed with regard to the Messiah coming from the house of David (2 Sam. 7:14–15; Ps. 89:30–31). Some in David's line may have failed to participate in the blessings of the promised line because they did not believe, but they had to transmit the blessings of the promise on to the next Davidic descendant in the line because God was overseeing and ensuring the success of the whole project. Likewise, many in Israel may have failed to believe, just as that generation in the wilderness had failed, but that did not halt the initial entrance into the land; neither will future unbelief unseat the eternal promise of God.

The Land in the New Testament

When it is asked what Christ and the apostles taught about a Jewish return to the land, the answer that is triumphantly given by our objectors is "Nothing!" There is no return to the land, no restoration, no repossession of Jerusalem, no rebuilding of the temple! So the New Testament principle of interpretation must take precedence over any alleged Old Testament abiding promise.

But it could just as well be asked: Where do Christ and the apostles teach anything about a prohibition on marrying one's own sister, aunt, or the like? Or where do they say a word against abortion? The answer, of course, is "Nowhere!" But very few would then contend that there is no teaching that is relevant for the Christian believer on these and other similar points! The point is that we misjudge the revelation of God if we have a theory of interpretation which says the most recent revelation of God is to be preferred or substituted for that which came earlier.

The fact is that the "state" and people of Israel are very much a part of the soteriological and eschatological plan of God in Romans 9–11. Our Lord is still waiting for a "full number" of Jews who will believe after the "full number" (*pleroma*) of the Gentiles is accomplished. When this is put together with what God had previously promised, it makes a complete picture.

Nevertheless, if it be insisted that there is no reference whatsoever to the land in the New Testament, we must demur, for a number of passages imply that this must be the case if the New Testament assumptions are to be upheld. Consider the following New Testament texts:

> O Jerusalem, Jerusalem, you who kill the prophets and stone those who are sent to you. . . . Look, your house is left desolate. For I tell you that you will not see me until you say, "Blessed is he who comes in the name of the Lord" (Matt. 23:37–39).

Jesus was in the land when He uttered this prediction, and He is therefore referring to the land as the place that will see Him and the people of Jerusalem in particular.

> So when you see standing in the holy place the abomination of desolation, spoken through the prophet Daniel . . . then let those who are in Judea flee to the mountains (Matt. 24:15–16).

The abomination of desolation will take place in the temple which is located in the land of Israel. Those who are to flee are to exit the land of Judea!

> And he will send his angels with a loud trumpet call and they will gather his elect from the four winds, from one end of the heavens to the other (Matt. 24:31).

Again, the question must be asked, from where will He regather the Jewish people being addressed, and to what place will He take them? Again the land is the answer.

So when they met together, they asked him, "Lord, are you at this time going to restore the kingdom to Israel?" (Acts 1:6).

The issue at stake here was not whether the land would be restored to Israel but only the issue of timing. Others have disagreed, saying that Jesus was trying to give a new understanding of the kingdom of God by telling them to be His witnesses in Jerusalem, Judea, Samaria, and to the ends of the earth.[27] But how, then, does that fit with verse 7, which follows? Jesus corrected their understanding of timing: "It is not for you to know the times or dates the Father has set by his own authority." Once again, there was both a physical and spiritual aspect to the kingdom concept of our Lord, but the land issue was not to be denied.

And so all Israel will be saved, as it is written: "The deliverer will come from Zion; he will turn godlessness away from Jacob. This is my covenant with them when I take away their sins" (Rom. 11:26–27).

These promises are quoted from Isaiah 59:20–21; 27:9; and Jeremiah 31:33–34, where a strong affirmation of a return of the people of Israel to the land is espoused. The geographical location is in Zion and the people are from Jacob. Where else is Zion but in the land?

Even the Book of Revelation places its actions in the streets of "the city [God] loves" (Rev. 20:9) and the "holy city" (Rev. 11:1–13), which has to be Jerusalem. Where else is the final gathering of the kings of the earth at "Armageddon" (Rev. 16:16) if it is not in the land, which some say is not mentioned in the New Testament!

The land is indeed a part of the New Testament revelation, even though we do not generally tend to think in those terms. And the people of Israel are directly tied into the entire plan of redemption. It is impossible to treat Romans 9–11 as a parenthesis or an interruption in the whole discussion of God's salvation offered to all peoples, for the Jew's participation and key role in that plan is announced from the thesis statement of the book in Romans 1:16, "I am not ashamed of the gospel, because it is the power of God for salvation of everyone who believes: first to the Jew, then to the Gentile." The land, Israel, and the kingdom of God are inextricably intertwined in this masterful book on our Lord's gracious offer of salvation.

CONCLUSION

It is difficult to talk about the nation of Israel apart from the land which it has been given. While many Christians find it difficult to see how God's work of salvation should have any attachments to geography, the fact remains that God Himself linked the two from the very beginning with the call of Abraham in Genesis 12. This is simply another way of affirming that God's activities do not take place in an abstract vacuum but in the midst of the concrete space and time of human history. The events of our salvation have strong attachments to Canaan, Bethlehem, Jerusalem, Nazareth, the Mount of Olives, and Golgotha.

If the dispersion was a mark of God's judgment, according to the prophets, then Israel's return to the land is the mark of God's grace. In fact, so astounding will be this future return of Israel that it will make the exodus from Egypt seem small in comparison. That is what the prophet Jeremiah held out for in his prophecies:

> However, the days are coming, declares the LORD, when men will no longer say, "As surely as the LORD lives, who brought the Israelites up out of Egypt," but they will say [instead], "As surely as the LORD lives, who brought the Israelites up out of the land of the north and up out of all the countries where he had banished them." For I will restore them to the land I gave their forefathers (Jer. 16:14–15; cf. Jer. 23:7–8).

As Hendrikus Berkhof has analyzed it:

> Since God's judgment is not the last word but is followed by a new acceptance of grace, it is clear that this takes the form of Israel's return to Canaan. This, too, is for Jewish prophecy a divine matter-of-fact. I mention Deut. 30.1–10; Isa. 11.11f; 14:1; 27:12f; 35:1, 10; 43:5f; 49:22; 62:4–7; 66:18–20; Jer. 16:14–15; 31:8–12; 32:36f; Ezek. 36:8–12, 24, 28, 33–36; Amos 9:11–15; Zech. 8:10:9f. Two quotations will make clear how closely connected people and country are in the eschatological salvation. "I will plant them upon their land, and they shall never again be plucked up out of the land which I have given to them, says the LORD your God" (Amos 9:15). "You shall no more be termed Forsaken, and your land shall no more be termed Desolate; but you shall be called My Delight Is in Her, and your land married" (Isa. 62:4 NRSV).[28]

Berkhof concludes, as we must, in a most powerful way on this subject of Israel's return to the land. He warned:

> At any rate, with the surprising geographical and political fact of the establishment of the State of Israel [in 1948], the moment has come for us [Christians] to begin to watch for political and geographical elements in God's activities, which we have not wanted to do in our Western dualism, docetism, and spiritualism.[29]

DISCUSSION QUESTIONS

1. How prominent is the theme of the land in the Old Testament (i.e., the Tanakh) and in modern Jewish thought? Give some statistics of usage in the Old Testament and some examples in modern Jewish life.

2. Was God's promise of the land contingent on Israel's obedience or on the grace of God? Explain the apparent tension between biblical passages that seem to point in opposite directions.

3. Which of the Old Testament prophets stressed the future return of Israel to her land and with what kind of analogies, comparisons, or expressions did these prophets emphasize this hope?

4. What promises (set in parallel lines) in Zechariah 10:6 indicate that the prophet Zechariah would not have identified the future return of Israel to her land as being the return of Judah from Babylon? How does the 518 B.C. dating of this passage add to the same argument?

5. Describe the future boundary lines of the land of Israel as promised in Scripture.

6. Name three of the four objections given in this chapter to the fact that God will bring Israel back to her land again and indicate what replies can be given to these objections?

ENDNOTES

1. W. D. Davies, *The Gospel and the Land* (Berkeley: University of California Press, 1974), 24.
2. Gerhard von Rad, *The Problem of the Hexateuch and Other Essays* (London: Oliver and Boyd, 1966), 79.
3. H. H. Schmid, *"['eres],"* *Theologisches Handworterbuch zum Alten Testamentt*, vol. 1, Ernst Jenni and Claus Westermann, eds. (Munich: Chr. Kaiser Verlag, 1971), 227–35, especially 234 and *"['adamah],"* 58, 59, cited by Elmer Martens, "Motivations for the Promise of Israel's Restoration to the Land in Jeremiah and Ezekiel," (Ph. D. Dissertation, Claremont Graduate School, 1972), 2.
4. Unless otherwise noted, all translations in this chapter are from the New International Version.
5. This is the Sabbath prayer for the synagogue as the ark is opened and the scrolls are taken out. Joseph H. Hertz, *The Authorized Daily Prayer Book*, rev. ed. (New York: Bloch Publishing Co., 1961), 472. Cf. A. J. Herschel, *Israel: An Echo of Eternity* (New York: Farrar, Straus, and Giroux, 1969), 43–44.
6. Heschel, *Israel*, 41 as cited by David E. Holwerda, *Jesus and Israel: One Covenant or Two?* (Grand Rapids: Eerdmans, 1995), 87.
7. On this general subject, see as well, Ole Chr. M. Kvarme, "The Theological Implications of the State of Israel," *The Hebrew Christian* 54 (1981): 83ff.; Mark Hanna, "Israel Today: What Place in Prophecy?" *Christianity Today* 26 (January 22, 1982): 14–17. Contrast William Hendriksen, *Israel in Prophecy* (Grand Rapids: Baker, 1968).
8. David J. A. Clines, *The Theme of the Pentateuch* (Sheffield, England: JSOT Press, 1978), 36–37 lists the following passages (with some additions and subtractions of

my own): Gen. 12:1, 7; 13:15, 17; 15:7, 18; 17:8; 22:17; 24:7; 26:3–5; 28:13, 15; 35:12; 46:3–4; 48:4; 50:24; Exod. 3:8, 17; 6:6–9; 23:23–33; 34:24.

9. Willis J. Beecher, *The Prophets and the Promise* (New York: Thomas Y. Crowell, 1905; Grand Rapids: Baker, 1963; repr. of 1905), 220.

10. Walter C. Kaiser Jr., *Toward an Old Testament Theology* (Grand Rapids: Zondervan, 1978), 90–91.

11. Martens, "Motivations for the Promise of Israel's Restoration," 12. See also the earlier study of Hans-Reudi Weber, "The Promise of the Land: Biblical Interpretation and the Present Situation in the Middle East," *Study Encounter* 7 (1971): 7–10 (= "La Promesse de la Terre," *Foi et Vie* 71 [1972]: 19–46).

12. Martens listed the explicit ones as Jer. 3:11–20; 12:14–17; 16:10–18; 23:1–8; 24; 28:1–4; 29:1–14; 30:1–3, 10–11; 31:2–14, 15–20; 32:1–44; 42:1–22; 50:17–20; Ezek. 11:14–21; 20:39–44; 34:1–16; 35:1–36:15; 36:16–36; 37:1–14; 37:15–28; 39:21–29. The indirect ones were Jer. 30:17b–22; 31:23–25; 33:1–18; Ezek. 28:20–26; 34:17–31 (Martens, "Motivations for the Promise of Israel's Restoration," 172–96).

13. Carol L. Meyers and Eric M. Meyers, *Zechariah 9–14*, The Anchor Bible, eds. William Foxwell Albright and David Noel Freedman (Garden City, NY: Doubleday, 1993), 207; note that the syntax of this bicolon (couplet) juxtaposes Judah with Joseph by having "house of Judah" follow the verb in the first half of the bicolon (couplet), but reverses the syntax in the next half by placing "house of Joseph" immediately after "house of Judah," thus making all Israel the central feature of the poetic line.

14. David Baron, *The Visions and Prophecies of Zechariah: "The Prophet of Hope and Glory"* (Fincastle, Va.: Scripture Truth Book Co., 1962 [repr. 1918]), 358–59.

15. Meyers and Meyers, *Zechariah 9–14*, 215, cites the study by K. Hoglund, *Archaemenid Imperial Administration in Syria-Palestine and the Missions of Ezra and Nehemiah,* SBL Dissertation Series no. 125 (Atlanta: Scholars Press, 1992).

16. Baron, *Visions and Prophecies of Zechariah*, 367, n. 2.

17. Meyers and Meyers, *Zechariah 9–14*, 222–23.

18. See my earlier discussion, Walter C. Kaiser Jr., "The Promised Land: A Biblical-Historical View," *BibSac* 138 (1981): 302–12, especially pp. 303–4. The Euphrates River and the river running through the valley that currently serves as the boundary between northern Lebanon and southern Syria, *Nahr el-Kebir*, "the great river," served as the two northern extremities for the land promised to Israel.

19. Benjamin Mazar, "Canaan and the Canaanites," *Bulletin of the American Schools of Oriental Research* 102 (1946): 9; cf. Jean Simons, *Geographical and Topographical Texts* (Leiden: E. J. Brill, 1959), 99–102. See also George W. Buchanan, *The Consequences of the Covenant* (Leiden: E. J. Brill, 1970), 91–109.

20. For example, John R. Wilch, "The Land and State of Israel in Prophecy and Fulfillment," *Concordia Journal* 8 (1982): 173.

21. The "analogy of faith" is that method of gathering groups of biblical texts (regardless of the time period from which they are derived) that pertain to the same subject or topic in a particular doctrine as we develop a systematic theology.

22. For a detailed explanation of this assertion, see Walter C. Kaiser Jr., "The Promise Theme and the Theology of Rest," *BibSac* 130 1973:135–50. *Idem. Toward an Old Testament Theology* (Grand Rapids: Zondervan, 1978), 127–42.

23. Wilch, 173.

24. Allan A. MacRae, "*ʿolam*," *Theological Wordbook of the Old Testament*, eds. R. Laird Harris, Gleason L. Archer Jr., and Bruce K. Waltke (Chicago: Moody, 1980): 2:672–73. With this definition E. Jenni is in agreement in E. Jenni and C. Westermann, *Theologisches Handbuch zum Alten Testament*, II, 230, as quoted by MacRae, 672–73.

25. James Barr, *Biblical Words for Time*, 2nd edition (1969), 73 as quoted by MacRae, 672–73.
26. Colin Chapman, "One Land, Two Peoples—How Many States?" *Mishkan* 26, 1 (1997): 6.
27. Chapman, "One Land, Two Peoples," 10.
28. Hendrikus Berkhof, *Christ the Meaning of History* (Richmond, Va.: John Knox, 1966), 148.
29. Ibid., 153.

PART FOUR

THEOLOGICAL ISSUES

Praying at the Western Wall of the Temple Mount.

CHAPTER NINE

THE DISPERSION AND RESTORATION OF ISRAEL TO THE LAND

John A. Jelinek

It is perhaps not too bold a statement to say that God's people have been think-ing about the end since the very beginning. That thinking, however, has not led to agreement on issues pertaining to the future. Even nominal Christians are not known for their doctrinal uniformity. It is not surprising, then, that a variety of viewpoints have emerged concerning the dispersion and the possibility of a na-tional future for Israel. Although evangelical and orthodox scholars find much to agree upon, including the ultimate source of appeal for the matter—God's Word—significant differences remain as to how God will fulfill (or has already fulfilled) His promises.

To attempt to address the theological dimensions of any topic in biblical the-ology in such a brief space may seem a bit presumptuous. Certainly, there are themes and supporting evidences that could be traced beyond the scope of a chap-ter such as this. The depth of treatment here, however, is not because the issues are of minor importance. In order to understand God's overall purpose in his-tory, it is imperative to know something of Israel's place in history and eschatology.

PRESUPPOSITIONS AND LIMITATIONS

Some presuppositions influence the results of this chapter. First, there is a hermeneutical issue related to the perspicuity of Scripture. Simply put, Scripture unfolds toward a goal. What is revealed at first in Scripture (or precedes in God's revelation) is not contradicted by what follows in Scripture. What OT authors wrote had a comprehensible meaning for their contemporary audiences and has a revelatory significance in its own right. What these audiences understood depended on both the prophetic message itself and the previously revealed prophetic messages from God. It is a problematic hermeneutic that must either resignify the OT message or see some aspect of an OT theme reiterated in the NT before it can lend legitimacy or permanency to its relevance. Language that says one thing concerning authorial intention but actually means something else is some form of allegory. Allegorical approaches to texts run the risk in this postmodern age of being understood as subliminal forms of reader-response criticism.

A historically sensitive study reveals that the NT develops OT teaching as divine history progresses, but the teaching of the OT is not lost in the process.[1] Promises that are made to Israel, therefore, must be fulfilled by God. God can do more than He promised, but He cannot do less. The primary question the exegete of texts on the land of Israel must ask is, Do I have sufficient biblical data to indicate that God is doing more or less than He promised with respect to the land promises to Israel?[2] At least the original promises concerning the land must be fulfilled, lest God be found unfaithful.

Biblical theology is best developed with a healthy respect to the progressive nature of biblical revelation. In a response to progressive dispensationalists' defense of their hermeneutic, Kaiser warned of a potential slippery slope facing the exegete:

> . . . dispensationalism . . . seems to have shifted from its former strength in making its case from the kingdom and restoration promises in the Old Testament to a biblical theology that is satisfied to rest the majority, if not all, of its case on the New Testament texts alone. If history is any kind of guide to the future, that could be a bad omen for the future of dispensationalism and the church at large. History has shown this to be the first step in capitulating to the anti-Israel mood of post-Constantine theology.[3]

Kaiser has identified a potential weakness in many approaches to biblical theology. It will not do to define biblical themes solely as they are developed in the New Testament.[4] Indeed, one may question whether they are adequately defined unless the foundational revelation of the OT is considered first. For this reason, in this chapter, the theology of the dispersion and the restoration are developed first from the standpoint of the land theology of Scripture. The supposition is that what God *first* said about what He would do is consistent with what He *later* said He *did* and what He says He *will do* in the future.

It would be possible to discuss the issues of land,[5] exile,[6] and restoration early in Scripture.[7] One might, for instance, begin with Adam and Eve in the Garden of Eden as prototypical of the relationship between Israel and the land, as some have done.[8] One might also go to the Abrahamic promises concerning the land and the covenant contexts in order to demonstrate the conditional and unconditional aspects of those promises.[9] The present chapter, however, will focus on the foundational warning passages concerning the nation's relationship to the land, survey Leviticus 26 and Deuteronomy 28–32, and then attempt to trace the trajectories of fulfillment within the remainder of Scripture.

The thesis of the chapter is that the key components of a theology of exile and restoration can be traced from Leviticus 26 and Deuteronomy 28–32 throughout the Bible and then organized into a consistent viewpoint concerning the Bible's portrait of a national future for Israel. These passages, therefore, provide the blueprint (the theological dimensions, if you will) from which the structure of a theology of Israel's exile and restoration can be erected. The validity of this approach is supported from the evident concern of all prophets subsequent to Moses to align with the pattern established in Deuteronomy 13. Moses, as the prophet *par excellance*, provided the authoritative words inscribed (and therefore safeguarded) by God's own hand.[10] The reflection of Torah themes in latter prophets is an expression of this concern to align with Moses.[11]

In the process of surveying and tracing the trajectories from these passages, some fundamental questions can be considered. What were the theological (or biblical) reasons for the dispersions? Certainly judgment of the nation emerges as a leading candidate. But judgment for what? On what bases? To what extent? Were the promises of restoration fulfilled in the first return under Ezra/Nehemiah? Is Israel still under the curse? Is her restoration to the land to be understood literally or figuratively for the church? To suggest that Israel is to be restored to the land in the last days as a part of God's program is to suggest that the Scripture teaches that there is indeed a future for national Israel. If this restoration is literal, does it take place under grace (i.e., a redeemed Israel is regathered) or under curse (i.e., a regathered Israel is redeemed)? To answer these questions is to establish what would constitute sufficient theological reasons for the restoration of national Israel to the land and to explain perhaps why the Jewish people continue to remain in dispersion until now.

Obviously, not every question indicated above can be answered to the satisfaction of every reader, but an attempt will be made to provide the broad strokes from which an answer may be formulated. Other chapters in this volume engage these questions in whole or in part and deal with textual particulars that cannot be addressed here.

LEVITICUS 26:14–46: THE NATURE OF AND RATIONALE FOR JUDGMENT AND DISPERSION

It is a common approach in biblical studies today to read the events of the exile backward into prior revelation. In other words, chapters like Leviticus 26 and Deuteronomy 28–32, which seem to anticipate failure on the part of Israel and predict exilic judgments, are handled as later additions to accommodate a changing Jewish theology.[12] The event of the exile, it is reasoned, led to inevitable changes in the way the prophets read the Torah, and eventually these changes were just written into the Torah by well-meaning redactors to accommodate various theodicies in the light of the national experience of exile.

It is generally recognized, however, that covenant forms such as are found in Leviticus 26 and Deuteronomy resemble the conclusions of Late Bronze Age Hittite vassal treaties' covenant codes.[13] If Leviticus 26 appears to anticipate failure on the part of Israel (vv. 14ff.), it is certain that such anticipation was a common feature in covenant treaties of that day.[14] The presence of a threat unto exile or dispossession of the land does not require attributing a late date for this text. In fact, the presence of such threats may serve to authenticate the origin of the threats as contemporary to the Mosaic period of writing. This is an important point to establish if these texts are the actual "launching points" for the projectile of exile/ restoration theology in Scripture.

Leviticus 26:1–13 served as a reminder to Israel of their covenantal obligation to keep the law, especially by abstaining from idolatry and sanctifying God's sanctuary. In return, the Lord promised that their obedience would be rewarded by the blessings of a fruitful and peaceable land as well as God's own presence with the nation. In verses 1–2 the Israelites are commanded to keep the fundamental aspects of the law (avoiding idolatry and sanctifying both the Sabbath and the sanctuary). In verses 3–13 the Lord promised that His response to faithful obedience would be the provisions of rain in due season and plentiful harvests (vv. 4–5), peace and protection within the land (vv. 6–10), and His presence to dwell with them as He had in Egypt, ensuring the rewards for obedience (vv. 11–13).

The rest of the chapter (26:14–46) revolves around the curses for disobedience. Verses 14 and 15 are emphatic in their assertion that this disobedience is not a mere indiscretion with regard to some technicality of law: "But if you do not listen to me and will not do all these commandments, and if you *despise* [(תִּמְאָסוּ) תּ from מאס, "to treat lightly, despise"] my statutes, and if your soul *abhors* [תִּגְעַל from געל, "consider as filth, dung"] my judgments, so that you will not do all my commandments, that you break my covenant, I will also do this to you" (emphasis mine).

Five stages to the curses may be discerned here. Each stage is characterized by an increasing severity in its consequence over the former.[15] (1) Disobedience would first result in sickness (physical disease) and defeat by their enemies (vv. 14–17).[16] (2) Persistent refusal to submit would lead, secondly, to broken pride through drought and an impoverished harvest and food supply (vv. 18–20).[17] Further hardness would result in (3) being overrun by cattle (vv. 21–22)[18] and (4) sword and pestilence (vv. 23–26).[19] If Israel refused to be warned and to repent, the severity of the penalty increased, culminating in (5) exile from the land (vv. 27–39).

It is possible for the modern reader to underestimate "exile" and "captivity" here as merely unfortunate results of war. In the context of covenant and biblical history, however, the implications for the nation would be far more devastating. If Israel would not be obedient to the covenant, God would move against His people in His fury. As a result, He lay them low in war, scattered their carcasses on the high places, devastated their cities, and scattered them among pagan peoples (2 Kings 25:1–7; 2 Chron. 36:14–21). The preaching of all of the prophets carried this message again and again to the people in rebellion against God. It is clear that the captivities and the diaspora were for disciplinary and theological reasons. God cursed those generations of His chosen people because of their spiritual apostasy. It is impossible to read these words without visualizing the wrath of God's fury visited upon Samaria and Jerusalem.

In Israel's perception, life without the land was scarcely life as God's people at all. The thought of "landedness" is vital to the idea of peoplehood in the OT. The pathos of the exile, therefore, can be felt in passages such as Psalm 137:1–3: "By the rivers of Babylon, there we sat down and wept, when we remembered Zion. Upon the willows in the midst of it we hung our harps. For there our captors demanded of us songs, and our tormentors mirth, saying, 'Sing us one of the songs of Zion.'"

After the destruction and scattering, the land would enjoy its Sabbath (Lev. 26:34–35; cf. 25:2–7). The purpose of these years of rest is to compensate for the sabbatical years in which the land was worked. Neglect of the sabbatical year within Israel would prove symptomatic of the evil that led to other social injustices.[20] Their stewardship of the land in these ways would provide the test of their submission to YHWH and the depth of their relationship to Him. In this sense, the true purpose of the exile cannot be understood apart from a biblical theology of the land in Israel.

One key to the biblical theology of the land is God's ownership of it (Lev. 25:23, "the land is mine"). God's Person and character are vitally linked to the land in Scripture, so much so that it may be said that He related to Israel through their land (cf. Lev. 25:33ff.).[21] God's discipline of Israel under the regulations of the Mosaic covenant were carried out in relation to the land. Land tenure is constantly linked to the fulfillment of ethical and cultic responsibilities on the part of the nation (Deut. 4:5, 14; 5:31; 6:1; 11:31–32; 12:1 et al.). Similarly, the blessing of rest (the security from outside interference or harassment by enemies, Deut. 25:19) was primarily a physical security (cf. Deut. 12:9–10) and a reversal of the wandering or nomadic conditions the fathers had endured in the wilderness. In other words, for Israel to retain land occupancy as the Lord's "tenants" in the land, they must submit to the Owner's regulations.

It is a mistake, however, to view the land as merely a spiritual symbol through which the Lord related to His people. Some have seen the seeming absence of the theme of land in the NT as an indication that land has been displaced in the promises of God, in the Person of Christ, or in the worldwide ministry of the church.[22] The problem with this view is that it implies something that the NT does not teach. Nowhere does the NT assume that it is *in itself* an adequate guide for the Christian faith. Instead, we recognize that the OT was the Bible of the early church. As observed above, the NT presupposes the OT understanding of God and His concerns, including the land. The multitudinous references to the OT within the NT are reminders that the OT must be taken seriously theologically. Wherever the testaments appear to take a differing view or where an OT subject is not explicitly treated, we are not justified in emasculating the OT by the virtues of the NT. Instead, we must consider the perspectives in some way complementary. Therefore, whatever else biblically attends to the land, it includes the physical area given to Israel as an inheritance. Thus, land in the OT is more than mere acreage or area, but it is not less than this physical territory. It is part and parcel of the promise God made to Abraham and furthered in subsequent generations.

God's ownership of the land and relationship to Israel through the land thus established the legal basis for the dispersion. Israel's moral failures in the land were said to have defiled and brought guilt upon the land (Num 35:29–34; Deut. 21:23; 24:4) in which YHWH is said to dwell.[23] It may sound overly simplistic, but the cumulative effect of the covenant violations brought about the exile. The very Person and character of God, His veracity with respect to His Word, and the relationship God intended for Israel to have with the surrounding nations was at stake. Leviticus 26:43–44 makes clear the standard that God's revelation is at stake in sending Israel forth: Literally "because and even because" they have despised God's laws and abhorred His decrees, the land will lie fallow for the sabbatical years.

The survivors of Israel's dispersion, Moses warned, would live in fear and waste away in the lands of their enemies (Lev. 26:36–39). So timid is their condition that even the sound of a wind-blown leaf sets them to flight (cf. Deut. 28:65) and their fear would lead to their eventual demise in the land of their enemies (v. 38). Others would languish away slowly (יִמַּקּוּ from מקק "to fester" [*of wounds*]) or rot, making a miserable life for themselves in enemy lands (cf. fulfillment in Ezek. 4:17; 24:23; 33:10).[24]

What greater curse could God pronounce as a warning upon this newly formed nation on their way to dwell in the land of promise? A curse of exile for disobedience was tantamount to a dispossession from the land, as Israel was about to do to the inhabitants of Canaan. Displacement from the land meant an inability to participate in the ongoing covenant according to the terms of that covenant. In the exile, God purged the rebels from within Israel, the unbelievers, but many righteous would have also died as a result (Ezek. 21:3–4). The punishment was physical and also temporal. Only God knows the spiritual status of those so disciplined.

As severe as this punishment would be, it would not signal total annihilation for Israel since Leviticus 26:40–46 address the possibility of repentance. The didactic lesson for Israel was (as is evidenced by the testimony of the prophets) that the exile was both *corrective* (exacting the requirements of the curses and the law) and *redemptive*. The exile was discipline in the sense that Israel corporately failed to live up to her obligations as God's elect people.[25] The exile was *mercy* in the sense that it was designed to tutor and preserve a remnant in Israel into the repentance that would lead to the hope of restoration. The threat of exile, then, was the Law's way of calling Israel back to allegiance to God. This balance of sovereignty and grace is often lost in OT theologies. There is a disciplinary sense, then, in which both believing and unbelieving Israel entered the exile under both the judgment and grace of God. God, in His mercy, preserved a remnant who could return again to the land.

The requirement for the restoration in vv. 40–46 (if such cursings were actually to play themselves out in Israel's history) is confession (v. 40, הִתְוַדּוּ *hithpael* [resultative] from ידה "know, confess") of sin. The confession would require an accompanying humility (יִכָּנַע, literally, "brought to their knees"), an internal recognition of sin, described here as a "circumcision of the heart" (cf. Deut. 30:6).[26] In seeking restoration, God prevailed upon Israel to confess not only her own sins of treachery (מַעַל, unfaithfulness, betrayal of trust) against Him, but the sins of their forefathers, the very practice later adopted by Daniel (cf. 9:4–19), Ezra (9:6–15), and Nehemiah (1:8–9; 9:6–37).[27]

The basis for the restoration revealed here (v. 42a) is announced as arising solely from God's direction. It is His remembrance (זכר) of the covenant promises to Jacob, Isaac, and Abraham.[28] This is further proof of the unilateral nature of the covenant promises including the land (42b) and that only participation in the *blessings* of the covenant was contingent upon obedience. From this standpoint it may be directly inferred that sufficient theological grounds for the restoration of national Israel are bound in the nature of the covenant-keeping God who honors His promises.

The theme of the legal basis for the dispersion (God's ownership of the land) is resumed briefly in verse 43 so as to contrast Israel's actions with God's reaction (v. 44). God had prescribed provisions for sabbatical rest for the land during Israel's occupancy of it (Lev. 25:1–7, 23; cf. 26:34–35). The sabbatical year was also intended to be a time of special instruction in the law of God (cf. Deut. 31:10–13). Hence, Leviticus 26:43–44 emphasizes that Israel's violation of the land-sabbath legislation is the equivalent to a rejection of God's law (מִשְׁפָּטִים, "laws" and חֻקֹּתַי "my decrees"). It is clear that the resumption of the ecological integrity of the land is another issue addressed by the dispersion of Israel from its land.[29] Another of God's purposes, then, in exiling Israel from the land was to preserve His earlier claims to sanctification of His land. God employs even the distresses of His people to achieve what is good.

God's reaction to Israel's breach of covenant fidelity (v. 44) is not to reject or even destroy them and so break His covenant. He would continue to show fidelity to His promises (cf. v. 42 and Gen. 12:2–3; 26:24; 35:9–15) and to the generation who has the first covenant (cf. v. 45 and Exod. 19:5–6) with Him.

DEUTERONOMY 28–29

Having established many of the preliminary details related to the exile and restoration in Leviticus 26, it is now possible to survey the complementary section in Deuteronomy 28–30 and observe additional nuances or refinements to these same themes as provided by these chapters.[30] Deuteronomy 28–30 has the aspects of conditionality of blessing (discussed above) and cursing, as well as other features in common with Leviticus 26. The pivotal information provided in these chapters also appears in Deuteronomy 30:1–10, which we shall treat in some detail below.

The information found in Deuteronomy 30 is the climax of the theme introduced earlier by Moses near the end of his second address (in 28:36–37): "The Lord will bring you and your king, whom you shall set over you, to a nation which neither you nor your fathers have known, and there you shall serve other gods, wood and stone. And you shall become a horror, a proverb, and a taunt among all the people where the Lord will drive you." Moses warned that for Israel's failure to keep the covenant, she would be driven to a distant foreign land unknown to their fathers. Moses described a reversal of roles between Israel and the nations (28:36–46). Two major elements of concern appear in Deuteronomy 28 that are added to the nature of exile predicted in Leviticus 26. The first is that the dispersion would occur with their governmental leaders, notably, their king (v. 36a).[31] The second is that Israel would worship idols in captivity and become objects of horror, scorn, and ridicule among the nations (36b). If they gave themselves over to idolatry in the land (Lev. 26:1ff.), the Lord would punish them by giving them over fully to idolatry. In addition, the severity of conditions during the siege of the land is foretold in vivid detail in 28:47–57.

Deuteronomy 28:58–68 introduces the theme of the reversal of Exodus typology. Violations of the covenant would ultimately "undo" the events of the exodus and place Israel back into bondage (28:58–29:1). It is from this context of bondage and exile that chapter 30 proceeds. Chapter 29 recapitulates the wilderness wanderings (vv. 2–8), clarifies the covenant-treaty situation Israel finds itself under (vv. 9–21), and reiterates the warnings proffered earlier (cf. Deut. 4:25–31) concerning punishment both within (vv. 22–24) and without (vv. 25–28) the land.

The maxim in Deuteronomy 29:29 has been understood both retrospectively (concluding the argument of chapters 17–28)[32] and as an anticipation of what is to follow (introducing 30:1–34 or the rest of the book).[33] In light of 29:29b ("the revealed things belong to us and to our sons forever"), it would appear that a link is intended to the "sons" of 30:2 and the "things revealed" to the covenant promises concerning a future for national Israel, something not immediately evident to the surrounding nations.

DEUTERONOMY 30:1–10:
THE CONDITIONS FOR RESTORATION TO THE LAND

The passage of primary interest for dispersion and restoration theology is Deuteronomy 30:1–10.[34] The passage is an *inclusio*. In verses 1–2 and 10, Moses reiterated the conditions for Israel's restoration to the land.[35] Within the pericope, the verb שׁוּב ("turn back, return") appears seven times in various forms (vv. 1, 2, 3 [twice], 8, 9, 10), making turning or repentance the dominant theme of the section.[36] The temporal particle כִּי ("when") is conditional and points to three prerequisites on Israel's part to the forgiveness God offers. Forgiveness and restoration from among the nations are offered when Israel: (1) "takes or brings back to heart" ("recalls" the blessings and curses of chapters 27–28, v. 1); (2) "return(s)" to the Lord their God (v. 2); and (3) "obeys" Him (שָׁמַעְתָּ, "hear," in the sense of "obey" His voice, v. 2). Similarly, in verse 10, God's forgiveness follows both obedience ("obey [here תִשְׁמַע] Yahweh your God") and "turning" (שׁוּב). The force of the repentance God requires of Israel is expressed in the repeated phrase, "with all your heart [inner volition] and with all your being [soul, essential person]" (vv. 2, 6, 10; and cf. Deut. 6:4–5).[37] Such a radical change of heart could be called nothing less than a regeneration.

As is known from her later history, it was precisely the failure of Israel to accomplish what the Shema required that led the nation into exile with her leaders and their idols. What would be different about this renewed presence of Israel in the land with national fortunes restored (vv. 3–5)? What is to be gained by the presence of a people unable to obey and thus fully receive the land and its benefit? The answer is plain: nothing, unless Israel's propensity to disobey can somehow be circumvented.[38] Thus, the call to repentance is accompanied by a recognition that genuine repentance is beyond the people's reach without God's help. God Himself (v. 6) must (and will) "circumcise their hearts" to accomplish the turning of heart and soul required for restoration. In the argument of verses 1–6, it is not a matter of whether God will do this, but when.[39] Only an obedient Israel can receive back her land. Only an Israel with a new heart can (as Israel has learned) be fully obedient.

The order of restoration presented here, then, is a renewed heart for Israel and *then* a regathering. Israel's full "prosperity" comes only after they return to the Lord and the Lord then, and only then, regathers a believing remnant to the land. Apart from belief, the remnant has no claim to the land. It is, therefore, not a regathered Israel that is regenerated (cf. Moses' song in Deut. 32:21 where the nation is made jealous by a "no-people"), but a regenerated Israel that is regathered (cf. Deut. 32:43, wherein both people and land are atoned for by the Lord). This would run counter to the claims of some groups that it is necessary that all Jewish people return to the land in order to usher in the restoration promises to Israel.[40]

TOWARD A THEOLOGY OF DISPERSION AND RESTORATION

The nascent elements of a theology of Israel's dispersion and restoration have thus been defined. First, concerning the theological purposes of Israel's dispersion, we have observed that Israel's spiritual apostasy, defined by her violation of the conditional aspects of the covenant, provided sufficient grounds for the covenant curses to be unleashed upon her. Those covenant curses included and predicted the prospect of exile (Lev. 26:14–46; Deut. 4:25–31; 28–30) with a view to reconfirming God's sovereign ownership of the land in which Israel served as tenant (Lev. 25:23). As God related to Israel through His land (cf. Deut. 4:5, 14; 5:31; 6:1 et al.), Israel's stewardship of the land served as an indicator of their submission to Him; therefore discipline was carried out in relation to the land. God's ownership of the land established the legal basis for the dispersion. God purposed, through the removal of Israel in exile, to provide Sabbath rest for the land (Lev. 26:34–35), confirming His sanctification of the land itself and resuming its ecological integrity. God's faithfulness to His word, His justice, and therefore His very Person (reflected in Israel's fear of His name, cf. Deut. 28:58), required the fulfillment of what He had spoken.[41] Finally, His patience spent, God sent Israel into exile as a corrective, disciplinary measure (Lev. 26:40–46), designed ultimately to tutor her unto the need for repentance. The exile proved that many Israelites were unwilling to keep the law by grace, and only a remnant understood their continual need for God's presence and mercy in so doing.

Second, concerning the theological purposes of Israel's restoration, we observe that these are bound up in the Person of God and His mercy. The theology of restoration proceeds solely from God's initiatives and stated purposes. It is His remembrance of His covenant promises that prompt His action (Lev. 26:42). It is His initiative that replants Israel in the land with a circumcised heart (Deut. 30:6). What Israel is unable to do for herself, God purposes to do when she turns with all her heart and all her being to Him (Deut. 30:2, 6, 10). Only an obedient Israel can possess the land thus sanctified by God. God will take upon Himself the task of seeing to this necessity by turning her heart back to Himself.

All of this is in prospect at the end of the Pentateuch. Still ahead of Israel lay the task of occupation of the land of promise. Still ahead were the turbulent years of the judges and the monarchy. Still ahead were the years of the divided kingdom and, ultimately, the exile. Each era proved to have both moments of faith and moments that tested the patience of God.

TRACING THE TRAJECTORIES OF A
THEOLOGY OF DISPERSION AND RESTORATION

As the strands of pentateuchal history and subsequent revelation were inter-woven, the colors of this theology of exile and restoration submerge and re-emerge. Many of the implications of Leviticus 26 and Deuteronomy 28–30 have been discussed in separate chapters in this volume. It is our purpose here to sur-vey the later biblical revelation to determine to what extent this proposed theol-ogy of dispersion and restoration is reflected.

Dispersion and Restoration Theology in the Prophets and Writings

Once Israel took up initial occupancy of the land, God constantly sent His mes-sengers, the prophets, to call His disobedient people to repentance and obedience; to return to a posture under which they might be blessed under His covenant (Dan. 9:6, 11).[42] The concern of each prophet was to align His message with Moses as the prophet par excellence (cf. esp. Deut. 12:32–13:18 and 18:15–22).[43] Leviticus and Deuteronomy contain the warnings and the promises of the land in their es-sence, and thus served as the basis for the later prophetic warnings and calls for a repentant Israel (cf. Hos. 14:1–4; Zeph. 3:15–20). The unbelievers within Israel, however, continued in their intractability and rejected the message of the prophets (cf. Ezra's prayer in Neh. 9:26); at times they were the ones who even persecuted and killed them.

The question may rightly be asked, Were the warnings of covenant curses is-sued by Moses brought to fruition in the OT? If so, in what ways?

In view of her intransigence, God's wrath burned against the northern king-dom of Israel in 722 B.C. and, as Isaiah had predicted (Isa. 8:6–8; 10:5–6), the people were sent into exile, including the believing remnant. Isaiah's prophecy fit into the pattern of Moses' predictions, for accompanying the prediction of ex-ile was the theme of a remnant to return to the land (10:20–27). Here God's warn-ing through Moses was experienced literally through an actual dispersion of Israel from her land. Only the remnant remained or returned, as Isaiah had foretold (cf. further Paul's argument in Rom. 9:27–29). Again, in 587/6 B.C., the southern king-dom of Judah was dispersed according to the judgment principles of the cov-enant. Judah was literally removed from her land (Jer. 39:1–10; 2 Chron. 36:14–21) until a remnant returned under the decree issued by Cyrus (2 Chron. 36:22–23).

During the prolonged exile, Israel still had the opportunity to repent of her sin. The pre-exilic prophets foretold this prospect (e.g., Jer. 30:9–11; 31:16–20), and the prophets of the return echoed its refrain (Hag. 1:5, 7; Zech. 1:3–6). In-deed, as Steck and others have observed, in at least one stream of Jewish tradi-tion, the curse of exile was considered as still upon Israel down through the second temple period (Baruch 1:13–22; 2:27–33; Jub 1:12; 1 Enoch 89:51).[44]

A key question must be addressed here: Were the promises of a national restoration fulfilled in this first return under Ezra, Nehemiah, and Zerubbabel or in subsequent returns to the land?

Cyrus' edict allowed for the return of the deported Jews to their homeland as well as for the rebuilding of the city of Jerusalem and the Temple. Many exiled Jews, however, did not avail themselves of the opportunity to return to Palestine. Some Babylonian Jews had found ways of making life comfortable, even in exile. Only a remnant of the northern tribes ever returned. One might speculate that those who failed to return were never "true Israel." However, several factors mitigate the position that the return promises were completely fulfilled in this era.

First, elements of the theology of restoration detailed in Deuteronomy 30:1–10 are absent from this period. Specifically, Israel's history (subsequent to the exile) is marked by partial attempts at restoration to the land but never actual full tribal reconstruction as was anticipated.[45] Further, the returns under Ezra/ Nehemiah never maximized the promise of Israel under its own king, reuniting north and south (cf. e.g., Hos. 1:11 [a king over a united Judah *and* Israel]; Zech. 10:6; Isa. 11:12; Jer. 23:5). Zerubbabel, Ezra, and Nehemiah saw partial returns, but many refused to go or had to be persuaded to return (Ezra 8:15); certainly not the "whole-hearted" return that Deuteronomy 30 anticipated.

Finally, there are anticipations of future elements of a national restoration present in books as late as Zechariah, which clearly indicate that, although many in Israel did return to the land, there is still a sense in which Israel awaited a wholistic national regathering (cf. Amos 9:15 and esp. Zech. 10:6 where Judah and Joseph are brought back to the land).[46] It is this position that informs the forward-looking perspective of Jesus and His disciples who anticipate a coming messianic reign. It is precisely this position that informs not only Luke in his anticipations (see Luke-Acts below) but Paul's perspective on a future national restoration for Israel (see also below).

It is difficult, therefore, to see all of these predictions as fulfilled in the Babylonian deportation and subsequent return. Clearly, there are in these contexts references not only to individually fulfilled elements of the theology of exile and restoration (cf. James 1:1 to the dispersed Twelve Tribes) but to the unfulfilled eschaton as well (such as the national confessional elements of Hos. 6:1–3). It will not do to refer the fulfillment of many of these prophecies to the eternal state when all people already know God, for passages such as Isaiah 2:2–4 and 51:4 teach that the nations will assemble in Zion to learn the Word of God and His ways. A particular people, whether national Israel or the church, could not serve the mediating function of bringing societal deliverance and salvation to other peoples in the eternal state where such a task is unneeded.

Dispersion and Restoration Theology in Jesus' Teaching

It is frequently argued that there is no doctrine of the restoration of Israel in Jesus' teaching. Some aver that there is no explicit statement by Jesus indicating that He anticipated a restoration of Israel to her land (apart perhaps from Matt. 23:37–39 [parallel to Luke 13:34–35]). Neither, however, are there any explicit statements from Jesus that Israel is forever rejected by God. Can an implicit case be made for either of these options?

Jesus did predict a further dispersion of the remnant of the Jews in His day "to all nations." In Matthew 24:2 and Luke 19:41–44 and 21:20–24, Jesus foretold the destruction of the city of Jerusalem and its temple. Jesus speaks here in the vein of an OT prophet, invoking images of judgment and captivity for unfaithfulness (cf. Deut. 18:15). Did not Jesus, in the spirit of the prophets, make repeated calls to national repentance (cf. Matt. 18:12–14; Luke 15:4–7)? There is no note of finality in Jesus' teaching as though this dispersion were the end of Israel. Neither is there an explicit transference of the promises to another group of persons in prospect or in retrospect (by Luke or Matthew). Instead, Jesus Himself follows the pattern established by Moses concerning God's actions on an unrepentant Israel (Deut. 28:64).

The phrase "until the times of the Gentiles are fulfilled" in Matthew and Luke, when associated with the fall of the city of Jerusalem, at least implies that the fall is of limited duration.[47] A contrast between Israel and the Gentile nations is also implicit. Further, Jesus' portrait here corresponds both to Moses' words in Deuteronomy 32:21 and Paul's subsequent use of those words in Romans 10:19.[48] The Gentiles are now prominent, and God's hand of blessing is extended toward them. Ultimately, however, God follows up His reproof of Israel with vindication in His future plan (Rom. 11:25–26).[49] Israel's rejection cannot thwart God's overall purposes.

This perspective is in concert with Jesus' words as prophet in Matthew 23:37–39 (cf. also Luke 13:34–35): "You will not see me again until you say, 'Blessed is he who comes in the name of the Lord.'" In these passages Jesus cites Psalm 118:26 in anticipation of a favorable response from the Jewish people. Until the nation acknowledges Him as blessed by God, judgment befalls her. God desired to regather Jerusalem, but her unwillingness to allow Him this desire was expressed in her continual killing of God's prophets (Matt. 23:37). The irony Matthew envisions is that, once again, the nation will reject the messenger God sends (cf. Deut. 18:15–19), this time in the person of the Messiah, and so lose out on the then present opportunity to experience the blessing aspects of the promise.

At least two other implicit arguments can be raised in support of Jesus' perspective of a national restoration. First, Jesus' appointment of the twelve disciples may point to Jesus' expectation that Israel will ultimately be fully restored through Jesus' ministry (since twelve is the number of the tribes of Israel).[50] Jesus' promise to the disciples in Matthew 19:28 (cf. Luke 22:30 to follow) that at the renewal of all things, "you who have followed me will also sit on twelve thrones, judging the twelve tribes of Israel." At first, this may appear to be a two-edged sword, for one may utilize the number twelve to read the church back into the

OT,[51] but the broader consensus of Scripture (harmonizing Jesus with Paul) suggests that such a reading backward is gratuitous without some severe restrictions.[52] The apostles, who are the foundation of the church, will lead and exercise judgment over the Israel who (in the context of Matthew and Luke) will reject Jesus.[53] Though the nation and its leaders reject Jesus, the nation will continue to exist. The disciples will have a future role in an administration that will encompass the nation.

A second implicit argument arises from the preaching of Jesus concerning the kingdom. E. P. Sanders has argued that Jesus, in common with the rest of Judaism, assumed the salvation of all of Israel. According to Sanders, Jesus preached in anticipation of the final restoration of Israel.[54] As Jesus preached, He announced a coming kingdom (Matt. 4:17; 10:7; Mark 1:15; Luke 10:9). The coming of the kingdom was not merely one of Jesus' themes, it was the summary theme of His preaching ministry. Such preaching in Jesus' context would have been understood in terms of a national restoration. Jesus' kingdom announcement carried with it an implicit idea of Israel's land and fortunes restored. Yet Jesus' portrayal of that restoration, in passages such as Matthew 23:39, 25:31–46, and Luke 13:35, is not of an immediate but an eschatological restoration at a time when Israel makes national confession of His identity in praise at His second coming (Ps. 118:26; cf. Acts 1:6–8; 3:21; and treatment to follow).

The fact that Jesus taught that there were spiritual aspects to the kingdom (e.g., Luke 17:21, Jesus' own presence as indicative of the advent of the kingdom) does not preclude the possibility of a literal land kingdom. There have always been spiritual aspects to the kingdom promises/relationships which did not preclude literal fulfillment of the land promises (cf. Dan. 2:44; 7:13–14).[55] Further, in OT biblical theology there is no thought of a future kingdom existing metaphysically separate from the earth, and nothing in Jesus' teaching ministry indicated a radical departure from this theology.

Dispersion and Restoration Theology in Luke-Acts

Luke's record of Jesus' theology of dispersion and restoration can be seen from the perspective of the collective gospels (as above) or from within Luke-Acts itself. The task here is to harmonize Luke's perspective on national Israel within Luke-Acts with the foregoing data.[56] Luke-Acts provides potential confirmatory insight as to the early apostolic preaching to Israel and to Gentiles of the need for repentance.

In Luke-Acts the promises to the nation are prominent, and Luke does little to dissuade hope of literal fulfillment of national and/or land promises. From the outset in Luke's gospel, the national perspective is prominent. Gabriel announces to Mary that the Davidic covenant concerning David's throne will be fulfilled in her son (Luke 1:32–33). It is difficult to imagine a throne in this context as understood by Mary as anything less than a literal fulfillment of the restoration of

Israel.[57] Indeed, Mary herself looks for the fulfillment of Israel's national covenant hopes (Luke 1:54–55), choosing the OT image of the nation as God's servant (Isa. 41:8–9; 44:1–2, 21).[58] Zacharias also looks for a restoration of the fortunes of Israel (Luke 1:68–69), including deliverance from enemies (vv. 71, 74; clearly alluding to Roman occupation of the land) and fulfillment of covenant promises (v. 72). He is in the land of promise as he speaks his hope. Similarly, Simeon awaits the "consolation of Israel" (2:25), a phrase pregnant with implications of the exile theology of Isaiah 40–55 (Luke 2:29–32). Certainly at the outset in Luke's gospel, the prospect for the "restoration of Israel" (2:25) and the "redemption of Jerusalem" (2:38) burn brightly in the minds of those affected by the advent of Messiah.

As noted above, Luke's gospel suggests no replacement theology, no explicit treatment of the twelve apostles or their followers as new Israel (Luke 6), but it does hold out hope for national Israel's future (Luke 13:35).[59] This national hope is spelled out in direct and indirect ways in the remainder of the gospel. Jesus' response to the Pharisees concerning the signs of the coming of the kingdom in Luke 17:20–21 is no exception. The necessary elements for identifying the kingdom were in their midst; responding properly to the King would enable them to see that. Jesus elaborated on the "days of the Son of Man" before His disciples in Luke 17:22–37. There He anticipated a rule that fulfilled God's plan of redemption (as in Peter's estimation in Acts 3:18–26) upon His return, which brings about the consummation of the kingdom. The kingdom is "near" in one sense: Jesus the King is here (Luke 10:9–11; 17:20–21). That kingdom, however, will only be inaugurated in its fullness when Jesus, the Son of Man, returns (Luke 17:22–37).[60]

The kingdom perspective unfolds further in Luke 21:24 where Jesus described Jerusalem's fall in the current age "until the times of the Gentiles are fulfilled." The expectation of a literal kingdom runs throughout Luke. As late as Luke 22:24, the disciples are presented as arguing their status in the hierarchy of the kingdom. In Luke 22:30, Jesus pictures the apostles, not as rebuked for cherishing national promises (including that rule), but sitting on thrones judging the twelve tribes of Israel! Why would Jesus/Luke portray a rule over Israel (the nation) here if they intend a more general rule over all of humanity? Does this not suggest a prominence for national Israel in their thinking?

Is this emphasis on literal fulfillment of national promises sustained in Luke's portrait of the post-resurrection apostolic ministry of Acts? A pivotal text for confirmation or denial of our suspicions is Acts 1:6.[61] Here, the eleven disciples ask Jesus a final question just prior to His ascension: "Lord, is it at this time You are restoring the kingdom to Israel?" (Acts 1:6 NASB). In the disciples' question, there are at least three key expectations: (1) they expected Jesus to be the executor of the divine promises; (2) fulfilling the promises involved restoration of something that once existed (namely, the earthly national kingdom); and (3) the restoration would be to Israel, not the church. Jesus' response does not rebuke their nationalistic hopes as misguided. Instead He sends them first to Jerusalem and Judea as witnesses of the gospel message.

As the disciples went forth with the message to Israel, their message retains the elements of repentance defined in Leviticus 26 and Deuteronomy 30 as precursors to a national restoration. According to Peter, Israel must repent and return to the Lord with circumcised hearts in order to receive forgiveness and "times of refreshing" (Acts 3:19–20; cf. "refreshment" [ἀνάψυξις] from Symmachus' LXX of Isa. 32:15) in which Jesus is sent from heaven to "restore all things" (Acts 3:21). Peter calls the nation to repent in order that the promises be fulfilled. Again, as in Acts 1:6, Peter expects Jesus to be the executor of the promises to Israel (3:20); he anticipates a restoration of all things (3:21); and he expects this to take place within and to Israel (since it is evident from the context that Peter did not include the Gentiles in his scenario of the future). Thus understood, Peter did not offer the Jews the kingdom, something he was unable to do in view of Acts 1:6–8, but offered repentance that his generation might receive the promised blessing (Acts 3:26).[62]

The same emphases on repentance for restoration discernible in Peter's speech to men of Israel are present in Paul's speeches in the Book of Acts and will be considered below.[63] This need for repentance in Israel, however, is proclaimed in the Book of Acts with a view toward hastening the fulfillment of the Levitical/ Deuteronomic promises concerning national restoration. Peter even issues a warning that the prophet like Moses has come (Acts 3:22–26)! There remain other aspects of Acts to harmonize within this perspective (such as James' anticipation of the restoration of David's tent in Acts 15:15ff.; "after these things"),[64] but these basic observations undermine the understanding that the church received the land promises in a replacement or transference of the covenant blessings.[65] Luke thus portrays the beginning stages of the fulfillment of the OT promises in the person of Jesus (through whom the church derives its benefits),[66] but this does not require that what he records dissipates the fulfillments that the OT intended and still expects for the nation. The rest of the story is yet to come. Peter's call to repentance and "restoration of all things" thus leads, in Luke's view (as in Jesus' view above), to a re-enfranchisement of Israel according to the ancient promises of Leviticus 26 and Deuteronomy 30.

Dispersion and Restoration Theology in Paul

Within Luke's narrative in Acts, Paul is portrayed as the apostle to the Gentiles on behalf of Israel. The reasons for this designation become apparent in both the defenses and speeches Paul makes before the Jews (cf. Acts 13:16–46) and later in his epistolary teaching concerning the Jews and their future (Romans 9–11; 1 Thessalonians 2:14–16).

I submit, as have others, that Paul perceives the vital relationship between people, land, and covenant in the OT requires that land be retained as an essential component of the original promises.[67] It makes little sense to affirm the literality of one aspect of God's promise while denying the same literal benefit to other aspects of that same promise.

In this vein, it has been observed elsewhere that Deuteronomy contains, *in nuce*, everything necessary for Paul to construct his argument that there is a future for Israel, in Romans 9–11.[68] The main elements of a theology of dispersion/cursings observed in Leviticus 26 are present throughout Romans. Israel has a recalcitrant heart (Rom. 2:4–5, 10:21; citing Isa. 65:2 in a Deuteronomic context) that has led to divine judgment (Rom. 9:1–3; cf. 2:24). The hardening is partial for, according to Romans 11:7–8 (citing Deut. 29:3 and Isa. 29:10), "the elect obtained it, but the rest were hardened."

In Romans 11:25 the hardening of Israel provides an opportunity for mercy toward others. God's mercy to Gentiles was extended as an opportunity resulting from the disobedience of Israel. God's mercy to Gentiles in Christ (Rom. 10:19, cf. Deut. 32:21) provides an opportunity by which He will provoke Israel to jealousy and again extend His mercy to His chosen ones (Rom. 11:30–31; 1 Thess. 2:14–16). Paul thus suggests, in keeping with Moses' prediction in Deuteronomy 32:21, that one purpose for the exile was that God would seek to make Israel jealous by means of the Gentiles in order to provoke Israel to repentance and emulation (1 Thess. 2:14–16; Rom. 10:19; 11:11, 14).

Paul, therefore, is seen in the Book of Acts working urgently to evangelize the Gentiles to bring the "full number of the Gentiles" in (Rom. 11:25; so also Luke 21:24) to provoke Israel to repentance so that all Israel might be saved (Rom. 11:25–26) and compose a bride for Christ, composed of both Jewish and Gentile peoples (cf. Isa. 42:6; 49:6). This provides a reaffirmation of Paul's view of the end: the salvation of Israel follows the salvation of the Gentiles (Rom. 11:11–15).

Israel was herself a special possession of God (Exod. 19:5–6), set apart from other nations to be a light to those nations. As such, Israel served and serves God's ultimate purpose of bringing glory to Himself in this world (Zech. 2:8; Isa. 43:7). If this is the case, why do many Jewish people continue in dispersion now? Part of the answer is that, as Paul explained, they are under a curse for their failure to abide by the Law (Gal. 3:10; Deut. 27:26). It was that curse that sent them into exile under judgment (Leviticus 26; Deuteronomy 30). It is that curse that they remain under until the veil is lifted (2 Cor. 3:13). The veil is lifted for individual Jews when they come to Christ. The veil is finally lifted for the nation when God gives them the new heart they need in order to see their Messiah Yeshua and the kingdom He brings. In the meantime, the Jewish people are not prohibited by the curse from returning to the land of their own volition. Paul, however, viewed his apostolic task as an urgent one, as a prophetic messenger bringing the message to the full number of Gentiles so that he might see the arrival of the day of national repentance and salvation for his people, the Jews.

CONCLUSION

We who stand in the present, looking back on the past, are often able to make more critical and analytical judgments about the nature of past events. Such a vantage point, however, is no guarantee of objectivity. Indeed, evangelicals who take the Word of God at face value for its promises to Israel are often subjected to harsh criticism for their reflections. The forward-looking promises in the NT need not consider the actual restoration of Israel to her land as integral to their fruition except that this is precisely the fulfillment anticipated early on in Leviticus and Deuteronomy and still awaited in the prophecies of Zechariah. It is the pattern of literal fulfillment of God's promises in the past that causes evangelicals to anticipate a literal fulfillment of those promises in the future.

In the unfolding of biblical history, God promised the nation Israel the right to the land unconditionally. In unconditionally promising the land, God anticipated Israel's failure to live up to the covenant stipulations to remain in that land and therefore: (1) warned of and promised a national exile in response to/for that national failure; and (2) promised a national restoration in a future time when Israel repented with a circumcised heart. This promise is sustained as a hope and an anticipation throughout the prophetic writings. It is further sustained in Jesus' anticipations of a national future as recorded in the Gospels (especially Luke) which picture the promises/return as yet unfulfilled. The Book of Acts pictures the national promises as yet to come but supplies the means of Israel's restored heart—the indwelling Holy Spirit. The apostles in Acts preach repentance to unbelieving Israel so that times of refreshing and restoration may come in. Even Paul's picture of Israel in Romans is still that of a nation with an uncircumcised heart in need of repentance and made jealous through God's work among the Gentiles (Rom. 2:24–25; 9:1–3).

Thus, faith and practice come into play in terms of the personal and practical experience of the nation Israel. Both believing Jews and unbelieving Jews constitute and remain throughout the apostolic preaching in Acts the one Israel, the people of God. They are the people of God in the sense that the transmission of the benefits of the covenant are still available to them. In Acts, believing Jews are part of the end-times remnant of God's people that calls unbelieving Israel to repentance.[69] Though united with Gentiles in the body of Christ, believing Jews are also part of the one people of God. This unique relationship, however, does not dissolve the biblical distinctions between Israel and the church.

Israel continues in its elected role, serving two primary purposes in the Bible.[70] First, Israel serves a revelatory purpose through which we have received the canonical OT and the ultimate perseverance of Israel unto salvation. Second, Israel serves a blessing purpose (Gen. 12:3) through which the promise of the Redeemer came. In Israel's election as a corporate nation, God accomplishes these ends. As indicated above, this is not simply an ethical election but an election for purposes of sanctification. The channel is not automatic. There is a remnant that remains faithful in spite of being cast off as a result of the Levitical/Deuteronomic curses. God's corporate election is no guarantee of salvation for particular Israelites.

The picture that a biblical theology of dispersion and restoration presents is ultimately that Israel is grafted back into God's salvific promises by means of a marvelous intervention of God's own power in their hearts. Then God's promises to Abraham will be fulfilled as promised in both a spiritual and national sense.

DISCUSSION QUESTIONS

1. Which Testament, Old or New, takes priority in understanding God's purposes for Israel? How would you support your answer?

2. Why is it insufficient for Bible students to develop eschatological themes solely from the New Testament?

3. What do Leviticus 26 and Deuteronomy 28–32 suggest concerning future dispersions and regatherings for national Israel? What reasons do these texts suggest will constitute sufficient grounds for the dispersion? What spiritual conditions do these same texts suggest will comprise the ultimate regathering of the nation?

4. Why is it a mistake to view the land as merely a spiritual symbol through which the Lord related to His people?

5. How were the warnings of covenant curses and return brought to fruition in the OT? What aspects of promise remain unfulfilled?

6. Did the NT authors and characters (such as Jesus and Paul) downplay the role of national Israel in the future? What specific texts (Gospels and Acts) suggest that Jesus and others continued to hold forth the literal promises to the nation?

7. How do the trajectories of the biblical themes of dispersion and restoration of Israel in the remainder of the OT and NT align with the original revelation given in Leviticus and Deuteronomy?

ENDNOTES

1. These statements arise from a presupposition concerning appropriate theological method as applied to the testaments. Which Testament, Old or New, takes priority in understanding God's purposes for Israel? This presupposition or starting point ultimately affects the conclusions drawn about the outcome of divine promises. The present article uses the OT as the starting point and attempts to trace the development

of the theme progressively through Scripture. NT authors often make an analogical or typological use of an OT motif. They do so in order to be able to employ OT materials to give answers to the (contemporary) questions which the NT authors are asking. The NT is thus not trying to interpret the OT in the light of the theological/authorial concerns which are intrinsic to the OT itself. NT authors do not, in other words, restrict their focus on the *meaning* those texts had as part of the communication between God and his people before Christ. Instead, they attempt to find answers to their own questions and issues, as other Jews of their day would utilize the Scriptures, without displacing the OT meanings. See further Paul D. Feinberg, "The Hermeneutics of Discontinuity" in John S. Feinberg, ed. *Continuity and Discontinuity: Perspectives on the Relationship Between the Old and New Testaments* (Westchester, Ill.: Crossway, 1988), 109–28; and Mike Stallard, "Literal Interpretation, Theological Method, and the Essence of Dispensationalism" *Journal of Ministry and Theology* 1.1 (1997), 5–36.

2. A complementary hermeneutic, thus defined, has a latent potential for subjectivity. Where can the boundaries be found which demarcate where NT expansions of OT promises have occurred? Certainly the NT establishes the appropriate parameters, but how does the OT meaning relate to those parameters? One supposition of this article is that however the tension between meaning/meanings is resolved, the NT expansion must include the meaning of the original OT promise. I thereby reject a *sensus plenior.*

3. Walter Kaiser, "An Evangelical Response," in C. A. Blaising and D. L. Bock, editors, *Dispensationalism, Israel, and the Church: The Search for Definition* (Grand Rapids: Zondervan, 1992), 369–70. Kaiser's observation here suggests the willingness of progressives to engage covenant theology on its own turf, in exegesis of specific NT texts, but to the neglect of OT promise. The reader of progressive dispensational writings must decide for himself whether or not the progressives have let the covenant theologians set the agenda for their response.

4. Reformed theologians often object that the NT itself does not suggest more than one or two debatable texts suggesting a regathering for Israel. They argue that another means of interpreting the NT is required by the silence of the NT on the matter. This argument is engaged in some detail below.

5. See "Israel the Land" by Ronald Allen in this volume. See further William D. Davies, *The Gospel and the Land* (Berkeley: Univ. of California Press, 1974), who suggests that the theme of the land is dispensable to Christians as evidenced by the lack of treatment in the NT. By way of contrast, W. Breuggemann, *The Land: Place as Gift, Promise and Challenge in Biblical Faith* (Philadelphia: Fortress, 1976), 3, sees in the land "a central, if not *the central theme* of biblical faith." Breuggemann suggests that the theme of the (literal, materialistic) land is prominent, though subtle, in the NT. Walter C. Kaiser, *Toward Old Testament Ethics* (Grand Rapids: Zondervan, 1983) and Elmer A. Martens, "God's Design: Land," Chapter 6 in *God's Design: A Focus on Old Testament Theology*, 2d edition (Grand Rapids: Baker, 1994), in arguing from the themes of promise and covenant, suggest that an approach to land "according to the Scriptures" must proceed according to both testaments. See further C. J. H. Wright, *God's People in God's Land: Family, Land, and Property in the Old Testament* (Grand Rapids: Eerdmans, 1990) and Peter Diepold, *Israel's Land* (Stuttgart: W. Kohlhammer, 1972), 187, concludes that the land is "konstitutiv für Israel's existenz."

6. See P. R. Ackroyd, *Exile and Restoration: A Study of Hebrew Thought of the Sixth Century B.C.* (Philadelphia: Westminster, 1968); Thomas M. Raitt, *A Theology of Exile: Judgment/Deliverance in Jeremiah and Ezekiel* (Philadelphia: Fortress, 1977).

7. Volumes of material (both pro and con) have been written on Israel's restoration in Romans 11:25–32. For bibliographic references see James D. G. Dunn, *Romans 9–16, Word Biblical Commentary,* 38B (Dallas: Word, 1988), 517–18; 675–76; and Douglas Moo, *The Epistle to the Romans, NICNT* (Grand Rapids: Eerdmans, 1996), 547–54 footnotes, 710–39, footnotes. See further the article by Harold Hoehner in this volume, "Israel in Romans 11."

8. See, for example, Christopher J. H. Wright, *An Eye for an Eye: The Place of Old Testament Ethics Today* (Downers Grove, Ill.: InterVarsity Press, 1983), 46–90. In pages 90ff., Wright extends his model to accommodate the future redeemed humanity in relation to the new heavens and earth.

9. For an overview of the conditional/unconditional aspects of the promises to the patriarchs, see Bruce K. Waltke, "The Phenomenon of Conditionality Within Unconditional Covenants," in *Israel's Apostasy and Restoration: Essays in Honor of Roland K. Harrison,* ed. A. Gileadi (Grand Rapids: Baker, 1988), 123–39. I find little to disagree with in Walter C. Kaiser, *Toward Rediscovering the Old Testament* (Grand Rapids: Zondervan, 1987), 46–58 and 153–154. Kaiser argues for the unilateral nature of the Noahic, Abrahamic, Davidic, and New Covenants as well as for the Covenant of the New Heavens and New Earth. In Kaiser's view, obedience is a condition for participation in the blessings or benefits of the covenant and does not thwart God's plan revealed in the covenant. Covenant benefits can be lost through disobedience, but are transmitted even by those who lose them to their successors as part of the messianic line. For an alternate but approximate position based on revelation rather than promise as the essence of covenant, see John H. Walton, *Covenant: God's Purpose, God's Plan* (Grand Rapids: Zondervan, 1994), 108ff.

10. The first and only biblically recorded instance of God "writing something down" occurs in the giving of the decalogue to Moses (Exod. 20–24). In Exodus 20:1–17, the words of the covenant were given audibly to Moses. In Exodus 24:12, God gave to Moses, וְהַמִּצְוָה אֲשֶׁר כָּתַבְתִּי לְהוֹרֹתָם, "the commandments which I have written for the people's instruction." Later in the same narrative (Exod. 31:18; 32:15, 16), these tablets are identified as that which is written "by the finger of God" and "God's writing" and delivered directly into the hands of Moses. The same emphasis on the nature of these writings continues into Exodus 34 where, following the idolatry and repentance of the nation (Chapters 32 and 33), God again pledged to write the words which were on the former, shattered tablets (v. 1, וְכָתַבְתִּי) and Moses described the finished product as what God wrote (v. 28). The idea of God as a *direct* Author or Scribe for certain texts, therefore, comes early in biblical revelation. Before Moses took pen to hand in composing Genesis, God is said to be at work in actual writing, thus safeguarding the foundational component of the Hebrew (and later Christian) ethic.

11. See the development of this theme below in the sections on "Dispersion and Restoration Theology" in Jesus' Teaching, in Luke-Acts and in Paul's writings.

12. See Donald E. Gowan, "Losing the Promised Land —The Old Testament Considers the Inconceivable," in *From Faith to Faith: Essays in Honor of Donald G. Miller,* ed. D. Y. Hadidian, PTMS 31 (Pittsburgh: Pickwick, 1979), 247–48. Obviously, advocates of a seventh-century date for Deuteronomy (such as Gerhard von Rad, *Deuteronomy,* OTL (Philadelphia: Wesminster, 1966), 25–28, 183) would reject the witness of Leviticus as even later (circa 450 B.C.). Such tradition-history analyses are invariably subjective.

13. See George Mendenhall, *Law and Covenant in Israel and the Ancient Near East* (Pittsburgh: Biblical Colloquium, 1955); F. Charles Fensham, "Clauses of Protection

in Hittite Vassal-Treaties and the Old Testament," *Vetus Testamentum* 13 (1963), 141ff.; and Meredith Kline, *Treaty of the Great King* (Grand Rapids: Eerdmans, 1963), for an introduction to the concept. The idea is that the great king, YHWH in this case, has redeemed the people from the bondage of another nation (here Egypt) and so their absolute loyalty belongs to him. The sovereign will continue to act benificently with them if they are faithful to the covenant.

14. See K. A. Kitchen, "Ancient Orient, 'Deuteronism,' and the Old Testament," in *New Perspectives on the Old Testament*, J. B. Payne, ed. (Waco: Word, 1970), 3–13. Kitchen demonstrates that other peoples in the ancient Near East knew of the threat of exile as part of the curses attendant to a covenant. Gowan, "Losing the Promised Land," 248, is correct in his assertion that this does not *prove* that these curses/threats are early, but it does move a substantial burden of proof to those who would assert that they are late. A thorough discussion of dating is beyond the scope of this article. Some preliminary information on the date of these texts may be found in John E. Hartley, *Leviticus, Word Biblical Commentary*, 4 (Dallas: Word, 1992), 459–62. Hartley lists seven reasons commending an early date for this text. The need to posit the exile as an event read into these texts arises only if one finds the possibility of predictive prophecy unbearable.

15. Several factors lend themselves to this conclusion. Each set of curses displays a variation in the lead formula of the curse ("and if . . . if in addition . . . and if in spite of . . . ," etc.) and each curse reiterates the fact of Israel's disobedience before listing the curse (suggesting an increasing obstinacy). The use of the term *yāsar* ("to discipline, to punish") also indicates that the purpose of the discipline was remedial as well as punitive.

16. This first stage of the cursing for covenant violators is the appointing (וְהִפְקַדְתִּי, "I will appoint," from פקד, "visiting") of terror (26:16). פקד describes YHWH's visitation for either blessing or judgment. Instead of peace and safety (26:6–8), there would be terror and sickness. This sudden terror is actually a helplessness. The "sickness" (הַשַּׁחֶפֶת —NASB "consumption") is a rare word, found only here. The LXX rendered it "scurvy" (ψώραν, "itch, mange, scurvy"). קַדַּחַת, likely "fever," is found only here and in Deuteronomy 28:22, another curse section of the covenant.

17. The expression that "your land shall not yield its increase" is perhaps reminiscent of the curse on Cain (Gen. 4:12, "it shall no longer yield its strength to you"), who also refused to be reasoned out of his sin by God.

18. Israel's continued disobedience is stressed in the remainder of this section through the repetition of the term קֶרִי, (literally "opposition" or "contrariness"). It occurs seven times in Lev. 26 (vv. 21, 23, 24, 27, 28, 40, 41) as an adverbial modifier of הלך ("to walk," figurative for the sense of "living"). It is always accompanied by forms of עִמִּי, suggesting Israel's antithetical relationship to YHWH. The LXX translates it with πλαγιοι, "walk perversely."

19. The sword represents war against the whole nation. The cities will be besieged so that the "staff of bread" or food supply is endangered. When they take refuge within their walls, YHWH's armies will enter in the form of pestilence, weakening the hands of the defenders to make the fifth stage, captivity, inevitable.

20. Wright, *God's People in God's Land*, 150–51. There were, of course, other causes for the exile such as idolatry, rejection of God's Word and messengers (2 Chron. 36:14–21), and failure to keep covenant, but all of these causes related directly to Israel's right to retain the land.

21. God's relationship to the people through the land is seen in the Jubilee requirements in Leviticus 23:10ff. and 25:2.

22. See, for example, Bruce K. Waltke, "A Response," in Blaising and Bock, eds. *Dispensationalism, Israel and the Church*, 347–59. Replacement theology advocates suggest that spiritual realities have replaced the physical (including the "landed") aspect of the covenant promises. In other words, what the OT promised physically, the NT provides in a spiritual manner (through the blessings of Messiah). The difficulties of this approach cannot be addressed in full here, but the replacement approach to texts in a postmodern setting may border on a reader-response approach in which the reader imports his perceptions into a text, distorting the original intention of the author. For further literature on the hermeneutical issue see Grant R. Osborne, *The Hermeneutical Spiral* (Downers Grove, Ill.: InterVarsity Press, 1991), 287ff., and Walter C. Kaiser, "What About the Future? The Meaning of Prophecy," Chapter 8 in Walter C. Kaiser & Moises Silva, *An Introduction to Biblical Hermeneutics: The Search for Meaning* (Grand Rapids: Zondervan, 1994), 148–58; 193–206.

23. Similarly, the Canaanites are said to have defiled the land by their practices (Lev 18:24–25) and this was one basis for the extermination of the nations within the land.

24. The same root is used in Zech 14:12 to describe the reversal of the curse and the fortunes that befall those who war against Jerusalem. See also Psalm 38:6 ("grow foul, fester") and Isaiah 34:4 ("wear away, moulder").

25. The corporate perspective of the OT with regard to the national promises is one key to understanding the various perspectives on national Israel. Whereas NT soteriology is individual in focus, the OT tends toward a corporate perspective. The harmonization of these two perspectives between the testaments is a key issue. A theologians' desire to find individual election in the OT will frequently lead him to read NT soteriological aspects back into the OT.

26. Moses (and later Jeremiah, Stephen, and Paul [Jer 4:4; Acts 7:51; Rom. 2:29]) used עָרֵל of the heart rather than the foreskin (cf. Deut 10:16; 30:6). The reference to the heart is to the volitional seat of decision making. Their hearts would have an attitude devoid of faith. To have a circumcised heart is to possess sanctification through faith. In the Levitical context the expectation would be a preparedness, an inclination to obey God's word. The covenant curses do not come upon pious believers who fall short of God's perfection. They come on a wicked generation, uncircumcised in heart, that needs to turn to the Lord (cf. Rom. 9:6–8). See the treatment of Deuteronomy 30 and surrounding context below.

27. Hartley, *Leviticus*, 469 observes a threefold repetition of "iniquity" in verses 40–41 and suggests that this forms a link between vv. 40–41 and the last curse of v. 39.

28. In context, זכר stands in contrast with הפר. God "remembering" His covenant (v. 42) is the antithesis of Israel's "breaking" the covenant (v. 44).

29. As observed above, God related to His people through their land. At least one passage (Lev. 18:4–5) makes the land an *active* participant in dispelling wicked inhabitants from within it.

30. An earlier reference to the portending exile and restoration occurs in Deuteronomy 4:25–31. It appears at the outset of the first inner frame (chapters 4–11) section and corresponds to the last half of the inner frame of the book (chapters 27–30). As Duane L. Christensen has observed, "the focus of attention in Deut. 4–11 is on the ideal Israel, those who are called to obey Yahweh's commandments as they set forth to conquer the land. The focus of attention in Deut. 27–30 is already directed to a more distant future in its call to a renewal of the covenant and subsequent prosperity after their dispersal 'among the nations' (Deut. 30:1)." See his *Deuteronomy 1–11* in *Word Biblical Commentary*, 6a, D. Hubbard et. al eds. (Waco: Word, 1991), 69. The focus in this paper is on the latter half of this inner frame (for obvious reasons), but it is

important to observe the absence of any conditionality in this earlier text. The driving force to repent is something God Himself will embed in them to encourage them to return to Him and to the land (cf. Lev. 26:40–45; Jer. 31:27–34; Ezek. 36:22–31).

31. The institution of monarchy had been long promised to Israel (Gen. 17:6, 16; 35:11; 36:31; 49:10) and provided for in Deuteronomy 17:14–20.

32. See H. F. van Rooy, "Deuteronomy 28:69—Superscript or Subscript?" *Journal of Northwest Semitic Languages* 14 (1988), 215–22.

33. See Norbert Lohfink, "Dtn 28:69—Überschrift oder Kolophon?" *Biblische Notizen* 64 (1992), 40–52.

34. Clearly, in the near context, the force of these verses is to present a compelling case for Israel's obedience in the present. The predictive element is contingent, as was the case with Leviticus 26, upon Israel's failure to keep covenant. See Peter C. Craigie, *The Book of Deuteronomy*, NICOT (Grand Rapids: Eerdmans, 1976), 364.

35. Craigie, *Deuteronomy*, 364, observes that this verse "indicates the new covenant, when God would in his grace deal with man's basic spiritual problem." There is a return to a contingent (if/then) sense in verse 10 as contrasted with the unconditional promise of verse 6.

36. The verb also later became a prominent term in the prophets for calling Israel to repentance in a covenantal context (cf. Jeremiah 48 uses; Isaiah 10 uses; Hos 6:1; 7:10; Amos 4:6). See William L. Holladay, *The Root SÛBH in the Old Testament* (Leiden: Brill, 1958). See further, A. Rofé, "The Covenant in the Land of Moab (Deut. 28:69–30:20)" in *Das Deuteronium. Entstehung, Gestalt und Botschatt*, ed. N. Lohfink, BETL 68 (Leuven: University Press, 1985), 310–20. In Deuteronomy 30:3, שׁוּב is used in the sense of "restoration" to the land. Though שׁוּב is used in more literal senses, it often implies a metaphorical "turning" from or toward something.

37. Here Moses returns to the essence of the Deuteronomic covenant principle and requirement of Deuteronomy 6:4–5.

38. J. Gordon McConville, *Grace in the End: A Study in Deuteronomic Theology* (Grand Rapids: Zondervan, 1993), 136ff., recognizes this same problem, and attributes it to a major tension which, he posits, the Deuteronomic History attempted to resolve. See further his "1 Kings VIII 46–53 and the Deuteronomic Hope" in *Vetus Testamentum* XLII, 1 (1992): 71–79.

39. As observed by Eugene Merrill, *Deuteronomy, The New American Commentary* (Nashville: Broadman & Holman, 1994), 4:389: ". . . the conditional clauses of vv. 1–6 require a nuance not of contingency but of time. The issue was not whether Israel and/or the Lord would do thus and so but when. Such lack of qualification requires that all of the blessings of restoration promised to Israel be seen as acts of divine initiative and grace, ones reserved for eschatological times and embracing the nation as such."

40. See, for example, David H. Stern, *Messianic Jewish Manifesto*, 2d edition (Jerusalem: Jewish New Testament Publications, 1991), 227–38. Stern calls for Jews, believing and unbelieving, to make *aliyah* (immigration to Israel). He teaches that self-examination of motives for remaining "in dispersion" is incumbent on messianic Jews in the present era and profitable even to unbelieving Jews. Messianic Jews, like all Christians, should reflect on their situation in life to determine whether they are in the will of God. Within the perspective of Deuteronomy and later Ezra/ Nehemiah, however, such immigration is permitted, but not required. Only those whose spirits were sovereignly stirred by God (Ezra 1:9) returned. The returns under Zerubbabel, Nehemiah, and Ezra with their accompanying problems illustrate that the remnant's return was not whole-hearted. God must create the heart in Israel

to seek Him and return and Jewish people cannot hasten this repentance by returning to the land when God's purposes with regard to Israel will make no distance too great for preventing their return. Arnold Fruchtenbaum, in his *The Footsteps of the Messiah: A Study of the Sequence of Prophetic Events* (Tustin, Calif.: Ariel Ministries Press, 1982), 65–68, has attempted to directly connect the present State of Israel as a fulfillment of prophecy by observing that there are two international returns. In the first return, there is "a regathering in unbelief in preparation for judgment" (cf. Ezek. 20:33–38; 22:17–22; Zeph. 3:11–20). This first return precedes and corresponds to the tribulational judgments. In the second return, the regathering is in belief, in preparation for the millennial blessings (Isa. 11:11–12). God may choose to use the presence of modern Israel to bring about these purposes, but whether He does or not, the remnant of Israel *will* be regathered in repentance.

41. Later, Ezekiel dwelt upon the implications/necessities of the restoration for the sake of God's holy name (Ezek. 36:22–24). Ezekiel's portrait of the restoration included not only a regathering of the nation, but a renewal of the land and its products (36:34–35) and a new covenant accompanied by cleansing and the presence of the Spirit within them (36:24, 27).

42. The exceptions to this rule, of course, were those prophets sent to deliver a message of impending judgment (cf. Amos 7:17; Isa. 6:9–13; Jer. 1:10; 18:7–17) before the exile. The language of those warnings, however, often served as reminders of the covenant warnings and, hence, would have alerted the nation to the reasons for impending disaster and the opportunity the covenant provided for repentance.

43. A history of the prophetic movement in Israel may be found in W. J. Beecher, *The Prophets and the Promise* (Grand Rapids: Baker, 1963), 36–65. See also J. Blenkinsopp, *A History of Prophecy in Israel* (Philadelphia: Westminster, 1983), 36ff. Accompanying signs and wonders had to be tested against the message of the prophet so that he would not lead Israel astray (to other gods). Additional revelation had to coincide and be consistent with what had been divinely revealed by God. It is in this sense that Moses' message is foundational: Every prophet subsequent to Moses had his "revelation" tested by the divinely given words of the Pentateuch, some of which are described as "inscribed by God's own hand" (Exod. 20:1–17, 24:12, 31:18; 32:15–16).

44. See Odil H. Steck, "Das Problem theologischer Strömungen in nachexilischer Zeit," *Evange-lische Theologie* 28 (1968), 445–58 (Steck argues that the Deuteronomic view of Israel's history permeated Judaic literature from 200 B.C. to 100 A.D. and also affects Paul's perspective in 1 Thess. 2); and George W. E. Nickelsburg, *Jewish Literature Between the Bible and the Mishnah: A Historical and Literary Introduction* (Philadelphia: Fortress, 1981), 18ff.

45. On the need for a tribal reenfranchisement, see Stephen D. Ricks, "The Prophetic Literality of Tribal Reconstruction," in *Israel's Apostasy and Restoration*, 273–81.

46. See further, Walter C. Kaiser, "Zechariah 10: The Land of Israel and the Future Return," in this volume. The designation "Judah and Joseph" indicates both the northern and the southern kingdoms and their tribes.

47. The arguments here are adapted from Darrell L. Bock, *Luke 9:51–24:53*, ECNT 3B (Grand Rapids: Baker, 1996), 1680–81; supported by D. L. Tiede, *Prophecy and History in Luke-Acts* (Philadelphia: Fortress, 1980), 87–96; and Craig A. Evans, *Luke*, NIBC 3 (Peabody, Mass.: Hendrickson, 1990), 313–14.

48. See further Rom. 11:11–12, 15, 30–32; 1 Thess. 2:14–16 and the partial development of these themes later in this article.

49. See, once again, the article by Harold Hoehner, "Israel in Romans 9–11," in this volume.

50. See Michael J. Wilkins, *Following the Master: A Biblical Theology of Discipleship* (Grand Rapids: Zondervan, 1992), 149–50. There is "both a backward and a forward look" to the number 12 in Scripture: Backward in terms of the 12 tribes of Israel and forward in terms of Matt. 19:28, Acts 1:15–26; Rev. 7:1–8; and 21:12–14. Cf. Karl H. Rengstorf, "δώδεκα," *TDNT* 2:326–28.

51. As William Hendriksen does, calling the church the "new Israel." See his *Exposition of the Gospel According to Luke* (Grand Rapids: Baker, 1978), 327.

52. For arguments contra a direct Israel-church connection, see Ben Witherington III, *Jesus, Paul and the End of the World: A Comparative Study in New Testament Eschatology* (Downers Grove, Ill.: InterVarsity Press, 1992), 225–31; and idem, *The Christology of Jesus* (Minneapolis: Fortress, 1990), 128–29.

53. Luke places the statement in the setting of the last supper. The passage calls to mind the thrones of Dan 7:9ff., where the saints of the Highest One receive the kingdom (v. 18) at the end of the period of the Gentile kingdoms (vv. 19–25) and the court sits for judgment (v. 26) sometime prior to the establishment of the everlasting kingdom (vv. 27–28).

54. See Sanders, *Jesus and Judaism* (London: SCM Press, 1985), 13–78. Sanders, as part of the Third Quest for the historical Jesus, attempts to reclaim the Jewishness of Jesus in his analyses. He portrays Jesus as an eschatological restorationist preacher who understood his ministry in the light of the widespread eschatological doctrine of the restoration of Israel within the Judaism of his day. According to Sanders, Jesus' task was to gather the outcasts of Israel so as to assure that all Israel would be included in the blessings His ministry entailed. The difficulty with this view, of course, is that it may lead to the perspective that Jesus failed in his restoration purposes (a conclusion with scant differences from that of Albert Schweitzer). The author affirms Sanders' desire to place Jesus within Judaism, but rejects the conclusions associated with Jesus as a restorationist preacher within Sanders' system.

55. By "spiritual" we mean the presence of God with His creation in which He renews and blesses that creation. It does not necessitate metaphysical connotations. The kingdom has "*of God qualities*" and thus has this spiritual dimension (cf. Rom. 14:17; 1 Cor. 4:20; 15:50; etc.).

56. The author rejects historical critical methodologies that suggest that Luke redacted Jesus' words in order to teach something different than Jesus taught. The attempt at harmonization between Luke-Acts and Jesus' teaching in this section proceeds with a recognition that Luke-Acts is a compendium and that Luke-Acts may provide additional information not found in the other synoptics and John's gospel which contribute to the NT teaching. It is legitimate to explore the ways in which Luke has arranged his material in terms of his purposes in writing these volumes. In my view, Luke's purpose(s) and record can be legitimately harmonized with what Jesus taught elsewhere concerning Israel's dispersion and restoration.

57. So Bock, *Luke*, 1:115; Schmitz, *TDNT* 3:164ff.

58. I. Howard Marshall, *Commentary on Luke*, NIGTC (Grand Rapids: Eerdmans, 1978), 85. According to Bock, *Luke*, 1:159: "The phrase clearly reveals Mary's national focus and suggests that she is awaiting a political deliverance, as well as a spiritual one from Jesus."

59. On this, see further John McLean, "Did Jesus Correct the Disciples' View of the Kingdom?" *BibSac* 151 (April–June 1994), 221–22. McLean observes that the term Israel is found twelve times in Luke and an additional twenty times in Acts. On each occasion it refers to national Israel and/or its people. McLean interacts on a more extensive level with the positions of Christological interpretations and replacement theologies.

60. Compare Luke 11:2 where the Lord instructs the disciples to pray for the coming of the kingdom. This future kingdom was to include (in Luke's/Jesus' thinking) the patriarchs, prophets, and apostles (cf. Matt. 8:11; Luke 13:28–29; 22:30).

61. See McLean, "Did Jesus Correct the Disciples' View" for a developed treatment of the issues related to this passage. The treatment of Acts 1–3 presented here leans on McLean's treatment, and the reader is referred there for further discussion. McLean argues that the fact that Jesus corrected the disciples' misperceptions on other occasions but did not do so here suggests that the disciples' concept of a future kingdom for Israel was correct (p. 227). See further the corroborating details in Larry R. Helyer, "Luke and the Restoration of Israel," *JETS* 36/3 (September 1993): 317–29.

62. McLean, 226–27.

63. See David P. Moessner, "Paul in Acts: Preacher of Eschatological Repentance to Israel" in *NTS* 34 (1988), 96–104. Moessner argues that Jesus and Paul employ the language and imagery of Temple destruction in Ezekiel 9–11; Jeremiah 7:8–15 and 12:7–13 to forewarn their listeners of the judgment that awaits those unresponsive to their messages. He concludes that the judgment preached by Paul and others in the apostolic community was of a final nature ("the final judgment of destruction for an unrepentant people," his Tenet D, p. 101), though he must imply that destruction at the close of the Acts (p. 103). The force of the apostolic message is a warning to repent, but, in my view, not a denial of God's faithfulness to fulfill his promises or a signal that the church has thus replaced Israel as the final path of God's blessing. Invoking the curses of exile, as we have noted above, was a prophetic means of summoning repentance in Israel.

64. "After this" can be understood as located temporally after the events of the Gentile inclusion given in v. 14, but see Darrell L. Bock, "Evidence from Acts," in *A Case for Premillennialism: A New Consensus*, D. K. Campbell and J. L. Townsend, eds. (Chicago: Moody, 1992), 195–97. The assumption James makes is that the house of David is in the process of being rebuilt and that Gentiles are somehow included, as Peter's experience demonstrated.

65. P. M. L. Walker, *Jesus and the Holy City: Perspectives on the Holy City* (Grand Rapids: Eerdmans, 1996), 57ff. argues for the restoration of both Jerusalem and Israel "through Jesus and the Spirit." Walker adds his voice to a host (beginning with Hans Conzelmann [1960]) of those opposing any physical restoration "voice" in Luke. He fails to adequately explain how abandonment of political aspirations coincides with the literal nature of the OT promises. Restoration within a Person or persons does not account for Jesus' anticipation of thrones or kingdom and identifies the wrong tension within the apostolic community. The issue in Acts was not "the repentance of ethnic Israel before evangelizing the Gentiles" (p. 97), but God's priority in using Gentiles to provoke His people to repentance (Rom. 10:19).

66. The OT promises to Israel are, as indicated above, reserved *for* and fulfilled *in* a restored Israel. The church gains only those aspects of the promise extended to us by Christ and this without the forfeiture of what God had promised unconditionally to the nation.

67. Compare, for example, John Goldingay, "The Jews, the Land, and the Kingdom," *Anvil* 4 (1987), see especially pp. 10–16.

68. As argued by Richard B. Hays, *Echoes of Scripture in the Letters of Paul* (New Haven/London: Yale University Press, 1989), 163–64.

69. The remnant is, in this sense, the earnest or down payment guaranteeing God's future work of the redemption of Israel. This would seem to overcome the difficulty experienced by Willem Van Gemeren in "A Response" in Blaising and Bock, eds,

Dispensationalism, Israel, and the Church, 341. See further "The Remnant of Israel" by Ray A. Pritz in this volume.
70. For development of these themes of Israel's role in biblical theology see Robert L.
    Saucy, "Israel and the Church: A Case for Discontinuity" in *Continuity and Discon-
    tinuity*, 257–59; and his earlier "A Rationale for the Future of Israel" *JETS* 28/4 (De-
    cember 1985), 433–42.

The Dome of the Rock, an Islamic mosque dating from A.D. 691, erected on the site of the Second Temple.

CHAPTER TEN

THE MISSION OF ISRAEL AND OF THE MESSIAH IN THE PLAN OF GOD

Robert L. Thomas

God has a plan for this world. As the personal Creator of all things, He had a goal in mind when making the universe the way He made it. He put human beings into the world to play a vital part in achieving His goal. He has assigned them a mission.

In particular, it is God's servant who has the task of carrying out the mission of God. Scripture applies the words *My servant*[1] to ten individuals and one corporate body.[2] One of the individuals referred to by this title is God's Servant, the Messiah.[3] His mission is paramount in the fulfillment of God's plan. Another primary participant in God's program is God's corporate servant Israel. This chapter will focus on the mission of these two servants in implementing the plan of God.

THE MISSION OF THE MESSIAH

Of special interest are references to God's Servant in the Servant Songs in Isaiah's prophecy. The prophet records the four songs in 42:1–9;[4] 49:1–13;[5] 50:4–11;[6] 52:13–53:12.

The First Servant Song (Isa. 42:1–9)

It is God who speaks in the first song. Westermann points out how Isaiah 42:1 relates to the Servant's God-given mission: "The first words [i.e., 'Behold, My Servant' or 'This is My Servant'] plainly describe a designation. This means that someone with the right so to do designates or appoints someone else to perform a task or to hold an office."[7] He notes three descriptions of the Servant's task in the first song: to bring forth justice to the nations (v. 1c), to bring forth justice in truth (v. 3c), and to establish justice in the earth (v. 4b).[8] To Westermann's list of tasks, the Servant's appointment as a covenant to the people[9] and a light to the nations[10] (v. 6c, d) is an additional responsibility. Westermann's three tasks interpret "justice" as having a special meaning in the context of Isaiah's prophecy, that of refuting the claim of Gentile gods that they are deity because the Lord alone is God.[11] The Servant's task is to spread this message worldwide. That is the illumination He must bring to all mankind. A further mission He is to fulfill comes out in 42:3 where the figurative language tells of the comfort and encouragement He will bring to the weak and oppressed. In addition, He will during His earthly reign replace Israel's spiritual blindness with clear vision and restore her captives to freedom (42:7; cf. Isaiah 29:18; 32:3; 35:5; 61:1).

One feature of the first song that renders improbable the identification of the Servant as corporate Israel lies in 42:3–4. The picture of gentleness and patience in verse 3 and of the absence of hesitation or discouragement in verse 4 is inapplicable to the nation as a group in fulfillment of their mission of bringing justice and light to the nations (cf. Isa. 41).[12]

The Second Servant Song (Isa. 49:1–13)

In the second song, the Servant speaks. This song includes other tasks for the Servant: bringing Jacob back to God (49:5b); restoring the preserved ones of Israel (49:6b); serving as a light to the nations so as to extend the Lord's salvation to earth's extremities (49:6c, d); and functioning as a covenant of the people Israel to restore the land (49:8c, d) and release the captives (49:9a, b). The return of captives will be much more miraculous than the exodus from Egypt under Moses. Though not directly stated, the Servant's task through all this activity is also to glorify the one true God (49:3). Thus the broader scope of the Servant's office extends to the Gentile world as a whole, though its immediate scope aims at Israel and bringing her back to God.[13] In the accomplishment of these tasks, the Servant must endure humiliating treatment that will for the moment appear to doom His mission to failure (49:4a, b, 7b, c), but He will eventually reign as the supreme ruler throughout the earth because of the Lord's blessing upon Him (49:4c, d, 7e, f, g).

The survey of the Servant Songs has thus far assumed the Servant's identity as an individual person. In the second song, however, that simple identification is insufficient because the prophet specifically identifies "My servant" as Israel (49:3a). Identification of the servant as corporate Israel has strong attestation elsewhere in Isaiah and the OT (e.g., Isa. 41:8–9; 42:19; 43:10; 44:1–2, 21, 26; 45:4; 48:20; Jer. 30:10; 46:27–28; Ezek. 28:25; 37:25). God affirms His choice of the nation frequently (e.g., Isa. 41:8–9; 43:10; 44:1–2; 45:4). Yet spiritual blindness and deafness have beset God's servant Israel (Isa. 42:19), causing them to turn their back on the Lord. Nevertheless, He will not forget them (Isa. 44:21)

but will eventually—after a period of chastening (Jer. 30:11d, e; 46:28f, g)—
redeem them and install them as the head of all peoples (Isa. 44:26; 48:20d; Jer.
30:10–11c; 46:27–28e; Ezek. 28:25; 37:25).[14]
Identifying the Servant as a single person is also necessary in some passages—
in the Servant Songs especially.[15] In this connection, Hugenberger comments,

> [A]lthough surrounded by texts that refer to corporate Israel as a ser-
> vant, the servant of the servant songs, who innocently and obediently
> suffers for the transgression of the people (53:4–12) and who brings sal-
> vation to the Gentiles and restores Jacob/Israel to Yahweh (49:5–6), is
> not to be equated with corporate Israel. By allowing him to share the
> servant designation of corporate Israel, however, and in one verse even
> the name 'Israel' (49:3), the prophet may be suggesting that this one is
> everything Israel should have been as he faithfully fulfills the role to
> which Israel had been called.[16]

Baron suggests essentially the same:

> Here [i.e., in 49:3] God says to him "Thou art My servant, O Israel" (or
> "Thou art Israel"). He is invested with the name of Israel because He,
> "as Israel's inmost centre, as Israel's highest head," realizes the idea and
> carries out the mission to which the nation which had originally been
> called to the task of carrying out God's saving purpose in relation to the
> world does not respond.[17]

In the second song, several features point to an individual. He will be a human
being, conceived in and born from a mother's womb (49:1b, c).[18] This distinguishes
Him from the personified group of Israel. Other indications of individuality include
God's giving effect to the Servant's word (49:2a), keeping Him safe (42:2b), and
the Servant's regard for His work as a failure (42:4a, b) with the realization that
God nevertheless approves of it (42:4c, d).[19] In particular, the individual Servant
stands in bold contrast to the corporate servant in that the latter receives the redemption provided by the former (49:6a, b).[20] A further distinction lies in the moral
perfection always attributed to the individual Servant as opposed to the shortcom-
ings of corporate Israel (e.g., cf. 42:1–9 with 42:18–25).[21]
Other reasons for concluding the Servant of the Servant Songs to be an individual emerge from the fourth song. The words, "He was cut off . . . for the transgression of my people" (53:8c, d),[22] distinguish the Servant from "my people" who
can hardly be other than the people of Israel.[23] Further, the subject of chapter 53 is
an innocent sufferer (v. 9c, d) who suffers for the guilt of others (v. 4). He is a
voluntary sufferer (v. 12), an unresisting sufferer (v. 7), and His sufferings ended
in death (vv. 8c, 9b, 12c).[24] None of these is applicable to a body of people.

In spite of the differences, however, a unity binds the individual Servant to the corporate servant. That is what emerges in Isaiah 49:3. Through the Servant's redemptive work on behalf of the nation (cf. Isa. 53:6), the nation will eventually be one with Him and thereby glorify the Lord. When the Lord says to the Servant, "You are My Servant, Israel" (Isa. 49:3), He views the unification that will eventually occur during the Messiah-Servant's reign upon the earth. The Servant will become a light to all the nations, extending His salvation to all (Isa. 49:6c, d) and using the nation to bring the nations to God (cf. Isa. 19:24). At that point the mission of the Messiah and Israel will coincide.[25]

The Third Servant Song (Isa. 50:4–11)

The Servant's soliloquy about being perfected through sufferings comprises the third Servant Song (Isa. 50:4–11). His task resembles the commission to Jeremiah the prophet, that of listening as a disciple and teaching as a disciple (Isa. 50:4a, 4d with Jer. 15:16; 18:20).[26] Of interest is the absence of the term *'ebed* ("Servant") from the earlier verses of this song. *Limmud* ("disciple") replaces it. Everywhere else in the OT *limmud* designates a disciple of some human teacher (e.g., Isa. 8:16), but here the Servant is a disciple of God in a direct sense.[27] His mission as a disciple also entails His obedience to God (50:5). "Opening the ear" is a figure of speech to denote obedience as in Psalm 40:6–8 (cf. Phil. 2:8; Heb. 5:8; 10:5–7). The Servant's unwavering obedience to God's will is an aspect of His moral perfection.

An additional task this song assigns to the Servant—one that His obedient spirit necessitates—is that of being persecuted, submitting Himself to cruel treatment by His enemies (50:6). Though some might construe verse 6 as implying the attacks, blows, and insults against the Servant as justifiable, with God on the side of His opponents, the ultimate explanation lies in the plan of God for His Servant to experience this type of treatment (cf. Isa. 53:10; Acts 2:23).[28]

The close of the third Servant Song offers encouragement to those who fear the Lord and obey the voice of His Servant (50:10) and proclaim judgment against perpetrators of injustice (50:11). Of particular help in identifying the Servant in verse 10 is the parallelism of the verse's first two lines. Obeying the voice of God's Servant is inseparable from fearing the Lord because the Lord has made His Servant's mouth as a sharp sword (cf. Isa. 49:2). This factor renders it difficult to comprehend how the Servant could be the nation Israel or the best part thereof. The Servant stands in an absolutely unique relationship to God, at least raising the possibility, if not requiring that the Servant be deity.[29]

The Fourth Servant Song (Isa. 52:13–53:12)

The fourth Servant Song speaks of the Servant in the third person and divides into three parts (52:13–15; 53:1–9, 10–12), the first and third of which speak of His humiliation and exaltation and the second of His humiliation only. The first section summarizes the whole song by speaking briefly of the Messiah's sufferings and glory. The second is the lament and confession of penitent Israel in the future, and the third tells of the fruit of His sufferings and His subsequent exaltation.[30] The fourth song corresponds to the first song (42:1ff.). Giving the culmination of the Servant's work as that earlier song shows His work's origin—that is, His appointment to the Servant's office.[31]

Implied tasks of the Servant in 52:13–15 include prudent dealings[32] as an exalted world ruler (v. 13), enduring inhuman cruelty to the point of disfigurement beyond semblance to a human being (v. 14), and an unprecedented rise to leadership that will amaze all the world (v. 15).[33] In the process of rising to the forefront He will "sprinkle many nations" (v. 15a), that is, perform the priestly work of cleansing not only Israel but also many outside the nation.[34]

In the second part of the fourth song (53:1–9), the speakers are those who confess that their guilt has caused the Servant's suffering.[35] The first person plural pronouns represent the prophet speaking on behalf of Israel and, contrasted with the third person singular pronoun, distinguish between the Servant and Israel.[36] Their confession reflects the Servant's suffering as a substitute for themselves and the consequent change in themselves this realization has brought. So the clear mission of the Servant is substitutionary suffering for the sins of others (53:4–6, 8d). His entire lifespan has the mark of lowliness and suffering, lacking in beauty and outward appeal (53:2–3).[37] The confessors acknowledge their agreement with general public opinion about the Servant's being despised and smitten by God, but emphasize that the suffering of such a one empowers Him to be a substitute and to atone for their iniquities (53:4–6).

Following the confession of verses 4–6, the report resumes from verse 3 and confirms earlier evidence from the second song that the Servant is an individual, not a corporate entity. Only an individual can be born (v. 3), suffer (v. 7a), die (v. 8c), and be buried (v. 9a, b).[38] In particular, His burial with malefactors points to an individual rather than a group.[39] The wording of verses 7–8a points to suffering at the hands of others in contrast to verses 4–6 which focus on suffering without reference to its cause. The Servant incurs death for no fault of His own (v. 9c, d), but because of the sins of His people (v. 8d). This accords with the moral faultlessness of the Servant observed in connection with the second song. His vicarious suffering receives specific mention at least nine times in this song (53:4a, b, 5a, b, c, 6c, d, 8c, d, 11d, 12e, f).

Sequential to the report about the Servant's suffering, the song continues in its third part by recounting God's plan for Him to die and for His exaltation following death (vv. 10–11b).[40] That this exaltation included resurrection from the dead is not explicit, but the promise to prolong His days (v. 10d) strongly implies it. That life after death will be satisfying (v. 11b). The closing part of the report adds to the word about the Servant's exaltation in 52:13, 15. Intermingled with words repeating His undertakings on behalf of sinners, 53:11c–12 tell of

His portion with the great and sharing the booty with the strong. All this was part of the Servant's mission in the plan of God. The mystery of it all is how one so lowly could eventually ascend to the throne as the King of kings and the Lord of lords.

An interesting feature of Isaiah's prophecy is that the fourth Servant Song marks the end of applying "servant" to the nation corporately. From this point on, references to Israel are always plural, "servants" (Isa. 54:17; 56:6; 63:17; 65:8, 9, 13–14, 15; 66:14). "Servant" does not occur in the singular in the remainder of the book after the fourth song.[41]

Pusey has summarized the teachings of the fourth Servant Song thus:

> The characteristics in which all agree are, that there would be a prevail-
> ing unbelief as to the subject of the prophecy, lowly beginnings, among
> circumstances outwardly unfavourable, but before God, and protected
> by Him; sorrows, injustice, contempt, death, which were the portion of
> the sufferer; that he was accounted a transgressor, yet that his sufferings
> were, in some way, vicarious, the just for the unjust; his meek silence;
> his willing acceptance of his death; his being with the rich in his death;
> his soul being (in some way) an offering for sin, and God's acceptance
> of it; his prolonged life; his making many righteous; his continued inter-
> cession for transgressors; the greatness of his exaltation, in proportion
> to the depth of his humiliation; the submission of kings to him; his abid-
> ing reign.[42]

Summary of the Servant Songs

The following summarizes various facets of the Messiah-Servant's mission as reflected in the Servant Songs' direct and indirect statements about the role He is to fulfill. That mission falls into two rather distinct phases.

Phase 1. Lowliness and suffering will mark His entire life, depriving Him of attractiveness and outward appeal (53:2–3). Yet He will bring comfort and en-couragement to the weak and oppressed (42:3a, b). He will listen as a disciple and teach as a disciple. He will obey God with an unwavering obedience that marks His moral perfection (50:5). Because of His obedience to God, He must endure persecution and cruel treatment at the hands of His enemies (50:6). Hu-miliating treatment will for the moment appear to doom His mission to failure (49:4a, b, 7b, c). His persecution will be so violent that it disfigures His outward appearance to the point of making Him unrecognizable as a human being (52:14).

He will die from such ill treatment, not because of any fault of His own (53:9c, d) but because of the sins of His people (53:8d). He will die as their substitute to atone for their iniquities (53:4–6, 8d). The general opinion of people will be that God despised and struck Him with these harsh measures (53:4c, d) but this is not so. It happened because God planned for Him to die thus (53:10a, b, c). Through

His death He will accomplish the priestly work of cleansing Israel as well as many other nations (52:15a). But it is also God's plan for Him to rise from the dead, thereby prolonging His days with a life after death that is satisfying (53:10e–11b).

Phase 2. The Servant's appointment as a covenant to the people of Israel (42:6c; 49:8c) elaborates on His prolonged life. He will restore Israel's land (49:8d) and release her captives (49:9a, b). He will replace her spiritual blindness with clear vision when He gives her captives their freedom (42:7). His dealings with Israel will be a means toward a further goal, that of bringing light to the nations (42:6d; 49:6c) and sending the Lord's salvation to earth's extremities (49:6d). He will establish justice in truth throughout the earth (42:1c, 3c, 4b), impressing all mankind with the truth that the Lord alone is God. He will reign as supreme ruler over the world because of the Lord's blessing on Him (49:4c, d, 7e, f, g). Prudent dealings will mark His reign (52:13), following a rise to leadership that will amaze all people (52:15). He will share a portion with the great and booty with the strong (53:11c–12).

Through all of this, His mission is to glorify the one true God (49:3).

Identification of the Servant

The Servant in the Servant Songs possesses characteristics that no individual in OT history can fulfill. Also, it is impossible to identify the Servant of the songs with corporate Israel for reasons already stated.[43] His unique relationship to God poses the possibility of His equality with God (Isa. 50:10), distinguishing Him from every other person who has ever lived. The only possible identification is the promised Messiah of Israel who was in Isaiah's time still to come. The life, death, and resurrection of Jesus of Nazareth perfectly fit Isaiah's portrayal of phase 1 of that Servant's mission.

NT writers frequently capitalize on the accuracy of that identification. The first gospel notes the fulfillment of Isaiah 42:1a in Christ at His baptism (Matt. 3:16–17) and transfiguration (Matt. 17:5). All four gospels observe the fulfillment of Isaiah 50:6 in the ill-treatment of Christ during His trial (Matt. 26:67; 27:26, 30; Mark 14:65; 15:19; Luke 22:63; John 18:22). Luke speaks of the resoluteness of Christ to complete His mission (Luke 9:51) as does Isaiah 50:7. John 12:38 ties Israel's failure to recognize her Messiah with Isaiah 53:1. Philip identifies Jesus as the one about whom Isaiah wrote in Isaiah 53:7–8 (Acts 8:32–33). All four gospel writers recorded the silence of Jesus throughout His trial (Matt. 26:63; 27:12–14; Mark 14:61; 15:5; Luke 23:9; John 19:9; cf. 1 Peter 2:23) just as Isaiah predicted regarding the Servant (Isa. 53:7). Several NT writers focus on Jesus' fulfillment of Isaiah 53:7 when they call Him the Lamb of God (John 1:29; 1 Peter 1:18–19; Rev. 5:6). Nor does the complete innocence of the Servant (Isa. 53:9) escape the notice of Peter (1 Peter 2:22). Isaiah's prediction of the Servant's crucifixion with wicked men (Isa. 53:12) also matches with Jesus' death according to Luke's description (Luke 22:37).

Such literal fulfillments of prophecies about phase 1 of the Servant's mission leads inevitably to the expectation that prophecies about phase 2 of His mission will receive that type of fulfillment also. The Servant at His second advent will serve in the precise manner that Isaiah predicted He would.

Further Explanation of Phase 2 of the Servant's Mission

Daniel 7 is a passage that, among others, furnishes specifics regarding phase 2 of the Messiah-Servant's mission. Daniel had a vision of a sea stirred up by the four winds of heaven and four large beasts emerging from it, the first resembling a lion with an eagle's wings, the second like a bear with three ribs in its mouth, the third like a leopard with four bird-wings from its back and four heads, and the fourth different from the other three and having ten horns (Dan. 7:2–8). As the vision continued, the next scene before him featured a blindingly brilliant picture of the Ancient of Days (i.e., God the Father) upon His throne with His surrounding retinue (Dan. 7:9–10).[44] Daniel next witnessed the slaying of the fourth beast and the divesting of dominion from the rest of the beasts (Dan. 7:11–12). At that point the Son of Man[45] came with the clouds of heaven, approached the Ancient of Days, and received dominion over all peoples, a kingdom that would never end (Dan. 7:13–14). All this troubled Daniel, so he asked for an interpretation of what the vision meant. He learned that the large beasts represented four kings (or kingdoms—i.e., Babylon, Medo-Persia, Greece, and Rome)[46] that were to arise from the earth, but that the saints would eventually possess the kingdom forever (Dan. 7:15–18).[47] Daniel then asked for further clarification regarding the fourth beast and regarding the ten horns and the horn that came up among them, uprooting three of the horns. He saw that last horn warring against the saints until the arrival of the Ancient of Days to deliver the saints and give them the kingdom (Dan. 7:19–22). The continuing explanation to him divulged that the fourth beast would be a fourth kingdom that would subdue the whole earth and that the ten horns would be ten kings within that kingdom. The additional horn would be a king who conquers three others, speaks out against the Most High, and wears down the saints, being permitted to change things his way for three and a half years (Dan. 7:23–25). But he will have his dominion removed, and control over the world will pass to the people of the saints of the Most High. The kingdom of the Most High will continue forever with all His subjects serving and obeying Him (Dan. 7:26–27).

A convenient way to survey Daniel 7 is through the eyes of John's Apocalypse, which alludes to Daniel 7 over thirty times.[48] In fact, the purpose of the entire Apocalypse is to develop a phrase derived from Daniel 2: "things that must happen soon" (Rev. 1:1; cf. Dan. 2:28 [LXX]; cf. also 2:29, 45).[49] Since Daniel 2, like Daniel 7, looks forward to the crushing and displacement of the kingdom of Rome by the kingdom of God, the two chapters speak of the rise and fall of the same four empires and the collapse of the last with the arrival of the messianic Son of Man.[50] Revelation as a further detailing of Daniel 7's prophecy, then, provides helpful insights.

Like both Daniel 2 and Daniel 7, the Apocalypse describes the outworking of God's program instituting the everlasting kingdom that will replace other earthly temporary kingdoms. "The things that must happen" (Rev. 1:1) comprise steps in the development of that program. That is part of the mission of the Messiah. Revelation uses the title "Son of Man" from Daniel 7:13 to designate the Messiah (Rev. 1:13; 14:14) and describes Him in terms similar to those speaking of the Ancient of Days in Daniel 7:9 (Rev. 1:14). The numbering of the throngs of angels around the heavenly throne in Revelation 5:11 has its origin in Daniel 7:10. The four winds of the earth held by angels in Revelation 7:1 derive from the four winds of heaven in Daniel 7:2. The warfare of the beast against the saints and victory over them are subjects in Daniel 7:21 and Revelation 11:7 (cf. also Rev. 13:7). Rulership of the Son of Man over a worldwide kingdom in Daniel 7:14, 27 finds further development in Revelation 11:15. Revelation 12:3 refers to ten horns of the beast as do Daniel 7:7, 20, 24 (cf. also Rev. 13:1; 17:12). The beast's persecution of the woman in Revelation 12:13 is an elaboration of his wearing down of the saints in Daniel 7:25. The picture of the beast emerging from the sea in Revelation 13:1 traces back to the emergence of beasts from the seas in Daniel 7:3 (cf. also Rev. 11:7). The beast arising from the sea of Revelation 13:1 recalls the fourth beast that was different from the other three in Daniel 7:7. Revelation 13:2 likens that beast to a leopard, a bear, and a lion, comparisons that allude to the first three beasts of Daniel 7:4–6. The "mouth speaking great things and blasphemies" of Revelation 13:5 recalls the "mouth uttering great boasts" of Daniel 7:8, the "boastful words" of Daniel 7:11, and the "mouth uttering great boasts" of Daniel 7:20. The blasphemies of the beast in Revelation 13:6 allude to the little horn's speaking out against the Most High in Daniel 7:25. Revelation 19:20 tells of the beast's slaying and his casting into the lake of fire burning with brimstone, adding details to Daniel 7:11. Revelation 20:4 tells of the saints' possessing of the kingdom in following up Daniel 7:9, 22, 27. Daniel 7:10 briefly mentions the seating of the court for judgment, but Revelation 20:12 reveals more about the opening of the books for judgment. Revelation 22:5 tells of the eternal reign of the saints, an allusion to Daniel 7:18, 27.

The alignment of the Apocalypse with Daniel 7 at so many points underscores the fact that the last book of the Bible is a further detailing of phase 2 of the mission of the Messiah. First, He will inflict upon a rebellious world unparalleled wrath for seven years, at the beginning of which He delivers the body of Christ from the scene of that wrath. He then will initiate Israel's promised kingdom on earth for a thousand years and follow it with an everlasting kingdom in the new heavens and the new earth.

THE MISSION OF ISRAEL

As noted above, the OT refers to corporate Israel also as "My servant." In fact, *Israel* or *Jacob* is the only name given for "My servant" (Isa. 41:8; 44:1–2; 45:4) since the text never assigns a name to the Servant individual except in the special occurrence of Isaiah 49:3. Many statements about the Messiah-Servant also apply to Israel as God's servant. For example, God has chosen both and upheld both with His right hand (Isa. 41:10; 42:1, 6; 43:10; 44:1). He has called both to be His witnesses to the nations (42:6; 43:10, 21; 49:3, 6; 60:3).[51] So the Servant and the servant relate closely to each other.

In the context of Isaiah 43:10, corporate Israel receives the charge to witness to the accuracy of God's prophecies. Since the gods of the surrounding nations could not match His predictive feats (43:9, 12), Israel is to bear testimony to this fact (43:12). This they will do in their promised future kingdom under the Messiah's leadership.

The servant Israel is to function as the Lord's messengers proclaiming the bright days ahead for the nation (44:25–26). A further part of Israel's mission is to manifest God's holiness in the sight of the nations (Ezek. 28:25).

The international scope of the servant's mission to all peoples is quite clear. That goal is evident from the very beginning of the nation, in God's promise (and commission) to Abraham that through his seed all the families of the earth would be blessed (Gen. 12:3). God's choice of Israel was His way of dealing with mankind as a whole, meaning that as Israel fares, so fares the rest of mankind (cf. Rom. 3:19). After a manner of speaking, Israel serves as God's test tube for sampling the whole human race.

In contrast to the Messiah-Servant, however, God's servant Israel has defaulted in her mission. Isaiah 42:18–22, 24, for example, elaborates on the nation's disobedience and failure. This reflects a definite discontinuity and distinction from the Servant whose character and mission are described in verses 1–9 of the same chapter.[52] Will the servant's ministry go unfulfilled, then?

No, but Israel must undergo a spiritual restoration before she can resume her mission. How will that spiritual restoration come? It must come through the Messiah-Servant, a part of whose mission is to "bring back Jacob and gather Israel to Himself" (Isa. 49:5).[53] The mission of the Servant to rest of the world does not preclude His restoration of Israel; rather, His restoration of Israel furnishes the channel for bringing salvation to the nations (Isa. 49:6). Though the Servant is distinct from Israel in His task of restoring her, He also identifies with Israel in enabling her to fulfill her original mission.[54] "The universal purpose of the election of Israel is to be achieved through the mission of the Servant."[55] Ultimately, in Israel He will show forth His glory (Isa. 49:3; 44:23).

When will the restoration of Israel come? It certainly did not come at the resurrection of Christ as Wright contends because subsequent to that event, His disciples asked about the yet unfulfilled restoration of Israel's kingdom (Acts 1:6).[56] Jesus did not deflect the disciples' question, nor did He correct it.[57] The restoration of Israel was still future at that point. Under the guidance of the Spirit, Peter later invited his Jewish listeners to repent in order to bring about the (future) restoration of Israel (Acts 3:19–21). Later, in Romans 11:26–27 Paul prophesied about the future restoration of Israel. Clearly, Israel is not fulfilling her mission today because she is still in a state of disobedience. She rejected her Messiah at His first advent and cannot function as His witness until a national repentance applies the benefits of His substitutionary atonement to the nation's sins.

That repentance will come in conjunction with phase 2 of the Servant-Messiah's mission. The mission of the servant Israel is in abeyance during this period while God is visiting all nations to call out a people for His name (Matt. 28:19–20; Acts 15:14). The mission of the church during this interim period is separate from God's mission for servant Israel.[58] God's purposes for the church were undisclosed during OT times (cf. Eph. 3:4–7).

So Israel will fulfill her mission in the promised future kingdom. God has not rejected His servant (Isa. 41:9). He will yet restore the nation to the role of being His witnesses to the nations (Isa. 43:10).

But He will do so in several steps after the church goes to be with the Lord Jesus in heaven. The seventieth week of Daniel 9 will immediately precede that kingdom. During the last three and a half years of that week, 144,000 Israelites will be God's major witnesses to the world.[59] Revelation 7:1–8 introduces these servants of God who are sealed on their foreheads to protect them from God's wrathful visitation against earth's rebels. They will bear the brunt of the dragon's anger while the bulk of believing Israelites find protection from that anger (Rev. 12:17).[60] In their faithful witness for Christ they will suffer martyrdom but subsequently will rise from the dead to join Christ on Mount Zion in His kingdom on earth (Rev. 14:1–5). At some point near the end of that seventieth week, a great revival will come in Jerusalem (Rev. 11:13), perhaps provoking the massive attack on Israel resulting in the battle of Armageddon (cf. Rev. 16:16).[61]

Then the King of kings and Lord of lords (Rev. 19:16) will usher in the millennial kingdom. In that kingdom Jerusalem, "the beloved city" (Rev. 20:9), will be the focus of all activity. Christ will rule sitting on David's throne as indicated throughout the Apocalypse (Rev. 1:5; 3:7; 5:5; 22:16). Servant Israel will be in the forefront, ruling with Him and shining as a light to all nations.

He will help His people (Isa. 44:2), redeem them, and wipe away their transgressions (Isa. 44:22; 48:20). He will show His glory in redeemed Israel (Isa. 44:23). Jerusalem and Judah will again prosper (Isa. 44:26). Then the Messiah's salvation will reach to the ends of the earth through the channel of Israel (Isa. 49:6). Israel will fulfill God's purpose for her.

THE MISSION OF ISRAEL IN THE PRESENT AGE

Wright builds a case to prove that Jesus' disciples began implementing the prophesied mission of Israel to the Gentiles immediately after Pentecost.[62] He cites Luke 24:46–48 and Acts 1:8 as fulfillments of Isaiah 43:10, 12 regarding Israel's responsibility as God's witness. He reasons that Peter and others were mistaken in thinking that God could not turn to the Gentiles until the restoration of Israel.[63] He insists that James' words in Acts 15:13–18 prove, however, that the restoration of Israel had already transpired, that the Davidic kingdom was present, and consequently, the light was going to the Gentiles in fulfillment of Isaiah's prophecy.[64] He sees Paul as concurring with this perspective as evidenced by his writing in Romans 9–11 and his preaching in Acts 13:46–47.[65]

Besides missing the point already cited—that is, that in no sense was the resurrection of Christ a restoration of Israel—Wright misses other important aspects of references to the OT in the NT. For instance, he overlooks the different direction the plan of God took in light of Israel's rejection of her Messiah at His first coming. That difference was well known in advance to God, but He did not see fit to reveal it to man in the pages of the OT. The new direction in His dealings with mankind resulted in additional meanings[66] being assigned to OT passages by authoritative NT writers.[67] For example, Paul's use of Isaiah 42:6 (cf. Isa. 49:6) in his speech of Acts 13:47 applies to his own ministry as he preached in Pisidian Antioch God's words to Isaiah's Messiah-Servant. In the Isaianic context, that promised salvation to the ends of the earth was to come in conjunction with repentant Israel's liberation from foreign oppressors. No strict application of grammatical-historical hermeneutics to the Isaiah passage could have interpreted it to refer to a Jewish Christian preacher, himself a fugitive wanted by Israel's authorities, offering international peace and prosperity to a mixed audience of Jews and Gentiles. Israel had not yet repented and still remained under foreign domination. Paul's meaning, inspired by the Holy Spirit, went beyond anything intended for Isaiah's original readers.

That was not a fulfillment of Isaiah's prophecy; it was an additional meaning furnished through the apostle to the Gentiles during the period of Israel's rejection. Isaiah's original promise will yet see realization after the fullness of the Gentiles has joined the body of Christ (Rom. 11:25). Wright is correct in allowing that the restoration of Israel is still future, but he is wrong is contending that it lies in the past also.[68] Fulfillment in the future is the only meaning that consistent grammatical-historical interpretation will yield. NT writers did not always assign additional meanings to OT texts. They sometimes depicted literal or direct fulfillment of OT prophecies, but any that they used relating to the new program and new people of God, the church, of necessity took on a different nature simply because OT prophecy did not foresee the NT church.

The new meaning of OT prophecies applied to the church introduced by NT writers did not cancel the original meaning and their promises to Israel. God will yet restore the nation of Abraham's physical descendants as He promised He would.

Failure to realize how the NT uses the OT has led some recent scholars to suggest that interpretation of the OT is not a one-way street, that NT writers' preunderstanding determined the meanings they found in the OT.[69] This has led them to label the literal understandings about political dimensions of predictions of a restored monarchy as "unfortunate misappropriations of prophecy in our day, with unhappy consequences for Christian consciousness, and conscience, in relation to Palestine."[70] The suggestion is that "a suitable appropriation of even these clearly messianic prophecies still has to pass through a rather subtle theological process."[71] That apparently refers to a removal or alteration of the meaning understood by the original readers of the prophecies.

It is quite true that a remnant in Israel according the election of grace (Rom. 11:5) within the body of Christ is currently providing great benefit to the Gentile world.[72] For example, the evident fact that all the books of the NT except two have Jewish authors is a reminder of the immeasurable profit of that remnant to the body of Christ and the world as a whole. God's wisdom in using people of Abraham's lineage as channels of His special revelation to the world has wrought untold spiritual value to countless numbers of the world's inhabitants. Many outstanding Christian leaders of Jewish lineage furnish a further illustration of the benefit of that remnant to the church and thereby to the rest of the world. But the grafting in of the wild olive branches—that is, God's direct dealings with Gentiles—has come during the period of corporate Israel's rejection of her Messiah (Rom. 11:11). That will not be the manner of Israel's illumination of the Gentiles according to Isaiah. Isaiah's ingathering of Israel will provide that illumination and will come in conjunction with the nation's repentance (cf. Rom. 11:12).

Israel in her rejection is currently distinct from the body of Christ, and the nation will remain distinct in the millennial kingdom and in the new heavens and the new earth. The Jewish people are and will always be God's chosen. Neither the church nor any other people will usurp their role of joining with Christ in His millennial rule.[73] Otherwise, Isaiah's OT promises about their future have undergone revision. God promised the land and the rulership to Israel and to Israel alone in the future kingdom.

John tells which mortals will inhabit the earth at the beginning of the millennium. He refers to them as "the nations" (Rev. 20:3). Of the possible identification of these nations, the most probable is that they will be the redeemed who have survived the rule of the beast during the last half of Daniel's seventieth week (Rev. 11:13; 12:13–17).[74] They will be largely of Jewish extraction as identification of the woman of Revelation 12 requires, but will also include a significant number of Gentile believers who have befriended the Jewish remnant of those days (cf. Matt. 25:31–46). In the millennium, the world's population will multiply rapidly because of ideal conditions and a relatively low death rate, bringing into existence a new set of nations in a relatively short period.[75] Among these, the Jewish nation will be the leader as the reference to "the beloved city"

Jerusalem in Revelation 20:9 reflects. During this time, the church will be present on earth with Christ but will exist in a resurrected state. God will fulfill the land promises to the generation of mortal Israelites alive at that time, not to immortal people subsequent to their resurrection.

The distinction between Israel and the church will continue into the new creation also. The twelve tribes of Israel will function as city gates in the new creation (Rev. 21:12), and the twelve apostles (i.e., the church) function as foundation stones (Rev. 21:14). Israel's role differs from that of the twelve apostles of the Lamb. Though finite man may not comprehend precisely the nature of those roles in the new creation, the text is clear that a distinction between the two peoples of God will remain.

THE ULTIMATE MISSION

Old Testament messianic prophecies begin as early as Genesis 3:15, a verse that depicts the Messiah's mission of bruising the serpent's head.[76] It was some time before revelation of the mission of Israel, however. That awaited the call of Abraham (Gen. 12:1–3). From that point on, the mission of Israel paralleled that of the Messiah in many ways. Why did God single out Abraham and his descendants from the rest of mankind? It was His chosen method of dealing with humans as a whole to limit His special attention to one segment of them. He gave this segment a mission to the rest of the world so that the rest of the world could fulfill His ultimate mission for all people. In light of Israel's failings along the way, the Messiah has filled and will fill the gap in redeeming Israel so that Israel can eventually fulfill her responsibility to the rest of the world.

So the mission of Israel and the Messiah in the plan of God is a means to fulfilling the mission of all mankind in God's plan. What is that ultimate mission? Is it a redemptive mission? That is certainly a part of God's plan, but God's plan is far greater in scope that just the redemption of lost mankind. Is man's mission to rule over God's creation (cf. Gen. 1:26)? That too is part of what God's plan entails, but it is not the ultimate goal. Both of these missions are anthropocentric, not theocentric.

Ephesians 1:3–14 expresses man's ultimate purpose three times: "to the praise of the glory of His grace" (1:6), "to the praise of His glory" (1:12), and "to the praise of His glory" (1:14). The first expression connects with God the Father, the second with God the Son, and the third with God the Spirit. Together they express the ultimate mission of the human race to glorify the Triune God. God receives glory through His grace manifested in the body of Christ. Similarly, God receives glory because of His gracious dealings with Israel. The ultimate mission of Israel (Isa. 44:23) and the Messiah (Isa. 49:3) is to bring glory to God because God will not give His glory to anyone or anything else (Isa. 42:8). As Israel and the Messiah fulfill their mission, so will the rest of humankind. The new Jerusalem will feature God's glory in the final realization of His plan for all of creation (Rev. 21:23–26; 22:5).

DISCUSSION QUESTIONS

1. Describe phase 1 of the Messiah-Servant's mission in light of Isaiah's four Servant Songs.

2. Discuss the Messiah-Servant's identity in light of phase 1 of His mission.

3. Give aspects of phase 2 of the Messiah-Servant's mission.

4. Trace the fulfillment of phase 2 of that mission in Daniel and Revelation.

5. Discuss the mission of Israel as indicated in Isaiah's prophecy.

6. Point out features related to the mission of Israel during the present age.

ENDNOTES

1. English translations of biblical expressions and texts in this chapter come from the New American Standard Bible unless otherwise indicated.
2. The individuals receiving the designation "My servant" include Abraham (Gen. 26:24); Moses (Num. 12:7, 8; Josh. 1:2, 7; 2 Kings 21:8; Mal. 4:4); Caleb (Num. 14:24); David (2 Sam. 3:18; 7:5, 8; 1 Kings 11:32, 34, 36, 38; 14:8; 2 Kings 19:34; 20:6; 1 Chron. 17:4, 7; Ps. 89:3; Isa. 37:35; Jer. 33:21–22, 26; Ezek. 34:23–24; 37:24–25); Job (Job 1:8; 2:3; 42:7–8); Eliakim (Isa. 22:20); the Servant of the Lord (Isa. 42:1; 49:6; 52:13; 53:11; Zech. 3:8; Matt. 12:18); Nebuchadnezzar (Jer. 25:9; 27:6; 43:10); Zerubbabel (Hag. 2:23); Christ's follower (John 12:26). The people of Israel (or Jacob) compose the corporate body that God calls "My servant" (Isa. 41:8–9; 42:19; 43:10; 44:1–2, 21, 26; 45:4; 48:20; Jer. 30:10; 46:27, 28; Ezek. 28:25; 37:25).
3. This chapter will capitalize the first letter—i.e., "Servant"—whenever the term applies to God's Servant, the Messiah, and will leave all other references to a servant in lower-case letters.
4. Claus Westermann (*Isaiah 40–66, A Commentary*, trans. David M. G. Stalker [Philadelphia: Westminster, 1969], 92) limits the first Servant Song to 42:1–4. He considers 42:5–9 to be a later addition to the song (101), but does so without convincing evidence.
5. Ibid., 206–7. Westermann limits the second Servant Song to 49:1–6. He considers 49:7ff. to be a later addition to the song (213), but does so without convincing evidence.
6. Westermann limits the third Servant Song to 50:4–9 (ibid., 225–26). He considers 50:10–11 to be a later addition to the song (233), but does so without convincing evidence.
7. Ibid., 93.
8. Ibid., 95.
9. I.e., He embodies the blessings of salvation promised to God's people Israel.
10. I.e., the Servant will use Israel to shine and enlighten all nations when He reigns in His kingdom (49:6; cf. Isa. 19:24).
11. Westermann, 95.
12. Allan A. MacRae, *The Gospel of Isaiah* (Chicago: Moody, 1977), 69–70.

13. Cf. ibid., 212.
14. Ezek. 37:22–25 is also a recognized messianic text in its reference to "My servant David" and His future reign (cf. Daniel I. Block, "Bringing Back David: Ezekiel's Messianic Hope," in *The Lord's Anointed*, ed. by Philip E. Satterthwaite, Richard S. Hess, and Gordon J. Wenham [Downers Grove, Ill.: InterVarsity Press, 1995], 177–83). It speaks of the future reign of David's descendent over Israel in fulfillment of the promise to King David in 2 Samuel 7.
15. The fourth Servant Song (52:13–53:12) in particular must refer to an individual. Various attempts to apply it to Jeremiah, Isaiah himself, Hezekiah, Josiah, and Job have been fruitless because of the many discrepancies between either of these individuals and the Servant described in that song. A generally accepted interpretation among Jewish people applies the song to the Jewish nation, a view dating at least as far back as Origen (David Baron, *The Servant of Jehovah: The Sufferings of the Messiah and the Glory That Should Follow, An Exposition of Isaiah LIII* [London: Morgan & Scott, Ltd., n.d.], 18). Baron suggests three reasons for this interpretation: the repugnancy to Rabbinic Judaism of a suffering expiatory Messiah, the inability to reconcile this picture of the Messiah with one of His coming in power and glory, and the impression that the Jewish nation through the centuries has been the innocent sufferer for the guilt of the other nations (18–20). According to the figurative interpretation of the fourth song that sees a reference to corporate Israel, the death of the servant is Israel's suffering and captivity which results in benefit to the rest of the world, but that suffering is hardly vicarious and does nothing to mediate between God and man (39; cf. Gordon P. Hugenberger, "The Servant of the Lord in the 'Servant Songs' of Isaiah: A Second Moses Figure," in *The Lord's Anointed, Interpretation of Old Testament Messianic Texts*, ed. by Philip E. Satterthwaite, Richard S. Hess, and Gordon J. Wenham [Grand Rapids: Baker, 1995], 108). That suffering was the penalty for Israel's own sins. Neither has the nation suffered voluntarily or without resistance as this Servant has (Baron, 42–44). Whenever Isaiah uses the servant in a collective sense, it is always with the addition of "Jacob" or "Israel" (Isa. 41:8; 44:1–2, 21; 45:4; 48:20) or through use of plurals alongside the singular (e.g., 43:10–14; 48:20–21) to indicate the corporate use (Baron, 45).
16. Hugenberger, 111.
17. Baron, 37.
18. Isaiah has earlier spoken of Immanuel's virgin birth (7:14).
19. Westermann, 211.
20. Baron, 37.
21. Hugenberger, 108, contrasts the sinlessness of the Servant (50:5; 53:9) with the sinfulness of Israel (40:2; 42:18–25; 43:22–28; 47:7; 48:18–19; 50:1; 54:7; 57:17; 59:2ff.; cf. also 43:22; 46:3, 12; 48:1, 8; 53:6, 8; 55:7; 58:1ff.; 63:17; 64:5–7). He also lists four passages that distinguish the Servant from the repentant remnant of Israel: Isa. 42:3, 6; 49:8; 53:8 (109).
22. According to Zech. 3:8–9, "My Servant the Branch . . . will remove the iniquity of that land in one day."
23. MacRae, 141.
24. Baron, 38.
25. The assigning of the name "Israel" to the servant in 49:3 has provoked much discussion. Westermann gives four reasons for suggesting it is a later addition to the text: (1) "Israel" is absent from one MS. of the LXX; (2) apart from 49:3, "Israel" never occurs in Isaiah 40–66 except when parallel to "Jacob"; (3) the other Servant Songs never assign 'eḏ eḏ a name; (4) the servant called "Israel" in v. 3 has a mission to

Israel in v. 5 (Westermann, 209). The omission suggested by Westermann lacks substantial support, however. Hugenberger resolves the difficulty by identifying "Israel"
in 49:3 as the "prophet like Moses" (p. 131). This is part of his theory that the Servant in all the Servant Songs is the "prophet like Moses" referred to in Deuteronomy
18:14ff. and 34:10ff. (ibid., 119).

26. Westermann, 227.
27. Ibid., 229.
28. Ibid., 230.
29. Edward J. Young, *The Book of Isaiah*, vol. 3 (Grand Rapids: Eerdmans, 1972),
303–4.
30. Baron, 51–52.
31. Westermann, 258.
32. I.e., He will act wisely in fulfilling the task entrusted to Him (Baron, 56). This contrasts with servant Israel's unwise dealings in failing to fulfill her mission.
33. Edward J. Young unfortunately limits the exaltation of the Servant in 52:13, 15 to
Christ's first coming—His resurrection, His ascension, and His session at the Father's
right hand—and refers the shutting of the mouths of kings to their amazement
regarding His saving work (*Isaiah Fifty-Three, A Devotional and Expository Study*
[Grand Rapids: Eerdmans, 1952], 12, 20–21). Yet the earlier context of Isaiah 52
speaks of Israel returning from exile (cf. George A. F. Knight, *Servant Theology, A
Commentary on the Book of Isaiah 40–55, International Theological Commentary*
[Grand Rapids: Eerdmans, 1984], 164–65). This factor locates the scene of the
Servant's exaltation on earth rather than in heaven, necessitating a reference to His
second advent rather than His resurrection and ascension. Young's explanation is
typical of covenantalists who are willing to understand prophecies of Messiah's first
advent—i.e., His sufferings and substitutionary death—in a literal way, but back away
from a literal interpretation of those related to His earthly rule during a future
kingdom.
34. Young, *Book of Isaiah*, 338–39.
35. Westermann, 257, 263–64. The tenses in the second part of the fourth song are "perfects, the future being regarded prophetically as already past" (Baron, 67).
36. Hugenberger, 110.
37. The inconspicuous beginning of the Servant, the "tender plant," alludes to the de-
cayed stump of Jesse of Isa. 11:1. After the "proud cedar" of David's monarchy fell
in that earlier messianic prophecy, a strong vigorous shoot proceeded from the root.
In Isaiah 53, however, it is a frail "tender twig" that struggles from the ground. The
passage here speaks of His sufferings and rejection while Isaiah 11 tells of His future reign and exaltation (Baron, 70–71).
38. Westermann, 264. Some advocates of a corporate identification of the Servant point
out that the prophet speaks of the nation as being born in Isa. 44:2, 24, thereby
claiming to nullify part of this argument for an individual identity (cf. Hugenberger,
107–8).
39. Westermann, 266.
40. Baron summarizes the "pleasure" (or "will")—i.e., mission—of the Lord for the Servant thus: "The regathering of Israel, the bringing back of Jacob, not only to his land
into a new covenant relationship with God, of which He Himself will be the bond;
the illumination of the Gentile world with the light of the knowledge of the true and
living God; the establishing of judgment and justice in the earth; the deliverance of
men from spiritual blindness and the bondage of sin, and the bringing near of God's
salvation to all men throughout the whole world" (125).

41. MacRae, 146–47.

42. E. B. Pusey, *The Jewish Interpreters of Isaiah* 'iii [sic, liii], cited by Baron, 16–17.

43. Cf. Hugenberger, 106–19.

44. John F. Walvoord, Daniel, *The Key to Prophetic Revelation* (Chicago: Moody, 1971), 164.

45. I.e., God the Son. The suggestion of J. A. Montgomery (*A Critical and Exegetical Commentary on the Book of Daniel*, ICC [New York: Scribner's, 1927], 319) that the son of man is a personification of the Jewish nation (cf. Dan. 7:7, 22, 27) is untenable, because Dan. 7:21–22 distinguishes between the saints and the Son of Man. On earth they suffer defeat at the hands of the horn before receiving the kingdom (7:21–22), but in heaven the Son receives power to rule the whole earth without any prior warfare (Dan. 7:13–14; Gleason Archer, "Daniel," *Expositor's Bible Commentary*, vol. 7, Frank E. Gaebelein, gen. ed. [Grand Rapids: Zondervan, 1985], 90). Note also that the followers of the Son of Man are "the saints, the people of the Most High," indicating the equivalence of the Son of Man with the Most High. The plural "saints" compared with the singular Him in the final clause of 7:27 further eliminates the possibility of identifying the nation of saints with the Song of Man (ibid., 94–95). Jesus Himself appears to be the one who connected the Son of Man with the Servant of Isaiah's Servant Songs. He did so in such passages as Mark 10:45: "For even the Son of Man did not come to be served, but to serve, and to give His life as a ransom for many" (Christopher J. H. Wright, *Knowing Jesus Through the Old Testament* [Downers Grove, Ill.: InterVarsity Press, 1992], 154).

46. Cf. E. J. Young, *The Prophecy of Daniel* (Grand Rapids: Eerdmans, 1949), 143–47, 275–94.

47. "The saints" can be none other than God-fearing Jews, as Robert D. Culver describes: "The 'saints' I hold to be no different from 'the people of the saints' [Dan. 7:27] in the passage before us. . . . They are the Israelites of the end time who will at last inherit the kingdom of David with Christ Himself reigning as their king" (*Daniel and the Latter Days* [Westwood, N.J.: Fleming H. Revell, 1954], 128, cf. 132–34; cf. A. C. Gaebelein, *The Prophet Daniel*, 17th ed. [New York: Our Hope, 1911], 80). Surprisingly, Walvoord sees the saints to be "the saved of all ages as well as the holy angels which may be described as 'the holy ones'" (p. 172), but this interprets the term anachronistically insofar as its referring to saints of all ages, and in its inclusion of angels it cannot explain the expression "the people of the saints" in 7:27.

48. Eugene H. Merrill, "Daniel as a Contribution to Kingdom Theology," in *Essays in Honor of J. Dwight Pentecost*, eds. Stanley D. Toussaint and Charles H. Dyer (Chicago: Moody, 1986), 222–23; cf. G. K. Beale, "The Influence of Daniel upon the Structure and Theology of John's Apocalypse," *JETS* 27, 4 (December 1984]: 419 n. 31; Robert L. Thomas, *Revelation 8–22, An Exegetical Commentary* (Chicago: Moody, 1995), 555 n. 40.

49. Robert L. Thomas, *Revelation 1–7, An Exegetical Commentary* (Chicago: Moody, 1992), 53.

50. Merrill, "Daniel as a Contribution," 222–23; Walvoord, *Daniel*, 146, 153. Revelation alludes to Daniel 2 over ten times (Thomas, *Revelation 8–22*, 553 n. 32). Gleason L. Archer Jr., writes, "Chapter 7 parallels chapter 2; both set forth the four empires, followed by the complete overthrow of all ungodly resistance, as the final (fifth) kingdom is established on earth to enforce the standards of God's righteousness. The winged lion corresponds to the golden head of the dream image (chap. 2); the ravenous bear to its arms and chest; the swift leopard to its belly and thighs; the fearsome ten-horned beast to its legs and feet. Lastly, the stone cut out without hands that in chapter 2 demolishes

the dream image has its counterpart in the glorified Son of Man, who is installed as Lord over all the earth. But chapter 7 tells us something chapter 2 does not—*viz.*, that the Messiah himself will head the final kingdom of righteousness" ("Daniel," 85).

51. Wright, 158–59.
52. Ibid., 159–61.
53. Ibid., 161.
54. Ibid., 162.
55. Ibid., 163.
56. Ibid., 164, 167.
57. Contra ibid., 167.
58. The next section of this chapter—"The Mission of Israel in the Present Age"—discusses the role of the faithful remnant of Israel within the body of Christ. That "remnant according to the election of grace" (Rom. 11:5) plays an important part in the church's discharge of her mission during the present.
59. Thomas, *Revelation 1–7*, 472–78; *idem., Revelation 8–22*, 141–43, 191–92; cf. J. A. Seiss, *The Apocalypse*, 3 vols. (New York: Charles C. Cook, 1909), 2:382, 3:27–28; J. B. Smith, *A Revelation of Jesus Christ* (Scottdale, Pa.: Herald, 1961), 191–92.
60. Thomas, *Revelation 8–22*, 141–42.
61. Ibid., 98–99, 216–63.
62. Wright, 165–74.
63. Ibid., 167–68.
64. Ibid., 169–70.
65. Ibid., 170–72.
66. "Additional meanings" refers to meanings beyond those discerned through grammatical-historical interpretations of the OT passages. Many use the expression *sensus plenior* (i.e., "fuller sense") to refer to those additional meanings.
67. Kaiser's rejection of a reader-response hermeneutic that assigns new meanings by the process of *sensus plenior* is quite valid (Walter C. Kaiser Jr., *The Messiah in the Old Testament* [Grand Rapids: Zondervan, 1995], 27–28). What is proposed here, however, is not a reader-response hermeneutic of just any reader. It is an additional meaning provided through inspired NT Scripture. Kaiser's objection to this explanation lies in an alleged loss of apologetic advantages of appeals to OT texts by the apostles and gospel writers (ibid., 23–24). An answer to that objection, however, lies in the fact that the apostles and writers also appealed to direct prophecies of the coming Messiah from the OT, ones that did not depend on meanings added by NT writers. Even Kaiser has prophetic categories that lie outside the "direct prophecy" category (ibid., 33–35), though in his system they are far less numerous. The literal fulfillments of grammatical-historical understandings of OT prophecies were ample to answer the skeptics with whom the earliest Christians had to deal.
68. Cf. Wright, 171.
69. E.g., J. Gordon McConville, "Messianic Interpretation of the Old Testament in Modern Context," in *The Lord's Anointed*, ed. Philip E. Satterthwaite, Richard S. Hess, and Gordon J. Wenham (Grand Rapids: Baker, 1995), 12.
70. Ibid., 15.
71. Ibid.
72. The continuing existence and distinctiveness of the Jewish people is in itself a testimony to God's faithfulness to His promises to Abraham, Isaac, and Jacob. Even in her unbelief, corporate Israel stands as a witness to the world. But the witness of the remnant according to the election of grace goes far beyond that because of the remnant's special relationship to God as part of the body of Christ.

73. Blaising and Bock appear to merge others with Israel in the nation's future inheritance: "We can illustrate this progressive dispensational view of the church in the case of Jewish Christians. A Jew who becomes a Christian today does not lose his or her relationship to Israel's future promises. Jewish Christians will join the Old Testament remnant of faith in the inheritance of Israel. Gentile Christians will be joined by saved Gentiles of earlier dispensations. All together, Jews and Gentiles will share the same blessings of the Spirit, as testified to by the relationship of Jew and Gentile in the church of this dispensation. The result will be that all peoples will be reconciled in peace, their ethnic and national differences being no cause for hostility. Earlier forms of dispensationalism, for all their emphasis on the future for Israel, excluded Jewish Christians from that future, postulating the church as a different people-group from Israel and Gentiles" (Craig A. Blaising and Darrell L. Bock, *Progressive Dispensationalism* [Wheaton: Victor, 1993], 50). That viewpoint in essence eliminates Israel's uniqueness in God's future program. Yes, the church will join with Christ in His earthly rule too, but in a capacity different from chosen Israel.

74. Thomas, *Revelation 8–22*, 410–11; cf. John F. Walvoord, *The Revelation of Jesus Christ* (Chicago: Moody, 1966), 302; Charles Caldwell Ryrie, *Revelation, Everyman's Bible Commentary* (Chicago: Moody, 1968), 116.

75. Walter Scott, *Exposition of the Revelation of Jesus Christ* (Swengel, Pa.: Bible Truth Depot, n.d.), 407.

76. T. Desmond Alexander, "Messianic Ideology in the Book of Genesis," in *The Lord's Anointed*, ed. by Philip E. Satterthwaite, Richard S. Hess, and Gordon J. Wenham (Grand Rapids: Baker, 1995), 27–32; cf. Kaiser, *Messiah in the Old Testament*, 37–42.

The date palm tree, which Josephus reports was found in forests in Israel in the first century.

CHAPTER ELEVEN

ISRAEL AND THE NATIONS IN GOD'S REDEMPTIVE PLAN

A. Boyd Luter

The waning years of the twentieth century have witnessed on-again, off-again efforts to mediate the ongoing tensions in the Middle East. From a political standpoint, though, Israel and the surrounding nations seem to have almost nothing in common except an intense desire to occupy and control the same historic real estate.

That would seem to be the sobering current reality. That is not the last word, however, on the relationship between Israel and the nations. That final, decisive word belongs to the Lord God as reflected in His overarching redemptive plan revealed in Scripture.

"Never the twain shall meet" is an inaccurate reflection of the historical phase in which Israel and the Arab nations came into being. The Bible portrays a profound interconnectedness between Israel and her neighbors at their infancy stage of growth as well as in their later history. Even more surprising to some, there is a clear biblical basis for understanding that a special aspect of blessing is readily available today for both those in Israel and the nations.

The following chapter will explore the nature of: (1) the foundational connection between Israel and the nations; (2) the unique election of Israel and her blessings and the significant national blessings available to other peoples (including the Arabs) through Israel, as seen in the Hebrew Scriptures; (3) the focal point of the blessings in the personal sense for both, seen in the New Testament; (4) the future chapters of the blessings to Israel and the nations, as seen in key eschatological passages; and (5) how the blessings are still readily available to be received today personally by those among both Israel and the nations.

THE EMERGENCE OF THE NATIONS

The apostle Paul confronted the ethnically proud philosophers in Athens with this fact of biblical history: "And He has made from one blood every nation of men to dwell on all the face the earth, and has determined their preappointed times and the boundaries of their dwellings" (Acts 17:26 NKJV).[1] Given the audience, Paul's proclamation of common ancestry and divinely designed historical[2] and geographical placement[3] includes both Israel and the nations.

What is the apostle to the Gentiles referring to when he says that God "has made from one blood every nation [πᾶν ἔθνος; *pan ethnos*] of men" (17:26)? At first, it seems that he has creation in mind and its aftermath (Genesis 1–5).[4] However, the following phrase, "all the face of the earth" (παντος προσώπου τῆς γῆς; *pantos prosopou tes ges*) likely looks back to the repopulation of the earth after the Flood (Genesis 9–11). It echoes the divinely forced spread of the nations "over the face of all the earth" (11:8–9; πρόσωπον πάσης τῆς γῆς; *prosopon pases tes ges* [LXX]) after the Tower of Babel.

Genesis 9–11 depicts the descent of the nations from one man, Noah, and his three sons: Shem, Ham, and Japheth (10:1). The genealogies in chapter 10 are from a point in time well before there was a nation of Israel.[5] As repeated in 10:5, 20, 31–32, they deal with *families* (מִשְׁפָּחָה; *mishpaha*) beginning to speak different *languages* (i.e., after the confusion of languages at Babel, 10:10) and occupying different *lands,* growing into *nations* (גּוֹי; *goy*).[6] While these growing nations are growing apart, so to speak, their family trees are all, ultimately, interconnected by their roots in Noah's family.

Among these nations are many with whom Israel must deal at a later stage. The most obvious of these geographic neighbors (often enemies) are Mizraim (Egypt, 10:6), the Philistines (10:14), various Canaanite peoples (10:15–19), the Assyrians and Arameans (10:22), and inhabitants of the Arabian Peninsula (10:27–30).[7]

THE ELECTION OF ISRAEL

Even at this early historical vantage point, however, there have been indications of which emerging peoples/nations will be distinctively blessed by God. The oracle of Noah clearly placed the Shemites in the position of honor (and the Canaanite wing of the Hamites as the recipients of a curse; 9:25–27).[8] Next, the line of Shem is emphasized in the Table of Nations (chapter 10) by mentioning his name first at the beginning of the chapter (10:1) but delaying the discussion of his descendants until last (10:21–31). Finally, the descendants of Eber are clearly spotlighted among the Shemites (10:21, 25).

After the crucial explanation of the scattering of the nations in 11:1–9, the genealogies of Shem (11:10–26) and Terah, the father of Abram (11:27ff.) set up the divine call to Abram.[9] From among the nations, out of the honored Shemite line, "Abram the Hebrew" (14:13) is chosen by God as the channel for His sovereign plan.[10]

However, there is a problem in regard to Abram that Scripture recognizes from the beginning. Abram's wife Sarai "was barren; she had no child" (11:30). Given the foundational "begot" (יָלַד; *yalad*; i.e., father and physical descent)[11] nature of the genealogies in Genesis 10 and 11, taking into account the eventual national and geographical aspects after generations of multiplication, the Lord's choice of Abram at this point in the narrative is intriguing to say the least.

But that does not stop God from making an astounding promise to the individual He had sovereignly selected. The striking initial statement[12] of what develops into the Abrahamic covenant is found in Genesis 12:1–3.[13] Immediately after the Lord directs Abram to relocate "to a land that I will show you" (12:1), He declares, "I will make you a great nation" (12:2).

Abram was already seventy-five years old when he received this mind-boggling promise (12:4). It would be twenty-five stretching years (17:17; 21:5), however, before the Lord God miraculously fulfilled the first step of His promise to make Abram's descendants (13:16) into "a great nation" (12:2): the birth of Isaac, the child of promise (17:16, 19). The Lord's unwavering choice of yet-unborn Isaac over Ishmael, Abram's son by Sarai's handmaid, Hagar (17:18–19), secured the bloodline that would become His elect nation. God's later direction to Abraham to send away Ishmael and Hagar clearly indicates that same resolve (21:9–13).

THE BLESSINGS TO ISRAEL

After the birth of Isaac, the rapid growth of Abram's family began to take place. Isaac's son, Jacob, had twelve sons. By the time "the house of Jacob" went to Egypt under Joseph's protection to avoid the great famine, they were a large family of seventy (Gen. 46:27). At the time of the Exodus, over 400 years later (Gen. 15:13), the nation-to-be numbered two million or more (Exod. 12:37).[14] God's promise to Abram of becoming a fully populated elect nation, Israel (Gen. 12:2), had come to fruition.

That was undoubtedly a significant part of what was meant by the Lord saying to Abram, "I will bless you" (12:2; cf. 22:17). Earlier in Genesis, both the creation account (1:28) and the beginning of the repopulation of the world after the Flood (9:1) closely connect God's blessing with mankind multiplying and filling the earth. Simply put, "In blessing man, God bestows good, at the time or later."[15] In the case of Abram (and Sarai) this aspect of blessing was much later but certainly worth waiting for.

However, that is surely not all that is meant by God's blessing on Abram. Some years into that period, Abram's frustration with childlessness (i.e., failure to be "blessed" with children) came to the foreground (15:2–3). At that point, the Lord restated His promise to make Abram's descent "a great nation." He committed Himself to multiply Abram's descendants to be as numerous as the stars of the heavens (15:4–5).

Abram's response to this unlikely promise becomes the biblical prototype for proper response to God and His plan. Genesis 15:6 records the kind of faith (אָמַן; *aman*)[16] that "justified" Abram before the Lord.[17] It is also utilized in the NT by both Paul (Rom. 4:1ff.; Gal. 3:6ff.) and James (2:23)[18] to make the same point in regard to any believer, Jew or Gentile (Rom. 1:16).

Though Genesis 15 does not say it in so many words, God's justification of Abram is also part of His blessing (Gen. 12:2), according to Galatians 3:9. Thus, not only would Abram's physical descendants be "blessed," based on the promise related to the initial statement of the Abrahamic Covenant. They could also participate in the blessing by individually following the spiritual example of Abram's faith. This aspect will be dealt with in more depth later in the chapter.

The rest of Genesis 15 describes the unilateral covenant (15:18) ceremony that the Lord chose to answer Abram's question about his inheritance of the land (15:8).[19] God's promise to bless Abram, originally made in Genesis 12:2, had further been manifested in an unconditional "contract," guaranteed by God!

An apparent final aspect of God's blessing to Israel is found in the restatement of the covenant to Abraham in Genesis 22:17: "Your descendants shall possess the gate of their enemies." Clearly, the imagery here is to defeat and displace an opposing force, in this case the enemies of the (later) nation of Israel.[20]

However, it is much more difficult to know how far this *blessing* can be extended historically. Some restrict the meaning to being able to "dispossess the Canaanites" in order to occupy the promised land (cf. 15:19–21).[21] That certainly is true, as far as it goes. Yet, it appears likely that this Abrahamic blessing refers generally to "the success of his descendents when they encounter enemies."[22] Thus, it could be as far-reaching as "any enemy of any time."[23]

This underplayed aspect of national blessing upon Israel may help explain why, even today, the Israeli military is phenomenally successful.[24] On the other hand, you need look no further than the spiritual dynamics behind Israel's devastating initial defeat at Ai (Joshua 7) to realize that this promise in Genesis 22:17 cannot be construed as completely ironclad.

THE BLESSINGS TO THE NATIONS THROUGH ISRAEL

As wondrous as the blessings were that Israel received through the Abrahamic covenant, they did not exhaust the Lord's blessings through Abram. In Genesis 12:3 God promised, "I will bless those who bless you"[25] and "in you all the families of the earth shall be blessed."

There are numerous plausible examples of blessings being bestowed on those who blessed Abraham or his descendants in some fashion. For example, in very close proximity textually, Lot was blessed financially (13:5); then he later owed his very survival to Abraham's intercession on behalf of any righteous residents of Sodom (Genesis 18–19). Two generations later, Laban realized he had been blessed because of Jacob (30:27). After he had earlier stolen Esau's blessing from

Isaac (Genesis 27), Jacob chose to bestow a very generous financial "blessing" (בְּרָכָה; *beraka*; 33:11) on his twin brother, from whom he had been estranged. Then, after Joseph was sold by his brothers into slavery, he initially became the stated vehicle of blessing for Potiphar's household in Egypt (39:1–6).[26]

These examples may appear to be merely personal, not national, in their scope. However, it should be realized that Lot's national descendants, the Moabites and Ammonites (19:37–38), humanly owed their opportunity to exist to Abraham because of Lot's survival. Esau's growing family, having been blessed by Jacob, the heir of promise, became the nation of Edom (36). Even more striking, Joseph's leadership role in Egypt made possible the blessing of survival through the seven-year famine for the Egyptian nation as well as many other surrounding nations (likely at least several of the locales of peoples/nations found in the Table of Nations in Genesis 10) disastrously impacted by the famine (41:53–57).

The Arabs are a particularly interesting case in regard to the Abrahamic blessings to the nations. Some of the peoples that lived in the Arabian Peninsula (i.e., Arabs) were listed in the Table of Nations. However, many others are descended from Ishmael, Abram's son by Hagar, Sarai's handmaid (25:12–18). Still others come from the children of Abraham by Keturah, his later concubine (25:1–6).[27]

Ishmael was, of course, the beloved older son of Abraham (21:11), for whom Abraham cared so much that he asked God to name Ishmael the child of promise: "Oh, that Ishmael might live before You!" (17:18). That request was denied, and the Lord's choice of Isaac (17:19), who would be born the next year (17:21), was made clear.

However, Abraham's request on behalf of Ishmael (and his descendants) had been heard by the Lord. Even though "redemptive history does not proceed through him," Ishmael is still greatly blessed.[28] God immediately promises to multiply him into a great nation with twelve princes (17:20), a promise fulfilled within the span of the Book of Genesis (25:16).

Through his participation in the covenant sign of circumcision with Abraham (17:9–14, 23–27), Ishmael was also very much part of the covenant and blessed accordingly.

Relatedly, Ishmael had already been blessed with the promise of a multitude of descendants before he was even born, in the context of his mother, Hagar, fleeing from Sarai's wrath (16:6–10). Then, when Ishmael was a teenager, and he and Hagar were finally required to leave by God's direction to Abraham (21:9–12), the Lord again promised to make a nation of Ishmael's descent (21:13). The reason given is because Ishmael is Abraham's son.

Thus, while Ishmael is not *the* heir of the Abrahamic covenant, he is an honored son of Abraham and highly blessed as a result. Further, even though there was a divinely sanctioned geographical distance placed between Ishmael and Isaac (21:9–21), either to prevent friction or a claim to Abraham's "estate," the return of Ishmael for Abraham's burial indicates (25:9–10) that there could still be some "family unity" between the stepbrothers.[29] Similar honorable treatment was accorded to Abraham's children by Keturah (25:1–6). Like Ishmael, they were purposefully distanced from Isaac (25:6). Also like Ishmael, they were each given gifts by their father (25:6; cf. 21:14) before leaving him.[30]

These passages have implications for the place of the Arab nations in God's plan. As seen above, they have been recipients of God's gracious blessing in biblical history. And, despite the ongoing seething rage of the surrounding Arab states toward Israel, who may well be "reaping the whirlwind" of the Abrahamic curse (12:3) as a result, they still deserve great respect as descendants of Abraham through Ishmael or Keturah's children. This will be a focus of the concluding section of this chapter.

In later restatements of the covenant to Abraham (22:18) and Isaac (26:4), the wording is "in your seed all the nations of the earth shall be blessed." Then, to Jacob (28:14) it becomes "in you and in your seed all the families of the earth shall be blessed." These passages strongly imply that blessings to the nations could flow through the generations of Israel after Jacob ("your seed").

In surveying the rest of the Hebrew Scriptures, some classic instances of apparent Abrahamic blessing to the nations mediated through his descendants emerge. For example, Jeremiah 29:7 directs the Jews in exile to be a blessing to Babylon, including praying for its peace.[31] Also, it seems that the presence of Daniel and his friends in Babylon proves to be a great blessing, especially during the times of King Nebuchadnezzar's incapacity to rule (Daniel 4).[32] Ezra 6:10 records the Medo-Persian King Darius's desire for the prayers of the Jewish priests. In the book of Nehemiah, that a blessing accrued to the Medo-Persian Empire because of Nehemiah, King Artaxerxes' cupbearer (Neh. 1:11), is certainly implied by the king's generous response (2:1–8).[33]

THE FOCUS OF PERSONAL BLESSINGS: JESUS CHRIST

Chris Wright is correct in asserting that Israel's election involved God's use of particular means for a universal goal.[34] In the Lord's grand redemptive plan, Abraham and Israel were chosen so that "all the nations" might be blessed. Paul goes so far as to say that there is an anticipation of the NT gospel being preached contained in Genesis 12:3 and 22:18 (Gal. 3:8).[35] He then ties the wider intent of the blessing of the Lord's covenant with Abraham to his ultimate "seed" (σπέρματί;[36] cf. Gen. 22:18, LXX) that the covenant looked forward to—Jesus Christ (Gal. 3:16), particularly in regard to His redemptive work on the cross (3:13–14).

As explained above, the national physical blessings for both Israel and the nations under the Abrahamic covenant were indeed extraordinary. However, Abram's blessing in being justified before God (Gen. 15:6) was even more so, given that it was spiritual and eternal in scope. That same aspect of blessing is also readily available to any person who will, by faith, follow Abraham's lead

(Gal. 3:9). Paul even says it is legitimate to call such believers "sons of Abraham" (3:7), whether they are Jewish or not, since faith is the means of entry to this spiritual, eternal aspect of blessing (3:9).

This should not be taken as a blurring between the purposes of God in relation to Israel and the nations, though. Certainly, in the church that Jesus Christ is currently building (Matt. 16:18), Jews and Gentiles are together (Eph. 2:11–18) in God's redemptive plan. However, in the conclusion of the same letter to the Galatians, for example, Paul refers to "the Israel of God,"[37] most likely meaning the current remnant of believing Jews (Rom. 11:2, 7), who are both Abraham's physical and spiritual children (Gal. 3:6–9).[38]

Significantly, it is the Lord Jesus' stated intent that the blessing of being justified by faith (Gal. 2:16) should be proclaimed to "all the nations" ($\pi\acute{a}\nu\tau a$ $\tau\grave{a}$ $\acute{\epsilon}\theta\nu\eta$; Matt. 28:19; Luke 24:47), the same intended scope as the statements of the Abrahamic blessing in Genesis 22:18 and 26:4 ($\pi\acute{a}\nu\tau a$ $\tau\grave{a}$ $\acute{\epsilon}\theta\nu\eta$, LXX).[39] This Great Commission for Christ's disciples is to continue unabated until "the end of the age" (Matt. 28:20).

Paul expressed the scope of his apostolic evangelistic ministry as "all the nations" (Rom. 1:5; 16:26), though he clarified that it was to be preached to the Jew first, but also to the Greek (i.e., non-Jew; Rom. 1:16). At the end of his life, with the Great Commission (and likely the Abrahamic covenant) in mind, the apostle to the Gentiles indicated that his preaching had had a significant impact toward reaching "all the nations" (2 Tim. 4:17).

Thus, the spiritual and eternal blessing aspect of the Abrahamic covenant continues to flow to both individual Jews and Gentiles as the gospel of Christ's redemptive work on the cross has been preached in the carrying out of the Great Commission. But, what will happen at the "end of the age" (Matt. 28:20)?

THE ESCHATOLOGICAL FUTURE OF THE BLESSING TO ISRAEL

At present, relatively few Jews are coming to faith in Jesus Christ, according to God's sovereign redemptive plan (Rom. 11:5).[40] That scarcity was so emotionally difficult for Paul that he was willing to give up his own salvation if, by doing so, his Jewish brethren, who possessed the Abrahamic national blessing (Rom. 9:2–5), might become believers as a result.[41]

Such an exchange was, of course, not possible. Paul's presentation of the Lord's grand redemptive scheme indicates that, until "the fulness of the Gentiles" (11:25)—the full complement from "all the nations" to be saved comes into the fold—the spiritual hardening (9:18) and blindness (11:7, 25) of the bulk of Israel toward the ultimate "seed" of Abraham (Gal. 3:16), Jesus Christ, will not end.[42] Widespread rejection of the Messiah has been, is, and will continue to be the rule during "the times of the Gentiles" (Luke 21:24) in God's plan.

However, that was not the case during the glorious initial chapter of the church's history, at Pentecost and immediately thereafter (Acts 2–6). Besides the fact that thousands of Jews were saved (Acts 2:41; 4:4; 6:1), it is particularly striking where many of these new believers came from geographically and what happened. They were Jews of the Diaspora, coming to Jerusalem for the Feast of Pentecost from "every nation [παντὸς ἔθνους] under heaven" (2:5). They came from countries of the New Testament era (2:9–11), which roughly parallel the Table of Nations in Genesis 10. Most astoundingly, they each heard the gospel in the language (γλῶσσα, 2:11) of the country in which they resided, a miraculous reversal of the Lord's confusion of the languages (γλῶσσα, Gen. 11:7, LXX) at Babel.

Perhaps these aspects of the beginning of the church at Pentecost (Acts 11:15) were meant to indicate that the Jews were intended to play a spotlighted role in taking the blessing of the gospel to "all the nations" (Matt. 28:19–20; Luke 24:47; Acts 1:8) throughout the age. Unfortunately, beyond Paul (Rom. 1:5; 16:26) it appears that few other Jewish believers chose to accept this crucial evangelistic responsibility.

By God's grace, this situation will improve drastically at the end of the age. The 144,000 Jews described in Revelation 7:1–8 and 14:1–5 are apparently miraculously protected ("sealed") in order to spread the message of Christ's redemptive death (5:9).[43] There is, unfortunately, not enough information provided biblically to know whether any of this group were already believers or are converted at the same time they are sealed.

Nor is this the only large-scale conversion of Jews seen in the Apocalypse. After the death, resurrection, and ascension of the two witnesses in 11:7–12, there is a devastating earthquake in "the great city," Jerusalem (11:8),[44] which kills 7,000 people (11:13). The survivors, surely primarily Jews, fear and give glory to God, exactly the commanded (saving) response to the climactic preaching of "the everlasting gospel" in 14:6–7.

At the very least, it appears that a revival of epic proportion will have broken out in Jerusalem.[45] More likely, this is the location of what is meant by "all Israel will be saved" in Romans 11:26. Though it is highly doubtful that this passage depicts a complete national conversion, as some understand Romans 11, it could easily be speaking of a group of hundreds of thousands, if not millions of Jews, gloriously brought into the fold of redemptive blessing.

These events take place after the conclusion of the two witnesses' three-and-a-half-year ministry (Rev. 11:3, 7), before the basically unrivaled reign of the Beast (11:7), also for three and a half years (13:7). Hence, this large group of new Jewish converts may well be the Jewish "woman" described in 12:6–17, who is miraculously protected from the Devil (12:9, 13–17) for that latter three-and-a-half-year period (12:14).

Suffice it to say that the eternal Abrahamic blessing of salvation by faith (Gen. 15:6) will be entered into by a great company of his descendants during the Tribulation period. Though there is no description of distinctively Jewish believers in Revelation ruling with Christ during the thousand years of the earthly messianic kingdom following the Second Coming (19:11–20:6), they are included, given Jesus' promise of judgment over Israel to the apostles in Matthew 19:28.

The final biblical clue in regard to Israel has to do with eternal blessedness. The unbreakable (unconditional) nature of the Abrahamic covenant guarantees that redeemed Jews will have a key part in the new Jerusalem. That never-ending role is portrayed as the twelve gates to the city (Rev. 21:12–13). Thomas is certainly correct in understanding this description as "explicit notice of the distinct role of national Israel in this eternal city in fulfillment of their distinct role in history."[46] Thus, it is not farfetched to say that, through Jesus Christ, the ultimate "seed" of Abraham (Gal. 3:16), and the role of Israel in the New Jerusalem (Rev. 21:12), the Jews will continue to bestow an eternal blessing!

THE ESCHATOLOGICAL FUTURE
OF THE BLESSINGS TO THE NATIONS

There is a bright ray of light in the midst of Matthew's dark description of the Tribulation period at the end of the age: "This gospel of the kingdom will be preached in all the world as a witness to all the nations, and then the end shall come" (24:14).[47] This means that the Lord is *promising* that "all the nations," the same group that the Abrahamic covenant promises to bless, will have the opportunity to hear the gospel before Christ comes to judge! We see just how serious the Lord Jesus is about the worldwide preaching of the gospel in His Great Commission statements in Matthew 28:19–20 and Luke 24:47.[48] In both, the scope of the commission, like Matthew 24:14, is "all the nations." In Luke 24, the commission begins in Jerusalem (progressing to the ends of the earth, Acts 1:8). In Matthew 28, the commission continues until the end of the age, as does the eschatological promise of 24:14.

We see the outworking of Jesus' promise of offering the redemptive message to "all the nations" in two important passages describing events at "the end of the age" in the Apocalypse. The first is the appearance before the heavenly throne of an innumerable redeemed multitude from "all nations, tribes, peoples and tongues" in Revelation 7:9.[49] But, not only does this description seem to at least partly fulfill the promise of Christ in Matthew 24:14 and the Great Commission, it also echoes the wording of the Table of Nations in Genesis 10.[50] Thus, it seems that the salvation of this great multi-ethnic multitude (like Pentecost; see above) at least partly reverses the forced spread of the nations after the arrogant, united disobedience of mankind at Babel, before the Lord's intervention through the Abrahamic Covenant and its promised blessing to all the nations.

There is a second great wave of salvation from among all the nations in Revelation 14:6–7, 14–16, and 15:2ff.[51] The 144,000 redeemed and sealed Jews (cf. 7:1–8) are said to be "firstfruits" (14:4), implying that a much larger harvest would follow.[52] The climactic preaching of the eternal "gospel" in 14:6–7[53] (perhaps by the 144,000 or others) leads to the reaping of the grain harvest, a figure for evangelistic ingathering and the image of many saved martyrs in heaven (15:2). Thus, between Revelation 7:9–17 and the "harvest" in 14, we see the blessed salvation of an amazingly vast throng from the nations at the end of the age.

Passages in the Hebrew Scriptures like Isaiah 25 prophesy a glorious future for the nations in which death will be swallowed up and all tears will be wiped away (25:8), and they will rejoice in the Lord's salvation (25:9). This description clearly foresees the eternal blessedness described in Revelation 21:1–4. In that radically new creation (21:1, 5), the nations (who are saved eternally) will "bring their glory and honor" (21:24, 26) alongside that of the redeemed Jews (21:12–13). They are still distinct but very closely related in the eternal outworking of God's redemptive plan.

CONCLUSION: ONGOING BLESSINGS TO ISRAEL AND THE NATIONS

In Acts 17:26–27, Paul told the Athenian philosophers that the Lord God's purpose for creating "from one blood every nation of men to dwell on all the face of the earth" was "so that they should seek the Lord." While both Israel and the nations could claim ignorance to an extent (17:30), with the divinely ordained death and resurrection of Jesus, the promised "seed" of Abraham, came the necessity of repentance (and faith) for all men (17:30–31).[54]

In effect, what the Lord now expects is for every individual Jew or Gentile to follow the example of Abraham's faith and justification in Genesis 15:6. This crucial applicational point is underlined by an artistic chiastic (i.e., inverted parallel) arrangement of the blessing element of four of the Abrahamic covenant passages (Gen. 12:3; 22:18; 26:4; 28:14).[55]

As seen below, the two outer passages (A, A') in the chiasm (12:3; 28:14) emphasize the foundational unconditional nature of God's covenant with Abraham. This aspect is only available to the Jews, God's sovereignly chosen people.

The emphasis of such mirroring structures is, however, in the middle layer (B, B').[56] There is seen the secondary conditional aspect of the covenant, in both cases emphasizing Abraham's obedience (22:18; 26:4). In both cases (i.e., God's commands to sacrifice Isaac and to not leave the promised land in spite of a severe famine), trust in the Lord in challenging situations was required, even as it had been in 15:6 when a divine promise to Abraham that came in the face of hopeless childlessness.

    A (12:3) In you all the families (מִשְׁפְּחֹת) of the earth shall be blessed *(Promise/Unconditional)*

    B (22:18) In your seed all the nations (גּוֹי) shall be blessed, because you have obeyed my voice *(Faith Needed/Conditional)*

    B' (26:4) In your seed all the nations shall be blessed, *because Abraham obeyed my voice* . . . *(Faith Needed/Conditional)*

    A' (28:14) In you and in your seed all the families of the earth shall be blessed *(Promise/Unconditional)*

In addition, the change from the use of "families" in 12:3 and 28:14 to "nations" in 22:18 and 26:4 is not merely stylistic. It points to the likely presence of such an inverted structure. In addition, the use of *families* recalls the divine choice of Abraham and Israel from among "the families of the sons of Noah" (10:32).

However, in the overall biblical usage, "all the nations" is picked up as the chord that is replayed over and over in the NT in the offering of the blessing/redemptive aspect of the Abrahamic Covenant to all who would believe in Jesus Christ (e.g., Matt. 28:19–20; Luke 24:47; Gal. 3:6–9; Rev. 14:6–7). So, not only is there a past historic interconnectedness between Israel and the nations dating back to Noah's family, well before the national aspects of the Abrahamic covenant; it is also the intention of the Lord's redemptive plan that the Abrahamic blessing provide the basis for a present and future connection through faith (Gen. 15:6) in Christ (Gal. 3:6–9). It is a blessing that can, one by one, person by person, overcome even the tensions between Jews and Arabs in the Middle East.

DISCUSSION QUESTIONS

1. What is Paul probably referring to when he states that God "has made from one blood every nation of men" (Acts 17:26)?

2. What is the relationship between God's promised blessings to Abram (Gen. 12:2–3) and Abram's example of faith (Gen. 15:6) as Paul applies them in Galatians 3:6–9?

3. Is there an ongoing significance to the promise to Abraham that his "descendants shall possess the gate of their enemies" (Gen. 22:17)?

4. List blessings to the nations, especially the Arab peoples, that occurred because of the Abrahamic covenant.

5. Is there biblical evidence that many Jews and Gentiles will come to saving faith in Jesus Christ, the ultimate "seed" of Abraham (Gal. 3:16), at the end of the age?

ENDNOTES

1. Unless otherwise indicated, all citations are from the New King James Version (NKJV) of the Bible.
2. F. F. Bruce, *The Book of the Acts*, rev. ed., *NICNT* (Grand Rapids: Eerdmans, 1988), 337–38, observes that "the times of the Gentiles" (καιροὶ ἐθνῶν; *kairoi ethnon*) in Luke 21:24 may be an example of such "preappointed times" (Acts 17:26).
3. I. H. Marshall, *The Acts of the Apostles: An Introduction and Commentary*, *TNTC* (Grand Rapids: Eerdmans, 1980), 288. Bruce, *Acts*, 338, cites Deut. 32:8 as the *locus classicus* in regard to divine geographical allocation.

4. E.g., Marshall, 287.
5. The emphasized initial placement of Eber (from which is derived the name "Hebrew" in Gen. 10:21) among the Shemite line (10:21–31) looks ahead to God's election of "Abram the Hebrew" (14:13) in chapter 12.
6. A. P. Ross, *Creation and Blessing: A Guide to the Study and Exposition of Genesis* (Grand Rapids: Baker, 1988), 227, helpfully describes "families" as "physically related clans, normally a national subdivision."
7. H. G. Stigers, *A Commentary on Genesis* (Grand Rapids: Zondervan, 1976), 121–28, takes great care in making the identification of each name/nation.
8. See, e.g., Ross, 218–19, for a helpful discussion.
9. Ross, 250–52, makes a likely case for parallelism between the genealogies in Gen. 5 and Gen. 11, developing their linkage in the line of promise and blessing.
10. This is the wording of V. P. Hamilton, "Genesis," *Evangelical Commentary on the Bible,* ed. W. A. Elwell (Grand Rapids: Baker, 1989), 19.
11. D. J. Wiseman, "Genesis 10: Some Archaeological Considerations," *Journal of the Transactions of the Victoria Institute* 87 (1955), 17.
12. Restatement or progressive clarification of various key aspects of the Abrahamic Covenant in Genesis are found in 13:14–18; 15 and 17, 18:1–18, 22:1–19, 26:3–5, 26:24 and 35:9–15. For a helpful visualization and explanation of how most of these passages develop as the Abrahamic Covenant, see the *Nelson Study Bible,* gen. ed. E. D. Radmacher (Nashville: Thomas Nelson, 1997), 35–36.
13. For varying evangelical discussions of the Abrahamic Covenant, see G. L. Archer, "Covenant," *Evangelical Dictionary of Theology,* ed. W. A. Elwell (Grand Rapids: Baker, 1984), 277; C. C. Ryrie, *Basic Theology* (Wheaton: Victor, 1986), 453–57; and T. M. McComiskey, "Covenant," *Baker Encyclopedia of the Bible,* ed. W. A. Elwell (Grand Rapids: 1988), 1:532–33. See also the somewhat older major contribution to this discussion by D. J. McCarthy, *The Form and History of the Abrahamic Covenant Traditions* (Amsterdam: Vandevelder, 1967).
14. The figure of "600,000 men" in Exod. 12:37 must be expanded by the number of women and children that accompanied the men out of Egypt, making for a conservative estimate of two million, but perhaps as many as three million or more.
15. W. J. Cameron and G. W. Knight, III, "Bless, Blessed, Blessing," *Evangelical Dictionary of Theology,* 162.
16. It should be noted that Heb. 11:8 states, "By faith Abraham obeyed when he was called to go out to the place which he would receive as an inheritance." That means Abram was already a man of faith before Gen. 15. However, his faith is apparently focused on in Gen. 15 because of its proximity to the solemnizing of the covenant in that chapter (Ross, 309–10).
17. For compact discussions of the doctrine of justification by faith from different evangelical perspectives, see, e.g., Ryrie, 298–300; and J. I. Packer, "Justification," *Evangelical Dictionary of Theology,* 593–97.
18. Since James 2:14–26 is a notoriously thorny passage, consult, e.g., D. W. Burdick, "James," *Expositor's Bible Commentary,* gen. ed. F. E. Gaebelein (Grand Rapids: Zondervan, 1981) 12:185; or D. J. Moo, "James," *Evangelical Commentary,* 1157.
19. E.g., Ross, 308; McCarthy, 300; C. L. Rogers, Jr., "The Covenant with Abraham and Its Historical Setting," *BibSac* 127 (1970): 241–56.
20. Stigers, 190–91.
21. Ross, 400.
22. H. C. Leupold, *Exposition of Genesis* (Grand Rapids: Baker, 1975 ed.), 2:635.
23. Stigers, 191.

24. See the excellent compact discussion of the modern State of Israel's remarkable military exploits in D. L. Larsen, *Jews, Gentiles and the Church: A New Perspective on History and Prophecy* (Grand Rapids: Vision House, 1995), 199–213.

25. The reverse was also true: ". . . and I will curse those who curse you" (12:3), with the initial example being Pharoah and the Egyptians in 12:17–20.

26. Ross, 625.

27. See, e.g., F. V. Winnett, "The Arabian Genealogies in Genesis," in *Translating and Understanding the Old Testament,* eds. H. T. Frank and W. L. Reed (Nashville: Abingdon, 1970), 171–96; and R. H. Smith, "Arabia," *Anchor Bible Dictionary*, vol. 1, gen. ed. D. N. Freedman (New York: Doubleday, 1992), 327.

28. Stigers, 167.

29. The conclusion by Stigers, 185, that Ishmael is here "disinherited," as well as expelled, seems to be overstated.

30. It defies belief that the only "gifts" given to Ishmael, his beloved older son, by Abraham were "bread and a skin of water" (Gen. 21:14a). Undoubtedly, these were mentioned because of the focus on survival in that passage (21:14b–20).

31. Indeed, it was possible for Israel to "be a blessing" (Gen. 12:2) to another nation while being "cursed" by exile herself (Deut. 28:15ff., esp. 28:64ff.; 30:1). See also the helpful related discussion of C. L. Feinberg, "Jeremiah," *EBC*, vol. 6 (Grand Rapids: Zondervan, 1986), 553–54.

32. J. D. Pentecost, "Daniel," *The Bible Knowledge Commentary: Old Testament,* eds. J. F. Walvoord and R. B. Zuck (Wheaton: Victor, 1985), 1343; for a parallel view by the present writer, see A. B. Luter, "Daniel," *The Complete Who's Who of the Bible,* ed. P. Gardner (London: HarperCollins, 1995), 124.

33. See the related discussions in A. B. Luter and B. C. Davis, *God's Good Hand: Expositions of the Books of Ezra and Nehemiah* (Expositor's Guide to the Historical Books; Grand Rapids: Baker, forthcoming).

34. C. Wright, "A Christian Approach to Old Testament Prophecy concerning Israel," in *Jerusalem Past and Present in the Purposes of God,* ed. P. W. L. Walker (Cambridge: Tyndale House, 1992), 1.

35. Consult the careful treatment of R. Y. K. Fung, *The Epistle to the Galatians* NICNT (Grand Rapids: Eerdmans, 1988), 138–40. From a different, more theological perspective, see J. D. G. Dunn, *The Theology of the Book of Galatians,* New Testament Theology (Cambridge: Cambridge University Press, 1993).

36. In an interpretation that has frequently been contested because of its subtlety, Paul takes the implication of the use of the singular "seed" in Genesis and focuses on the individual descendant who would fulfill the Abrahamic promise: the Lord Jesus Christ. For a helpful discussion, see Fung, 155–56.

37. The classic scholarly discussion of this generation is P. Richardson, *Israel in the Apostolic Church* Society of New Testament Studies Monograph Series 10 (Cambridge: Cambridge University Press, 1969), 74–84.

38. W. S. Campbell, "Israel," *Dictionary of Paul and His Letters* eds. G. F. Hawthorne, R. P. Martin and D. G. Reid (Downers Grove: InterVarsity Press, 1993), 441–42. See also the conclusion of the present writer in *NSB*, 1980.

39. For in-depth discussions by the present writer of the various Great Commission statements at the conclusions of the Gospels, see A. B. Luter, *A New Testament Theology of Discipling* (Dallas: Dallas Theological Seminary/Ann Arbor: University Microfilms, 1985); Luter, "Great Commission," *Anchor Bible Dictionary* 2:1090–91; Luter, "Women Disciples and the Great Commission," *Trinity Journal* 16NS (1995): 171–85; Luter and Kathy McReynolds, *Disciplined Living: What the New Testament Teaches*

about Recovery and Discipleship (Grand Rapids: Baker, 1996); and Luter and McReynolds, *Women as Christ's Disciples* (Grand Rapids: Baker, 1997).

40. See the significant treatment of Rom. 11 in regard to the salvific future of the Jewish nation elsewhere in this volume by H. W. Hoehner.

41. R. G. Gruenler, "Romans," *Evangelical Commentary*, 943, presents a balanced discussion of this difficult passage.

42. Gruenler, 948–49; see also Hoehner's discussion.

43. Larsen, 291–92; R. L. Thomas, *Revelation 1–7: An Exegetical Commentary* (Chicago: Moody, 1992), 474–75.

44. The wording "where also our Lord was crucified" (Rev. 11:8) cinches the identification of "the great city" here as Jerusalem.

45. R. L. Thomas, *Revelation 8–22: An Exegetical Commentary* (Chicago: Moody, 1995), 99. See also Thomas's related discussion in "The Mission of Israel and the Messiah in the Plan of God," in the present volume, as well as Hoehner's treatment of Rom. 11:25–26.

46. Thomas, *Revelation 8–22*, 463.

47. The significance of this passage, as well as Rev. 7, 14, for the blessed conversion of the nations, is developed by the present writer in A. B. Luter, "End Times and Mission," in the *Evangelical Dictionary of World Missions,* gen. ed. S. Moreau (Grand Rapids: Baker, forthcoming).

48. Luter, "Great Commission," 1090–91; Luter and McReynolds, *Women,* 16–21, esp. the chart on page 19.

49. For an up-to-date, scholarly discussion of this passage by the present writer, see A. B. Luter, "Martyrdom," in the *Dictionary of the Later New Testament and Its Developments,* eds. P. H. Davids and R. P. Martin (Downers Grove: InterVarsity Press, forthcoming).

50. Thomas, *Revelation 1–7*, 401, believes "the origin of the expression is the prophecy of Daniel." However, the similar usage in Daniel 3, 5, 6, and 7 contains three elements, while Gen. 10 has four, as do the passages in Revelation.

51. R. Bauckham, *The Theology of the Book of Revelation,* New Testament Theology (Cambridge: Cambridge University Press, 1993), 95–98, argues at some length for a positive grain harvest in Rev. 14:14–16 and a negative grape harvest in 14:17–20. See also the more developed treatment in chapter 9 ("The Conversion of the Nations") of R. Bauckham, *The Climax of Prophecy: Studies on the Book of Revelation* (Edinburgh: T & T Clark, 1992). C. H. Talbert, *The Apocalypse: A Reading of the Revelation of John* (Louisville: Westminster/John Knox, 1994), 67, also concludes 14:14–16 describes a grain harvest and 14:17–20 a grape harvest, as Thomas does cautiously, *Revelation 8–22*, 218–24.

52. Some understand "firstfruits" here (14:4) to refer only to the quality of the offering. With "harvest" imagery following within just a few verses (14:14ff.), that conclusion is rendered highly unlikely.

53. Surely it is highly significant that the term "gospel" is found only here in the Apocalypse. A very plausible explanation for its inclusion is that it echoes Matt. 24:14, esp. since "every nation . . ." is also found in 14:6, likely echoing "all the nations" in Matt. 24:14; 28:19.

54. The NT usage of "repent" in regard to unbelievers implies/includes faith. See the present writer's discussion in A. B. Luter, "Repentance (NT)," in *Anchor Bible Dictionary* 5:672-74. See also the brief, but helpful, discussion of Marshall, 289–90.

55. An example of a chiastic pattern spread throughout an entire biblical book (in this case, Rev. 1 to 22), with significant theological ramifications is found in Bauckham,

Revelation, 57–58. Examples of standard chiasmus in Genesis are presented in Ross, 436, 446, 474, 498, 631, 649.

56. For in-depth development of the potential significance of chiastic structures for the interpretation of extended passages or entire books of Scripture, see A. B. Luter and B. C. Davis, *God Behind the Seen: Expositions of the Books of Ruth and Esther* (Expositor's Guide to the Historical Books; Grand Rapids: Baker, 1995).

PART FIVE

CONCLUSION: A DOXOLOGY

The Eastern or Golden Gate of the Temple Mount seen from the Kidron Valley. The gate was mortared shut following the expulsion of the Crusaders in A.D. 1187.

CHAPTER TWELVE

A CELEBRATION OF THE LORD OUR GOD'S ROLE IN THE FUTURE OF ISRAEL

David L. Larsen

Solid, exegetically based theology must be doxological. The theological task must lead to praise and worship of the living God. Orthodoxy after all is "right praise." So the apostle Paul, in heralding the mystery of Israel in God's plan, shows us how "Israel has experienced a hardening in part until the full number of the Gentiles has come in. And so all Israel will be saved" (Rom. 11:25–26). He reaches into two OT prophets for substantiation:

> The deliverer will come from Zion; he will turn godlessness away from Jacob.

> And this is my covenant with them when I take away their sins. (Rom. 11:26–27)

The inspired apostle then argues that Israel is loved, "for God's gifts and his call are irrevocable," and that indeed Israel and the church alike are recipients of God's mercy, fulfilling the divine purpose and pleasure, "For God has bound all men over to disobedience so that he may have mercy on them all" (Rom. 11:29, 31–32). Then Paul can repress an outburst of praise to God no longer, and he concludes his classic discussion of Israel and her future with a rapturous doxology:

> Oh, the depth of the riches of the wisdom and knowledge of God! How unsearchable his judgments, and his paths beyond tracing out! Who has

301

known the mind of the Lord? Or who has been his counselor? Who has
ever given to God, that God should repay him? For from him and through
him and to him are all things. To him be the glory forever! Amen. (Rom.
11:33–36)

Four celebratory axioms bring this study into sharp biblical and practical
focus.

WE OUGHT TO CELEBRATE GOD AND HIS SOVEREIGNTY— AS SEEN IN THE MYSTERY OF ISRAEL'S ELECTION

The God who made the world and everything in it is the Lord of heaven
and earth and does not live in temples built by hands. And he is not served
by human hands, as if he needed anything, because he himself gives all
men life and breath and everything else. From one man he made every
nation of men, that they should inhabit the whole earth; and he determined the times set for them and the exact places where they should live.
God did this so that men would seek him and perhaps reach out for him
and find him, though he is not far from each one of us. For in him we
live and move and have our being (from the apostle Paul's sermon in
Athens found in Acts 17:24–28).

The God of the Bible is sovereign and almighty. God has taken initiatives in
creation, providence, and redemption. He is in His essence a self-sufficient being and is not dependent on anything He creates for His own fulfillment. God
does not need us. But He has made us in His image and likeness, and He loves
and cares for all human beings with "an everlasting love" (Jer. 31:3; John 3:16;
Rom. 5:8). Out of His great compassion and love He has formulated a plan of
redemption and salvation for His lost and rebellious creatures. Though all human beings share a common ancestry and a common dignity by virtue of being
created by God, we also share alike in the condemnation and consequences of
our arrogant revolt against a holy God and His divine law.
   In devising a plan of deliverance and redemption to be accomplished by His
one and only Son, Jesus Christ, God in His sovereign determination sent His Son
into time-space as the God-man to be the ransom and substitutionary atonement
for human guilt and sin. God's own nature defines what is the good, and His plan
and "his eternal purpose which he accomplished in Christ Jesus our Lord" (Eph.
3:11) are set forth and declared in His supernaturally given revelation which is
Holy Scripture. Here we are told that at the dawn of history God sovereignly
chose one nation out of all the nations to be the special instrument of effecting
blessing for all the nations (Gen. 12:1–3). The nation of Israel was elected not to
salvation but for service, just as the younger Jacob was chosen for a unique place

in the unfolding plan of God and Esau the older was designated "to serve the younger" (Gen. 25:23). The principle of concentration is seen repeatedly in Scripture, as when our Lord makes a disproportionate investment of time and effort in the twelve apostles in order to foster an exponential multiplication of persons for His kingdom. The fact is that God chose a nation through whom He would give His special revelation, the Bible; through whom He would send His only Son, the Messiah; and through whom He would bear testimony and witness to the Gentile nations. This nation selected in sovereign grace was not the United States, Great Britain, China, or any other nation except Israel. So the Scriptures bear reiterated testimony:

> The LORD your God has chosen you out of all the peoples on the face of the earth to be his people, his treasured possession. (Deut. 7:6)

> The LORD did not set his affection on you and choose you because you were more numerous than other peoples, for you were the fewest of all peoples. (Deut. 7:7)

> "You are my witnesses," declares the LORD, "and my servant whom I have chosen, so that you may know and believe me and understand that I am he." (Isa. 43:10)

> "But now listen, O Jacob, my servant, Israel, whom I have chosen." (Isa. 44:1)

> "You only have I chosen of all the families of the earth." (Amos 3:2)

Two-thirds of our Bible consists of the history of God's ancient people. That Jesus the Savior "was a descendant of David" (Rom. 1:3) and all of the apostles were Jewish bear irrefutable evidence that God diverted one small ethnic stream in human history in order to accomplish His very special and gracious redemptive purpose for the whole of humankind. This chosenness has been a heavy burden for Israel, as Tevye in *Fiddler on the Roof* laments: "I am tired of being one of the chosen. Could you choose someone else for awhile?"[1] We must bear in mind that this election of Israel was not based on inherent or moral superiority but solely in God's gracious providence, as Paul emphasizes in describing "God's purpose in election." It is "not by works but by him who calls" (Rom. 9:11–12).

God's particularity in executing the elective decree has been a major scandal for the power brokers of a sinful race. Great ridicule and resistance have always been manifest toward God, His decree, and those who have been elected (not a small part of the etiology of anti-Semitism).[2] The same ridicule and resistance have attached to the later chosen people of God, the church "which is Christ's body." Here again God has gone counter to the prevailing wisdom of benighted culture in His election (1 Peter 2:9–10; 1 Cor. 1:26–31). Our argument here is that the later choice of the church as the people of God does not and cannot displace or supersede the unique function of ethnic Israel, who have yet to fulfill God's total and complete purpose. In either case many moderns find it very difficult, if not impossible, to accept what has been called "the specificity of biblical particularity." The Lutheran theologian Robert Jenson has described this "balking" at God's particularity as a new form of "gnosticism," that is seeking "categories more amenable to the contemporary mind."[3] A brief factor-analysis of this mind-set suggests several critical components.

The Issue of Authority

The primary issue of our time is that of authority. Sin itself is the assertion of human autonomy, and from the Garden of Eden the question has been, "Has God said?" (Gen. 3:1). In the growing anthropocentrism of the Renaissance and then in the Enlightenment's enthronement of human reason (with Kant's banishment of religious knowledge to sheer subjectivity), and no less in the painful skepticism of postmodernity, we human beings most tragically will brook no rival in the contest for control. The idea of a divine-command morality is out because it would call for our capitulation to God and obedience. Heresy is out because in pluralism "all the cows are gray." And sadly, in all of this, teleology has been lost in western civilization because we have been sundered from any vital sense of the sovereign God's purpose for history. Modern biblical criticism liquidated the authority of Scripture, and the result has been a Babel of confusion and chaos.[4] Without the indefectible authority of Holy Scripture, we are all on our own. Thus the Jesus Seminar comes up with an entirely new Jesus along with a denial that Jesus ever taught of future divine intervention and judgment, and indeed, a denial of the Jewishness of Jesus. So one scholar is commended for "refusing to let guilt sneak in and make a system of redemption out of Christianity."[5] The contemporary move away from the centrality of the atonement, seen even in evangelicalism today, is but another symptom of cultural accommodation resulting from the vacuum created by the abdication of biblical authority.

The Impact of the Enlightenment

The Enlightenment, in its admirable concern for equality in human rights and human dignity before the law (as reflected broadly in our nation's founding documents), basically demolished all social hierarchies and any expectation of "honor" in society itself.[6] What the late William Henry termed "liberalism's deeply misguided egalitarianism" replaced the necessary dialectic between elitism and egalitarianism with an inevitable "influx of mediocrities" and a lowering of standards. The Bible abounds with hierarchies in leadership, in government, in the home, and in the church. This is increasingly unpalatable in our time. Needless to say, this mood, resentful of a special privilege or duty, finds God's electing decree offensive. Henry argues that "some ideas are better than others, some values more enduring, some works of art more universal, some cultures more accomplished and worthy of more study."[7] Similarly, Aaron Wildavsky traces in a thoughtful work "the rise of radical egalitarianism" and the ridiculous notion that social engineering must dedicate itself to the drastic reduction, if not the elimination, of differences.[8] In the face of this immense societal pressure for uniformity, the believer is countercultural in affirming the great differences that are vital to biblical faith, one of them being God's election of Israel.

Relativism and the Absence of Authority

One more strand in this fabric is represented in the kind of thinking heard in Amitai Etzioni's Communitarianism, with its laudable insistence on tolerance and acceptance in communities of integrity but subject to a paralyzing relativism and absence of objective authority for guiding moral behavior.[9] So history is flattened out and horizontalized to the point that the only nod toward God's sovereign election becomes the reluctant concession that the Lord's original choice of Judas "shows that God can make mistakes too." Frequently, generous doses of romanticism flavor Communitarianism, a belief system more at home with Rousseau's original virtue than with historic Christianity's original sin. Radical evil has left us convoluted and skewed, producing both the Holocaust and the gulag. God's dramatic and decisive intervention on His own terms is absolutely necessary. Human nature is profoundly flawed, and we are incapable of redressing our plight. God is the Prime Mover in the amelioration of our disastrous escapade of rebellion. Thus romanticism as well as rationalism lacks the key we desperately need. Only God possesses the key, and He has not been silent or passive. God has acted and is acting, and He does so in His sovereign good pleasure. It is thus fitting and appropriate that we begin our response by celebrating God's glorious sovereignty in His election of Israel from among all the nations of the earth.

> Oh, the depth of the riches of the wisdom and
>   knowledge of God!
> How unsearchable his judgments, and his paths
>   beyond tracing out! (Rom. 11:33)

WE OUGHT TO CELEBRATE GOD AND HIS FIDELITY—AS SEEN IN THE TRAGEDY OF ISRAEL AND HER PRESERVATION

"I the LORD do not change. So you, O descendants of Jacob, are not destroyed." (Mal. 3:6)

The election of Abraham and his descendants for a specific role in divine providence, and the donation of the land, are inseparable in the biblical presentation of history.[10]

To fulfill the Word of God, the restoration of Israel is an absolute necessity.[11]

The aims and the activities of the God of the Bible stem from His character and His moral attributes. The prophet Malachi argues for the survival of ethnic Israel based on who God is and His essential unchangeableness. Both Israel and the church are contingent, depending on the truthfulness and faithfulness of God to His promises and His Word. Indeed the whole universe would plunge into moral and ethical chaos if God were to become contradictory or unreliable. The nature of truth itself depends on God's fidelity, and with the apostle Paul we exclaim, "Let God be true and every man a liar" (Rom. 3:4). Israel may fail, but God is faithful. Christians may fail, but God is faithful. Indeed, "If we are faithless, he will remain faithful, for he cannot disown himself" (2 Tim. 2:13). God's purposes will find fulfillment, and His purpose for Israel has been unequivocally stated: "the people I formed for myself that they may proclaim my praise" (Isa. 43:21). The immutability of God does not make Him any less feeling or compassionate but does assure the moral and ethical stability of His universe.

God's covenants of promise are the key to understanding how God has intended to implement His purposes through Israel. Promissory covenants are agreements which may be conditional or unconditional. God has made covenants that are conditional, and He has made covenants which are unconditional. He is a covenant-making and covenant-keeping God. The covenant made after the flood with Noah and his sons would be an example of an unconditional covenant (Gen. 9:8–17). God commits Himself without any stipulations whatever. The covenant God made with Abraham in calling him out of Ur of the Chaldeans had one stipulation, and that was met when Abraham obeyed God and came to Canaan (Gen. 12:1–3). To the original articles of the covenant concerning nationhood and blessing, God now unconditionally adds the land (Gen. 13:14–17; 15:17–21; 17:3–8). I cannot see any conditions attached to Israel's title to the land. It is *Eretz Israel*. God has made many promises to other nations as set forth in the Old Testament (e.g., to the Egyptians and Assyrians in Isaiah 19) and to all Jews and Gentiles who are part of the church (2 Cor. 1:20; 2 Peter 1:3–4).[12] Still, some covenants of promise are conditional. While Israel's title to the land is inviolable, her possession of and prosperity in the land are markedly conditioned on her obedience to God (cf. Deut. 27–28). The book of Deuteronomy should be seen as a covenant renewal document.

Not all Jewish scholars see their history in terms of covenant. Norman F. Cantor's history of the Jews sees neither their ritual life nor their sacred texts as anything more than fictitious sagas, and in a bizarre fashion concedes validity to the anti-Semitic case. This approach makes a total capitulation to deconstructionism and postmodernism.[13]

Preferable is David Novak's probing study of various positions and his tilt toward the Orthodox Jewish philosopher Michael Wyschogrod and his book, *The Body of Faith: Judaism as Corporeal Election*. Yet Novak wants to advance even more strongly the premise that "the election of Israel involves an altogether special relation with God that is central to cosmic redemption" and that the Torah articulates universal moral law.[14] Still better in my judgment is Eugene B. Borowitz and his lament of "our love affair with modernity." He sees modernity as the betrayer and Hermann Cohen's surrender to Immanuel Kant as leading to the present Jewish espousal of liberal religion and its deification of the self. "Modernization has become our Messiah."[15] He stands with Abraham Heschel for the accuracy of the biblical record and thereupon asserts that God's contractual agreement with Israel continues on in full force.[16] He argues forcefully that the people of universal history need a particular land. Borowitz presents a classic analysis of serious cultural default because of the abdication of covenant responsibility. In moving away from the Documentary Hypothesis now in academic shambles, he boldly states that "Jews know their people will survive." This is because, as a nation, Israel is covenanted to God and awaits the culmination of the covenant in the days of the Messiah. Borowitz sees clearly that "the covenant depends on Jewish biologic-historic continuity until the messianic days."[17] This is essentially the argument of the prophet Jeremiah:

> This is what the LORD says, he who appoints the sun to shine by day, who decrees the moon and stars to shine by night, who stirs up the sea so that its waves roar—the LORD Almighty is his name:
> "Only if these decrees vanish from my sight," declares the LORD, "will the descendants of Israel ever cease to be a nation before me."
> This is what the LORD says:
> "Only if the heavens above can be measured and the foundations of the earth below be searched out will I reject all the descendants of Israel because of all they have done," declares the LORD. (Jer. 31:35–37)

The OT documents are bursting with lament for Israel's loss of vision and her egregious apostasy. Yet likewise the documents glow with the hope and promise of outpoured blessing. Are the judgments and plagues to be taken literally (as indeed they must be) and the promises of blessing to be spiritualized and allegorized beyond ethnic Israel to the church? This very critical hermeneutical issue is at the crux of our understanding of God's fidelity and His character. If the church displaces Israel forever and indeed ethnic Israel is superseded by the church (a view that has regrettably fueled anti-Semiticism across the centuries), then have we not abandoned the historical-grammatical exegesis of the Old Testament with all of the disastrous consequences thereof, including the effective loss of the plain, direct meaning of the biblical text? Have we not moved back again from the Antiochene to the Alexandrian nemesis of spiritualizing Scripture? Are we not back with Philo and Origen and those who through the centuries have seen the biblical text as a nose of putty to be shaped and formed at will? Are we not out on the high seas of subjectivity, bereft of the navigational aids and skills afforded to us by sound hermeneutics and exegesis?

How did God's ancient people reasonably understand the plethora of promises? Is all of their common-sense understanding and reasonable confidence in the meaning of words and sentences to be wrenched away from them in favor of a higher spiritual meaning which, in point of fact, they could not have understood? We must weigh thoughtfully and carefully the cumulative data of OT prophetic insight (to say nothing here of the other genres of OT literature).

> In that day the Lord will reach out his hand a second time to reclaim the remnant that is left of his people from Assyria, from Lower Egypt, from Cush, from Elam, from Babylonia, from Hamath and from the islands of the sea. He will raise a banner for the nations and gather the exiles of Israel; he will assemble the scattered people of Judah from the four quarters of the earth. (Isa. 11:11–12)

The first reclamation is clearly the return of the remnant as described in Ezra and Nehemiah. What is the second reclamation but something not yet experienced fully for ethnic Israel at the end of the age? If this is a prophecy of the church, who are Egypt and Babylon?

> "However, the days are coming," declares the LORD, "when men will no longer say, 'As surely as the LORD lives, who brought the Israelites up out of Egypt,' but they will say, 'As surely as the LORD lives, who brought the Israelites up out of the land of the north and out of all the countries where he had banished them.' For I will restore them to the land I gave their forefathers." (Jer. 16:14–15)

> "The days are coming," declares the LORD, "when I will raise up to David a righteous Branch, a King who will reign wisely and do what is just and right in the land. In his days Judah will be saved and Israel will live in safety. This is the name by which he will be called: the LORD our Righteousness. So then, the days are coming," declares the LORD, "when people will no longer say, 'As surely as the LORD lives who brought the Israelites up out of the Egypt,' but they will say, 'As surely as the LORD lives, who brought the descendants of Israel up out of the land of the

north and out of all the countries where he had banished them.' Then they will live in their own land." (Jer. 23:5–8)

Interwoven with this majestic prophecy of Jesus the Messiah is certainly something very special concerning the land and the people which has not yet occurred.

"For I will take out of the nations; I will gather you from all the countries and bring you back into your own land. I will sprinkle clean water on you, and you will be clean; I will cleanse you from all your impurities and from all your idols. I will give you a new heart and put a new spirit in you; I will remove from you your heart of stone and give you a heart of flesh. And I will put my Spirit in you and move you to follow my decrees and be careful to keep my laws. You will live in the land I gave your forefathers; you will be my people, and I will be your God. . . . They will say, 'This land that was laid waste has become like the garden of Eden'. . . . Then the nations around you will know that I the LORD have rebuilt what was destroyed and have replanted what was desolate. . . . Once again I will yield to the plea of the house of Israel and do this for them: I will make their people as numerous as sheep." (Ezek. 36:24ff.)

Has this ever been literally fulfilled? Or does this involve a spiritual resurrection and renewal, as described in Ezekiel 37:1–14, which has not yet taken place?

At that time Michael, the great prince who protects your people, will arise. There will be a time of distress such as has not happened from the beginning of nations until then. But at that time your people—everyone whose name is found written in the book—will be delivered. (Dan. 12:1)

History or prophecy?

For the Israelites will live many days without king or prince, without sacrifice or sacred stones, without ephod or idol. Afterward the Israelites will return and seek the LORD their God and David their king. They will come trembling to the LORD and to his blessings in the last days. (Hos. 3:4–5)

When did this take place? Or is dispersed and suffering Israel justified in seeing this as fidelity to the covenant of promise?

"I will bring back my exiled people Israel; they will rebuild the ruined cities and live in them. They will plant vineyards and drink their wine;

they will make gardens and eat their fruit. I will plant Israel in their own land, never again to be uprooted from the land I have given them says the LORD your God." (Amos 9:14–15)

This is clearly a declaration of a permanent possession of the land of promise. Has it been voided?

But on Mount Zion will be deliverance; it will be holy, and the house of Jacob will possess its inheritance. (Obad. 17)

A virtually unanimous witness bespeaking "the harmony of the prophetic word."

Who is a God like you, who pardons sin and forgives the transgression of the remnant of his inheritance? You do not stay angry forever but delight to show mercy. You will again have compassion on us; you will tread our sins underfoot and hurl all our iniquities into the depths of the sea. You will be true to Jacob, and show mercy to Abraham, as you pledged on oath to our fathers in days long ago. (Mic. 7:18)

The blessings envisioned embrace spiritual and moral new birth and cleansing. Will this really happen?

The LORD will restore the splendor of Jacob like the splendor of Israel, though destroyers have laid them waste and have ruined their vines. (Nah. 2:2)

The last word will be redemptive and regenerative.

LORD, I have heard of your fame; I stand in awe of your deeds, O LORD. Renew them in our day, in our time make them known; in wrath remember mercy. . . . You came out to deliver your people, to save your anointed one . . . yet I will rejoice in the LORD, I will be joyful in God my Savior. (Hab. 3:2, 13, 18)

In the grim reality of captivity and oppression, the prophet clings to God's salvific purpose. God can be depended on.

At that time I will gather you; at that time I will bring you home. I will give you honor and praise among all the peoples of the earth when I restore your fortunes before your very eyes, says the LORD. (Zeph. 3:20)

Ultimately, Satan and all his minions will not thwart the gracious purposes and promises of God.

> "For I am with you," declares the LORD Almighty. "This is what I covenanted with you when you came out of Egypt. And my Spirit remains among you. Do not fear." (Hag. 2:4bff.)

The covenant is reliable.

> "For whoever touches you touches the apple of his eye. . . . Shout and be glad, O Daughters of Zion. For I am coming and I will live among you," declares the LORD. "Many nations will be joined with the LORD in that day and will become my people. I will live among you and you will know that the LORD Almighty has sent me to you. The LORD will inherit Judah as his portion in the holy land and will again choose Jerusalem." (Zech. 2:8c, 10ff.)

God always expands and enlarges but never reduces the scope of His covenant.

> "Ever since the time of your forefathers you have turned away from my decrees and have not kept them. Return to me, and I will return to you," says the LORD Almighty. . . . "Then all the nations will call you blessed, for yours will be a delightful land," says the LORD Almighty. (Mal. 3:7, 12)

Without minimizing the seriousness and enormity of sin and guilt, God has made a way of salvation in which justice and righteousness link with love and faithfulness (Ps. 89:14). Hallelujah to the Lamb!

Any thoughtful and reflective person would have to conclude that there is still something very special for ethnic Israel which has yet to be fulfilled on the basis of this outpouring of prophetic promises.

In turning now to the NT, we immediately face the question of continuity and discontinuity with the OT promises. Clearly the church built on Christ and founded at Pentecost is absolutely unique and through the Spirit's baptizing work is an organism in which there are neither Jews nor Greeks, neither slave nor free (1 Cor. 12:13). The creation of the church and the definition of her destiny must not be seen as negating or nullifying the promises of God to Israel or God's purpose for her. The Lord Jesus seems to assume that people living at the time of His coming could recognize and identify Him correctly on the basis of the perspicuity of the OT prophecies.[18] Jesus does not rebuke or correct the apostles' expectation of the restoration of ethnic Israel as we read in Acts 1:6. He does not say, "There is no future for Israel."[19] Indeed, Peter proclaimed that Jesus the Messiah would "restore all things" (Acts 3:20–21). Barker quotes Van Ruler on "the surplus in the Old Testament" that the church cannot itself assimilate. Van Ruler goes on to say:

> Does everything end in the church? Does everything, not only Israel, but history and creation, exist for the sake of the church? Or is the church only one among many forms of the kingdom of God, and does its catholicity consist precisely in the fact that it respects, acknowledges, and holds dear all forms of the kingdom, for example, even the people of Israel?[20]

The very literally fulfilled prophecies of Christ's first advent would incline us to expect a similar literality in connection with the prophecies of His second advent and the events surrounding it. Matthew's gospel stresses the fulfillment of messianic prophecy and chronicles the preaching of the kingdom by John the Baptist and Jesus without any redefinition or corrective. Jesus speaks of the messianic banquet in Matthew 8:11 in which "many will come from the east and west, and will take their places at the feast with Abraham, Isaac and Jacob in the kingdom of heaven." Jesus does not suggest a cancellation of the promised feast or a scratching of Israel from the guest list. When Jesus describes "the renewal of all things when the Son of Man sits on his glorious throne," He indicates that "you who have followed me will also sit on twelve thrones, judging the twelve tribes of Israel" (Matt. 19:28). Jesus foresees the day when the Jews would see Him and receive Him (Matt. 23:37–39). He seems to speak of Israel's receptivity to the Antichrist in the time of the end (John 5:43). While it is impossible to characterize a single and comprehensive NT hermenuetic in the use of the OT, it is instructive to note that the Gentile writer, Luke, shares with us the angel's promise to Mary that her son would receive "the throne of his father David, and he will reign over the house of Jacob forever; his kingdom will never end" (Luke 1:32–33). Luke also shares with us Zechariah's song in which reference is made to God's remembrance of "his holy covenant, the oath which he swore to our father Abraham" (Luke 1:68, 72). Demonstrably Luke uses the word *Israel* in both Luke-Acts in an ethnic and national sense.[21]

The evidence accumulates and finally culminates in the apostle Paul's treatment of Israel's election and future in Romans 9–11. Something very special awaits ethnic Israel in the final wrap-up of human history in the end time. Paul is quite clear:

> God did not reject his people, whom he foreknew. (Rom. 11:2)

> Did they stumble so as to fall beyond recovery? Not at all! (Rom. 11:11)

> For if their rejection is the reconciliation of the world, what will their acceptance be but life from the dead? (Rom. 11:15)

And if they do not persist in unbelief, they will be grafted in, for God is able to graft them in again. (Rom. 11:23)

Even nonpremillennialists like Charles Hodge[22] and many of the Puritans, as well as Karl Barth,[23] G. C. Berkouwer,[24] and D. Martyn Lloyd-Jones,[25] to say nothing of John Murray[26] and the commentators C. E. B. Cranfield[27] and C. K. Barrett,[28] all agree that Romans 11 is not describing the experience of the church but has to do with ethnic Israel. As the Danish scholar Johannes Munck vigorously argued, "God is storing up eschatological wrath but plans in the meanwhile to save all Israel in the last days."[29] Of course these writers do not agree with the full premillennial projection of the literal establishment of Israel in her land at the end, but the essential survival and preservation of the Jewish people for a particular purpose in God's ongoing work has been granted. We have yet to trace Christ's mediatorial ministry as basic to this fulfillment, but we can at this juncture readily recognize how appropriate it is for us to celebrate and praise God for His magnificent fidelity to His covenant promises. We see them most especially in Israel's tragedy and in her providential preservation down through the centuries. Analogously, we who are part of the church, which is Christ's body, can be encouraged and heartened to rest in the faithfulness of our God. Were Israel to be stripped of the clearly understood covenant promises made unconditionally, we would have to consider ourselves as standing in serious and uncertain jeopardy. So we need not fear or become faint of heart. God and His Word can be depended on.

Let Israel say: His love endures forever. Let the house of Aaron say: His love endures forever. Let those who fear the LORD say: His love endures forever. (Ps. 118:2–4)

The LORD has sworn and will not change his mind. (Ps. 110:4)

WE OUGHT TO CELEBRATE GOD AND HIS MERCY—AS SEEN IN THE DESTINY OF ISRAEL AND HER SALVATION

Just as you who were at one time disobedient to God have now received mercy as a result of their disobedience, so they too have now become disobedient in order that they too may now receive mercy as a result of God's mercy to you. For God has bound all men over to disobedience so that he may have mercy on them all. (Rom. 11:30–32)

"I will have mercy on whom I will have mercy, and I will have compassion on whom I will have compassion." (Exod. 33:19)

. . . to give his people the knowledge of salvation through the forgive-ness of their sins, because of the tender mercy of our God, by which the rising sun will come to us from heaven to shine on those living in dark-ness and in the shadow of death, to guide our feet into the path of peace. (Luke 1:77–79)

"Praise be to the God and Father of our Lord Jesus Christ! In his great mercy he has given us new birth into a living hope through the resurrec-tion of Jesus Christ from the dead." (1 Peter 1:3)

> When all Thy mercies, O my God,
> My rising soul surveys,
> Transported with the view, I'm lost
> In wonder, love, and praise.
> —Joseph Addison

Mercy is one of the attributes of God related to His love, kindness, and grace. A. W. Tozer gives helpful definition to the quality of mercy: "Mercy is an at-tribute of God, an infinite and inexhaustible energy within the divine nature which disposes God to be actively compassionate."[30] Tozer goes on properly to insist that both Testaments set forth God as merciful always in proper tension (as we humanly perceive the reality) with God's justice and righteousness. His "kind-ness and sternness" (Rom. 11:22) seem to present an unresolvable tension but as we shall see, God, in the genius of His omniscience and wisdom, has found the way to perfectly express His great everlasting love and to sustain and support the righteous foundations of His moral universe. This is the story of salvation which issues from the very nature of God and who God is.

The object of God's mercy is the entire human race, created by God and loved by God as His creatures, yet plunged into the vicious vortex of alienation and estrangement from God because of rebellion and revolt against Him. Genesis 3 describes the complicity of our first parents with Satan, the fallen angel. Imme-diately upon transgressing the commandment of God, our forebears lost their spiri-tual poise and sought to hide from God. The disastrous consequences of human pride and willfulness are seen immediately as predicted (Gen. 3:16–19). The murder of Abel by Cain is but the beginning of fratricidal conflict in the world. In the days of Noah, "the LORD saw how great man's wickedness on the earth had become, and that every inclination of the thoughts of his heart was only evil all the time" (Gen. 6:5). Indeed, "now the earth was corrupt in God's sight and was full of violence" (Gen. 6:11). The hubris and arrogance of fallen humankind are seen in the presumptuous undertaking at the tower in Babel, "Come, let us build ourselves a city, with a tower that reaches to the heavens, so that we may make a name for ourselves and not be scattered over the face of the whole earth"

(Gen. 11:4). The OT relentlessly narrates the story of calamity and catastrophe, both for nations and individuals, which follow upon the undeniable fact of human depravity and lostness. Jeremiah 17:9 tells us that "the heart is deceitful above all things and beyond cure." This is one with the apostle Paul's argument in Romans that "there is no difference, for all have sinned and fall short of the glory of God" (Rom. 3:22–23).

But the unrelieved darkness of history's nightmare of suffering and death was challenged at the very outset by a divine promise of mercy, undeserved and unmerited mercy. In the bleakness of post-lapsarian Eden and our rebellion, God promises an intervention through a woman's offspring who would counteract and ultimately defeat humanity's spiritual nemesis (Gen. 3:15). This merciful promise was enlarged and expanded across the centuries. As Adam and Eve in their desolation stood trembling in the fig leaves with which they sought to conceal their shame, God interposed, killed animals, and clothed them with the skins of the animals (Gen. 3:21). Already the principle of benefit through the death of an innocent victim is set forth. The evolving picture of the coming "mashiach," or Anointed One, reveals He is to be God's king and God's Son (2 Sam. 7:14). He is to come through Abraham by Isaac (Gen. 12:1–3, 17:19) and through Judah, the fourth son of Jacob (Gen. 49:10). His lineage is to be supernaturally prepared and preserved. A meticulous examination of this massive evidential base is beyond the purview of this chapter, but suffice it to say that among the strands of messianic expectation to be seen in the Old Testament is "the hope of the eschatological appearance of a king of Davidic descent."[31] This was in considerable vogue at the time of Jesus of Nazareth, who was hailed by His followers as "Son of David."

The richness of this body of predictive and prophetic material completes a fairly full sketch of Messiah's earthly career, including His death and resurrection and a chronological scheduling of His first advent.[32] He is to be called Jesus (Yeshúa) "because he will save his people from their sins" (Matt. 1:21). At His birth He was acclaimed as "the Savior" (Luke 2:11), and after His resurrection He is called "our Savior, Christ Jesus" (2 Tim. 1:10). The long-awaited one came on a mission of mercy and redemption. "For the Son of Man came to seek and to save what was lost" (Luke 19:10). At the core of Israel's common experience was the sacrificial system, which was described at length in the Pentateuch and embodied the principle, "For the life of the creature is in the blood, and I have given it to you to make atonement for yourselves on the altar; it is the blood that makes atonement for one's life" (Lev. 17:11). The variety of animal sacrifice and the diversity of priestly function in the OT prefigure the perfect sacrifice which Messiah would make (as per Isa. 53:4ff.). The guilty sinner placed his or her hand on the innocent victim in an obvious transfer of guilt. Vicarious substitution in an actual transaction demonstrates what will constitute the essence of divine deliverance. Yet the rivers of sacrificial blood cannot remove sin, as the writer to the Hebrews insists: "It is impossible for the blood of bulls and goats to take away sin" (Heb. 10:4). The endless repetition of the sacrifices reinforces the fact that they were typical but not in themselves efficacious (Heb. 10:1, 11). Thus we see God's forbearance in leaving sin unpunished where persons brought sacrifice in trust and faith in God's ultimate provision for the forgiveness of sin (cf. Rom. 3:25–26; Gen. 15:6). When at last the Messiah came (Gal. 4:4), He was hailed as the sinbearer (John 1:19). He lived His life under the shadow of the death He had come to die for the ungodly (Mark 10:45). The centrality of the death of Jesus on the cross and the certainty of His bodily resurrection become the very heart and essence of the Good News, which the early church was to proclaim to Jews and Gentiles everywhere (Rom. 1:16–17; 1 Cor. 15:3–8). The inspired interpretation of the atoning death of Jesus becomes absolutely critical for an appreciation of the mercy of God to us as lost sinners:

> . . . and are justified freely by his grace through the redemption that came by Christ Jesus. God presented him as a sacrifice of atonement, through faith in his blood. . . . He did it to demonstrate his justice at the present time, so as to be just and the one who justifies those who have faith in Jesus. (Rom. 3:24–26)

> At just the right time, when we were still powerless, Christ died for the ungodly. . . . But God demonstrates his own love for us in this: While we were still sinners, Christ died for us. (Rom. 5:6, 8)

> For what the law was powerless to do in that it was weakened by the sinful nature, God did by sending his own Son in the likeness of sinful man to be a sin offering. (Rom. 8:3)

> For the message of the cross is foolishness to those who are perishing, but to us who are being saved it is the power of God . . . but we preach Christ crucified: a stumbling block to Jews and foolishness to Gentiles, but to those whom God has called, both Jews and Greeks, Christ the power of God and the wisdom of God. . . . For I resolved to know nothing while I was with you except Jesus Christ and him crucified. (1 Cor. 1:18, 24–25; 2:2)

> God was reconciling the world to himself in Christ, not counting men's sins against them. . . . God made him who had no sin to be sin for us, so that in him we might become the righteousness of God. (2 Cor. 5:19, 21)

> Christ redeemed us from the curse of the law by becoming a curse for

us, for it is written: "Cursed is everyone who is hung on a tree." (Gal. 3:13)

May I never boast except in the cross of our Lord Jesus Christ, through which the world has been crucified to me, and I to the world. (Gal. 6:14)

In him we have redemption through his blood, the forgiveness of sins. Now in Christ Jesus you who once were far away have been brought near through the blood of Christ. His purpose was to create in himself one new man out of the two, thus making peace, and in this one body to reconcile both of them to God through the cross, by which he put to death their hostility. (Eph. 1:7; 2:13, 15–16)

Many live as enemies of the cross of Christ. Their destiny is destruction, their god is their stomach, and their glory is in their shame. Their mind is on earthly things. But our citizenship is in heaven. And we eagerly await the Savior from there, the Lord Jesus Christ. (Phil. 3:18–20)

He forgave us all our sins, having canceled the written code, with its regulations, that was against us and that stood opposed to us; he took it away, nailing it to the cross. And having disarmed the powers and authorities, he made a public spectacle of them, triumphing over them by the cross. (Col. 2:14–15)

We believe that Jesus died and rose again and so we believe that God will bring with Jesus those who have fallen asleep in him. . . . He died for us so that, whether we are awake or asleep, we may live together with him. (1 Thess. 4:14, 5:10)

. . . God our Savior, who wants all men to be saved and to come to a knowledge of the truth. For there is one mediator between God and men, the man Christ Jesus, who gave himself as a ransom for all men. (1 Tim. 2:3–6)

But when the kindness and love of God our Savior appeared, he saved us, not because of righteous things we had done, but because of his mercy. He saved us through the washing of rebirth and renewal by the Holy Spirit, whom he poured out on generously through Jesus Christ our Savior, so that, having been justified by his grace, we might become heirs having the hope of eternal life. (Titus 3:4–6)

With respect to human salvation and forgiveness and its basis, there is no wedge between Jesus and Paul and no discontinuity between the Old and New

Testaments. Human beings, whether centuries before Christ, in this church age, in the tribulation to come, or in the millennium, all come into a right relationship with God and the reality of eternal life only through the mediatorial work of Jesus Christ once and for all accomplished on the cross. Whether grasping the principle of grace in anticipation or glorying in Christ's finished work retrospectively, salvation is a free gift to the repenting and trusting person (Eph. 2:8–9). No one of us can earn it, deserve it, or achieve it by ourselves. It is "not of works, lest anyone should boast." The remnant of Jews saved today is by grace (Rom. 11:6), and the mass of Gentiles saved today come on the same grounds of mercy and are together incorporated into the "body of which Christ is the Head." Those who are saved during the tribulation after the exit of the bridal church, whether they are the martyrs "under the altar" (Rev. 6:9ff.), the 144,000 Jewish vanguard converted to Christ, or the great multitude who come through Jewish witness and testimony now at long last faithfully borne, all come as trophies of God's super-abounding grace and mercy. God's purpose in every age is salvation. These very ancient special people, the Jews, are to be the recipients of this mercy in plain view of all the created intelligences of the universe. All praise be to God! He "delights to show mercy" (Mic. 7:18c).[33]

WE OUGHT TO CELEBRATE GOD AND HIS PERSISTENCY—AS SEEN IN THE RESPONSIBILITY OF THE CHURCH UNDER THE GREAT COMMISSION

For this is what the Sovereign Lord says: I myself will search for my sheep and look after them. As a shepherd looks after his scattered flock when he is with them, so will I look after my sheep. I will rescue them from all the places where they were scattered on a day of clouds and darkness. I will bring them out from the nations and gather them from the countries, and I will bring them into their own land. I will pasture them on the mountains of Israel, in the ravines and in all the settlements in the land. I will tend them in a good pasture, and the mountain heights of Israel will be their grazing land. There they will lie down in good graz-ing land, and there they will find in a rich pasture on the mountains of Israel. (Ezek. 34:11–14)

"What do you think? If a man owns a hundred sheep, and one of them wanders away, will he not leave the ninety-nine on the hills and go to look for the one that wanders off?" (Matt. 18:12)

Essentially I mean the moment you consider man's real need, and also the nature of the salvation announced and proclaimed in the Scriptures, you are driven to the conclusion that the primary task of the church is to preach and to proclaim this, to show man's real need, and to show the only remedy, the only cure for it.[34]

The gospel is either true for all, or it is not true at all.[35]

Jesus insisted, "As the Father has sent me, I am sending you" (John 20:21). The mission of the church to evangelize rises necessarily out of the commands of her living Lord and out of the conviction that Jesus Christ is the one way of salvation (John 14:6; Acts 4:12). The church has the responsibility under God to be salt and light in a corrupt world, but under her doxological calling to glorify and honor God her number one priority must be sharing the Good News of Christ with a perishing world. For this the Holy Spirit has been poured out in empowering fullness (Acts 1:8). Thus missionaries and evangelists have traversed the globe in the interest of planting churches and seeing men and women everywhere converted.

The apostle Paul acknowledged his inclusive obligation—"I am obligated both to the Greeks and non-Greeks, both to the wise and the foolish. That is why I am eager to preach the gospel also to you who are at Rome" (Rom. 1:14–15). Paul also asserts a certain priority for witness to the Jewish people (Rom. 1:16). Every local church should demonstrate sensitive obedience to the debt we owe the Jewish people by including a generous allocation to witness to the Jews. After all, "salvation is from the Jews" (John 4:22b). Christian love, instead of arrogance, ought to foster "envy or jealousy" among the Jews for what Christians possess in Christ (Rom. 11:11). How frequently has this phenomenon been in evidence in Christian history or now?

Most assuredly, however, there are some especially vexed obstacles and hindrances which we face right now in aggressively pursuing Christian witness to the Jewish people.

Modern Pluralism

There is a mistaken modern ecumenicity which concedes all to pluralism and thus has given away the store. In postmodernism there are no facts, only opinions. When doctrinal consensus is gone, mission dissolves. Dialogue replaces declaration. Every religious impulse is accorded equal status, and evangelism is out the window.[36] A salient example of this is the work of Hans Küng, the liberal Roman Catholic. He would like to see Judaism, Christianity, and Islam meld, but in order to promote such understanding, he abandons his trinitarian presuppositions and feels it necessary to jettison serious Christology by making concessions on the pre-existence, the incarnation, and the expiatory sacrifice of Christ.[37] How different from the apostle Paul who testified: "My heart's desire and prayer to God for the Israelites is that they may be saved" (Rom. 10:1).

Two-Covenant Theology

Another very bizarre twist found in many broad church circles and increasingly among evangelicals is what is commonly called the two-covenant idea that asserts that God will save Jews today under the terms of the Old Covenant without their coming to Christ. One leading American television preacher is quoted as saying, "I'm not trying to convert the Jewish people to the Christian faith. . . . In fact, trying to convert the Jews is a waste of time. I believe that every Jewish person who lives in the light of the Torah has a relationship to God and will come to redemption." This is a very serious error. I much prefer the response of Fuller Theological Seminary's late president, David Hubbard, when a group of prominent rabbis protested to him and urged the seminary to abandon "proselytizing." Hubbard replied: "If Jesus is not the Messiah of the Jewish people, he can hardly be the Christ of the Christian faith."[38]

Rise of Universalism

There is also a move to universalism and the fallacious assumption that everybody will be saved. This view is by no means new but has always been regarded as a heresy. Sighs of relief seem to emanate from those quarters where the hard and difficult fields for evangelism (such as Jewish or Muslim evangelism) continue to test faith and courage. But Paul's own conversion (as unlikely as any from a human standpoint) is "an example for those who would believe on him and receive eternal life" (1 Tim. 1:16). With God there is no impossible case, and God relishes the opportunities to show His mercy. Universalism is the death knell of all evangelism and is undercutting vigorous witness today.

The Holocaust

We must also face the enormity of Jewish suffering in the Holocaust, the declining strength of Judaism as such in the United States and Europe,[39] and the anguish and divisions among the Israelis in *Eretz Israel* itself. Some spokesmen characterize Jewish evangelism as anti-Semitic in its essence and tantamount to launching another pogrom calculated to destroy the Jewish people. On the contrary, I would argue, failure to include the Jewish people in the proclamation of the gospel would represent anti-Semitism at its very worst. If I have good news, I must share it, certainly without undue pressure or any manipulative strategies. Many ideologies and competitive worldviews are presented to the Jewish people as with all of us. How conceivably could we fail to present them with the option of belief in Jesus as the Messiah sent from God?

Thus are we summoned to worship and praise our great God—in whom we see such an incomparable and unique sovereignty, fidelity, mercy, and persistency in relation to Israel.

Our model and our motivation in service and in ministry can be none less than our persistent and patient God "who wants all men to be saved and to come to a knowledge of the truth" (1 Tim. 2:4). Indeed, "the Lord is not slow in keeping his promise, as some understand slowness. He is patient with you, not wanting anyone to perish, but everyone to come to repentance" (2 Peter 3:9). Why does God not thrust in the sickle of judgment and end the nightmare of human history? God wants all to be saved who will be saved. Our shepherd God is out on the mountain looking for lost sheep. What a grounds for celebration and worship. He has found us, to the praise of His glory!

> And none of the ransomed ever knew
> How deep were the waters crossed;
> Or how dark was the night that the Lord passed thro'
> Ere he found His sheep that was lost.
>   —Ira D. Sankey

DISCUSSION QUESTIONS

1. Why has Israel's special election been a serious problem for many in our time?

2. Why is Israel's destiny of extreme importance to the church?

3. What are the implications in the present and in the future for Israel and the church having the same way of salvation?

4. What are some of the obstacles to the evangelism of the Jews today?

5. How can Christians today counteract anti-Semitism?

ENDNOTES

1. For amplification and discussion of these points, cf. my *Jews, Gentiles and the Church* (Grand Rapids: Discovery House, 1995), 20ff.
2. H. H. Rowley, *The Biblical Doctrine of Election* (London: Lutterworth, 1950).
3. Robert Jenson in "A Lutheran Debate on Theological Integrity," in *Christian Century* (June 27–July 4, 1990): 623.
4. Gene Edward Veith, Jr., "The Fascist Moment," in *Chronicles of Culture* (September 1993), 35.
5. Pheme Perkins, commending Robert Farrai Capon's *The Mystery of Christ, First Things*, 39 (January 1994): 39.
6. Charles Taylor, *Multiculturalism and "The Politics of Recognition"* (Princeton: Princeton University Press, 1992), 49.
7. William A. Henry III, "In Defense of Elitism," in *Time*, August 29, 1994, 63ff., taken from the book, *In Defense of Elitism* (New York: Doubleday, 1994).
8. Aaron Wildavsky, *The Rise of Radical Egalitarianism* (New York: American University Press, 1991), 42.

9. J. Budziszewski, "The Problem with Communitarianism," in *First Things*, March 1995, 22ff. For a penetrating analysis of sin, Andrew Delbanco, *The Death of Satan: How Americans Have Lost the Sense of Evil* (New York: Farrar, Straus and Giroux, 1995). Etzioni's exposition is best found in his *The Spirit of Community: Rights, Responsibilities, and the Communitarian Agenda* (New York: Crown, 1993).

10. Paul Johnson, *A History of the Jews* (New York: Harper & Row, 1987), 19.

11. D. M. Stearns (a Reformed Episcopalian who died in 1920) in Allen C. Guelzo, *For the Union of Evangelical Christendom: The Irony of the Reformed Episcopalians* (University Park: Penn State University Press, 1994), 243ff.

12. Wilbur M. Smith, *Egypt in Biblical Prophecy* (Boston: W. A. Wilde, 1957). A very rich study.

13. Norman F. Cantor, *The Sacred Chain: The History of the Jews* (New York: HarperCollins, 1995).

14. David Novak, *The Election of Israel: The Idea of the Chosen People* (Cambridge: Cambridge University Press, 1996).

15. Eugene B. Borowitz, *Renewing the Covenant* (Philadelphia: Jewish Publication Society, 1991), 19.

16. Ibid., 45.

17. Ibid., 298.

18. John S. Feinberg, "Systems of Discontinuity," in *Continuity and Discontinuity: Perspectives on the Relationship Between the Old and New Testaments* (Wheaton: Crossway, 1988), 124.

19. John A. McLean, "Did Jesus Correct the Disciples' View of the Kingdom?" in *BibSac* 151 (April–June 1994): 218.

20. Kenneth L. Barker, "The Scope and Center of Old and New Testament Theology and Hope," in ed. Craig A. Blaising and Darrell L. Bock, *Dispensationalism, Israel and the Church: The Search for Definition* (Grand Rapids: Zondervan, 1992), 304. Also see A. A. Van Ruler, *The Christian Church and the Old Testament* (Grand Rapids: Eerdmans, 1971), 89.

21. McLean, 221ff.

22. Charles Hodge, *Epistle to the Romans* (Grand Rapids: Eerdmans, 1886, 1953), 371ff.

23. Karl Barth, *Church Dogmatics*, vol. 2 (Edinburgh: T & T Clark, 1936), 300.

24. G. C. Berkouwer, *The Return of Christ* (Grand Rapids: Eerdmans, 1972), 351.

25. D. Martyn Lloyd-Jones, in "From Buckingham to Westminster: Interview with Carl F. H. Henry," *Christianity Today* (February 8, 1980): 33.

26. John Murray, *Romans*, vol. 2, NIC (Grand Rapids: Eerdmans, 1965), 89ff., 99.

27. C. E. B. Cranfield, *Romans*, vol. 2, ICC (Edinburgh: T & T Clark, 1979), 562, 575, 577.

28. C. K. Barrett, *The Epistle to the Romans*, vol. 2 (New York: Harper & Row, 1957), 215ff.

29. Johannes Munck, *Christ and Israel* (Philadelphia: Fortress, 1967); cf. my discussion in *Jews, Gentiles and the Church*, 52.

30. A. W. Tozer, *The Knowledge of the Holy* (New York: Harper, 1961), 96–99; Arthur W. Pink, *The Attributes of God* (Swengel, Pa.: Bible Truth Depot, 1962), 65–69.

31. Oscar Cullmann, *The Christology of the New Testament* (Philadelphia: Westminster, 1959), 115.

32. David L. Cooper, *Messiah: His Nature and Person* (Los Angeles: Biblical Research Society, 1933, 1961); *Messiah: His Redemptive Career* (Los Angeles: Biblical Research Society, 1935, 1963); *Messiah: His First Coming Scheduled* (Los Angeles: Biblical Research Society, 1939, 1967). These volumes are some of the most carefully researched and thoroughly done studies of messianic prophecy.

33. For discussion on conversion, cf. David L. Larsen, *The Evangelism Mandate: Recovering the Centrality of Gospel Preaching* (Wheaton: Crossway, 1992), 22–42.

34. D. Martyn Lloyd-Jones elaborates in "The Primacy of Preaching" in *Preachers and Preaching* (Grand Rapids: Zondervan, 1971), 9, 25.

35. Robert E. Speer argues this point in *The Finality of Christ* (New York: Fleming H. Revell, 1933), 5.

36. S. Mark Heim, "The Next Ecumenical Movement," in *Christian Century* (August 14–21, 1996): 780ff.

37. Hans Küng, *Judaism: Between Yesterday and Tomorrow* (New York: Crossroad, 1992), 317ff.

38. Arthur Glasser quotes David Allan Hubbard in the memorial issue of *Fuller Focus* (Fall 1996): 11.

39. For a very searching study, cf. Bernard Wasserstein, *Vanishing Diaspora: The Jews in Europe since 1945* (Cambridge: Harvard University Press, 1996). Careful attention is given to the drastically diminishing Jewish presence in the new European disorder. Jewish population will soon be chiefly in Israel and in the United States, although there are ominous signs of the disappearance of the Jewish family even in American society. "We witness the end of Jewish culture in Europe," 284. A similar note of warning is to be found in Alan M. Dershowitz, *The Vanishing American Jew: In Search of Jewish Identity for the Next Century* (Boston: Little, Brown, 1996). Dershowitz is entirely secular and is critiqued by Elliott Abrams, former Assistant Secretary of State, in *Fear or Faith* (New York: Free Press, 1997) where he argues that "Jewishness without Judaism cannot be transmitted from generation to generation."

SUBJECT INDEX

AUTHOR INDEX

SCRIPTURE INDEX

OLD TESTAMENT

NEW TESTAMENT